ANCIENT INDIAN TRADITION & MYTHOLOGY

Translated by

A BOARD OF SCHOLARS

And Edited by

Dr. G.P. BHATT

VOLUME 56

ANCIENT INDIAN TRADITION AND MYTHOLOGY SERIES

[PURĀṆAS IN TRANSLATION]

VOLUMES

ŚIVA 1-4
LIṄGA 5-6
BHĀGAVATA 7-11
GARUḌA 12-14
NĀRADA 15-19
KŪRMA 20-21
BRAHMĀṆḌA 22-26
AGNI 27-30
VARĀHA 31-32
BRAHMA 33-36
VĀYU 37-38
PADMA 39-48
SKANDA, PARTS I-VIII 49-56

VOLUMES UNDER PREPARATION

SKANDA, PARTS IX-XXIV
BHAVIṢYA
BRAHMAVAIVARTA
DEVĪBHĀGAVATA
KĀLIKĀ
MĀRKAṆḌEYA
MATSYA
VĀMANA
VIṢṆU
VIṢṆUDHARMOTTARA

THE

SKANDA-PURĀṆA

Translated and Annotated by

Dr. G.V. TAGARE

PART VIII

MOTILAL BANARSIDASS PUBLISHERS
PRIVATE LIMITED • DELHI

First Edition: Delhi, 1995

ISBN: 81-208-1232-2

Also available at:

MOTILAL BANARSIDASS

41 U.A. Bungalow Road, Jawahar Nagar, Delhi 110 007
120 Royapettah High Road, Mylapore, Madras 600 004
16 St. Mark's Road, Bangalore 560 001
Ashok Rajpath, Patna 800 004
Chowk, Varanasi 221 001

UNESCO COLLECTION OF REPRESENTATIVE WORKS—Indian Series
This book has been accepted in the Indian Translation Series of the UNESCO Collection of Representative Works, jointly sponsored by the United Nations Educational, Scientific and Cultural Organization (UNESCO) and the Government of India

PRINTED IN INDIA
BY JAINENDRA PRAKASH JAIN AT SHRI JAINENDRA PRESS,
A-45 NARAINA, PHASE I, NEW DELHI 110 028
AND PUBLISHED BY NARENDRA PRAKASH JAIN FOR
MOTILAL BANARSIDASS PUBLISHERS PVT. LTD.,
JAWAHAR NAGAR, DELHI 110 007

PUBLISHER'S NOTE

The purest gems lie hidden in the bottom of the ocean or in the depth of rocks. One has to dive into the ocean or delve into the rocks to find them out. Similarly, truth lies concealed in the language which with the passage of time has become obsolete. Man has to learn that language before he discovers that truth.

But he has neither the means nor the leisure to embark on that course. We have, therefore, planned to help him acquire knowledge by an easier course. We have started the series of Ancient Indian Tradition and Mythology in English Translation. Our goal is to universalize knowledge through the most popular international medium of expression. The publication of the Purāṇas in English Translation is a step towards that goal.

Acknowledgements

It is our pleasant duty to put on record our sincere thanks to Dr. R.N. Dandekar and the UNESCO authorities for their kind encouragement and valuable help in the publication of the volumes in this series.

CONTENTS

SKANDA PURĀṆA
Book III: BRĀHMA-KHAṆḌA
Section I: SETU-MĀHĀTMYA

Chapters

EDITORIAL

This part of the Purāṇa treats of the Setu currently known as Adam's Bridge between India and Sri Lanka, forming a chain of islets, the island of Rāmeśvaram being the first link. The bridge is supposed to have been constructed in the remote past by Nala, the chief engineer of Rāma's Army, in order to enable it to cross the ocean when Rāma had planned to invade the Rākṣasa kingdom of Laṅkā for rescuing Sītā from the clutches of Rāvaṇa, the cruel Rākṣasa king. Being intimately associated with the sacred life of Rāma who is held in the highest esteem as a near-full incarnation of God Viṣṇu, it has since acquired a great religious importance and a pilgrimage to it is enjoined as a giver of great merit and freedom from great sins. The existing Setu actually represents the remains of the original Setu which was demolished by Śrī Rāma himself at the instance of Vibhīṣaṇa, the new king of Laṅkā installed by Rāma, who was afraid that invaders could use the Setu as an easy access to Laṅkā.

Twenty-four Tīrthas are located on the Setu, such as Cakratīrtha, Vetālavarada, Koṭitīrtha etc. A pilgrim should take his holy bath in each. One is exhorted to visit them even if one has to beg or borrow the funds.

All these Tīrthas are glorified with the help of a number of inspiring stories and incidents. Among those most are new and a few repetitions from the Mahābhārata, the Upaniṣads and other Purāṇas, for instance, the killing by Aśvatthāmā of the sleeping warriors, the story of King Jānaśruti and Sage Raikva, and of the killing of Demon Mahiṣa by Goddess Durgā.

The section gives a list of twenty-eight hells which include a number of new names incorporating perhaps torturing methods of punishing the criminal current at the time when the Purāṇa was composed.

The five major sins enumerated by all the Purāṇas and Smṛtis include killing of a Brāhmaṇa or the intellectual guide and leader of the society, drinking, stealing particularly gold, having sex with one's teacher's wife and associating with those who have committed these sins. This section declares some more sins as equivalent to these major sins in chapter 1, vv 53-67.

A number of sins are listed in chapter 36, vv 212-219, for which no expiation can be prescribed and they include ungratefulness and breach of trust, and in chapter 41, vv 67-73 it is stated that even if one could somehow devise a means of getting rid of such sins no atonement can be laid down for one who being competent to save a patient does not try to save him.

An interesting geological phenomenon is alluded to in chapter 4. vv 53-59. It is said that formerly mountains had wings and they used to fly at a tremendous speed causing colossal damage, infuriated at which Indra cut down their wings and they entered the sea out of fear. Geologists say that something like that did take place ages ago, say, about twenty million years back in the early stage of the formation of the earth's crust.

G.P. BHATT

ABBREVIATIONS

Common and self-evident abbreviations such as Ch(s)—Chapter(s), p—page, pp—pages, v—verse, vv—verses, Ftn—Footnote, Hist. Ind. Philo.—History of Indian Philosophy are not included in this list.

ABORI	*Annals of the Bhandarkar Oriental Research Institute*, Poona
AGP	S.M. Ali's *The Geography of Purāṇas*, PPH, New Delhi, 1973
AIHT	*Ancient Indian Historical Tradition*, F.E. Pargiter, Motilal Banarsidass (MLBD), Delhi
AITM	*Ancient Indian Tradition and Mythology* Series, MLBD, Delhi
AP	*Agni Purāṇa*, Guru Mandal Edition (GM), Calcutta, 1957
Arch. S.Rep.	Archaeological Survey Report
AV	*Atharva Veda*, Svādhyāya Maṇḍal, Aundh
BdP	*Brahmāṇḍa Purāṇa*, MLBD, Delhi, 1973
BG	*Bhagavadgītā*
BhP	*Bhāgavata Purāṇa*, Bhagavat Vidyapeeth, Ahmedabad
Br	*Brāhmaṇa* (preceded by name such as Śatapatha)
BsP	*Bhaviṣya Purāṇa*, Vishnu Shastri Bapat, Wai
BVP	*Brahma Vaivarta Purāṇa*, GM, 1955-57
CC	*Caturvarga Cintāmaṇi* by Hemādri
CVS	*Caraṇa Vyūha Sūtra* by Śaunaka, Com. by Mahīdāsa
DB	*Devī Bhāgavata*, GM, 1960-61
De or GDAMI	*The Geographical Dictionary of Ancient and Mediaeval India*, N.L. De/Dey, Oriental Reprint, Delhi, 1971
DhS	*Dharma Sūtra* (preceded by the author's name such as Gautama)
ERE	*Encyclopaedia of Religion and Ethics* by Hastings
GP	*Garuḍa Purāṇa*, ed. R.S. Bhattacharya, Chowkhamba, Varanasi, 1964
GS	*Gṛhya Sūtra* (preceded by the name of the author such as Āpastamba)
HD	*History of Dharma Śāstra*, P.V. Kane, G.O.S.
IA	*The Indian Antiquary*

IHQ	*The Indian Historical Quarterly*
JP	*Purāṇa* (Journal of the Kashiraj Trust), Varanasi
KA	*Kauṭilya Arthaśāstra*
KP	*Kūrma Purāṇa*, Veṅkaṭeśvara Press Edn., Bombay; also Kashiraj Trust Edn., Varanasi, 1971
LP	*Liṅga Purāṇa*, GM, 1960; also MLBD, Delhi, 1981
Manu	*Manusmṛti*
Mbh	*Mahābhārata*, Gītā Press, Gorakhpur, VS 2014
MkP	*Mārkaṇḍeya Purāṇa*
MN	*Mahābhārata Nāmānukramaṇī*, Gītā Press, Gorakhpur, VS 2016
MtP	*Matsya Purāṇa*, GM, 1954
MW	M. Monier-Williams' *Sanskrit-English Dictionary*, MLBD, Delhi, 1976
NP	*Nāradīya* or *Nārada Purāṇa*, Veṅkaṭeśvara Press, Bombay
PCK	*Bhāratavarṣīya Prācīna Caritrakośa*, Siddheshwar Shastri, Poona, 1968
PdP	*Padma Purāṇa*, GM, 1957-59
PE	*Purāṇic Encyclopaedia*, V. Mani, English Version, MLBD, Delhi, 1975
PR or PRHRC	*Puranic Records on Hindu Rites and Customs*, R.C. Hazra, Calcutta, 1948
ṚV	*Ṛg Veda*, Svādhyāya Maṇḍal, Aundh
Śat Br	*Śatapatha Brāhmaṇa*
SC or SMC	*Smṛti Candrikā* by Devanna Bhaṭṭa
SEP	*Studies in Epics and Purāṇas*, A.D. Pusalkar, Bharatiya Vidya Bhavan (BVB), Bombay
SkP	*Skanda Purāṇa*
SP	*Śiva Purāṇa*
VāP	*Vāyu Purāṇa*
VR	*Vālmīki Rāmāyaṇa*
VdP	*Viṣṇudharmottara Purāṇa*
VmP	*Vāmana Purāṇa*
VP	*Viṣṇu Purāṇa*
VrP	*Varāha Purāṇa*

SKANDA PURĀṆA

Book III: BRĀHMA-KHAṆḌA

Section I: SETU-MĀHĀTMYA

CHAPTER ONE

The Merit of Visiting Setu[1]

Obeisance to Śrī Gaṇeśa
Obeisance to Veda-Vyāsa

1a. For the prevention of all obstacles one should meditate upon the four-armed, moon-complexioned Lord Viṣṇu, clad in white garments, whose kindly disposed countenance exudes pleasure (everywhere).

1b-6. In the highly meritorious forest of Naimiṣa[2] conducive to liberation, their abode, many sages of noble souls such as Śaunaka and others performed great penance. They were engaged in the practice of Yoga consisting of eight limbs (i.e. stages). They were interested solely in the realization of Brahman. They were desirous of attaining salvation. Those great souls were free from the sense of 'mine'. They were the expounders of Brahman. They were conversant with Dharma and free from jealousy. They were devoted to observance of the vow of truthfulness. They had conquered the sense-organs and anger. They were compassionate towards all living beings. They worshipped the eternal Lord Viṣṇu with great devotion.

Once, those noble-souled sages convened an excellent assembly.

---

1. *SETU*: Adam's Bridge between India and Śrī Laṅkā. The island of Rāmeśvaram is the first link in the chain of islets forming the Setu (De 1984). Our Text states that as per advice of the Ocean-god, Rāma commissioned Nala, the son of Tvaṣṭṛ, to build the Setu (*infra* 2.87-90). Nala built the Setu in five days (*infra* 7.57). This is contradicted in the next Section, Dharmāraṇya-Māhātmya (30.47-48) which states that Nala began to construct the Setu on the 10th day in the bright half of Pauṣa and completed it on the 13th day of the bright half of Pauṣa, i.e. within four days.

In the Text Rāmasetu signifies the region around Setu and is also called Setubandha.

2. *NAIMIṢA*: Modern Nimsar on Gomatī in Sitapur District of Uttar Pradesh.

They were engaged in telling highly meritorious stories destructive of sins. They were eager to know the means for the achievement of both worldly pleasures and salvation. They were discussing that matter mutually. There were twenty-six thousand sages of purified souls. It is impossible to mention the number of their disciples and disciples' disciples.

7. In the meanwhile, Sūta,[1] the great sage, the highly learned disciple of Vyāsa, the most excellent one among persons conversant with Purāṇas, came to Naimiṣa forest.

8. On seeing the sage coming, refulgent like a blazing fire, the sages, Śaunaka and others, honoured him with *Arghya* etc.

9. When Sūta was comfortably seated on a splendid seat, the sages, with a desire to bless the world, asked him (questions about) highly esoteric matters.

10-15a. "O Sūta, O great sage conversant with the principles of Dharma, welcome unto you. You have heard the Purāṇas from Vyāsa, the son of Satyavatī. Hence you know the contents of all the Purāṇas, O great sage. Which of the places are holy? Which Tīrthas are meritorious on the earth? How will salvation be obtained from the ocean of worldly existence by individual souls? How is *Bhakti* (devotion) to Hari or Hara generated (in the minds) of men? By what means is the benefit of the three types of Karma[2] obtained? O son of Sūta Romaharṣaṇa, be pleased to narrate this and everything else. Preceptors should disclose even secret doctrines to an affectionate disciple."

On being asked thus by the inhabitants of Naimiṣa forest, Sūta, at the outset, bowed down to Vyāsa, his preceptor, and began to recount:

Śrī Sūta said:

15b-18a. Your questions are very well put, O Brāhmaṇas, regarding what is conducive to the welfare of the universe. I shall speak out this secret to you. Listen respectfully, O great sages.

---

1. This text elevates the status of the Purāṇa-narrator Sūta. He is called Śrī Sūta and a sage, though his father Romaharṣaṇa was killed by Balarāma as a punishment for occupying a higher seat in the assembly of Brāhmaṇa-Sages, while narrating the Purāṇa. Romaharṣaṇa was a disciple of Vyāsa, but this Sūta (Ugraśravas) also is called a disciple of Vyāsa.

2. Performed by body, speech and mind (of physical, oral and mental types).

This has never been disclosed to anyone before by me. Having controlled your minds, O eminent Brāhmaṇas, listen with devotion.

There is a sacred spot named Rāmeśvara in Rāmasetu. It is the most excellent one among holy places and Tīrthas.

18b-19. There is no doubt about it that the moment one sees Rāmasetu, one gets liberation from the sea of worldly existence, that devotion either to Hari or Hara will be generated, that one will have abundance of merit and that the fruit of the three types of Karma will be achieved.

20. Listen, O great sages, I shall tell the merit of one who, in the course of his life, devoutly visits Setu.

21. Along with two crores of generations of his maternal and paternal families, he will enjoy for a Kalpa in the company of Śaṁbhu and thereafter will attain salvation.

22. The dust particles on the earth can be counted. The stars in the firmament can be enumerated. But the merit resulting from a visit to Setu cannot be estimated even by Śeṣa.

23. Setubandha is glorified as the form of all the deities. Who is competent to reckon the merit of the man who has visited it?

24. By visiting Setu, O Brāhmaṇas, a Brāhmaṇa is declared (in Smṛtis) as one who has performed all sacrifices. He is on a par with one who has bathed in all the Tīrthas or with one who has performed all kinds of penances.

25. If anyone tells anyone else "Go to Setu", he too attains that benefit, O Brāhmaṇas. Of what avail is much talk?

26. A man who has taken his holy bath in Setu goes to the abode of Viṣṇu accompanied by seven crores of the members of his family and becomes liberated there itself.

27. It is true that a man who thinks about Setu, the Liṅga (named) Rāmeśvara and the Gandhamādana[1] mountain is absolved of all sins.

28. Accompanied by a hundred thousand crores of members of his paternal and maternal families, he goes to the abode of Viṣṇu

1. This is a sandy elevation on the shore of the 'Southern Sea'. It is at a distance of a mile and half west of Rameswaram temple. There is a storeyed Maṇḍapam on this. This is different from the Gandhamādana of Mbh, that is a part of Rudra Himalayas.

and becomes liberated there itself. He stays in the region of Śaṁbhu for a period of three Kalpas and becomes liberated there itself.

29. One who takes his holy bath in Setu, never sees the hells[1] Mūṣāvasthā, Vasākūpa, Śvabhakṣa, Mūtrapāna and the Vaitaraṇī river.

30. One who performs ablutions in Setu never sees (the hells) Taptaśūla, Taptaśilā, Purīṣahrada and Śoṇitakūpa.

31-32. One who visits Setu does not fall into the hells Śālmalyārohaṇa, Raktabhojana, Kṛmibhojana, Śvamāṁsabhojana, Vahnijvālāpraveśana, Śilāvṛṣṭi, Vahnivṛṣṭi, Kālasūtraka, Kṣārodaka and Uṣṇatoya.

33-34a. A man who regulary bathes in Setu, O Brāhmaṇas, may have committed five (great) sins. Yet, accompanied by a hundred crores of the members of his maternal and paternal families, he stays in the region of Viṣṇu for three Kalpas and becomes liberated there itself.

34b-36. A person who regularly bathes in Setu never sees the hells Adhaḥ-śiraḥ-śoṣaṇa (where the sinner is kept topsy turvy and dried), Kṣārasevana (where alkaline liquid is administered), Pāṣāṇayantrapīḍā (where pain is inflicted through stone-machines), Maruprapatana (where there is a desert precipice), Purīṣalepana (where filth is smeared), Krakacadāraṇa (where sinners are cut with saws), Purīṣabhojana (where sinners are compelled to eat faeces), Retaḥpānam (where sinners are compelled to drink semen), Sandhiṣu-dāhana (where the joints are burned), Aṅgāraśayyābhramaṇa (where a sinner has to roll on a bed of fires) and Musala-mardana (where a sinner is thrashed with threshing rods).

37-41. If anyone thinks like 'I will take my bath in Setu' and takes a hundred paces (towards it), he shall, even if he has committed great sins, become free of sins. He will not fall into any of the following hells: where a sinner is pulled and stretched between many wooden machines, where a sinner is pierced with weapons, where he is thrown up and made to fall, where he has to be crushed with iron clubs and staffs, where he is hit with the

1. Places of torture and punishment after death. Their number is generally regarded twenty-four but twenty-eight in 30.3-8. There is some difference of names in the list. This chapter however gives a list of about thirty hells. VV 29-47 give a terrible description of tortures in hells.

tusks of elephants, where he is bitten by different kinds of serpents, where he has to inhale smoke, where he is bound with nooses, where he is pierced with spears and lances of various kinds, where acrid and corroding liquids are poured into the mouth or nostrils, where saltish water is drunk and where heated iron needles are thrust into the mouth.

42-47. One who bathes in Setu does not see the following dreaded hells: where a sinner has to enter holes and pits filled with alkaline fluids, where a sinner is compelled to eat faeces, where sinners are cut, where sinners are burned, where bones are crushed, where phlegm is eaten, where bile is drunk, where extremely bitter liquids are administered, where a sinner is forced to drink very hot (boiling) oil, or to drink corrosive alkaline liquids, where a sinner has to drink astringent water, where he has to eat heated pebbles, where a sinner is showered (bathed) with extremely hot sand particles, where the teeth of a sinner are shattered, where a sinner has to lie on red hot iron, where a sinner's eyes, mouth and joints are pricked with needles, where weighty iron pieces are tied to the penis and the testicles, where a sinner is compelled to fall down from the top of a tree into a pit filled with foul-smelling (rubbish), where a sinner has to lie down on a bed of sharp-edged weapons and where a sinner has to imbibe semen virile.

48-51. If a person lies on the sand of Setu and the particles of sand stick to his body, O excellent Brāhmaṇas, as many sins of killing Brāhmaṇas as there are sand particles sticking to his body are destroyed. There is no doubt about it.

If anyone's body is completely in touch with the wind blowing from Setu, ten thousand sins of drinking liquor perish immediately.

If hairs are cut and they remain in Setu, ten thousand sins of defiling the preceptor's bed perish immediately.

If the bones are consigned to Setu by the sons or grandsons of anyone, he is rid immediately of ten thousand sins of stealing gold.

52. If a person thinks about someone and takes the holy bath in Setu, O excellent Brāhmaṇas, the sin of that one due to contact with one who has committed great sins shall get dissolved.

53-58a. A wayside plunderer, one who cooks for oneself only, a person who censures ascetics and Brāhmaṇas, one who eats too much, and one who sells the Vedas—these five are (regarded as) murderers of Brāhmaṇas.[1]

If a person invites Brāhmaṇas and promises to give them monetary gifts, etc., but afterwards refuses to give them anything, he is also declared as a Brāhmaṇa-slayer.

If a person gets instruction in Dharma from someone, and begins to hate that one, or if a person insults Brāhmaṇas, he is also mentioned as a Brāhmaṇa-slayer.

If a person prevents a herd of cows that has come to drink water near a tank or river, O Brāhmaṇas, he too is said to be a Brāhmaṇa-slayer. All these persons are liberated from sins and defects once they visit Setu.

O excellent Brāhmaṇas, all those persons who are on a par with Brāhmaṇa-slayers are liberated on arrival at Setu. There is no doubt about it.

58b-60. One who abandons the holy rite of Aupāsana, one who feeds himself on the food-offering intended for a deity, one who is in close contact with a woman liquor-addict, one who consumes the cooked rice of a prostitute, one who feeds himself with the food of a guild and one who eats the food of a fallen man—all these are said to be *Surāpins* (liquor-addicts)[2]. They are excluded from all holy rites. But, by taking holy bath at Setu, all these get rid of their sins and are liberated.

61-63. Others who are on a par with drink-addicts are liberated by taking a plunge at Setu.

Those who steal bulbous roots, roots and fruits, musk, woven silk, milk, sandalwood, camphor and areca nuts, honey, ghee, copper, bell-metal and Rudrākṣa-beads should be known as equal to those who steal gold.[3] On arriving at the holy spot Setu they are liberated. There is no doubt about it.

64. Other thieves too, O Brāhmaṇas, are absolved of all sins by taking holy bath at Setu. There is no doubt about this.

65-67. He who carnally approaches his own sister, son's wife, a woman in her monthly period, wife of a brother, wife of a friend, a woman addicted to liquor, other person's wife, a woman of low caste and a widow, should be known as a defiler of preceptor's

---

1. VV 53-58 enumerate the evil acts equivalent to a Brāhmaṇa-slaughter (*Brahmahatyā*).

2. VV 58b-60 state what acts come under the sin of liquor-drinking.

3. VV 61-63 list the acts which are as sinful as stealing gold.

bed.[1] He is excluded from all holy rites. These and others who are on a par with those who defile preceptor's bed become liberated by taking holy bath at Setu, O Brāhmaṇas.

68. Those who are in close contact with these and other sinners as well, shall attain salvation by means of the highly sacred bath at Setu.

69. O Brāhmaṇas, those who are desirous of enjoying Ghṛtācī, Menakā and other celestial damsels in the world of Devas without performing a sacrifice, should take their holy bath at Setu, the dispeller of sins.

70. A person who is desirous of auspiciousness without worshipping the Sun-god, without propitiating the Fire-god and other Suras, should devoutly take the holy bath at Setu.

71. Let those who wish for heaven without making gifts of gingelly seeds, plots of ground, gold, grains of corn and rice, O Brāhmaṇas, take their holy bath at Setu.

72. Let the men who are desirous of heavenly pleasures without giving any strain to their physical body by means of fasts and all other holy rites, take their holy bath at Setu, the bestower of salvation.

73-76. Indeed the holy bath at Setu bestows purity of the mind as well as salvation. It is mentioned in detail in the Purāṇas that sacred bath at Setu is superior to Japa, Homa, charitable gifts and even sacrifice and penance. It has been declared that holy bath performed without any desire at Setu, the destroyer of sins, causes cessation of rebirth. O excellent Brāhmaṇas, the truth has been spoken.

A man who joyously takes the holy bath at Setu with riches in view, shall attain abundant wealth, O great Brāhmaṇas. If one takes bath at Setu for the sake of purity, he shall obtain purity.

77. If one takes the holy bath for the sake of sexual pleasure with celestial damsels in heaven, he attains the same.

78. If one takes the holy bath at Setu, the bestower of salvation, for the sake of salvation, he attains salvation which is devoid of the necessity to return (to the world).

79. There shall be Dharma as a result of the holy bath taken at Setu. There shall be the destruction of sins due to the holy bath taken at Setu. The holy bath taken at Setu, O excellent Brāhmaṇas,

1. VV 65-67 enumerate the acts equivalent to the sin of defiling the teacher's bed.

is the bestower of all desired benefits.

80. It is proclaimed in Smṛtis that it is more meritorious than all the *Vratas*, much greater than all *Yogas*, and more excellent (meritorious) than all the Tīrthas.

81. If people have eagerness and desire for enjoyment of pleasures in the worlds of Indra and others, O excellent Brāhmaṇas, they must take the holy bath at least once at Setu built by Rāma.

82. Let those who have the desire to sport about in the world of Brahmā, in Vaikuṇṭha or in Kailāsa, the abode of Śiva, respectfully bathe at Setu.

83-87a. One who desires long life, good health and wealth, super-handsomeness and good qualities, mastery of the four Vedas with their ancillary subjects, ability to understand all sacred texts or becoming conversant with all the Mantras, should take his bath at Setu, the bestower of all objects. It is true. There is no doubt about it.

In this world, those men who are afraid of poverty or falling into hell, should take the holy bath at Rāmasetu, the bestower of salvation. Whether the man is endowed with faith or is devoid of faith, the man who regularly takes his holy bath at Setu, does not meet with any misery in this world or in the other world.

87b-94. The mass of sins of all perishes by virtue of the holy bath at Setu. The mass of piety and virtue enhances and flourishes like the Moon in the bright half (of a month). Just as different kinds of jewels increase in the ocean, so merits increase and flourish, O Brāhmaṇas, due to the holy bath at Setu.

Just as Kāmadhenu (wish-yielding cow) bestows all desires in the world, just as the Cintāmaṇi stone (philosopher's stone) grants all the desires of men or just as the wish-yielding celestial tree grants the desires of men, so also the holy bath at Setu yields all the desires of the men.

If anyone is unable to undertake a pilgrimage to Setu on account of poverty, he should request good people for the sum and perform the rite of the holy bath at Setu. There the donor (of the said amount) attains merit equal to that of taking holy bath at Setu. So also the recipient attains the full benefit.

With pilgrimage to Setu in view one should receive the sum from Brāhmaṇas. If the Brāhmaṇas do not give him the amount, he should borrow it from a Kṣatriya. If the kings do not give him, he should take from a Vaiśya.

95-96. The man shall not accept the requisite amount from a Śūdra. The man who gives money, foodgrain or clothes, etc. and encourages a man to go to Setu attains the excellent merit of a horse-sacrifice and other Yajñas.

97-99. He shall attain the merit of reciting the four Vedas. He shall obtain the merit of offering charitable gifts, the chief of which is Tulāpuruṣadāna.[1] The sin of murder of a Brāhmaṇa and similar sins shall perish. There is no doubt about it. Of what avail is much talk? He obtains all the desired things. Similarly the recipient too attains a benefit equal to that. If one were to beg for the sum for the sake of pilgrimage to Setu, it does not involve him in the sin of acceptance of monetary gifts.

100. After assuring a person by promising, "Go to Setu; I shall give you the required amount", if one says afterwards, "I do not have (money)", they call him a *Brahmaghātaka* (murderer of a Brāhmaṇa).

101. If out of greed a rich man were to beg the money like a poor man for the sake of pilgrimage to Setu, learned men call him a thief.

102. If by saying "I will go to Setu" a man accepts some sum but, out of greed, does not go to Setu, they call him a murderer of Brāhmaṇa.

103. By any means whatsoever, a man should joyously go to Setu. A man who is unable to go himself should make monetary gifts to an excellent Brāhmaṇa and make him go (to Setu).

104-106. Just as there is no sin in performing a Yajña after raising the required amount by begging, so also there is no harm in undertaking pilgrimage to Setu by raising the amount of expenses by begging.

A man should raise some amount by begging and give it to another for undertaking pilgrimage to Setu and the holy bath thereat. Like the man who takes the holy bath, he too shall attain the merit thereof.

In Kṛtayuga, they attain salvation by perfect knowledge. In Tretāyuga, sacrifice alone is the bestower of salvation. Similarly in the other two Yugas, they say that charitable gift is very excellent. But in all the Yugas holy bath at Setu is excellent for all men.

---

1. This is a *Mahādāna*. The donor is weighed in a balance against gold and valuables in the pan. The gold and valuables equal in weight to the donor is distributed among Brāhmaṇas. For the procedure of this *Dāna*, see HD II, ii 871-872.

CHAPTER TWO

The Construction of Setu

The sages said:

1-2. O illustrious Sūta, how was Setu (the bridge) made by Rāma of unimpaired activities, in the deep sea, the abode of Varuṇa?

How many Tīrthas are there in Setu, in the Gandhamādana mountain? O most excellent one among those conversant with the Purāṇas, recount this to us who have great faith and who listen with great attention.

Śrī Sūta said:

3. O eminent sages, I shall relate to you how Setu was built by Rāma in the abode of Varuṇa.

4. At the bidding of his father, Rāma stayed in Pañcavaṭī in the Daṇḍaka forest with a composed mind. He was accompanied by Sītā and Lakṣmaṇa.

5. While the noble-souled Rāghava was staying therein, O Brāhmaṇas, his wife was abducted by Rāvaṇa by deceiving him through Mārīca.

6. Searching for his wife, Rāma, the son of Daśaratha, went to the banks of Paṁpā. He was overwhelmed by grief and delusion.

7-10. Rāghava, the son of Daśaratha, saw a certain monkey there.[1] He was asked by the monkey, "Who are you, respectable Sir?"

He recounted his own particulars from the beginning, to him truly. Then the monkey too was asked by Rāghava, "Who are you?"

He informed the noble-souled Rāghava thus: "I am a monkey named Hanumān. I am the Minister of Sugrīva. He wishes to secure the friendship of both of you. Deputed by him, I have come to you. Welfare unto both of you. Do come immediately to the presence of Sugrīva."

11-17. Saying "So be it", O eminent sages, Rāma went to Sugrīva along with him and pledged friendship (with Sugrīva) with Fire-

---

1. Vide VR IV, cantos 2 to 5.

god as the witness. Rāma promised him that he would kill Vāli, O Brāhmaṇas, and Sugrīva promised to bring back Vaidehī (i.e. Sītā).

After making this mutual agreement and creating confidence in each other, the lord of men and the lord of monkeys experienced great joy. O excellent Brāhmaṇas, they then settled down on the Ṛṣyamūka mountain. In order to convince Sugrīva Rāghava hurled the body of Dundubhi to a distance of many Yojanas (1 Yojana =12 Kms) with the big toe of his foot. The seven palmyra trees were pierced (with one arrow) by the noble-souled Rāghava.[1]

Then much delighted in his mind, Sugrīva, the warrior, said to Rāma, "O Rāghava, I am not at all afraid of the Devas including Indra, since I have secured you as my friend of such great valour and I have made your friendship. Killing the lord of Laṅkā, I shall bring back your wife."

18. Then accompanied by Sugrīva and Lakṣmaṇa, Rāmacandra of very great power went immediately to Kiṣkindhā protected by Vāli.

19-25. Thereafter Sugrīva roared challenging Vāli to come (out for fighting). Unable to brook the challenging roar of his younger brother, Vāli came out from the inner apartment and fought with his younger brother.

Hit with his fist by Vāli, Sugrīva became extremely afflicted. He went away immediately to the place where Rāma of great strength was present. Thereupon, the mighty Rāma tied a creeper round the neck of Sugrīva as a mark of recognition and urged him to fight once again.

Sugrīva challenged Vāli again with a roar. Encouraged by Rāma, he fought a close hand-to-hand fight with him. Then Rāghava killed Vāli with a single arrow.[2]

After Vāli had been killed, Sugrīva returned to Kiṣkindhā. When the rainy season passed off, Sugrīva, the ruler of the monkeys, gathered together the vast army of monkeys quickly, in order to bring back Sītā. He came to the princes.

26-29. With a desire to search for Sītā, he sent the monkeys (to various places). After Sītā had been found in Laṅkā and the crest jewel was given to him by the son of Wind-god (i.e. Hanumān), Rāghava was both delighted and sad.

---

1. Vide VR IV.11.84-93 and 12.1-5.
2. *Ibid.* IV.16.35-39.

Rāma started under the auspicious influence of Abhijit[1], O Brāhmaṇas. He was followed by Sugrīva, brother (Lakṣmaṇa), the intelligent son of Wind-god and other monkeys, the chief of whom were Jāmbavān and Nala.

After crossing many lands, he went to the mountain Mahendra. Thereafter he went to Cakratīrtha and stayed there.

30. It was there that the virtuous-souled Vibhīṣaṇa, the brother of the lord of the Rākṣasas, approached him accompanied by four ministers.

31-32. Rāma received him with a large-hearted welcome. Sugrīva feared that he might be a spy. But by his activities and perfect conduct, Rāma found him free from (suspicious) defects and only then did he honour him.

33. He crowned Vibhīṣaṇa as the ruler of the kingdom of all the Rākṣasas[2]. He made him his chief minister equal in importance to Sugrīva, the son of Sun-god.

34-39. The glorious Rāma, the scion of the family of Raghu, who was staying at Cakratīrtha was plunged in thought. Then he spoke to Sugrīva and others thus in the presence of prominent monkeys: He spoke these words befitting the occasion : "What is the means by which you will cross this sea? This army is vast. The sea is impassable. This mass of water is blue with surging waves. The fishes jump about. It is exceedingly agitated by huge crocodiles, conchshells and oyster-shells. In some places the submarine fire assails it. It is exceedingly terrible on account of foams. The violent gusts of wind blowing over it, toss the blue clouds (here and there). Its sound is like that of the clouds at the time of the great deluge. It is powerful on account of the stormy winds. How can we cross the ocean, the abode of Varuṇa, the imperturbable (vast sheet of water)? All of you are surrounded by the armies of the exceedingly powerful monkeys.

40-45. (Let us find out) means whereby we can cross the lord of rivers. How can we go beyond the abode of Varuṇa along with our armies without any delay? It is a hundred Yojanas wide. It

1. This was on the 8th day of the dark half of Mārgaśīrṣa (*infra* Dharmāraṇya 1.30-42).

2. Vide VR VI.17-19. Dharmāraṇya 1.30-46 states that this was the 4th day of the bright half of Pauṣa.

is inaccessible even mentally. There are many obstacles. How can Sītā be redeemed?

We are without any support now. We have come to a miserable plight. We are in the stormy sea, a huge mass of water without any shelter. What means shall we employ for crossing by the monkeys? I was banished from the kingdom. I came to the forest. My father died. Sītā was abducted.

More unbearable than all these is the difficulty involved in crossing the sea. Fie, fie upon your roars, O sea! Fie upon your watery mass! How can the words of the great Pot-born Sage (Agastya) be false? 'After killing Rāvaṇa the sinner, go immediately to the holy Gandhamādana for dispelling the sins.' This is what he had said."

Śrī Sūta said:

46-50. On hearing these words of Rāma, Sugrīva and other prominent (monkeys) said with palms joined in reverence to Rāghava of great strength: "We shall cross this by means of various kinds of boats and rafts."

Then in the midst of the crores of monkeys Vibhīṣaṇa spoke thus: "It behoves King Rāghava to seek refuge in the sea. This sea, the abode of Varuṇa, has been dug by Sagaras. It behoves the sea to co-operate in the task of their successor Rāma."

On being told thus by Vibhīṣaṇa, the learned Rākṣasa, Rāghava pacified all the monkeys and said thus:

51-55. "All the monkeys cannot cross the exceedingly dreadful sea, a hundred Yojanas in width, by means of rafts, canoes and boats.

O great monkeys, there are not many ships and big boats sufficient for a large army. How can a person like me cause loss to the merchants? Our army is very large. The enemy may strike at vulnerable points. Hence the crossing by means of rafts and canoes does not appeal to me. O monkeys, what is said by Vibhīṣaṇa gives me delight. I shall worship this sea for the purpose of getting a way across. If he does not yield the path, I will burn him up by means of unobstructable great missiles blazing like fire urged by gusts of winds."

56-59. After saying this, Rāghava ceremoniously sipped water and lay on a bed of Kuśa grass along with the son of Sumitrā waiting for the favour of the sea.[1]

Rāma, of very powerful arms, lay on the shore of the sea over which Kuśa grass had been spread.

He (shone) like sacred fire in sacrificial altar. The scion of the family of Raghu kept his own arm as a pillow, his arm that resembled the body of Śeṣa. Keeping his right arm as the pillow, the clever (prince) propitiated the Sea.

For three days and nights Rāma lay like this on the ground over which Kuśa grass was spread. He never swerved from observance of restraints.

60-66. Rāma, who was conversant with good policies and was devoted to pious activities, spent three days thus and propitiated the Sea for the purpose of getting the pathway. Still the dull-witted Sea did not reveal himself to Rāma, although he was duly worshipped by Rāma with purity. When the Sea did not appear before Rāma, Rāma with extremities of the eyes reddened became infuriated. He spoke to Lakṣmaṇa who was near him: "O son of Sumitrā, within a moment I shall restrain the Sea through with my arrows. Along with its conchshells and oyster-shells, along with its fishes and sharks, the Sea shall be dried up by me by means of arrows and unfailing missiles. I am endowed with forbearance but this Sea regards me incapable of doing anything. Fie upon the forbearance in respect of such people! The Sea does not reveal himself to me by peaceful means.

67-70. O Lakṣmaṇa, bring me my bow and arrows resembling serpents. I shall dry up the Sea. Let the monkeys cross the Sea on foot. I shall wipe out with arrows the boundary of this Sea that is agitated with thousands of waves, as it has transgressed the limits of propriety. I shall dry up the great Sea agitated by great Dānavas, possessing great sharks and crocodiles and turbulent with enormous waves."

After saying this, Rāma took up the bow in his hand. With his eyes full of anger, Rāma became dreadful like Śiva, the destroyer of the three Puras.

71. He bent the bow with anger, he shook the world with his

1. Vide VR VI.21. Rāma started his *Satyāgraha* on the 6th day, bright half of Pauṣa as per Dharmāraṇya. The place of Rāma's *Satyāgraha* against the Sea-god is now called *Darbha-Śayana* or *Darbha-Śayyā* or Tiruppullani. It is a coastal village about 7 miles from Rāmanāthapuram Railway Station.

arrows and he discharged fierce arrows like Bhava (Śiva) on the three Puras.

72. The brilliant and dreadful arrows brightened the ten quarters and entered the waters of the Sea fully agitated by haughty Dānavas.

73. The Sea then got frightened. As he had no other refuge, he trembled with fear and with palms folded in reverence, he came up personally from the nether world.

74. He sought refuge in Rāghava, the cause of salvation. Having become (very humble) he eulogized Rāghava with pleasing words.

The Sea said:

75. O Rāghava, I bow down to your lotus-like feet. O Lord of Sītā, you are the bestower of happiness to those who serve your feet. I bow down to the dust of your glorious feet that absolved the wife of Gautama (from the curse) and that are worthy of being served by groups of Devas.

76. Obeisance, obeisance to you who pierced the body of Tāḍakā, who guarded the sacrifice of Viśvāmitra. Obeisance to you who broke the bow of Mahādeva. Repeated bows to the destroyer of multitudes of Rākṣasas.

77. O Rāma! O Rāma! I bow down (to you) the bestower of what is desired by devotees. You have incarnated in the family of Raghu with a desire to carry out the task of Devas.

78. You are Nārāyaṇa without beginning and end. You are the bestower of salvation, the auspicious one, the imperishable one. O Rāma, O Rāma of great and powerful arms, protect me. I have sought refuge (in you).

79-82. O great king, restrain your anger. O abode of mercy, forgive. The earth, the wind, the ether, the water and the fire, O scion of the family of Raghu, retain their respective natural characteristics with which they have been created by Brahmā Parameṣṭhin. Fathomlessness is my natural characteristic. Shallowness will be an aberration. This is the truth I am saying. I dare not at all to give up my ancestral quality on any account, out of covetousness, love, fear or attachment, O scion of the family of Raghu. But I will render help in getting your army across.

83-84. When the Sea, the lord of rivers, said thus, Rāma said to him: "I will go to Laṅkā protected by Rāvaṇa, along with my army. So do dry up yourself so that I may cross now."

On being told thus the Sea, the abode of Varuṇa, said to Rāghava again:

85-86. "Listen attentively, O Rāma. After hearing, do whatever you want to do. If I dry up at your bidding, because you are desirous of crossing along with your army, others also will command me on the strength of their bows. I shall tell another means whereby your army can cross.

87-90. There is a monkey here (in your army) named Nala. He is a highly respected architect. O descendant of Kakutstha, he is the powerful son of Tvaṣṭṛ, the architect of gods. Whatever he casts into me, a blade of grass, a log of wood or a piece of boulder, I shall hold it up and that shall be your bridge. By that bridge you go to Laṅkā ruled by Rāvaṇa."

After saying this the Sea vanished. Rāma said to Nala: "Construct a bridge over the sea, O highly intelligent one. Indeed you are competent to do it."

Then Nala spoke these words to Rāma, the most excellent one among the virtuous:

91-93. "I shall build the bridge over the fathomless sea. Boons have been granted to me by my father. I am equal to him in capacity. A boon was granted to my mother by Viśvakarman on the mountain Mandara: 'Your son will be on a par with me in Arts and Crafts.' I am his bosom-born son and I am on a par with Viśvakarman. Let the great monkeys build the bridge today itself."

94-97a. Commanded by Rāma, the extremely powerful monkeys of huge bodies and the velocity of Garuḍa and Wind-god, brought mountains, peaks of mountains, grass blades, creepers and trees and Nala built the great bridge in the middle of the sea. It was a hundred Yojana long and ten Yojana wide. Rāma, the Lord of Jānakī, thus got the bridge built by Nala, the great monkey, the son of Viśvakarman.[1]

97b-102. Resorting to this Setu built by Rāma, all men who have committed sins, are liberated from their sins. Śiva is not pleased so much with *Vratas*, charitable gifts, penances and Homas, as he is pleased with the holy plunge at Setu. Just as there is no other splendour comparable to the refulgence of the Sun, so also there is nothing equal to the holy bath at Setu. A tip of Setu is

1. Cf VR VI.22.44-62.

in Laṅkā where Rāma desired to go and therefore began the construction by the monkeys. It (the tip of Setu) is meritorious and destructive of sins. Afterwards it became well-known by the name *Darbhaśayana*. Thus, O Brāhmaṇas, the construction of Setu has been recounted by me. There are many meritorious Tīrthas here.

103. Even Śeṣa is incapable of counting all of them and telling their names. But I shall describe a few of those Tīrthas.

104-106. In the main there are twenty-four Tīrthas at Setu.[1] The first one is Cakratīrtha and then Vetālavarada. Then is the Tīrtha named Pāpavínāśārtha which is famous in all the worlds. Then is the meritorious Sītāsaras and Maṅgalatīrtha then. Thereafter is the Tīrtha named Amṛtavāpikā which is the destroyer of all sins. Beyond that is the Tīrtha Brahmakuṇḍa and thereafter the Tīrtha (Pool) of Hanumān.

107-109. Thereafter is Āgastya Tīrtha. Rāma Tīrtha is beyond that. Then Lakṣmaṇa Tīrtha and Jaṭātīrtha is beyond it. Beyond it is the great Tīrtha of Lakṣmī and Agnitīrtha is further beyond that. Away from it is the meritorious Cakratīrtha and beyond it is Śivatīrtha. Then is the Tīrtha named Śaṅkha and Yamunā Tīrtha is beyond it. Gaṅgātīrtha is further away and Gayātīrtha is the next one.

110-111. Beyond it is the Tīrtha called Koṭitīrtha and thereafter is the Amṛtatīrtha of the Sādhyas. Beyond it is the Tīrtha named Mānasa and Dhanuṣkoṭi is further.

These are the important Tīrthas. They are destructive of great sins. Thus the Tīrthas in Setu have been recounted, O excellent Brāhmaṇas.

112. How the great Setu was built across the sea by Rāma has been recounted, O leading Brāhmaṇas. It is meritorious and destructive of sins.

113-114. By listening to this and reading this, the man on the earth is liberated.

The man who reads this chapter or listens to this with great devotion, O leading Brāhmaṇas, attains infinite success in the other world. He shall never experience the distress of rebirth.

1. VV 104-111 give a list of important Tīrthas on Setu.

CHAPTER THREE

Dharmatīrtha Becomes Famous as Cakratīrtha[1]

The sages said:

1-2. Twenty-four Tīrthas have been recounted by you, O sage, as the most important Tīrthas at Setu that is destructive of sins. Of them the first one is famous as Cakratīrtha. How did it get that name and fame, O Sūta? Recount it to us even as we ask for it.

Śrī Sūta said:

3-9. Of the twenty-four important Tīrthas, O excellent Brāhmaṇas, the first one that is mentioned is well-known in all the worlds. By remembering that Tīrtha a devotee will cease to have rebirth in any species. Even the sins committed in the course of a hundred thousand births become dissolved by taking a single holy bath in that Tīrtha, by remembering it and by glorifying it. A Tīrtha superior to this or at least equal to it does not exist in the world, O excellent Brāhmaṇas. O excellent sages, the truth has been stated by me.

Gaṅgā, Sarasvatī, Revā, Pampā, Godāvarī, Kālindī, Kāverī, Narmadā, Maṇikarṇikā and other Tīrthas, and all the meritorious rivers on the earth are not equal to a ten-millionth part of this Tīrtha, O eminent Brāhmaṇas. Those who are conversant with ancient legends call that Tīrtha Dharmatīrtha.

How it became famous as Cakratīrtha, I shall recount now. Listen, O great sages.

10. It is called Setumūla. It is said to be *Darbhaśayana*. There itself is Cakratīrtha which crushes great sins.

11-12. Formerly there was a sage named Gālava.[2] He was devoted to Viṣṇu. He performed a great penance on the banks of Dharma Puṣkariṇī in the vicinity of village Phulla very near the lake Kṣīrasaras and not far from Hālāsya on the shore of the southern sea.

---

1. Dharma Tīrtha (Dharma Puṣkariṇī) alias Cakratīrtha is at Devipatnam (Devipaṭṭana, in the Text) or near Phullagrama. It is regarded as Setumūla. The place of Rāma's *Satyāgraha* against the Sea-god is near here and is called *Darbha-śayana* (v 10).

2. From the account of Sage Gālava as found in the Mbh, *Udyoga*, Chs. 106-118, this sage is different—his namesake only.

13-19. He performed penance for ten thousand Yugas, O Brāhmaṇas, eulogizing the eternal Brahman. He was compassionate and truthful. He abstained from food and conquered his sense-organs. He saw all the living beings like himself. He was free from desire for sensual objects. He was desirous of the welfare of all living beings. He had perfect control over all the sense-organs. He was unaffected by all mutually opposed pairs (e.g. pleasure-pain etc.). For several years he lived on withered leaves. For some time he took in only water. For some years he subsisted on air only. Thus, for five thousand years the great sage performed a severe penance which was difficult even for Devas (to perform).

The great sage spent the other five thousand years without food, without breathing, without any support (or abode) and without viewing anything.

During rainy season he suffered the heavy downpour. During early winter he lay under water. During summer he stood in the midst of five fires[1] and engaged himself in meditating on Viṣṇu. Repeating the eight-syllabled Mantra, meditating on Janārdana in his heart, Gālava, the great sage of very great refulgence, performed the great penance.

20-25. Thus the sage passed ten thousand years. The Lord of Lakṣmī became pleased with his penance. He appeared in front of him, holding the conch, the discus and the iron club. His eyes resembled petals of a full-blown lotus. He had the lustre of crores of suns. He was seated on Garuḍa (the son of Vinatā). He was remarkably splendid with his royal umbrella and chowries. He was adorned with necklaces, armlets, coronets, bracelets, etc. He was surrounded by Viṣvaksena, Sunanda and other servants. Songs describing his victories were sung by Nārada and others playing on lutes, flutes, Mṛdaṅga drums, etc. He shone in his yellow garment. Lakṣmī gracefully dazzled on his chest. He had the splendour of blue clouds. Madhusūdana shook (playfully) a lotus flower with one of his hands. On his two sides he was served by the great Yogins like Sanaka, etc.

26-30. With his gentle smile he fascinated the entire three worlds. With his refulgence he brightened everyone, O Brāhmaṇas,

---

1. This is called *Pañcāgnisādhana.* The person has four fires in four directions around him and the Sun is the fifth fire above the head. This is to be performed during summer.

and all the ten quarters. He appeared splendid with the jewel Kaustubha tied round his neck. He was accompanied by many chamberlains with golden staffs in their hands. His unimaginable and rare miraculous exploits, not shared by others, were sung by them. Lord Hari, the lover of Lakṣmī, easily accessible to his devotees, appeared before Gālava, the great sage. On seeing the yellow-robed Lord, whose chest was marked with Śrīvatsa, the great sage became delighted. The great sage who was endowed with great devotion eulogized the Lord of the universe.

Gālava said[1]:

31-36. Obeisance to the primordial lord of Devas holding the conch, discus and the iron club. Bow to the eternal and the pure one, having the forms of existence, knowledge and bliss.

Obeisance to the destroyer of the agony of devotees. Salute to you having the form of *Havya* and *Kavya*. Hail to you, the three-formed one, the cause of creation, sustenance and annihilation (of the world).

Obeisance to the great lord. Obeisance to the Lord of plentiful abundance. Obeisance to the Lord of Lakṣmī. Bow to the great creator. Hail to the Lord with the Sun and the Moon for his eyes. Obeisance to the Lord saluted by Viriñci and others.

Obeisance to that destroyer of Daityas, who is free from the notions of name, class, etc., who is bereft of all defects and who dispels the fright of worldly existence.

Obeisance to the Lord of Ramā, who can be comprehended through the Vedānta, whose abode is in Vaikuṇṭha, and who is the father of Creator Brahmā. Repeated obeisance to the Lord who dispels the agony and distress of the people of Satya (Loka). Obeisance to Nārāyaṇa of unmeasured valour.

Obeisance to you, to Lord Vāsudeva holding the Śārṅga bow. Again and again obeisance to you lying down on the couch of Śeṣa.

37-40a. After eulogizing Hari thus, O Brāhmaṇas, Gālava kept quiet.

1. It is the special feature of all these eulogies that the deity praised is shown to be equivalent to Brahman irrespective of its being Viṣṇu, Śiva etc. The same epithets implying identification with Brahman are freely used in common. Compare this eulogy of Viṣṇu with that of Rudra in vv 56-61 below.

On hearing the eulogy pleasant to the ears made by that noble-souled sage, Hari, the wielder of the conch, discus and the iron club, was greatly delighted. Śauri embraced him with all his four arm. With great pleasure he spoke these words: "Let the boon be chosen. I am pleased with your penance, eulogy and obeisance, O Gālava. I have come here as the bestower of boons on you."

Gālava said:

40b-46a. O yellow-robed Nārāyaṇa, O Lord of Ramā, (Lord) identical with the universe, O Janārdana, the abode of the universe, O Govinda, the slayer of Naraka, I am contented and blessed by seeing you. I am now superior to all.

Those who are violators of the path of virtue do not see you because you are the protector of Dharma. What boon is greater than this that I know that Supreme Soul whom Brahmā and Bhava do not know, whom even the three Vedas do not know!

What boon is greater than this that I see the Supreme Ātman whom the Yogins do not visualize and whom the steadfast followers of Karma do not see? I am contented with this, O Janārdana, O Lord of the universe.

I see that Janārdana (by) remembering whose name great sinners as well as sages attain salvation. Let me have steady devotion to the pair of your lotus-like feet.

Hari said:

46b-50. Let your devotion to me be steadfast and free from desire, O Gālava. Listen also to another statement of mine, O sage. Perform holy rites for my sake. Meditate on me. Be devoted to me. At the end of this physical body that has been assigned by destiny, you will attain my form. O great sage, stay in this hermitage itself.

This Dharmapuṣkariṇī is meritorious and destructive of sins. One who performs penance on its banks shall attain the *Siddhi* (fulfilment) of his penance.

Formerly Dharma came here and performed a penance on the shore of the Southern Sea, mentally meditating on Mahādeva.

51-52. For the purpose of (his) holy bath, O great sage, Dharma created a Tīrtha.[1] Since it was made by him, it became well-known

1. This is why it came to be called Dharma-Puṣkariṇī. The story of Dharma's penance is described in vv 52-53.

as Dharmapuṣkariṇī.

Just as the penance is performed by you now, O excellent sage, in the same manner a penance was performed by Dharma then who served Hara.

53. Being delighted with his penance, the trident-bearing Lord Maheśvara manifested himself before him, illuminating all the ten quarters with his brilliance.

54. Dharma who was extremely delighted eulogized the Lord, the Supreme Lord, the storehouse of mercy, who himself came to his hermitage.

Dharma said:

55-61. I bow down to the lord of the universe, to Īśāna of the nature of Praṇava, who has the forms of all the deities, who is devoid of beginning, middle and end, who has sublimated his sexual energy, who has uneven number of eyes (lit. of deformed eyes). who is of cosmic form and who is the support of the entire universe.

I bow down to the unborn, infinite and immutable lord. I salute that lord who makes nourishment increase, whom great Yogins honour.

Obeisance to the overlord of the worlds who moves about (in the heart), who goes to and fro unnoticed.

Obeisance to Nīlakaṇṭha. Salute to the lord of *Paśus* (individual souls). Obeisance to the destroyer of sins. Hail to the most bountiful one, to the most liberal one!

Obeisance to Lord Rudra. Obeisance to *Kadrudra.*[1] Obeisance to the noble-minded one. Obeisance to the Lord with the Pināka bow in his hand; obeisance to you, the trident-armed one.

Obeisance to the lord in the form of consciousness. Bow to the lord of nourishment. Obeisance to the five-faced lord; salute to the lord of holy places.

On being eulogized thus, Śaṅkara, the great lord, the benefactor of the worlds, became extremely pleased with Dharma. He spoke to him thus:

---

1. *Kadru* means a brown-coloured vessel for Soma-juice. This breaking of the Soma vessels probably refers to Śiva's destruction of Dakṣa's sacrifice.

Maheśvara said:

62. I am pleased with this prayer of yours, O Dharma of great intellect. Choose a boon from me. Do not delay.

63-64. On being told thus by Īśvara, Dharma spoke to the lord thus:

"I shall become your vehicle permanently, O Lord of Pārvatī. This boon alone should be granted to me, O destroyer of the three Puras. I shall be blessed and contented merely by bearing you, O lord."

65. On being told thus by Dharma, the Lord spoke thus to Dharma:

Īśvara said:

Become my vehicle, O Dharma. You will be always honoured by the world.

66. You will have never-failing power to bear me. Those who serve you shall always have devotion to me. There is no doubt about this.

67. When this was said by Śaṅkara, Dharma who assumed the form of a Vṛṣa (Bull), O Gālava, began to carry the great Lord ever since then.

68. Mahādeva rode on Dharma who had taken the form of a bull. He shone remarkably and spoke these nectar-like words to Dharma.

Īśvara said:

69. The Tīrtha made by you on the shore of the Southern Sea will become famous in the world as Dharmapuṣkariṇī.

70-71a. *Japa*, *Homa*, charitable gift and study of the Vedas performed on its banks shall bestow endless benefits. Other holy rites too, if performed joyously by men on its banks, should be known as the bestowers of infinite benefits. There is no doubt about it.

71b-72a. After granting this boon to that Dharmatīrtha, Śaṅkara rode on Dharma, the bull, and went to the Kailāsa mountain.

72b-73. Hence, O Gālava, you shall stay on the banks of Dharmapuṣkariṇī till your death. O tiger among sages, you should perform penance with great concentration. Afterwards, you will certainly attain me.

74-75a. Whenever there is any threat befalling you and frightening you, I shall destroy it by discharging my discus instantaneously.

After saying this Viṣṇu vanished there itself.

Śrī Sūta said:

75b-77a. After Viṣṇu had vanished, Gālava, the great sage, stayed on the banks of Dharmapuṣkariṇī meditating on Viṣṇu. The intelligent sage worshipped Viṣṇu three times every day in the Śālagrāma stone, the bestower of salvation. He was detached and he had conquered his sense-organs.

77b-80. Once, on the day of Hari (the eleventh day) in the bright half of the month of Māgha, he observed fast and kept awake during the night. He then worshipped Viṣṇu. On the next day, the twelfth day, he took his holy bath in the waters of Dharmapuṣkariṇī. He performed all the daily round of holy rites beginning with Sandhyā prayers and libations. Then he began the worship of Hari.

Gālava fetched Tulasī leaves and flowers, performed the worship of Kṛṣṇa and uttered this prayer:

Gālava said:

81-82. I bow down to the thousand-headed Viṣṇu, to Hari who had assumed the form of a fish. I bow down to Hṛṣīkeśa in the form of tortoise and boar. I bow down to the Man-Lion, the (incarnation) named Vāmana, the son of Jamadagni, Rāghava, Balabhadra, Kṛṣṇa and Kalki.[1] I bow down to Viṣṇu.

83-84. I bow down to Janārdana, Vāsudeva who needs no support, who destroys the distress of those who bow down and who is the support of all living beings. I bow down to Janārdana who is omniscient, who is the maker of all, whose form is constituted of existence, knowledge and bliss, who is beyond the range of thought and who cannot be pointed out specifically.

* * *

1. VV 81-82 give the list of Viṣṇu's usual incarnations. But instead of Buddha as an incarnation, here is Balabhadra along with Kṛṣṇa. It shows that this chapter was written before the recognition of the Buddha as an incarnation of Viṣṇu.

85. Eulogizing thus, Gālava, the great Yogin, the eminent sage stayed on the banks of Dharmapuṣkariṇī engaged in meditation.

86. In the meantime a certain dreadful Rākṣasa who was afflicted excessively with hunger, came there in order to devour Gālava.[1]

87-88. This Rākṣasa seized Gālava with force. On being caught thus forcibly by the demon, Gālava shouted piteously to Nārāyaṇa, the ocean of mercy, the ultimate refuge of those who are in great distress, the discus-armed lord, crying "Save me, save me" repeatedly.

89. "O great Lord, O supreme bliss, O protector of those who seek refuge (in you) ! Save me, O ocean of mercy. I have been caught within the clutches of a demon.

90. O Hari, O Viṣṇu, O Lord of Lakṣmī, O Garuḍa-emblemed Vaikuṇṭha! Save me. I have been assailed by the demon. Save me in the manner you saved the elephant seized by the crocodile.

91. O Dāmodara, O Lord of the universe, O crusher of the demon Hiraṇya! I am extremely harassed by the Rākṣasa. Save me as you saved Prahlāda."

92-95. As Gālava prayed thus, O excellent Brāhmaṇas, the discus-armed Viṣṇu came to know of the danger of his devotee and he despatched his discus for protecting the devotee.

Hurled by Viṣṇu, the powerful Lord, the discus of Viṣṇu came speedily to the shore of Dharmapuṣkariṇī.

On seeing Viṣṇu's Sudarśana that resembled infinite number of Suns, and had the lustre of infinite number of fires ablaze with great flames and with loud report, the discus that crushed the great Asuras, the demon fled.

96. Sudarśana that was unconquerable with its clusters of flames suddenly cut off the head of the fleeing demon.

97. On seeing the Rākṣasa fallen on the ground, Gālava was filled with great delight. He eulogized Sudarśana.

Gālava said:

98-101. O Discus of Viṣṇu, obeisance to you. O (weapon) always ready to protect the universe, obeisance to you, the ornament of the lotus-like hands of Nārāyaṇa.

---

1. VV 86-111 explain why it is called *Cakra-tīrtha.*

O Sudarśana of loud report, bow to you, an expert in the annihilation of Asuras in battles; salute to you, the destroyer of the distress of devotees.

Save me, I am extremely frightened. Redeem me from all the sins. O Lord Sudarśana, be present in this Dharmatīrtha forever for the welfare of the universe desirous of salvation.

On being told thus by Gālava, O eminent sages, that Discus of Viṣṇu spoke to sage Gālava delighting him as it were through close friendship.

Sudarśana said:

102-107. This excellent Dharmatīrtha is exceedingly meritorious, O Gālava.

I shall permanently stay here with a desire for the welfare of the people. Considering your molestation by the wicked Rākṣasa, I have been sent, O Brāhmaṇa. I have therefore come here hurriedly. The base Rākṣasa who troubled you has been killed by me. You have been relieved of the fear. Indeed you have always been a devotee of Hari. O great sage, I shall stay always in this Puṣkariṇī (Lake) of Dharma for the protection of the world. Since I will be present, O Brāhmaṇa, neither you, nor others will have any trouble from spirits or demons hereafter. Indeed this Dharmapuṣkariṇī is destructive of all sins.

108-111. This lake was made by Dharma formerly up to Devīpaṭṭaṇa. I shall always stay everywhere (within it) here, O great sage. Due to my presence this lake will become famous as Cakratīrtha.

Those who take their holy bath in Cakratīrtha that bestows salvation will be rid of all sins. Their sons and grandsons and all persons in their family shall be rid of all their sins. They will go to the great region of Viṣṇu.

Those who offer rice-balls here to the Manes will go to heaven and the Pitṛs who are propitiated will also go to heaven.

112. After saying thus the Discus of Viṣṇu suddenly entered Dharmapuṣkariṇī, the destroyer of sins, O Brāhmaṇas, even as Gālava and all other Brāhmaṇas were watching.

Śrī Sūta said:

113-117. How Dharmatīrtha came to be well-known as Cakratīrtha has been recounted to you all by me joyously, O eminent Brāhmaṇas. There has never been nor will there ever be a Tīrtha on a par with Cakratīrtha.

Those who take their holy bath here, O Brāhmaṇas, shall be liberated. There is no doubt about this.

One who glorifies this chapter or listens to this with concentration and mental purity, shall obtain the excellent benefit of taking the holy bath in Cakratīrtha. He will enjoy all pleasures here and then enjoy the pleasures in heaven.

He who remembers at least once Dharmatīrtha, Gālava who performed the severe rites of Samādhi and Yoga, and Sudarśana, the destroyer of the Rākṣasa, shall never become a sinner.

CHAPTER FOUR

Redemption of Durdama from a Curse

The sages said:

1. O Holy Lord Sūta, most excellent one among those conversant with the Purāṇas, who was that Rākṣasa who harassed the noble-souled Gālava, the devotee of Viṣṇu?

Śrī Sūta said:

2. I shall tell you about that cruel Rākṣasa, O Brāhmaṇas; listen respectfully. I shall tell you how that Rākṣasa came to be born by the power of a curse of sages.

3-10. Formerly, on the peak of Kailāsa, in the abode of Śiva in Hālāsya, twenty-four thousand sages, expounders of Brahman, and residents of Madhurāpura (Mathurā) headed by Vasiṣṭha and Atri, propitiated Lord Śiva, the lord of Hālāsya, the moon-crested lord of Umā, and the lord of spirits, for their salvation. All of them, the devotees of Śiva, had applied holy ash all over their bodies. They were of great spiritual splendour. They had the Tripuṇḍras (three sectarian horizontal parallel lines) on their foreheads.

They wore rosaries of Rudrākṣa beads. They were engaged in

the Japa of the five-syllabled Mantra, *namaḥ śivāya*.

Once a Gandharva, a powerful son of Viśvāvasu, named Durdama, being himself nude, was joyously engaged in aquatic sports with naked women. O great Brāhmaṇas, he was addicted to the company of an assemblage of viciously vulgar fellows. A hundred women surrounded him. It was the Tīrtha of Hālāsyanātha where they sported thus:

Desirous of performing the midday religious rites, Vasiṣṭha in the company of many sages went to that Tīrtha from the abode of Śaṅkara. On seeing those sages the young women became frightened and clothed themselves immediately. But the foolhardy Durdama did not. Infuriated by this, Vasiṣṭha cursed that shameless fellow.

Vasiṣṭha said:

11-14. O Durdama, O Gandharva, you did not feel ashamed on seeing us and did not put on your clothes at once. Hence, be turned into a Rākṣasa.

After saying thus, Vasiṣṭha, the eminent sage, said to those women: "O excellent young women, since you all put on your clothes on seeing us, I do not curse you. Do go to heaven."

On being told thus by Vasiṣṭha the young women bowed down to Vasiṣṭha with great humility. With their palms folded in reverence, they entreated Vasiṣṭha who was surrounded by groups of sages.

The young women said:

15-19. O holy lord, conversant with all Dharmas, O son of the Four-faced Lord (Brahmā), O ocean of mercy, look upon us with mercy. It does not behove you to be angry.

It is the husband who is called the greatest ornament of women. A woman may have a hundred sons, but if she has no husband, she is called a widow in the world. It is regarded as death in the case of women. Hence do us this favour. O sage, be pleased with our husband too. One offence should be forgiven by the sages who know the truth. Forgive, O ocean of mercy, Durdama who is (like a) disciple unto you.

On being requested thus by the womenfolk of Durdama Vasiṣṭha became pleased, O excellent Brāhmaṇas, and he spoke these words again:

20-26a. "O ladies of excellent eyebrows, my words shall never be false. I shall tell you a means. Listen with attention.

The curse given to your husband shall be limited to sixteen years. At the end of this period Durdama in the form of a Rākṣasa shall by chance go to Cakratīrtha, O celestial maidens. Gālava, a great Yogin, devoted to Viṣṇu, lives there. The Rākṣasa will rush at the sage with the intention of devouring him. Thereupon the excellent discus hurled by Viṣṇu for saving Gālava, O ladies, will take away his head. There is no doubt about it. Durdama will become rid of his curse and regain his own form. Your husband will come to heaven once again. There is no doubt about this. After coming to heaven with handsome features and beautiful dress, Durdama, your husband, will delight you all, O beautiful women."

26b-29. After saying this to the excellent wives of Durdama, Vasiṣṭha, the devotee of Lord of Hālāsya, immediately went back to his hermitage.

Then the young women in great agony embraced their husband Durdama and began to lament. They were grief-stricken. They were in the depths of the ocean of distress. Even as they were watching him, Durdama turned into a Rākṣasa.

He had great curved teeth, a huge body and red beard and hair. On seeing him, the young women became distressed with fear; they went back to heaven.

30-34. In his body of a Rākṣasa, Durdama of dreadful features wandered from country to country, from forest to forest, eating and devouring all living beings. With the velocity of wind he moved from place to place. Then he went to Dharmatīrtha. Thus sixteen years passed while he was moving from place to place. Then, at the end of the sixteenth year, O great sages, with the force of a violent gust of wind, this Rākṣasa rushed at sage Gālava, the resident of Dharmatīrtha, in order to devour him. He (Gālava) prayed to Janārdana. On being eulogized by Gālava, Viṣṇu hurled his discus in order to save sage Gālava who was harassed by the Rākṣasa. The discus of Hari came down and severed the head of the Rākṣasa.

35-41. Thereupon, he discarded the demoniac body and assumed a divine form. Durdama got into an excellent aerial chariot.

He was showered with flowers. He bowed down to Sudarśana and saluted it. With palms joined in reverence, he then eulogized it, in excellent words pleasing to the ears.

Durdama said:

O Sudarśana, I offer obeisance to you. O sole ornament of the hand of Viṣṇu, salute to you, the destroyer of Asuras. Bow to you having the refulgence of a thousand Suns. It was due to a bit of your kindness that I was able to get rid of my Rākṣasa form and regain my real form. O Discus, the weapon of Viṣṇu, salute to you. Permit me to go to heaven, O lover of Viṣṇu. There my wives, with their minds in agony due to separation, bewail me. Be merciful to me so that I shall be able to fix my mind on you. Obeisance to you, O Discus.

On being eulogized thus by Durdama with great devotion, the Discus of Viṣṇu blessed him quickly, O great sages, and said, "So be it".

42-48. Permitted by the Weapon Discus, Durdama bowed down to sage Gālava. On being allowed by him, the Gandharva went to heaven.

When Durdama went to heaven, Gālava the eminent sage prayed to the Discus, the excellent weapon of Viṣṇu:

"O Weapon Discus, I bow down to you, O crusher of great Asuras. Be present in the excellent Dharmatīrtha extending up to Devīpaṭṭaṇa. Let it be destructive of all sins of the sinners who take bath in it. Let it be sacred due to your presence. Do destroy the sins. Grant them permanent salvation. Make it famous as Cakratīrtha in the world. Henceforth let the fears of the sages here perish due to your presence. O Weapon Discus, obeisance to you. O lord, let there not be any danger from evil spirits, ghosts and vampires."

On being requested thus by Gālava, O leading sages, the Discus said, "So be it" and vanished there in the Tīrtha itself.

Śrī Sūta said:

49-50. Thus, O Brāhmaṇas, the origin of the Rākṣasa has been recounted by me. The glory of that Cakratīrtha, that is destructive of dirt (sins) is also recounted. On hearing this, a man on the earth is liberated from all the sins.

The sages said:

51-53a. O Sūta, O disciple of Vyāsa, of great intellect, O most excellent one among those conversant with Purāṇas, the excellent Cakratīrtha (originally) extended from Darbhaśayana to Devīpaṭṭaṇa. It was very large. How did it become split now? Tell us. It behoves you to dispel this doubt that occurs in our mind.

Śrī Sūta said:

53b-58. Formerly all the mountains had wings. They had the velocity of mind. They moved about here and there by the ethereal path along with the other mountains nearby. They glided and flew along and settled on cities and countries, villages and forests. Wherever these mountains settled down like this, men, cows and other living beings were crushed by them. They met with instantaneous death. When Brāhmaṇas and peoples of other castes too perished thereby, this prevented the performance of Yajñas, etc. On account of the absence of the Yajñas and other rites, Devas became distressed, Indra became infuriated. Seizing the thunderbolt he cut off the wings of the powerful mountains.

59. When their wings were thus being cut off by Indra, all the mountains had no other refuge. Out of fear they entered the sea.

60-63. When all the mountains thus fell into the salty sea, some of them fell into the Cakratīrtha too, mistaking it to be the sea itself.

By the mountains fallen thus, Cakratīrtha got filled in the middle. The highly meritorious Cakratīrtha became split in the middle.

By a lucky chance, the great mountains did not fall on the two sides. Therefore, it appears as though divided into two at Darbhaśayana as well as at Devīpura. On account of the mountains that fell in the middle Cakratīrtha (in the middle) became a land mass.

Śrī Sūta said:

64. Thus, O eminent sages, it has been recounted to you all how this Tīrtha became a land mass in the middle and how with their wings cut off by Indra, the lofty mountains fell down here suddenly.

CHAPTER FIVE

Redemption from Curse of Alaṁbuṣā and Vidhūma[1]

Śrī Sūta said:

1-3a. In the context of the meritorious Cakratīrtha that is destructive of sins, I shall tell something wondrous, O eminent sages. A Vasu named Vidhūma and a celestial woman named Alaṁbuṣā formerly attained human birth due to a terribly severe curse of Brahmā. By taking their holy bath in the highly meritorious Cakratīrtha they were redeemed from the curse.

The sages said:

3b-6. O Sūta, O Sūta of great intellect, O great expert in the Purāṇa topics, there is nothing not known to you, because of your intelligence and because of your being a disciple of Vyāsa. What was that offence for which Brahmā, the four-faced lord, cursed the Vasu named Vidhūma along with Alaṁbuṣā? Who were they to whom these two were born as children due to the terrible curse of Brahmā? How did they get redemption after having been cursed by Brahmā. It behoves you to recount this in detail to us who are strongly desirous of hearing it.

Śrī Sūta narrated:

7-12. Formerly, the self-born, four-faced Lord Brahmā was present in his assembly. Sāvitrī and Sarasvatī graced the sides. Sage Sanātana, intelligent Sanaka, Sanatkumāra, the noble-souled Nārada, Sanandana and other eminent sages waited upon (him). He was being eulogized by Indra, surrounded by a group of Devas. The Sun and the other Planets were engaged in praising his lotus-like feet. He was surrounded by Siddhas, Sādhyas, Maruts and Kinnaras as well as groups of Kiṁpuruṣas and the eight Vasus. He was now and then engaged in witnessing the charming dance and (hearing) the instrumental music of the celestial courtesans, the chief of whom

1. In glorifying the efficacy of Cakraīrtha, the author uses the curse as a motif and cleverly uses historical persons like Śatānīka, Sahasrānīka, Rumaṇvān, Yaugandharāyaṇa, giving their mythological background in heaven.

vital airs wandering outside, became sad. Their faces were filled with tears. They spoke these words to Vidhūma:

The attendants said:

All the three of us will not be able to bear the separation from you. Hence you shall take human birth along with us. The saintly king Śatānīka has a minister named Yugandhara; the commander-in-chief named Vipratīka who always goes ahead in the battle front and a close friend, a Brāhmaṇa named Vallabha, who is a very great man. We shall be born as the sons of these three surely. When you are born as the son of the saintly king Śatānīka we shall serve you in various ways.

Even as they told him thus Vidhūma spoke to them these words:

Vidhūma said:

44-47. I know the type of excellent affection that you all have for me. Still I shall tell you these words for the sake of your welfare. The despicable birth as a human being is brought about by the dreadful curse of Brahmā caused by my own evil action. I alone shall take it up. You are not called upon to experience the bitter taste of the curse. Hence do not feel inclined towards the despicable human birth now. So, be patient enough to endure separation from me till the end of the period of the curse.

48-51. As he spoke thus, all of them, the chief among whom was Mālyavān, bowed down their heads and spoke thus repeatedly requesting him:

"Hitherto you have been protecting us. Now do not take any great risk. You are abandoning us, your devotees, without any sins. We consider even the despicable human birth more honourable than the dreadful separation from you. Hence, O lord, save us now."

He permitted them to follow him when the attendants requested him so ardently. He desired to go to Kauśāmbī accompanied by those three.

52-57. In the meantime, Śatānīka, the king, ruled the earth. He was a scion of the family of the Moon-god born in the line of Arjuna. He was the son of Janamejaya. He was intelligent, just and eloquent. He was interested in protecting the subjects. He was

On being propitiated thus, the immutable Lord of Sarasvatī became overwhelmed with sympathy. He said to Vidhūma consoling him.

Brahmā said:

26b-31. The curse has already been given to you. I do not utter any lie. So I shall assign a limit to the curse upon you now. You will assume human form along with this Alaṁbuṣā. You will be born as a great king. After ruling the earth for a long time, you will beget a matchless son of her and crown him when he becomes competent to defend the kingdom. In order to quell this curse, you will perform the rite of holy bath in the great Cakratīrtha which is near Phullagrāma village on the shore of the Southern Sea. You will bathe there in the company of your wife. At that time you will cast off the human form like a serpent that casts off the rotten slough. You will then return to your own world along with your wife. A curse like this will never perish without holy bath in Cakratīrtha.

32-36. On hearing these words of Brahmā Vidhuma was not much pleased. He took leave of the Four-faced Lord and immediately entered his home. There he began to think thus, 'I am going to be born as a man. Who shall be my father on the earth? Who shall be my mother?' After pondering over this in various ways, Vidhūma decided thus. 'There is a king in the city of Kauśāṁbī[1] well-known as Śatānīka.[2] He is a great warrior and highly fortunate. His wife is a very chaste lady named Viṣṇumatī. She is his beloved like Śrī is that of Viṣṇu. I shall have him as my father and her as my mother. As a result of my own Karma, I shall be born in the terrestrial world thus.'

37-43. He called his three attendants Mālyavān, Puṣpadanta and Balotkaṭa and told them about this, "O my attendants, welfare unto you; listen. On account of the dreadful curse of Brahmā, I shall be born as the son of Śatānīka and Viṣṇumatī."

On hearing these words the attendants who were as though his

1. Mod. Kosam, a village on the left bank of Yamunā, about 30 miles west of Allahabad.

2. Son of Janamejaya (Parīkṣit's son) and Vapuṣṭamā (called Viṣṇumatī here) Mbh, *Ādi* 96.88.

vital airs wandering outside, became sad. Their faces were filled with tears. They spoke these words to Vidhūma:

The attendants said:

All the three of us will not be able to bear the separation from you. Hence you shall take human birth along with us. The saintly king Śatānīka has a minister named Yugandhara; the commander-in-chief named Vipratīka who always goes ahead in the battle front and a close friend, a Brāhmaṇa named Vallabha, who is a very great man. We shall be born as the sons of these three surely. When you are born as the son of the saintly king Śatānīka we shall serve you in various ways.

Even as they told him thus Vidhūma spoke to them these words:

Vidhūma said:

44-47. I know the type of excellent affection that you all have for me. Still I shall tell you these words for the sake of your welfare. The despicable birth as a human being is brought about by the dreadful curse of Brahmā caused by my own evil action. I alone shall take it up. You are not called upon to experience the bitter taste of the curse. Hence do not feel inclined towards the despicable human birth now. So, be patient enough to endure separation from me till the end of the period of the curse.

48-51. As he spoke thus, all of them, the chief among whom was Mālyavān, bowed down their heads and spoke thus repeatedly requesting him:

"Hitherto you have been protecting us. Now do not take any great risk. You are abandoning us, your devotees, without any sins. We consider even the despicable human birth more honourable than the dreadful separation from you. Hence, O lord, save us now."

He permitted them to follow him when the attendants requested him so ardently. He desired to go to Kauśāmbī accompanied by those three.

52-57. In the meantime, Śatānīka, the king, ruled the earth. He was a scion of the family of the Moon-god born in the line of Arjuna. He was the son of Janamejaya. He was intelligent, just and eloquent. He was interested in protecting the subjects. He was

On being propitiated thus, the immutable Lord of Sarasvatī became overwhelmed with sympathy. He said to Vidhūma consoling him.

Brahmā said:

26b-31. The curse has already been given to you. I do not utter any lie. So I shall assign a limit to the curse upon you now. You will assume human form along with this Alaṁbuṣā. You will be born as a great king. After ruling the earth for a long time, you will beget a matchless son of her and crown him when he becomes competent to defend the kingdom. In order to quell this curse, you will perform the rite of holy bath in the great Cakratīrtha which is near Phullagrāma village on the shore of the Southern Sea. You will bathe there in the company of your wife. At that time you will cast off the human form like a serpent that casts off the rotten slough. You will then return to your own world along with your wife. A curse like this will never perish without holy bath in Cakratīrtha.

32-36. On hearing these words of Brahmā Vidhuma was not much pleased. He took leave of the Four-faced Lord and immediately entered his home. There he began to think thus, 'I am going to be born as a man. Who shall be my father on the earth? Who shall be my mother?' After pondering over this in various ways, Vidhūma decided thus. 'There is a king in the city of Kauśāṁbī[1] well-known as Śatānīka.[2] He is a great warrior and highly fortunate. His wife is a very chaste lady named Viṣṇumatī. She is his beloved like Śrī is that of Viṣṇu. I shall have him as my father and her as my mother. As a result of my own Karma, I shall be born in the terrestrial world thus.'

37-43. He called his three attendants Mālyavān, Puṣpadanta and Balotkaṭa and told them about this, "O my attendants, welfare unto you; listen. On account of the dreadful curse of Brahmā, I shall be born as the son of Śatānīka and Viṣṇumatī."

On hearing these words the attendants who were as though his

1. Mod. Kosam, a village on the left bank of Yamunā, about 30 miles west of Allahabad.

2. Son of Janamejaya (Parīkṣit's son) and Vapuṣṭamā (called Viṣṇumatī here) Mbh, *Ādi* 96.88.

was (called by) Tilottamā. But since he was thinking about his beloved of whom Indra had been talking, and since he was pondering over the words of Indra without his mind being distracted by any other topic, the king did not see her. On being slighted and disrespected that lady of excellent eyebrows cursed him:

"O King Sahasrānīka, why did you ignore me though you were called by me? You are meditating on Mṛgāvatī and so neglect me. Proud women haughty on account of their good fortune do not brook disrespect. You will become separated for fourteen years from that lady of whom you are thinking after disrespecting me."

When Tilottamā cursed thus, the king spoke to her: "If I am going to get that daughter of Kṛtavarman, I shall very well endure the misery due to separation from her for fourteen years." After saying thus the king returned to his city with his mind fully engrossed in her.

104. Thereafter, in due course, the daughter of King Kṛtavarman, who was as it were the entire property of lord of Love, came to him as his beloved wife.

105. On getting Mṛgāvatī (who was like) the creeper twining round the tree of graceful sports, a gentle ripple in the ocean of amorous charm, the king who had the refulgence of god of Love, became delighted.

106. Like Bhavānī from the Moon-crested Lord, she conceived from him (the king). She shone with the white pale colour (all over the body) like a digit of the Moon washed by nectar.

107. When the symptoms of pregnancy appeared very clear, the crowned queen of the king shone like the Eastern cardinal point with the Moon in her womb.

108. As is usual with women during pregnancy, the queen had a craving for many things. Whatever she desired the king lovingly brought it immediately, even if it happened to be rare.

109. As the husband was ready to do whatever she desired, once Mṛgāvatī wished for taking a plunge into a tank of blood.

110. On coming to know of the desire of Mṛgāvatī the king immediately caused a tank to be built and it was filled with saffron waters.

111-112. The queen eagerly took her bath in that red water. Wet with red water, she resembled a Kiṁśuka flower in full bloom (*Butea frondosa*). As ill luck would have it, a hideous bird born of Garuḍa's family took away the beautiful queen thinking her to of the battle. The leader of Daityas as well as the king were killed in the battle in heaven. Then, at the instance of Indra, Mātali placed the great king who had died, in his chariot and went to Kauśāṁbī. Taking him to the earth, Mātali mentioned (everything) to his son. Sahasrānīka became very miserable and he lamented much. Together with the ministers, he performed the obsequial rites. Immediately after the realization that her husband had been killed, the queen too died. When the king along with his queen left nothing behind except his renown, the son of Śatānīka succeeded to the throne at the request of the ministers.

88-96a. When Yugandhara, Vipratīka and Vallabha died, their sons including Yaugandharāyaṇa began to be engaged in different services to the son of Śatānīka.[1] Thus the powerful son of the king protected the earth.

After lapse of some time, he was invited by Mahendra in the course of a great festival at Nandana park. There he listened to the future events recounted by him:

"The celestial courtesan Alaṁbuṣā is reborn in Ayodhyā as Mṛgāvatī, the daughter of King Kṛtavarman, on account of the curse of Brahmā. You are the Vasu named Vidhūma. Formerly in the abode of Brahmā, you gazed at that heavenly courtesan when her inner garments had been blown by the breeze. You were overcome by lust and so were cursed. Due to that curse you became a human being. O king, O my friend, she alone will before long become your wife. 'O king, after installing your son in the kingdom, you shall go to the highly meritorious Cakratīrtha near Phullagrāma, on the shore of the southern sea, along with your wife Mṛgāvatī. There you shall take your holy bath and you will be liberated from the curse'. So said Lord Brahmā in Satyaloka."

96b-103. On hearing these words of Indra, King Sahasrānīka became very enthusiastic about the prospective marriage. He took leave of Indra and proceeded towards Kauśāṁbī. On the way he

---

1. According to *Kathāsaritsāgara* and the plays of the great pre-Kālidāsa dramatist Bhāsa (viz. *Pratijñā-Yaugandharāyaṇa* and *Svapna-Vāsavadatta*) these were the companions and trusted ministers of Udayana, the son of Sahasrānīka.

The author of this text got a jumbled version of the traditional history. *Kathāsaritsāgara* differs. According to it, the serpent was Vasunemi, Vāsuki's elder brother. Out of gratitude he gave to Udayana the famous lute Ghoṣavatī and betels and taught him the art of making unfading garlands and unfading mark on the forehead.

ters, he started towards his city.

157-163. The excellent king entered the city of Kauśāmbī. Remembering the words of Indra, he already began to despise human birth. He gave the earth to his intelligent son Udayana. As his son Udayana had already become competent to protect the kingdom, he entrusted him with the burden of the kingdom.

In order to get redemption from the curse, he wanted to take his holy bath in the highly meritorious Cakratīrtha on the shore of the Southern Sea. By means of vehicles having the velocity of wind, he hurried to the briny sea without wasting time, to take the holy bath in the most excellent one of all the Tīrthas.

He was accompanied by Mṛgāvatī, his wife, Vasantaka, Rumaṇvān and Yaugandharāyaṇa, the son of the minister.

After reaching Cakratīrtha they all took the holy bath in accordance with the injunctions. As soon as the king and others took their holy bath in Cakratīrtha their highly disreputable human birth terminated instantaneously.

Getting rid of their sins, they regained their respective original forms.

164-167. All of them had divine garments, divine garlands and divine unguents. They were adorned well. They got into aerial chariots of great value.

They honoured that Tīrtha that had been the cause of the annulment of their curses. Even as all the worlds watched them, they proceeded towards the heavenly world.

Ever since then they continue to take their holy bath always in the sacred Cakratīrtha which has such power. All those men who come here and take their holy bath even once, become heaven-dwellers.

168. Thus, O Brāhmaṇas, the great story of Vidhūma has been recounted to you. He who reads this chapter or listens to it with attention, shall quickly obtain whatever he desires.

her delighted by informing her of the event. Then Mṛgāvatī became delighted in her heart.

141-142. In the meantime that hunter went to a merchant at Kauśāṁbī in order to sell the gem-set bangle marked with the name and seal of Sahasrānīka.

On seeing the royal seal in the bangle, the excellent merchant went to the king along with the hunter and told him everything.

143-145. On coming into possession of the gem-set bangle, Sahasrānīka became afflicted due to the fiery poison of separation from Mṛgāvatī. Since the bangle had been in contact with her hand, it was cool like nectarine spray. He placed the bangle on his chest and lamented miserably. Then he said, "O hunter, how is this bangle obtained by you?" On being told thus, he informed him about the way in which he had obtained it.

146. On hearing the words of the hunter, King Sahasrānīka started along with his ministers. He was very eager and impatient to see his wife.

147-152. He proceeded towards that self-same mountain where the moon, the sun and other (luminaries) rise at once. After traversing a part of the path, he halted and saw that the army got its rest. Eagerly engaged in thinking about (the impending) union with his wife, the king had no sleep. Vasantaka narrated to him various wonderful anecdotes. He spent that night listening to those stories. In due course, he proceeded to the direction protected by Indra (i.e. the eastern direction). He went to the hermitage of Jamadagni where lion and elephant did not bear any enmity to each other. On seeing the sage engaged in penance, he bowed down his head before him. The sage received the king with due words of benediction. The sage duly honoured him with *Pādya, Arghya* and *Ācamanīyaka.* He spoke to the king the following virtuous words:

153-155. "O king, this youth is your son born of Mṛgāvatī. He is a storehouse of fame. He has great refulgence. He is like another Rāmacandra. He is a youth with leonine body. He will conquer all the cardinal points. O illustrious one, this is your grandson, the son of Udayana. This is your wife Mṛgāvatī always devoted to chastity. Therefore, accept these three, O great king. Do not delay."

156. After saying thus, the sage handed them over. The king accepted them. Accompanied by his beloved wife and the minis-

of Vasus; O Brāhmaṇas, the nose was made out of the refulgence of Kubera.

40. The rows of teeth were shaped from the refulgence of the nine Prajāpatis. The pair of eyes was formed out of the brilliance of the Fire-god.

41-43. The two Sandhyās (dawn and dusk) became her eyebrows. The refulgence of the Wind-god became her ears. The other limbs of the lady were evolved from the dreadful refulgence of the other Devas. Thus Durgā of excessively brilliant form took birth. She appeared invincible to all—both Surās and the Asuras. Thus she was born of the amalgamation of the refulgences of the army of all the Devas. Seeing her, all those Devas who had been harassed by Mahiṣa became delighted.

44. Then, O excellent Brāhmaṇas, Devas headed by Rudra extracted spears and other weapons of their own and handed them over to her.

45-49. They gave her ornaments, garments, garlands and sandalpaste. Adorned and equipped with the ornaments, garments, flowers, weapons, garlands, sandalpaste, etc. that goddess, the dreadful goddess of frightening voice, laughed boistrously. She roared out loudly as if to shake heaven and earth. She was attended upon by gods. Due to terrific roar of the goddess the entire universe got agitated.

As the Devī rode on her vehicle, the lion, the immortal ones, sages, Siddhas, Gandharvas and others began to eulogize with shouts of "Be victorious".

Due to the extremely terrible shouts of the Devī the three worlds became agitated. On seeing it, Daityas, the enemies of the Devas, rose up with arms raised.

50. Mahiṣa was excessively infuriated. He lifted up his great weapons and surrounded by Asuras proceeded in the direction of that sound.

51-53. He saw the Devī pervading the three worlds by means of her refulgence. She had innumerable hands equipped with weapons. She shook the entire earth with her shouts. She made great serpents including Śeṣa excited thereby. On seeing the Devī, Asuras stood ready with their weapons lifted up.

Then a fight between the Asuras and the Devī ensued with missiles, weapons, arrows, discuses, iron clubs and big threshing rods.

54. Then the excessively powerful Mahiṣa, the suppressor of

25. The army of Devas fled due to fear, O Brāhmaṇas. Keeping Indra ahead of them, Devas went to god Brahmā.

26. Taking all those Devas with him, Brahmā went to the place where Nārāyaṇa and Śiva, the protectors of the universe, were present.

27. After going there, bowing to them and eulogizing them by means of various kinds of prayers, Brahmā reported to them the misdeeds of Mahiṣāsura.

28-31. He intimated the trouble inflicted on Suras by Asuras, to the Lords Śaṁbhu and Kṛṣṇa (i.e. Viṣṇu). (Then he said,) "He has dismissed Indra, Agni, Yama, the Sun-god, the Moon-god, Kubera, Varuṇa and others and has occupied their posts himself. He has usurped the powers of the other Devas too. The dismissed group of Devas has left the heavenly world on being harassed by Mahiṣāsura. They are now wandering over the earth like human beings. It is to intimate this to you two, my Lords, that I have come here along with the same groups of Devas. Do protect them who have come down here."

32. On hearing the words of Brahmā, Rameśvara (Viṣṇu) and Maheśvara became furious. Their faces became dreadful and very difficult to gaze at.

33-35. Then, O Brāhmaṇas, from the highly enraged blazing faces of Viṣṇu, Śaṁbhu and Brahmā, a great refulgence issued forth. From the bodies of Indra and other Devas too a dreadful splendour came forth. All these units of splendour joined together and formed a single mass. This mass of splendour resembled a blazing mountain. It was seen by the groups of the Devas as spreading its flames and enveloping every direction.

36. This mass of fiery refulgence took the shape of a woman. The refulgence of Śiva became her face; that of Viṣṇu her arms, O Brāhmaṇas.

37. The splendour of Brahmā became the feet; the splendour of Indra became the waistline. The tresses were formed with the refulgence of Yama and the breasts with the brilliance of the Moon.

38. The shanks and the thighs were evolved out of the refulgence of Varuṇa, O Brāhmaṇas. The refulgence of the Earth became the hips and the loins, and that of the Sun became the toes of the feet.

39. The fingers of the hands were shaped with the splendour

of Vasus; O Brāhmaṇas, the nose was made out of the refulgence of Kubera.

40. The rows of teeth were shaped from the refulgence of the nine Prajāpatis. The pair of eyes was formed out of the brilliance of the Fire-god.

41-43. The two Sandhyās (dawn and dusk) became her eye-brows. The refulgence of the Wind-god became her ears. The other limbs of the lady were evolved from the dreadful refulgence of the other Devas. Thus Durgā of excessively brilliant form took birth. She appeared invincible to all—both Suras and the Asuras. Thus she was born of the amalgamation of the refulgences of the army of all the Devas. Seeing her, all those Devas who had been harassed by Mahiṣa became delighted.

44. Then, O excellent Brāhmaṇas, Devas headed by Rudra extracted spears and other weapons of their own and handed them over to her.

45-49. They gave her ornaments, garments, garlands and sandalpaste. Adorned and equipped with the ornaments, garments, flowers, weapons, garlands, sandalpaste, etc. that goddess, the dreadful goddess of frightening voice, laughed boistrously. She roared out loudly as if to shake heaven and earth. She was attended upon by gods. Due to terrific roar of the goddess the entire universe got agitated.

As the Devī rode on her vehicle, the lion, the immortal ones, sages, Siddhas, Gandharvas and others began to eulogize with shouts of "Be victorious".

Due to the extremely terrible shouts of the Devī the three worlds became agitated. On seeing it, Daityas, the enemies of the Devas, rose up with arms raised.

50. Mahiṣa was excessively infuriated. He lifted up his great weapons and surrounded by Asuras proceeded in the direction of that sound.

51-53. He saw the Devī pervading the three worlds by means of her refulgence. She had innumerable hands equipped with weapons. She shook the entire earth with her shouts. She made great ser-pents including Śeṣa excited thereby. On seeing the Devī, Asuras stood ready with their weapons lifted up.

Then a fight between the Asuras and the Devī ensued with missiles, weapons, arrows, discuses, iron clubs and big threshing rods.

54. Then the excessively powerful Mahiṣa, the suppressor of

25. The army of Devas fled due to fear, O Brāhmaṇas. Keeping Indra ahead of them, Devas went to god Brahmā.

26. Taking all those Devas with him, Brahmā went to the place where Nārāyaṇa and Śiva, the protectors of the universe, were present.

27. After going there, bowing to them and eulogizing them by means of various kinds of prayers, Brahmā reported to them the misdeeds of Mahiṣāsura.

28-31. He intimated the trouble inflicted on Suras by Asuras, to the Lords Śaṁbhu and Kṛṣṇa (i.e. Viṣṇu). (Then he said,) "He has dismissed Indra, Agni, Yama, the Sun-god, the Moon-god, Kubera, Varuṇa and others and has occupied their posts himself. He has usurped the powers of the other Devas too. The dismissed group of Devas has left the heavenly world on being harassed by Mahiṣāsura. They are now wandering over the earth like human beings. It is to intimate this to you two, my Lords, that I have come here along with the same groups of Devas. Do protect them who have come down here."

32. On hearing the words of Brahmā, Rameśvara (Viṣṇu) and Maheśvara became furious. Their faces became dreadful and very difficult to gaze at.

33-35. Then, O Brāhmaṇas, from the highly enraged blazing faces of Viṣṇu, Śaṁbhu and Brahmā, a great refulgence issued forth. From the bodies of Indra and other Devas too a dreadful splendour came forth. All these units of splendour joined together and formed a single mass. This mass of splendour resembled a blazing mountain. It was seen by the groups of the Devas as spreading its flames and enveloping every direction.

36. This mass of fiery refulgence took the shape of a woman. The refulgence of Śiva became her face; that of Viṣṇu her arms, O Brāhmaṇas.

37. The splendour of Brahmā became the feet; the splendour of Indra became the waistline. The tresses were formed with the refulgence of Yama and the breasts with the brilliance of the Moon.

38. The shanks and the thighs were evolved out of the refulgence of Varuṇa, O Brāhmaṇas. The refulgence of the Earth became the hips and the loins, and that of the Sun became the toes of the feet.

39. The fingers of the hands were shaped with the splendour

71-73. Then Devī rode on her vehicle, the lion, of the velocity of the mind. She seized her dreadful bow of loud report like that of the cloud at the time of the world destruction. She made a twanging sound and discharged many arrows of adamantine strength and of the velocity of the wind. Daitya Mahāhanu equipped with a million elephants, ten million horses, ten million chariots and a thousand million foot-soldiers was killed by Devī in the battle.

74. In his army, O excellent Brāhmaṇas, thousands, hundred thousands and crores of the commanders of the principal units were killed by Devī with her arrows.

75. Mahiṣa had very powerful Asura leaders numbering thousands, hundred thousands and crores. Each of these leaders too had an army of four divisions.

76-77. Just as, O Brāhmaṇas, Mahāhanu had a great army, so others too had a vast army. The entire army was killed by Devī by means of arrows with golden feathers fixed to their tails. That was something of a miracle, O eminent Brāhmaṇas, that this was done within a (short) period of a Yāma (3 hours) only.

CHAPTER SEVEN

Mahiṣāsura Killed

Śrī Sūta said:

1. On seeing that his army had been destroyed by Devī, Mahiṣa, the lord of Dānavas, spoke with great anger to Caṇḍakopa:

Mahiṣa said:

2-6. O Caṇḍakopa of great vigour, fight with this vicious woman.

After saying "So be it", the valorous Caṇḍakopa showered a volley of arrows on Devī at the front of the battle. Aṁbikā sportingly split quickly the arrows of Caṇḍakopa; killed the charioteer and the horses of the Daitya. Then she cut down his flagstaff and bow. Then she crushed the chariot and hit the demon in his chest.

(Finding) the horses and the charioteer killed, the bow broken and the chariot shattered, Caṇḍakopa rushed at Devī wielding a sword and a shield. With his sword, the great Asura struck the lion, the vehicle of Devī.

7. He hit the left arm of Devī with his sword but it was broken into a thousand pieces on (the impact of) her hand.

8. Then Aṁbikā hit Caṇḍakopa in his chest with a great spear. He fell down dead.

9. When Caṇḍakopa of great vigour and excessive strength was killed, Citrabhānu mounted an elephant and rushed at Devī.

10. The demon hurled a divine Śakti tinkling with big bells. Without being agitated, Devī warded off that Śakti with her *Huṁkāra* ('hum' sound).

11. Then the Goddess tore Citrabhānu with her spear. When he died in the battle, Karāla rushed in.

12. Hitting him with her fist, Devī made him fall down. Then with her iron club Devī deprived the haughty fellow of his life.

13. Goddess Durgā despatched to the world of Yama Bāṣkala with her sharp spear and Antika with her discus, O excellent Brāhmaṇas.

14. Similarly she pierced with her spear the other huge-bodied ministers of Mahiṣa and sent them to the abode of Yama.

15-19. When his army was thus slain by Durgā, Mahiṣāsura assumed the form of a buffalo and devoured the Gaṇas of Devī. He killed a few with his snout and others by kicking with the hoofs. The infuriated demon toppled down others with the impact of his exhalation. After killing Devi's army of goblins, Mahiṣāsura (rushed) to kill her lion. He became infuriated and roared. Then the lion of great strength became furious. With his paws he dug the ground and broke the mountains. As Mahiṣāsura came near, he tore him up with his claws. The wrathful Caṇḍikā intended to kill him then.

20-24. In her excessive anger, Caṇḍikā bound Mahiṣa by means of ropes and nooses. The demon got himself released from the nooses and abandoned the guise of buffalo. The Daitya then adopted the form of a lion. By the time Devī was ready to cut off his head, the Daitya of great strength became a man with a sword in his hand. With multitudes of arrows of sharp points capable of tearing vulnerable spots, Devī struck that man with the sword in his hand. Then that man became an elephant with a trunk and two tusks. With its trunk it pulled the lion, the vehicle of Devī. Thereupon, the lion split its trunk by means of its claws.

25-27. Again he became a great Asura in the guise of a buffalo. Then the infuriated Bhadrakālī began to drink the great liquor.

On account of the drink she became inebriated. Her eyes became red and she (contemptuously) laughed. With his horns Mahiṣāsura proudly hurled boulders of rocks on Caṇḍikā. With her arrows she cut them off. Then Devī, the mother of the universe, spoke to Mahiṣāsura:

Devī said:

28-29. O stupid fellow, you can well be proud for a short while as long as I drink this liquor. After I finish drinking this liquor, I shall send you to Yama's abode.

After you have been killed, you who have been unassailable (so far), and have been a thorn to Devas, let Siddhas, Sādhyas and groups of Maruts resort to their respective posts.

30-34. After saying this, Devī dealt Mahiṣāsura a blow with her fist. On being struck by Devī, Mahiṣa became frightened and agitated. He immediately fled to the shore of the Southern Sea. Riding on her vehicle, the lion, Devī chased him. Thereupon, pursued by Devī, Mahiṣa, the lord of Dānavas, entered the waters of Dharmapuṣkariṇī, ten Yojanas in width.[1] Agitated by the blow of Durgā, he remained hidden therein. Then Durgā came to the banks of Dharmapuṣkariṇī. But Caṇḍikā did not see Mahiṣāsura there. Then an unembodied voice spoke to Goddess Durgā:

35-36. "O Bhadrakālī, O great Goddess, Mahiṣa, the Dānava who has been hit by you with the fist, has become extremely frightened. O gentle lady, he lies concealed in the waters of Dharmapuṣkarṇī. Slay him. Deprive him of his life by some means."

37. On being told thus by the incorporeal voice, Caṇḍikā who was ready to slay the demon, told the lion, her vehicle:

38. "O king of beasts of leonine valour and excessive strength, let the water of Dharmapuṣkariṇī be drunk up completely by you."

39. On being told thus by Devī, O Brāhmaṇas, the lion drank the entire quantity of water in Dharmapuṣkariṇī so that there was only dust (silt) left behind.

40-42. Thereupon the dejected Mahiṣa came out of the water

1. In order to increase their importance, the Sthala-Purāṇas claim that many important purāṇic events took place at their Kṣetra. SkP has now brought the final phase of the fight between Mahiṣāsura and Durgā at Dharmapuṣkariṇī. It is not ten Yojanas in width as stated here.

reservoir. As the Asura approached her, the infuriated Devī placed her foot on the head of the Asura and hit his neck with her spear. Then Devī seized (her) sword and cut off his huge head.

Thus, O Brāhmaṇas, the demon Mahiṣa was slain by Durgā along with his servants, army and vehicles. He fell down on the ground and died.[1]

43. Thereupon, Devas, Siddhas, Gandharvas, and the great sages eulogized Devī with prayers. They were satisfied and delighted.

44-46. Permitted by Devī, Devas went to different places in the manner they had come. Then Devī founded an excellent city named after her.[2] The mother of the universe built the city on the northern shore of the Southern Sea. Thereafter, at the bidding of Devī, Devas headed by Śakra filled Dharmapuṣkariṇī with nectar. Therefore, that excellent Tīrtha got the name *Amṛta Tīrtha.*

47-48. Then Devī who was joyous, granted this boon to her city: "Let this city be conducive to the welfare of all animals and be free from sickness." To the Tīrtha, she granted the boon: "The men who take their holy bath here shall attain Siddhi in accordance with their desires."

After saying thus she went to heaven.

Śrī Sūta said:

49. The excellent city which Devī built and named after her, is called Devīpaṭṭaṇa. It is the most excellent among all cities.

50-56. At a very auspicious hour, Rāma started from Devīpaṭṭaṇa, O Brāhmaṇas. At the outset, he bowed down to Vighneśvara (Gaṇeśa) and the Lord of waters (i.e. Varuṇa). Permitted by Mahādeva, Rāmacandra, the highly virtuous one, joyously laid down with his own hand the (first) nine boulders.[3] He inaugurated the construction of the Setu, O Brāhmaṇas. Till it was completed upto Laṅkā, he watched its progress alertly. While watching the progress of the work, Rāma occupied a splendid throne made by Nala. Through

1. In Mbh, *Vana* 231.26, *Śalya* 46.74, Skanda is credited to have killed Mahiṣāsura.

2. This explains why the place came to be called Devīpaṭṭaṇa, a reply to the query of the sages in *Supra* 6.1-4.

3. The nine boulders represent the nine Planets. The place is known as 'Navapāṣāṇam' now, and also called Setumūla (the root, i.e. the beginning of Setu). But as explained in vv 58-62, the place where Rāma lay on the bed of Darbha-grass to propitiate the Sea-god is to the west of Setumūla and Devīpaṭṭaṇa to the east of Setumūla. Hence both the places are known as Setumūla.

When your younger brother will see the lord of Vidyādharas named Vijñaptikautuka, he shall become liberated from the curse.

You are the actual perpetrator of a great sin like this. You will attain the human birth and in the very same birth you will attain the form of a Vetāla. You will wander over the world for a long time."

After saying this and cursing the Vidyādhara princes, Gālava took his daughter with him and went back to his hermitage along with the other sages.

45b-50. When that great sage, the illustrious one, had gone, the Vidyādhara princes named Sudarśana and Sukarṇa became extremely worried on account of the sage's curse. They began to ponder over this very much. Sudarśana and Sukarṇa came to a decision as to what they should do. They selected a Brāhmaṇa named Govindasvāmin, resident of a place on the banks of Yamunā, to be their father. Then they abandoned their real form and were born as his sons named Vijayadatta and Aśokadatta. The elder one named Sudarśana was born as the son named Vijayadatta. Sukarṇa, the younger one, became the son named Aśokadatta. Vijaya and Aśoka gradually attained the age of youth.

51. At that time, on account of absence of rain, there occurred a drought lasting for twelve years on the auspicious banks of Yamunā.

52-54. Observing his own city devastated by famine, the Brāhmaṇa named Govindasvāmin, master of all the Vedas, proceeded towards the city of Kāśī along with his sons and wife.

When he reached Prayāga and visited the meritorious Mahāvaṭa[1], he saw a sage in front of him wearing a garland of skulls. The Brāhmaṇa, named Govindasvāmin, bowed down to that sage.

55. That sage spoke to him, offering his blessings to him along with his sons and wife. He then spoke these words to Govindasvāmin:

56. "Now, O excellent Brāhmaṇa, very soon you will be separated from this elder son Vijayadatta".

57-58. On hearing his words, the Brāhmaṇa called Govindasvāmin, went away for his Sandhyā prayers as the sun had set. After concluding the daily rites, the Brāhmaṇa who was fatigued and vexed on account of a long travel, stayed for that night in a vacant temple along with his wife and sons.

1. This is probably the celebrated Akṣaya Vaṭa which is now in a subterranean chamber in the fort of Allahabad. That Banyan Tree is still worshipped by pilgrims.

59. Aśokadatta and the Brāhmaṇa lady who were utterly exhausted, spread a cloth on the ground and went to sleep.

60-61. Vijaya was greatly exhausted on account of the long journey. He was overwhelmed with fever with fits of cold. Although he was closely embraced by his father Govindasvāmin for dispelling the suffering from cold, he could not get rid of the affliction.

62. (Then the boy said:) "O father, an excessive chillness and fever with cold fits afflicts me very much. Fetch some fire to check completely this chillness. Do not delay."

63. On hearing these words of his son, he went in search of fire. Nowhere could he get the same. He returned to his son and said thus:

64-69. "O son, I am not able to get fire, though I have searched for it everywhere. It is midnight now. All the doors are closed. The citizens are overcome by sleep. They will not give fire." Thus Vijayadatta who was afflicted with fever was told by his father. Still in a piteous tone, he begged of his father to fetch him some fire. (He said:) "I am afflicted with chillness as a result of the shivering fever. The wind with icy sprays oppresses me with doubly increased severity. A lie has been uttered by you, O father, that fire could not be got. See, yonder, there, in front of us, a fire is blazing. It has clusters of flames. It licks the sky with shooting flames. O father, fetch that fire quickly for quelling the chillness."

As the son spoke thus, the father replied thus:

70-74. "I do not utter any lie now, my son. I am speaking the truth. The place that is seen from afar as having fire, know it to be the cremation ground, my son. The fire that blazes forth at present with its flames licking the sky, in front of us, know it to be the fire of the funeral pyre that generates fear. This fire (of the funeral pyre) is inauspicious. Its very touch defiles. It should not be resorted to. If anyone resorts to the funeral pyre, his span of life gets reduced. The inauspicious funeral fire unworthy of being touched is not brought here by me, dear son, lest there should be an adverse effect on your span of life."

As the father said thus, that miserable wretch replied:

75. "It may be the fire in funeral pyre or it may be the sacrificial fire. In any case let it be fetched. If not, it is sure that I will die."

76. Under the influence of filial affection, the Brāhmaṇa named

Govindasvāmī went immediately to the cremation ground in order to fetch the funeral fire.

77. When Govindasvāmin went away to bring the funeral fire, Vijayadatta too quickly followed him.

78. Coming very near the warm fire, the funeral fire, where the bones lay scattered, it appeared as though he was going to embrace it. Gradually he attained some relief.

79-80. He then asked his father: "What is this excessively brilliant and circular object that resembles a red lotus and shines in the fire?" On hearing these words of his son, the excellent Brāhmaṇa carefully looked at it and spoke these words:

Govindasvāmī said:

81. This piece of circular object is the skull with fiery flames. It is full of fat, flesh and hard bony stuff. It resembles a red lotus.

82. On hearing this, the son of the Brāhmaṇa hit it with the tip of a log of wood, whereat it broke. The fat that splashed about sprinkled his face.

83. When particles of blood from the broken skull stuck to his face, he began to lick them with his tongue repeatedly. He began to relish that blood.

84. After relishing it, he seized the skull and excitedly drank the melted fat. His body grew bigger in size and he became exceedingly dreadful.

85-88. Immediately he was transformed into a Vetāla (Vampire) with sharp teeth. At that hour of the night, the quarters, inter-spaces between the cardinal points, the heaven, the firmament and the earth began to burst as it were at the loud report of his boisterous laugh.

Then he rushed at his father with a great speed and attempted to kill him. Instantly a heavenly voice spoke: "Do not indulge in this rash, heinous act."

On hearing that divine utterance, the highly dreadful Vetāla let off his father. Without faltering in his steps, he rushed along the ethereal path with great speed.

89-90. After going a long way, he got into touch with (other) Vetālas. On seeing him arrived thus, all the Vetālas joined together and called him by the name 'Kapālasphoṭa' because it was by shattering the *Kapāla* (Skull) that he was transformed into a Vetāla.

91-92. Surrounded by all the Vetālas, this Kapālasphoṭa immediately went to the presence of the king of Vetālas named Narāsthibhūṣaṇa. Equipped with a great army, Narāsthibhūṣaṇa appointed him his Commander-in-chief.

93-95. Once a powerful Gandharva named Citrasena killed Narāsthibhūṣaṇa in battle. He too was killed. When Narāsthibhūṣaṇa was killed by the Gandharva, Kapālasphoṭa got into his position.

On account of the curse of the great sage, Sudarśana, son of the lord of Vidyādharas, at first became a man. Then he attained the state of a Vetāla and gradually became the lord of Vetālas.

CHAPTER NINE

Redemption of Sudarśana and Sukarṇa

1-2. Then that Brāhmaṇa in the company of his wife and (the other) son Aśokadatta began to lament on account of the grief for the (elder) son in the morning. On seeing the lamenting Brāhmaṇa Govindasvāmin, O Brāhmaṇas, a merchant named Samudradatta brought them to his house.

3-5. After bringing them there, he consoled them. The compassionate merchant-leader made him the guardian of all his assets.

The Brāhmaṇa frequently remembered the words of the great sage. He was eager to see his son once again. Thus he stayed in the house of the merchant along with his wife and son.

The second son of the Brāhmaṇa, named Aśokadatta, became a great expert in the use of weapons and also in the scriptural literature.

6. Similarly in the other lores too there was none like him on the earth. After the completion of his education, the son of the Brāhmaṇa became very famous in that city.

7-8. In the meantime, a certain powerful wrestler, the lord of Kāśideśa, came (as a challenger in wrestling) to the king named Pratāpamukuṭa. In order to defeat that wrestler, King Pratāpamukuṭa invited through his attendants that Brāhmaṇa's son of very great strength.

9-15. On seeing him arrived, Pratāpamukuṭa said: "O Aśokadatta, indeed you are the most excellent one among powerful persons. Defeat this invincible wrestler who is proud of his strength. Conquer him in a fight. If this great wrestler from the southern region is defeated by you, I shall give you whatever is desired by you. There is no doubt about it."

On hearing these words of his, the powerful son of the Brāhmaṇa struck the king of wrestlers from the southern region.[1] That powerful wrestler, on being struck by that powerful son of the Brāhmaṇa, fell down dead on the ground with the eyes suddenly rolling back. This act of the son of the Brāhmaṇa was something that was very difficult even for Devas.

On seeing it, Pratāpamukuṭa became very delighted in his heart. He gave him much wealth and many villages. Thereafter, he kept him near himself.

Once, that great king accompanied by the son of the Brāhmaṇa was riding a horse in a lonely spot at the time of dusk.

16-19. Accompanied by the son of the Brāhmaṇa (the king) heard a piteous appeal: "O king, my offence was very slight. On account of the repeated instigation of my enemies, the magistrate has impaled me on the spike ruthlessly. This is the fourth day since I have been impaled and I still continue to be alive. In the case of men of vicious deeds, the vital airs do not go out happily and easily. An unquenchable thirst oppresses me; satiate it, O king."

On hearing these piteous appeals the king spoke to the Brāhmaṇa's son named Aśokadatta who was very bold.

20. "O son of a Brāhmaṇa, water should be given by you to this innocent creature that has been impaled on the spike and that is exceedingly thirsty."

21. Immediately after being commanded thus by the king, the son of the Brāhmaṇa took a pot filled with water and hurried off.

22-23. He went to that cremation ground infested with evil spirits and Vetālas. He was eager to give water unto that (creature) impaled on the spike.

There he saw a woman in the prime of youth. The Brāhmaṇa saw that refulgent lady who appeared to be Rati (wife of the god of Love) in a bodily form.

24-25. On seeing her, the bold son of the Brāhmaṇa said: "O gentle lady, O beautiful lady, who are you? Why are you standing here in this lonely spot in the cremation ground? Why do you stand beneath this fellow who has been impaled on the spike?"

1. It appears that South Indian athletes were famous in Purāṇic times. The wrestlers maintained by Kaṁsa and used against Kṛṣṇa and Balarāma were also southerners.

On hearing these words of his, that lady of charming countenance said:

26-29. "This man is my lover. He has been impaled on the spike by the king. Just as a miser does not leave off his wealth, so also he does not leave off his vital airs. He is about to die and I am here to fellow him. He is thirsty and begs of me to give him water. This gives me incessant pain. He is on the top of the spike. My lover is about to die. I am not able to make him drink water standing as I am beneath him in a lower position." On hearing these words, Aśokadatta who was an ocean of mercy, spoke these words befitting that occasion:

Aśokadatta said:

30-31. Mother, step on my shoulder and give him the cool water.

Saying "This I will do" the young maiden, in a great hurry, stepped on the shoulder (of that Brāhmaṇa) and got up. Thereupon the son of the Brāhmaṇa saw fresh blood trickling down.

32-34. Wondering what it was, he lifted up his face and stared. He saw that (the body of the impaled man) was being eaten by her. On realizing this, the son of the Brāhmaṇa, Aśokadatta, caught hold of her foot along with the anklet. Thereupon, she left the valuable anklet studded with many jewels and went away.

Aśokadatta took that anklet studded with many jewels and started from the cremation ground to the presence of the king.

35. He reported to the king the incidents of the cremation ground and handed him the anklet studded with very costly jewels.

36. On coming to know of his heroic activities that could not be performed by others, the king gave him his daughter named Madanalekhā.

37-40. Once, gazing at that anklet, the king eagerly thought thus: 'From where can I get another anklet on a par with this?'

Aśokadatta came to know the desire of the king. He began to think of the ways and means of getting another anklet. 'It was from the cremation ground that this anklet was obtained by me before. Where else can I look for getting another anklet?' After considering various alternatives, the highly intelligent one came to a decision:

41-43. 'I shall go to the cremation ground and sell human flesh. The Rākṣasas, Vetālas, Piśācas and other beings can be invoked by means of Mantras. As they come, that demoness too will come there. As soon as she comes I shall catch hold of her and seize that anklet per force. A thousand Rākṣasas, ten thousand Piśācas and ten million Vetālas are very insignificant to me: now I am powerful enough.'

44-45. After making up his mind thus, he at once went to the cremation ground. After invoking the Rākṣasas by means of Mantras, he began to hawk human flesh.

He wandered in all the quarters shouting loudly "Take ye! Human flesh is on sale! Take ye, this 'great' (human) flesh. Take ye", and he made (the spirits in all quarters) hear it.

46. The Rākṣasas and the Vetālas, skeletons and ghosts and other evil spirits flocked there together with great delight.

47-52. "All of us shall consume the meat which is most desired by us", said they in great glee.

As all the Rākṣasas arrived, that Rākṣasī too came there surrounded by Rākṣasa girls eagerly desirous of eating that flesh. The Brāhmaṇa was on the lookout for her. When he espied the Rākṣasī, he immediately recognized her as the one seen by him formerly. The son of the Brāhmaṇa said to her, "Give me the other anklet".

On hearing his words, she was pleased. She spoke these words with great delight: "O leader of heroes, it was my anklet that was taken away by you previously. Accept this second anklet also very beautiful on account of the jewels."

After saying this (the Rākṣasī) gave him the anklet as well as her beloved daughter. The Brāhmaṇa was highly delighted on obtaining the beloved lady named Vidyutprabhā who was endowed with beauty and youth and was given (in marriage) to him by Vidyutkeśī.

53-55. Vidyutkeśī gave a gold lotus too to her son-in-law. After getting Vidyutprabhā, the anklet and the golden lotus, he took leave of his mother-in-law and came again to the presence of the king.

Delighted with the acquisition of the anklet, Pratāpamukuṭa praised the son of the Brāhmaṇa endowed with heroism and courage. Once the Brāhmaṇa spoke to Vidyutprabhā, his beloved, in secret:

56. "O my beloved, from where was this golden lotus obtained by your mother? From where can I obtain other (flowers) like this, O lady of excellent countenance?"

57-59. Vidyutprabhā spoke in secret to the son of the Brāhmaṇa, her husband: "O lord, there is a divine lake belonging to the king of the Vetālas named Kapālasphoṭa. It is adorned with golden lotuses. This golden lotus has been brought by your mother-in-law who was engaged in aquatic sports therein."

On hearing these words, he said: "Take me there." Immediately she took that Brāhmaṇa to the golden lake.

60-61. As that son of the Brāhmaṇa was about to pluck the golden lotuses, many Vetālas and others prohibited (caused obstacles to) him and he killed all of them. After all the soldiers had been killed, he himself saw the lord of the Vetālas named Kapālasphoṭa and set about to kill him.

62-69. In the meantime, the highly refulgent lord of the Vidyādharas named Vijñaptikautuka came there in his aerial chariot and spoke to him: "O Aśokadatta, O eminent Brāhmaṇa, do not be rash in your activity." The son of the Brāhmaṇa heard it and immediately saw the refulgent lord of the Vidyādharas in the firmament. He was seated in an aerial chariot. The moment he saw him, the son of the Brāhmaṇa became rid of his curse. He abandoned his human form and attained a divine form.

Vijñaptikautuka said to Sukarṇa who had been liberated from the curse, was seated in an excellent aerial chariot and was adorned with divine ornaments:

"O Sukarṇa, this is your brother, the sinner who touched the daughter of Gālava, the great sage. He attained the state of a Vetāla on account of his curse.

Since you were an abettor of his crime you too were cursed by him. Since your offence was of a minor character the curse was operative only till you saw me. This was ordained by that sage himself. But he has not granted any redemption from the curse to (your brother). Therefore, come along. You are free from the curse, O Sukarṇa, ascend to heaven." Thereupon Sukarṇa said to the overlord of the Vidyādharas:

70-71. "O lord of Vidyādharas, without my elder brother I am not eager enough to go to heaven, although it is full of all kinds of pleasures. Tell me the means whereby the curse of my brother may come to an end."

The highly brilliant Vijñapatikautuka said to him:

72-79. "This curse is very difficult to be counteracted. Who else can stop it? But I shall tell you a very great secret. This was told by Brahmā formerly to the sages including Sanaka. On the meritorious shore of the Southern Sea which is the receptacle of all the Tīrthas, there is an exceedingly great Tīrtha near Cakratīrtha.

Merely by visiting it, masses of great sins perish instantaneously. I do not know the benefit of taking the holy bath. If your brother goes there and takes his holy bath in that exceedingly great Tīrtha, he shall certainly be rid of the state of a Vetāla which is a result of the curse of Gālava."

On hearing his words, Sukarṇa immediately went to the shore of the Southern Sea along with his brother in the form of Vetāla.

The Tīrtha mentioned by Brahmā to Sanaka and others is to the south of Cakratīrtha and north of Gandhamādana. After reaching the banks of that Tīrtha he spoke to his brother thus:

"O Brother, for dispelling the dreadful curse of Gālava, take your holy bath immediately in this Tīrtha which is the most excellent of all the excellent Tīrthas."

80. At that time, O Brāhmaṇas, the sprays of water from that Tīrtha brought by wind fell on his limbs.

81. On account of the contact with the spray of water, he abandoned the state of Vetāla and regained the state of human being, i.e. that of the son of the Brāhmaṇa.

82. Thereafter with the ritualistic *Saṁkalpa* for dispelling his state of human being, the son of the Brāhmaṇa took the holy plunge in the most excellent one of all the excellent Tīrthas.

83-91. Rising up immediately, he attained divine form. He got into an excellent aerial chariot. Sudarśana was surrounded by celestial ladies. He was adorned with all ornaments. Accompanied by his brother, he praised that Tīrtha and bowed down to it repeatedly. Keeping Vijñaptikautuka at the head, he went to heaven.

Ever since then that Tīrtha came to be called *Vetālavarada* because the state of being Vetāla was dispelled merely with the touch of its sprays.

Those who come to this Tīrtha to the south of Cakratīrtha and take even a casual bath become living-liberated souls.

There has never been nor will there ever be a Tīrtha as meritorious as this Tīrtha.

He abandoned the terrible form of Vetāla and attained divine state.

The devotee should perform *Saṁkalpa* rite and take the holy bath in the splendid Vetālavarada and offer rice-balls to the manes with due observances. Thus, O Brāhmaṇas, the glory of that Tīrtha as well as how this Tīrtha came to be called by the name Vetālavarada has been recounted to you. He who reads or listens to this chapter becomes liberated.

CHAPTER TEN

The Sanctifying Power of Pāpavināśa[1]

Śrī Sūta said:

1. After taking the holy bath in the Vetālavarada Tīrtha, O excellent Brāhmaṇas, the man (i.e. the pilgrim) should slowly go to the Gandhamādana mountain.

2-8. The mountain Gandhamādana which is like a bridge on the sea, is the pathway to the world of Brahmā, built by the maker of the universe. There are hundred thousands and thousands of crores of lakes and rivers. There are highly sanctifying seas, forests and hermitages. There are meritorious groups of holy spots such as Vedāraṇya[2]. The following dwell here: Sages including Vasiṣṭha and others, Siddhas, Cāraṇas and Kinnaras, Lord Madhusūdana with Lakṣmī and Dharaṇī (Goddess Earth), the four-faced lord Brahmā with Sāvitrī and Sarasvatī, Heraṁba (Gaṇeśa), the six-faced lord (Kārttikeya), Devas with Indra as their leader, Planets including the Sun, the eight Vasus, Pitṛs, the Guardians of the Quarters as well as other groups of Devas. O Brāhmaṇas, all these live there on the mountain Gandhamādana which sanctifies the worlds and which is destructive of the masses of great sins. They stay there day and night. The delighted Gaurī dwells there always with Hara.

9. There the lively sports of Kinnara ladies go on continuously. Merely by witnessing them, people get mental satisfaction.

10. The young women of Siddhas and Cāraṇas who reside on its top, always worship Śaṅkara, Kāla, the Lord of the Daughter of the Mountain (Pārvatī).

11. If the gusts of wind coming from Gandhamādana come into contact with the limbs (of one's body), crores of the sins of Brāhmaṇa-slaughter and crores of the sins of carnal approach to forbidden women perish.

12. Standing in the middle of the great ocean with surging waves, this Gandhamādana was formerly served by groups of sages.

13. When the Setu came to be built by Nala at the behest of

---

1. This Tīrtha is in Vethilai Maṇḍapam (Mandapam Railway Station) near the seashore.

2. A forest in Tanjore, the hermitage of Agastya.

Rāma, Gandhamādana which was accessible in the middle (of the sea), became worthy of being served by human beings.

14-16. The devotee should pray to Gandhamādana, the mountain in the form of the Setu: "O mountain of great merit, who are bowed down to by all the Devas! Even the Devas including Viṣṇu serve you with faith. O excellent one among mountains! I am treading upon you with my feet. Kindly pardon me who am a sinner, for my striking you with my feet (by placing it upon you). Show me Śaṅkara who has made his abode on your top."

17. After praying to the excellent mountain in the form of the Setu, the man should gently step on the sacred Gandhamādana.

18. He should take his bath in the sea and offer rice-balls on the mountain Gandhamādana even if they were to be only as small as mustards.

19. The manes shall be delighted with it till the Yuga is concluded. Or the pilgrim should give the Pitṛs the rice-balls equal in measure to a Śamī leaf.

20-21. Those who are in heaven will attain salvation and those who are the denizens of hell will go to heaven.

There is a great Tīrtha above it, well known in all the worlds. It is the most excellent of all the Tīrthas. It is sanctifying. It is called Pāpavināśana. That extremely meritorious Tīrtha. O Brāhmaṇas, is on the sacred Gandhamādana.

22. Merely by remembering it, one will cease to have rebirth. After going there the pilgrim should take his bath for dispelling the dirt of the body. By taking his holy bath there, the pilgrim goes to Vaikuṇṭha. There is no doubt about it.

The sages said:

23. O Sūta, tell us the glory of the Tīrtha called Pāpavināśa. Indeed, enlightened by Vyāsa, you understand everything, O great sage.

Śrī Sūta said:

24. O excellent Brāhmaṇas, I shall recount to you the splendid story of events that took place in the penance-grove on the auspicious slopes of Himavān.

25. The penance grove is auspicious and the hermitage meritorious. It is full of different kinds of trees on the auspicious

slopes of Himavān.

26. It is full of many kinds of hedges, bushes and creepers. It is frequented by deer and elephants. It is reverberated by the sound of Siddhas and Cāraṇas. It is beautiful with the forest in full bloom.

27. It has a number of enclosures. It is rendered brilliant by the presence of ascetics and distinguished Brāhmaṇas resembling (in brilliance) the Sun and Fire-god.

28. It is fully occupied by ascetics pursuing holy observances and vows. The ascetics are initiated for performing sacrifices. They have restrained their diets and are self-possessed.

29-31. The hermitage is full of followers of Vedas who have studied the Vedas. There are persons of all the stages of life, i.e. religious students, householders, forest-dwellers and recluses. They are devotedly engaged in conduct preculiar to their respective stages of life. They regularly perform the rites laid down for their respective castes. Even the Vālakhilya sages and the Marīcis come there.

Once a certain Śūdra named Dṛḍhamati who was daring and jolly came to those Brāhmaṇas, O Brāhmaṇas.

32. The Śūdra named Dṛḍhamati came to the hermitage and was honoured by the ascetics. He prostrated in front of them with the eight limbs (touching the ground).

33. That Śūdra was much delighted to see multitudes of sages endowed with great refulgence and on a par with Devas, performing different kinds of sacrifices.

34. Then he felt inclined to perform an excellent penance. So he approached the Kulapati (Head sage of the hermitage) and spoke these words:

Dṛḍhamati said:

35-37. O ascetic, obeisance to you. Save me, O ocean of mercifulness. I wish, O eminent Brāhmaṇa, to engage in righteous conduct with your guidance and favour. Hence I have come here. O sage of good holy rites, initiate me in the Yāga rite. O Brāhmaṇa, I belong to the Śūdra community, O excellent one. I wish to render services to you. Be pleased with me who have sought refuge in you.

When this was spoken by the Śūdra, the Brāhmaṇa spoke to him:

Kulapati said:

38-41. A Śūdra being of low birth cannot be initiated in a sacrifice. Be pleased to listen. If you are so inclined, be engaged in service. No (religious) instruction is to be given to one of low caste. In instructing him, the preceptor incurs great sin.

A learned man shall not teach a Śūdra, nor should he perform a Yāga on his behalf. He shall not teach a Śūdra any of the following subjects: the scriptures including Grammar, Poetry, Drama, Rhetorics, Purāṇa, Epic, myths and legends.

42. If a Brāhmaṇa were to teach a Śūdra these subjects, the other Brāhmaṇas shall banish him from the village, from Brāhmaṇa community.

43. One shall abandon like a Cāṇḍāla, the Brāhmaṇa who instructs a Śūdra. One should avoid from afar a Śūdra who is literate.

44. Hence, welfare unto you. Render service unto Brāhmaṇas with reverence. Service to the twice-born has been prescribed by Manu and others (as the duty) of a Śūdra.

45. It does not behove you to forsake your natural duty.

On being told thus by the sage, the Śūdra thought thus:

46-47. 'What is to be done by me now? My faith in the holy rites is very firm. I shall strive in such a way as to acquire perfect knowledge.'

After resolving thus mentally, the Śūdra named Dṛḍhamati went a long distance from that hermitage and built a splendid hut.

48. There he built a temple and many holy shrines. He constructed flower-gardens and lakes, etc.

49. He constructed these as an aid for the attainment of (success in) penance. He performed ablutions (to deities), observed *Niyamas* (self-imposed religious vows) like fasts, etc.

50-51. After preparing *Bali* (food such as rice) and offering it into fire, he worshipped deities duly. With resolve and regulation he subsisted on fruits only and controlled his passions and senses. With fruits, roots and bulbous roots he duly honoured the guests who visited him.

52. Thus a great deal of time passed by. Once a Brāhmaṇa named Sumati came to his hermitage.

53a. This Brāhmaṇa was born of the family of Garga. He was truthful and he had controlled his passions and senses.

53b-55. (The Śūdra) honoured the sage with due (formalities of) reception. He pleased him with fruits and other things. Narrating holy stories he enquired about his welfare.

Honoured thus by means of various courteous actions such as prostrations, etc. (the sage Sumati) blessed him, received his hospitality, took leave of him with great delight and went back to his own hermitage.

56. The Brāhmaṇa developed great partiality and affection for that Śūdra. He visited his hermitage every day in order to see that Śūdra.

57. The association of the Brāhmaṇa with the Śūdra continued for a long time. Influenced by his affection he never refused any request of the Śūdra.

58-61. (Once) the Śūdra said to the Brāhmaṇa who had been won over by means of friendship, as he came (to his hermitage): "O great sage, recount to me the entire procedures regarding the offering of *Havya* and *Kavya* to Devas and Pitṛs respectively. Teach me the requisite Mantras to be uttered and the procedure to the adopted during *Mahālaya* (holy festival in honour of Pitṛs to be performed in the dark half of Bhādrapada). Tell me the duties regarding Aṣṭakā-śrāddha and whatever other Vedic rites there may be (apart from these). Say what the secret doctrines are and also all the details. Indeed you are considered to be my preceptor."

On being requested thus by the Śūdra, he taught him everything. He made him perform all the rites of the Pitṛs and other rites as well.

62-64. After the rites of the Pitṛs had been performed by him (the Śūdra) bade farewell to him and the Brāhmaṇa went away.

Thereafter, for a long time, he was maintained by the Śūdra. So he was abandoned by the Brāhmaṇa community. (Later) he passed away. He was taken away by the soldiers of Yama and cast into the hells. He experienced the tortures of the Narakas for thousands and crores of Kalpas, for hundreds and crores of Kalpas and at the end of that period, he became an immobile being.

65. Then he was born as a donkey; again a pig eating feces. Then he was born as a dog and then a crow.

66. Then he was born as a Cāṇḍāla and thereafter as a Śūdra. Thereafter he became a Vaiśya and later on a Kṣatriya.

67. As a result of very powerful Karmas he became a Brāhmaṇa then. In the eighth year of his life reckoned from the day of

conception, the Brāhmaṇa was invested with the sacred thread by his father.

68. He continued to stay in his father's abode. He was given to follow his own will in his actions. Once, when he went deep into the forest, he was haunted by an evil spirit known as Brahmarākṣasa.

69. He began to cry and wander (here and there). He faltered in his steps. He was deluded. Sometimes he cried and sometimes he laughed. Sometimes he began to lament. He always shouted "Alas, Alas!". He abandoned Vedic rites.

70. On seeing the son turned so, the father was afflicted with great misery. He affectionately took his son with him and sought refuge in Agastya.

71. The father of that son bowed down to the sage with great devotion and intimated to him the problem of his son.

72-77a. Then the Brāhmaṇa said to the great Pot-born Sage: "O holy Brāhmaṇa, this my son has been caught by a Brahmarākṣasa. O holy Brāhmaṇa, he is not at all happy. Protect him with your benign glance. I do not have any other son for the sake of repaying the debts unto the Pitṛs. Tell me the means of quelling the suffering of this (son of mine), O Pot-born Sage. There is no other ascetic on a par with you in the three worlds. Indeed you have been described as the leader of the devotees of Śīva by great sages. Without you my son cannot be saved at all. Be merciful towards (an unhappy) father. Indeed good people are habitually kind and merciful."

Śrī Sūta said:

On being entreated thus by him, the Pot-born Sage began to meditate. After meditating for a long time, he spoke to the Brāhmaṇa then:

Agastya said:

77b-81. O highly intelligent one, in a previous birth your son was a Brāhmaṇa named Sumati. That Brāhmaṇa imparted instruction to a Śūdra. He taught him all the Vedic rites. Hence he had to experience tortures in hells for a period of thousands and crores of Kalpas. At the end of that period he was born in different species beginning with one of immobile beings. Now he is born as a Brāhmaṇa and your son due to his remaining (good) Karma.

He was caught by a Brahmarākṣasa sent by Yama. It was due to a terrible sin committed in the course of a previous birth (that this happened). I shall tell you the means of destroying the Brahmarākṣasa.

82-85. Listen with great faith and with great concentration of mind. There is a great mountain in the form of a Setu, O Brāhmaṇa, in the Southern Sea. It is the sacred Gandhamādana worthy of being served even by Devas. There is a great Tīrtha named Pāpavināśana on it. It is meritorious, famous and destructive of even great sins.

That Tīrtha is known as the destroyer of Bhūtas, ghosts, evil spirits, vampires, Brahmarākṣasas and of great ailments too. Take your son and go to that Tīrtha in the middle of the Setu.

86. Be self-restrained and make your son bathe in the Tīrtha named Pāpavināśana. By taking holy bath for three days there the Brahmarākṣasa perishes.

87. There is no other means on the earth for destroying it. So go there quickly to Rāmasetu, the bestower of salvation.

88. There bathe your son in the Tīrtha called Pāpavināśa. Do not delay here. O Brāhmaṇa, go quickly.

89. On being told thus, that Brāhmaṇa prostrated flat on the ground before Agastya. Permitted by him, he went to Gandhamādana.

90-91. After going to Pāpavināśana along with his son, the great Brāhmaṇa performed the rite of Saṅkalpa and made his son bathe there for three days, O eminent Brāhmaṇas. He himself took his bath. Then his son was let off by the Brahmarākṣasa.

92-93. He became free from ailments. He attained normalcy and he assumed a beautiful form. He became richly endowed with all prosperity and enjoyed various kinds of pleasures. Due to the holy bath in Pāpavināśana, he attained salvation on death. His father too, by taking the holy bath, attained salvation on death.

94-98. The Śūdra who was instructed by him experienced the tortures of hells in succession. Then he was born in various despicable species. Ultimately he became a vulture on the Gandhamādana mountain.

Once he went to the Tīrtha called Pāpavināśana in order to drink water. He drank water and sprinkled his own body. Instantaneously he got a divine body. He was adorned with all ornaments. He wore divine garlands and garments. He smeared himself with red sandalpaste. He got into a divine aerial chariot. He was made splendid by means of umbrellas and chowries. Surrounded by excellent ladies he went to the abode of the immortal ones.

Śrī Sūta said:

99-101. This Tīrtha has such a great power. Pāpavināśana Tīrtha bestows heavenly pleasures and salvation. It is meritorious and it causes atonement (of sins). It is resorted to by all the Suras, by Brahmā, Viṣṇu and Śiva. O Brāhmaṇas, it is called Pāpanāśa because it destroys sins. Hence a man seeking ultimate welfare should take bath in Pāpavināśana.

Thus, O eminent sages, the secret has been told. The glory of Pāpavināśana has been narrated. It is by taking bath there that the Brāhmaṇa and the Śūdra of censurable activities were at once liberated.

CHAPTER ELEVEN

Glorification of Sītā Lake—Indra Absolved of the Sin of Brāhmaṇa-Slaughter

Śrī Sūta said:

1. After taking the holy bath in Pāpanāśa which destroys all sins, one should go to Sītāsaras in order to bathe there with due observances.

2-5. All the meritorious Tīrthas within the Cosmic Egg, includ ing Gaṅgā and other holy places, reside in Sītāsaras for the purification of their respective sins, as the lake Sītāsaras is destructive of great sins. For the purpose of suppressing their own sins, the highly esteemed holy spots, Kāśī, etc. serve (stay in) Sītāsaras day and night.

A lion's cub had been attracted to that lake by the quality of its music. It stays in the lake destroying the five great sins.

Formerly Indra came to this Tīrtha and took his holy bath here with great faith. Thereby, O Brāhmaṇas, he was freed from the sin of Brāhmaṇa-slaughter.

The sages said:

6. O sage, how did Indra incur the sin of Brāhmaṇa-slaughter? How did he become liberated (from that sin) by taking his holy plunge in Sītāsaras?

Śrī Sūta said:

7-10. Formerly there was a Rākṣasa named Kapālābharaṇa, O Brāhmaṇas. Due to a boon given by Brahmā, he became exempt from death at the hands of all Devas. He had an excellent minister named Śavabhakṣaṇa. He had a hundred Akṣauhiṇīs (of army) consisting of horses, elephants and chariots. His city was well-known as Vaijayanta. While living in this city, the mighty Kapālābharaṇa called his minister Śavabhakṣa, and spoke to him, O Brāhmaṇas:

11-12. "O Śavabhakṣa of great valour, expert in the treatises on Mantras (or Politics), we shall go to the city of Devas and conquer Suras in battle. We shall occupy the abode of Indra along with our armies. We shall sport about in his Nandana park in the company of the groups of Raṁbhā and other celestial ladies."

13. On hearing these words of Kapālābharaṇa, O Brāhmaṇas, Śavabhakṣa spoke, "We will do so."

14-18. Then the powerful Kapālābharaṇa installed in his city his heroic son Durmedhas. Desirous of fighting with the Devas, he went to Amarāvatī, surrounded by his army.

With dust particles raised by the elephants, horses, chariots and foot-soldiers, he dried up oceans and rivers. He made the mountains crumble down to powder. With the sound of the Niḥsāṇa drum, O Brāhmaṇas, he made heaven and earth reverberate. With the neighing sounds of the horses, the trumpeting sounds of the elephants, the dreadful sounds of the rims of the chariot-wheels and the leonine roars of the foot-soldiers, he deafened the ears of the elephants of the cardinal points.

Thus he went to the city of Devas with a desire to fight with the immortal beings.

19. On hearing the tumultuous sound of the army, O Brāhmaṇas, Devas headed by Indra set out from the city resolutely inclined to fight.

20. Then a fight ensued between Devas and Rākṣasas, the like of which has never been seen or even heard before.

21. Devas headed by Indra killed many Rākṣasas in the battle. The Rākṣasas too killed the Suras with a strong desire for conquest in the battle.

22. There were duels between the Suras and the Rāksaṣas. The enemy of Bala and Vṛtra (i.e. Indra) fought with Kapālābharaṇa in the battle.

23. O excellent Brāhmaṇas, Śavabhakṣa fought with Yama, Kauśika fought with Varuṇa and Rudhirākṣa with Kubera.

24-28. The four valorous brothers of Kapālābharaṇa, Māṁsapriya, Madyasevī, Krūradṛṣṭi and Bhayāvaha fought with Aśvinī Devas, Fire-god and Wind-god in the course of the battle.

Yama of great vigour wielded his Kāla Daṇḍa with great speed, struck Śavabhakṣa and slew him. Yama killed the thirty Akṣauhiṇīs that belonged to him. With his lance, Varuṇa chopped off the head of Kauśika in the battle. Kubera knocked off the head of Rudhirākṣa with his spear. The younger brothers of Kapālābharaṇa were killed by the Aśvinī Devas and Agni and Vāyu in the battle, O Brāhmaṇas. They went to the abode of Yama (i.e. died).

29. A hundred Akṣauhiṇīs were destroyed within half a *Yāma* (i.e. one hour and a half) by Devendra in that battle and they went to Yama's abode.

30-34. On seeing his army destroyed, Kapālābharaṇa took up a bow and very sharp and swift arrows. He then rushed at Indra for fight, and yelled "Stop, stop". Then he hit the head of Indra with five arrows. Even before they had reached him, Indra cut them by means of his own arrows. Then Kapālābharaṇa took up a spear and hurled it at Devendra. He struck it down with a Śakti. Then Kapālābharaṇa took up an iron club, a hundred Hastas long and made of five thousand Tulā weights of iron. With that he hit the chest of Indra.

35-40. Thereupon Indra swooned and sank down within the chariot. Bṛhaspati repeated the *Mṛtasañjīvanī* mantra and revived Indra in a miraculous manner.

Then Indra mounted the elephant Airāvata and came near Kapālābharaṇa. Then Mahendra, the chastiser of Pāka, furiously dealt a blow with his thunderbolt and smashed to smithereens Kapālābharaṇa along with his chariot, horse, bow, flagstaff, quiver and shield.

When the heroic Kapālābharaṇa was thus killed in battle, the world that had been miserable for a long time, became happy.

As a result of the killing of the Rākṣasa the sin of Brāhmaṇa-slaughter chased Indra, terribly causing reverberations in all the ten quarters.

The sages said:

41. O Sūta, O sage, Kapālābharaṇa, the Rākṣasa, was not a Brāhmaṇa. How did then the sin of Brāhmaṇa-slaughter pursue Indra after he was slain.

Śrī Sūta said:

42-47. O great sages, I shall tell a great and wonderful secret. Listen with great attention and concentration of mind.

Formerly there was a Rākṣasa named Trivakra in the region of Vindhya. His wife possessed all good qualities. She was very beautiful. The lady of beautiful buttocks was Suśīlā by name. She had all the characteristics (of a noble lady).

That beautiful lady of graceful charms, with fascinating dress and charming smiles, once wandered in the sylvan regions near the slopes of Vindhya.

There was a sage named Śuci in that forest. He was engaged in penance and meditation. He was devoted to the study of the Vedas.

That lady of excellent complexion went to his hermitage. On seeing her the sage became afflicted with erotic passion and he lost all his steadiness and composure. Approaching the beautiful lady, the excellent sage spoke thus:

Śuci said:

48-53. O young lady, welcome to you. O lady of bright smiles, whose wife are you? What is the task for which you have come to this extremely dreadful forest? You are excessively tired. Stay within this hut of mine.

On being told thus, that lady of beautiful buttocks replied to the sage: "O sage, I am the wife of a Rākṣasa named Trivakra. I am Suśīlā by name. I have come to this forest with a desire to gather some flowers. I have no son, O sage. My husband eagerly wishes for a son and hence I have been urged by him, 'Propitiate sage Śuci and get a son from him.'

On being directed by my husband thus, I have approached you. Beget a son of me, O sage. Take pity on me." On being told thus Sage Śuci spoke to her thus:

Śuci said:

54-58. O Suśīlā, I am highly delighted now on seeing you. Fulfil the ocean of the wishes of mine.

After saying thus the sage sported with her for three days. Then the delighted sage said to Suśīlā of beautiful features: "You will have in your womb a very powerful son named Kapālābharaṇa. He will rule the earth for a long time. Your dear child will perform penance for a thousand years and propitiate God Brahmā. Excepting Indra no other Deva will be able to kill him. Such a son will be born to you. He will have valour equal to that of Indra."

After saying this to that lady, the sage went to Kāśī, the city of Śiva.

59-60. Suśīlā gave birth to her son Kapālābharaṇa, O eminent sages. It was him that Indra killed in battle with his thunderbolt. Since Indra killed the son born of the seed of Śuci, Indra was seized by the sin of Brāhmaṇa-slaughter.

61. Indra was extremely frightened and he fled all over the worlds. The sin of Brahmahatyā pursued him all over there.

62. O eminent Brāhmaṇas, Indra was chased by the sin of Brāhmaṇa-slaughter and he went to the assembly of Brahmā with his heart afflicted very much.

63-64. Indra intimated to Brahmā everything and pointed out to the sin of Brāhmaṇa-slaughter: "O Lord of the worlds, this dreadful sin of Brāhmaṇa-slaughter oppresses me much. O lord of the subjects, tell me how to destroy it." On being told by Indra thus, Brahmā spoke to Indra, the lord of the heaven:

Brahmā said:

65-69. O Indra, go to Sītākuṇḍa on the Gandhamādana mountain. On the banks of Sītākuṇḍa, you should perform Yāgas unto Sadāśiva. You should take the holy bath in that splendid lake that dispels all sins. Thereby, O Indra, you shall become purified and liberated from the sin of Brāhmaṇa-slaughter. You shall be rid of all miseries and you shall return to the world of the Devas once again.

Sītākuṇḍa is meritorious and destructive of all sins. It bestows liberation. It is destructive of all great sins. It is the greatest cause of immortality. It suppresses all miseries. It dispels all penury. It bestows wealth and food-grains. It yields the (stay in the) region of Vaikuṇṭha, etc. Hence, O slayer of Vṛtra, perform a Yāga on the lake Sītāsaras.

70-71. On being told thus, the king of Suras went to Gandhamādana, O Brāhmaṇas. He reached Sītāsaras and took his holy bath there. He performed sacrifice on its banks. He was liberated from Brahmahatyā and he went back to his city. That Tīrtha, the Kuṇḍa of Sītā, is very excellent. It has such powers.

72-73. Maithilī, the daughter of Janaka, entered fire in the presence of all the Devas in order to create faith in Rāma. She then came out of it and stood there with a beautiful refulgent body. She then made an excellent Tīrtha for the sake of protecting the world. It is known after her name.

74-76. Sītā took her bath there. Hence it is remembered as Sītā-saras. One who takes his holy bath there shall obtain all desires.

One who takes the holy bath in and ceremoniously sips the water of that lake, should make charitable gifts of diverse kinds, O great Brāhmaṇas, and perform Yajñas with plenty of monetary gifts. He shall go to the world of Parameśvara.

Thus, O eminent sages, the glory of Sītāsaras has been recounted to you. He who listens to it or reads it, shall enjoy worldly pleasures here and enjoy happiness hereafter too.

CHAPTER TWELVE

Glorification of Maṅgala Tīrtha

Śrī Sūta said:

1-5. After taking holy bath in the highly meritoriou Sītākuṇḍa, O excellent Brāhmaṇas, one should proceed to the auspicious Maṅgala Tīrtha with a composed mind. It is the place where Kamalā, the beloved of Viṣṇu, always abides. All the Suras with Indra as their leader, come here every day in order to avoid Alakṣmī (ill-luck, misfortune).

So, O sages, I shall narrate an ancient legend connected with this Tīrtha, which sanctifies the worlds. It is meritorious and destructive of sins.

Formerly, there was a king of the lunar race named Manojava.[1] He righteously protected the ocean-girt, earth. He performed Yajñas to propitiate Suras and offered heaps of foodstuffs to propitiate Brāhmaṇas.

6. Every year he propitiated the deities called Pitṛs by means of *Kavyas*. He always studied the Vedas. He studied the scriptures along with their meanings.

7. He conquered the enemies by means of his valour. He worshipped Śiva and Viṣṇu. He studied with interest treatises on Ethics and Politics and read great Smṛti works like that of Manu.

8. Thus that king protected the earth righteously. As the king protected it, the kingdom became free from thorns (i.e. enemies).

9-14. He became proud, the result of which was the destruction of sons and wealth. Where there is pride there are also the defects like covetousness, haughtiness, lust, anger, violence as well as jealousy that causes delusion. All these are the causes of the destruction of wealth. One who has these (defects) perishes in a moment along with his sons, grandsons and the entire assets.

He became defiled by malicious jealousy causing the people to hate him always. He was vain. He became covetous and contaminated by lust and (so) he thought thus: 'I shall levy tax on the village of Brāhmaṇas.' Having decided thus he did accordingly.

---

1. This is a new story told for the glorification of this Tīrtha, as persons mentioned herein, viz. King Manojava and his enemy Golabha are untraced in PE and PI.

On account of his greed, the king confiscated the wealth and the foodgrains of Brāhmaṇas.

15-17. Out of greed, he confiscated the assets of the deities like Śiva, Viṣṇu, etc. This (king) whose intellect was deluded on account of haughtiness, confiscated the shrines and sacred spots of Śiva, Viṣṇu and other deities and the noble-souled Brāhmaṇas.

Since the king thus became very unjust and hostile to Devas and Brāhmaṇas, therefore as a disastrous result of these evil actions, O prominent Brāhmaṇas, an enemy, a powerful lord of a foreign land, laid a siege to his capital.

18-23. That hostile foreign king was Golabha by name, O great Brāhmaṇas. He was accompanied by armies having four divisions (viz. chariots, cavalry, elephants and infantry). The war between Golabha and Manojava, the vicious king of great haughtiness, continued for six months. Then he was defeated by Golabha and was ousted from the kingdom.

Manojava went to the forest along with his son and wife. Golabha occupied the city of Manojava and ruled it for a long time after defeating him in the battle. He was powerful and he had an army of the four divisions:

O eminent Brāhmaṇas, Manojava entered the great forest in the company of his son and wife. He bewailed (his ill-luck). He became emaciated on account of hunger. His steps faltered frequently. He entered the forest which was dreadful on account of tigers and other beasts of prey. It was noisy on account of crickets (and other insects). The trumpeting sound of elephants pervaded the entire region. It was teeming with boars and buffaloes.

In that terrible forest, the infant son of Manojava, who was afflicted with hunger requested his father for food.

24-29. Then the boy turned towards his mother and requested: "O mother, give me food. Hunger oppresses me very much."

On hearing the words of their son, the parents suddenly became grief-stricken. They became confounded. Then the king spoke to his wife named Sumitrā. He fainted repeatedly. His throat, lips and palate became parched: "O Sumitrā, what shall I do? Where shall I go? What is the wayout? Being afflicted with hunger this son of mine will die soon. O my beloved! Why did God Brahmā create me, an unfortunate wretch, in vain? Who is going to save me from this misery which is the result of my evil actions? Neither Śaṁbhu nor Hari were worshipped by me in my previous births.

30-31. O my beloved wife, the deities including the Sun and Fire also have not been worshipped by me. Hence, O splendid lady, it is on account of the evil actions that I have been overcome by egotism and conceit in this birth. I have confiscated the holy spots and the lands of Brāhmaṇas. The wealth belonging to Śiva, Viṣṇu and other deities has been taken away by me.

32. On account of this mass of evil actions, I have been defeated by Golabha and have come to this desolate forest along with you and our son.

33. I am poor and miserable. I have no food. I am hungry and thirsty. How can I provide food to my hungry son?

34-35. O lady of bright smiles, foodstuffs have never been given by me to Brāhmaṇas. Neither Śaṁbhu, nor Viṣṇu, nor any other deity has been worshipped by me. It is because of that sin that this misery has befallen me. I have never performed Homa in the sacred fire. No Tīrtha has been resorted to by me.

36-37. Śrāddha has not been performed by me for my mother or father on the anniversary of their death either individually or collectively. I have never done feeding of the masses, O gentle lady. It was on account of the sin thereof that this misery has befallen me today.

38-40. During the Citrā constellation in the month of Caitra, O my beloved one, sweet drinks, jackfruit and tasty plantains were not given by me to Vedic scholars. Similarly an umbrella, a walking stick, a beautiful pair of sandals, betel leaves, flowers, sandal-paste and unguents were not given by me to them for the propitiation of Citragupta. It is on account of the sin thereof that this misery has befallen me.

41-42. Neither a fig tree, nor a mango, nor a banyan tree, nor a tamarind, nor a Picumanda (*Azadirachta Indica*), nor a wood-apple tree, nor an *Embylic myrobalan*, nor a coconut palm has been planted by me for the purpose of alleviating the fatigue of wayfarers. It is on account of that sin that this misery has befallen me.

43-48. I have never swept the precincts of the temples of Śiva and Viṣṇu. No lake, well or pool has been dug by me. Neither a flower-garden nor a Tulasī grove has been grown by me. I have not built a temple of Śiva or Viṣṇu, O my beloved! It is on account of the sin thereof that this misery has befallen me. O splendid lady, in the month of the manes (i.e. Bhādrapada) neither Mahālaya nor the

Aṣṭakā Śrāddha has been performed by me. Neither Nitya Śrāddha, nor Naimittika Śrāddha, nor Kāmya Śrāddha has been performed by me. No Kratu (sacrifice) has been duly performed by me with plenty of monetary gifts, O my beloved one. Monthly fast has not been observed by me. I have never refrained from taking food on the eleventh lunar day. I have never worshipped Śaṁbhu, Viṣṇu and other deities early in the morning in the month of Dhanus and the food offering has not been done by me duly. It is on account of the sin thereof that this misery has befallen me.

49-54a. I have never glorified the names of Hari and Śaṅkara. I have never applied *Bhasma* all over my body, nor the three parallel lines of Tripuṇḍra have been made by me (on the forehead). I have not applied Bhasma in the seven ways prescribed by Jābāla. O gentle lady, a Rudrākṣa bead has not been worn by me. The Japa of *Rudrasūkta* or that of the five-syllabled Mantra (i.e. *śivāya namaḥ*) has not been performed by me. The recitation of the *Puruṣasūkta* or the Japa of the eight-syllabled Mantra (i.e. *om nārāyaṇāya namaḥ*) has not been performed by me, O gentle lady. Nor have I added to my store of merits by performing other religious rites. It is on account of that sin that this misery has befallen me." Addressing his wife thus, the king of dejected mind began to lament, O Brāhmaṇas. He then swooned and fell on the ground. On seeing him fallen the extremely dejected lady, his wife Sumitrā, embraced him and began to lament along with her son:

54b-60a. "O my lord, O great king, O leader of the Lunar race, where have you gone leaving me and your son alone in this desolate forest? I have no other lord. I have followed you. I am in the same plight as the hind frightened by a lion. If you are dead, O great king, I will immediately follow you. I will not remain a widow even for a moment. O my son Candrakānta, see, your father has fallen down on the ground."

On being told thus, Candrakānta, the son of the king, embraced his father and began to cry without uttering any word, as he was extremely oppressed by hunger.

In the meantime, a sage named Parāśara happened to come there by chance. O Brāhmaṇas, he had matted hair and was clad in bark garments. He had applied Bhasma all over his body. Tripuṇḍra mark shone on his forehead. He was adorned with garlands of Rudrākṣa-beads and had a white sacred thread.

60b-62. The sage Parāśara who is honoured by noble and good-natured people, came there following the sound.

On seeing Parāśara arrived, Sumitrā, the chaste lady, bowed down to his feet along with her son. Thereupon Sumitrā was consoled by Parāśara. The sage pacified her saying, "O beautiful lady, do not feel grief-stricken." Then the great sage, the son of Śakti, asked Sumitrā:

Parāśara said:

63-64. O beautiful lady, who are you? Who is this (person) fallen in front of us? How is this child related to you? O splendid lady, tell me all the facts.

On being asked thus by the sage, the chaste lady said to that great sage.

Sumitrā said:

65-71. O excellent sage, this is my husband. I am his wife. This is Candrakānta, the son born to us both.

This king of the Lunar race named Manojava is the son of Vikramāḍhya. He is strong and like Viṣṇu in heroism. I am his wife named Sumitrā and I have followed my husband. King Manojava was defeated by Golabha in battle. He has been exiled from the kingdom. He is without support. Followed by me and our son, O Brāhmaṇa-Sage, he entered the forest dreadful on account of the cruel beasts of prey. Our son who was afflicted with hunger requested us for food. On seeing his son afflicted with hunger the king who had no foodstuff with him became dejected and grief-stricken. O Brāhmaṇa, he has swooned and fallen on the ground.

On hearing these words of hers, the syllables of which (were not distinct), because she was highly miserable, the sage, the son of Śakti, spoke to that chaste lady Sumitrā, the wife of King Manojava. She was comparable to the flame of a fire:

Parāśara said:

72-73a. O wife of Manojava, do not at all be afraid. Everything inauspicious in your affairs will come to an end ere long. O gentle lady, your husband will get up in a trice free from his unconsciousness.

* * *

73b-75. Then the Brāhmaṇa Parāśara touched the king with his hand repeating a Mantra and meditating on the Three-eyed Lord. Thereupon, when touched by the great sage with his hand, King Manojava got up suddenly leaving off his unconsciousness born of Tamas. Then the king joined his palms in reverence. He bowed down to sage Parāśara. With great delight he spoke to the excellent Brāhmaṇa:

Manojava said:

76-78. O sage Parāśara, since I resorted to your lotus-like feet today, my unconsciousness has been dispelled quickly and my sin has perished. Those who are not meritorious will never get even your glimpse. Save me with your sympathetic glance. I have been exiled from my own city by my enemies.

On being told thus, the sage spoke to King Manojava.

Parāśara said:

79-85. I shall tell you the means, O king, for conquering your enemies. There is an auspicious Tīrtha named Maṅgalatīrtha on the highly meritorious Rāmasetu on the Gandhamādana mountain. It yields all kinds of prosperities. For the sake of helping all the people, O excellent king, Rāghava is always present there along with Lakṣmī (in the form of) Sītā. Do go there along with your son and wife and take the holy bath with great devotion. On its banks, O king, perform the rites of Kṣetra Śrāddha, etc. If everything is performed thus by you, O king, all ill-luck and misfortune that brings to you great distress shall undoubtedly perish on account of the glory of that Tīrtha. You will obtain all types of auspicious results, O king, ere long. After conquering the enemies in the battle, you will regain the kingdom. Hence, O Manojava, go to that Maṅgalatīrtha along with your wife and son. Go to that Tīrtha on the Gandhamādana mountain. I shall also come there with a desire to bless you.

86-91. After saying this, Parāśara started for Setu along with those three persons, the chief of whom was the king, in order to take the holy bath in Maṅgalatīrtha. Along with the king and others the sage crossed various forests, lands abounding in woodlands and many villages of the aboriginals called Dasyus. Then he reached Maṅgalatīrtha on the Gandhamādana mountain. After duly performing the rite of Saṅkalpa there, the eminent sage took his holy bath. He made the king and others too take their holy baths duly. For the propitiation of Pitṛs, the king performed Śrāddha too. There the king, his wife and son took the holy bath for three months. Sage Parāśara took his holy bath with due observance of rules, etc. Thus the eminent sage took his bath along with them for three months in the highly meritorious Tīrtha named Maṅgala that is destructive of all inauspiciousness.

92. Then at the end (of those three months), Sage Parāśara imparted to him the single-syllabled Mantra of Rāma, that is destructive of all misfortune.

93. For forty days the king repeated the single-syllabled Mantra in that Tīrtha as per procedure stated by the sage.

94. O Brāhmaṇa, as he performed the repetition of single-syllabled Mantra thus, a sturdy bow appeared in front of him due to the favour of the sage.

95-101a. Two inexhaustible quivers, two swords with golden handles, one shield, one iron mace, an excellent *Musala* (Threshing pestle), one conchshell of loud report, a chariot yoked with horses and manned by a charioteer and a flag rose up in front of them from the Tīrtha. A golden armour refulgent like fire appeared from the Tīrtha due to the favour of the sage. Many ornaments such as necklaces, armlets, coronets, bracelets etc. rose up in front of the king from that most excellent Tīrtha. A thousand divine garments came up from that Tīrtha then. A garland named Vaijayantī rendered splendid by golden lotuses (rose up from the Tīrtha). On seeing all these, the king dedicated all of them to the Sage. Then Sage Parāśara sanctified them by means of the Tīrtha water charged with Mantras and sprinkled the king with the same.

101b-103. Thus sprinkled by the sage, the king became refulgent. He got ready (for a campaign). He put on the armour, seized the sword (in his hand) and took up the bow and the arrows. Adorned with the necklaces, armlets, coronet, bracelets, etc. he shone like a youth. He wore the divine garments and occupied the chariot with horses. Thus the king appeared splendid and brilliant like the Sun at noon.

104-107. The great sage, the son of Śakti, taught the king the use of the missiles of Brahmā, etc. along with their ancillaries, the secrets, mode of discharge and the method of withdrawal. He taught everything to the husband of Sumitrā. Then King Manojava was directed by the sage with due blessings. He occupied the chariot after bowing down to the sage and circumambulated him and was duly permitted by the great sage. Accompanied by his wife and son, he started for conquest. After going to his city, the king blew his conchshell.

108. On hearing the blast from the conchshell, Golabha came out immediately along with his army in order to fight with King Manojava.

109-111. The battle lasted for three days between Golabha and the king. Then on the fourth day, King Manojava destroyed Golabha along with his army by means of his Brāhma missile. Then along with his wife and son, the king entered his city. He ruled the entire earth and enjoyed it along with his wife. Ever since then the king never became proud.

112. The king refrained from malice and other defects. He practised non-violence. He had perfect control over his sense-organs. He was always engaged and absorbed in virtuous activity.

113-114. Thus the king protected the earth for a thousand years. Then the king became unattached to worldly life. He installed his son as the ruler of the kingdom. He went to Maṅgalatīrtha on the Gandhamādana mountain. Meditating on Sadāśiva in his heart, he performed penance there.

115-116. Ere long thereafter, King Manojava abandoned his body and went to the world of Śiva, due to the power of that Tīrtha. O Brāhmaṇas, his wife Sumitrā embraced his body then and ascended his funeral pyre. She too attained the same world.

Śrī Sūta said:

117-119. That Maṅgalatīrtha has such power. It is glorious. By taking his bath in that great Tīrtha King Manojava conquered his enemies. On death he went to Śivaloka along with his wife. Hence Maṅgalatīrtha should be resorted to with great effort.

O excellent Brāhmaṇas, for the sake of salvation resort to this highly splendid Tīrtha which is auspicious and which always bestows worldly pleasures and salvation to men. It is (like) fire unto the grass and cotton in the form of masses of sins.

CHAPTER THIRTEEN

The Glory of Amṛtavāpī[1]: Salvation of Agastya's Brother

Śrī Sūta said:

1. After taking the holy bath in the great Tīrtha and getting rid of the sins, one should go to the holy spot named Ekāntarāmanātha.

2-3. There, O Brāhmaṇa, Rāma, the lord of the worlds, is always present along with Jānakī, Lakṣmaṇa and the monkeys, the chief of whom is Hanumān. He is present there with a desire to bless the worlds. There is a tank there named Amṛtavāpikā which bestows merits.

4-6a. Men who take their holy plunge there need not be afraid of old age or death. The man who faithfully takes his holy bath in this Amṛtavāpī attains immortality, due to the favour of Śaṅkara.

On its banks Hara is always present in order to grant immortality to those who take their holy bath in this tank that destroys great sins.

The sages said:

6b-7. For what reason is this called Amṛtavāpī? O disciple of Vyāsa, kindly tell this to us. So also state the glory of this tank named Amṛta. We who regularly drink the nectar of your words are not satiated.

Śrī Sūta said:

8-12. O excellent Brāhmaṇas, I shall particularly describe (the origin of) the name *Amṛta* given to this tank and its fascinating glory. Listen.

Formerly the brother of the Pot-born Sage (Agastya) lived and performed his penance on the sides of Himavān which is full of sages of various classes. It is resorted to by Siddhas, Cāraṇas, Gandharvas, Devas and Kinnaras. It is infested by various beasts of prey and wild animals such as lion, tiger, boar, elephant and buffalo. It abounded in trees like Tamāla, Tāla, Hintāla, Campaka

---

1. This Tīrtha is inside Ekānta Rāmar Temple. It is called here Ekāntarāmanātha and the story connected with Rāma is told to explain its derivation in vv 46-53.

and Aśoka. It is rendered beautiful by swans, cuckoos, gallinules, ruddy geese and other birds. It is surrounded by lakes full of lotuses, blue lotuses, red lotuses and lilies.

The sage was truthful and of good conduct. He was eloquent and had control over his senses and passions.

13-19a. He sought salvation. He was a devotee of Śaṅkara. With roots, fruits, etc. available in the forest, he worshipped Śaṁbhu three times everyday. With sylvan foodstuffs, he honoured guests who came to his hermitage. He performed *Sandhyā* and worshipped the sacred fire. At the proper times he repeated Gāyatrī and other great Mantras with great joy. He used to get up from his sleep in the Brāhma Muhūrta. He meditated upon Viṣṇu. He used to take the holy bath early in the morning. With a delighted mind he bowed down to the *Sandhyās*. O Brāhmaṇas, he repeated Gāyatrī and worshipped both Hari and Śaṅkara. He studied the Vedas regularly. He read the scriptures regularly. He honoured guests during midday. He regularly listened to the Purāṇas. He was active and very scrupulous with regard to the sacred rites in the fires. Everyday he performed the five Yajñas. He used to offer the Vaiśvadeva oblations. O Brāhmaṇas, every year he performed Śrāddhas to his parents and other Śrāddhas as well. Thus he spent his time regularly engaged in his daily routine of duties.

19b-22. Thousand years passed off thus as he performed the excellent penance with the mind attached to Śaṅkara. Still Śaṅkara did not appear before him. Therefore, the brother of Agastya performed a more terrible penance. During summer he stayed within five fires with his eyes fixed on the Sun. He observed the vow of silence. He stood motionless on the small toe of his left leg. He kept his hands lifted up. He had no prop as he performed the severe penance.

23-24. Mahādeva, the storehouse of mercy, became pleased with him then and appeared before him illuminating the ten directions by means of his own refulgence. Then the sage saw Śaṁbhu, Sāṁba (accompanied by Aṁbā, the goddess) seated on his Bull. On seeing the lord of Bhavānī, the sage bowed to him and eulogized him.

The sage said:

25-29. Obeisance to you, O lord of Pārvatī, O blue-throated great lord, O Śiva, O Rudra, O Mahādeva, O lord, obeisance to you, to Śambhu. O Śrīkaṇṭha, O lord of Umā, O trident-bearing lord, O destroyer of the eyes of Bhaga, O immutable one, O holder of Gaṅgā, O lord of unequal (i.e. three) eyes, obeisance to you, O Rudra, O Manyu. O enemy of Yama, O enemy of god of Love, O lord of the Devas, O lord of the universe, O master, O lord of Paśus (individual souls), obeisance to you, O Śarva of a hundred bows. Obeisance to the destroyer of Dakṣa's Yajña, to the lord of sinews* (*snāyūnāṁ? pataye).* Obeisance to you, *Niceru* (the gliding one); obeisance to the lord of the nourished ones. Again and again, obeisance to you, O Mahādeva, O ocean of mercifulness. O three-eyed one, enable me to cross the ocean of worldly existence.

30. Eulogized thus by the brother of Agastya, Śambhu delighted the sage, the younger brother of the Pot-born One (Agastya), by means of his words and spoke thus:

Īśvara said:

31-33. O younger brother of the Pot-born Sage, O sinless one, I shall tell you the means of salvation. In the middle of the Setu on the Gandhamādana mountain, not far from the Tīrtha named Maṅgala, there is a great Tīrtha. Go there and take your holy bath. Thereby you will attain salvation. There is no other easy means for you to obtain salvation than resorting to that Tīrtha. It is impossible for me to recount the excellence of that Tīrtha.

34. No doubt should be entertained by you in this matter, O excellent sage. Hence do go there, if you wish for the destruction of worldly existence.

35-36. After saying this, Lord Īśa vanished there itself. Then at the instance of the lord, the brother of Agastya went to Setu on the Gandhamādana mountain in the sea. He soon reached the Tīrtha spoken by Īśvara.

37-40. There is that highly meritorious Tīrtha which bestows salvation on those who take their bath therein, and which is a splendid ornament to the holy spot named Ekāntarāmanātha. That

---

* Probably a misprint for '*Dasyūnāṁ*', for '*Dasyūnāṁ pati*' is Rudra's epithet in *Rudrādhyāya.*

Brāhmaṇa duly took his holy bath for three years. In the fourth year the great sage entered into transcendent meditation. By means of Yogic power he directed the vital breath in the Brahma-nāḍī on the head. Then he made the vital breath come out through the *Brahmarandhra* (the aperture on the crown of the head). Then the younger brother of Agastya abandoned his body and attained the greatest salvation due to the power of that Tīrtha.

41-43. Agastya's younger brother got rid of all his miseries due to the power of the holy bath in that Tīrtha. Since he attained *Amṛtatva* (immortality), O eminent sages, this tank became famous by the name Amṛtavāpī. Men who regularly take their holy bath in this Tīrtha for three years will certainly attain immortality. Thus, O Brāhmaṇas, the reason for being famous by the name Amṛtavāpī as well as its power have been narrated by me to you. What more do you wish to hear?

The sages said:

44-45. O sage, how did that holy spot get the name Ekāntarāmanātha? O Sūta, it behoves you to recount this. O tiger among sages, our desire to hear about it is very intense.

Śrī Sūta said:

46-48. Formerly when the Setu was being built in the middle of the sea, Rāma, the son of Daśaratha, was mentally thinking about Sītā. With Sugrīva, Vibhīṣaṇa, his brother Lakṣmaṇa and Hanumān who was an expert in secret counselling, Rāma was taking counsel regarding the means of killing Rāvaṇa and others. At that time the sea rumbled much with the waves moving about up and down.

49. When the loud rumbling sound of the sea rose up in a terrific manner, they could not hear the words uttered by them to one another.

50-55. Thereupon, Rāma became a bit furious. He knitted his eyebrows and glanced at the sea furiously. Rāma brought the sea under control and continued his counsel with the others, O eminent Brāhmaṇas, for planning an attack on Rākṣasas and their slaying.

Since Rāghava took counsel with them in a lonely, quiet spot, O Brāhmaṇas, that holy spot came to be known by the name *Ekāntarāmanātha*.

The sea restrained by the graceful knitting of the eyebrows of

Rāma is seen even today in that area with still water.

This is the excellent holy spot named Ekāntarāmanātha. Those who come here, take their holy bath in Amṛtavāpī with due observances and serve Rāma and others shall attain salvation.

O great Brāhmaṇas, by taking the holy bath here those who are devoid of discrimination (of right and wrong) and knowledge of non-duality, those who have no detachment, those without (performance of) meditation and those who have never performed sacrifices attain immortality.

CHAPTER FOURTEEN

Brahmā's Redemption from Śiva's Curse

Śrī Sūta said:

1. After taking the holy bath in Amṛtavāpī and having visited Ekāntarāghava, one who has conquered his passions and senses should proceed towards Brahmakuṇḍa in order to take the holy plunge.

2. The great Tīrtha well-known as Brahmakuṇḍa in the middle of Setu on the Gandhamādana mountain is an antidote against poverty for everyone.

3. It is destructive of a hundred million sins of Brāhmaṇa-slaughter. A mere sight of Brahmakuṇḍa is destructive of mass of all sins.

4. What has he to do with many Tīrthas, penances, sacrifices and great charitable gifts (i.e. these are unnecessary to a person) who visits Brahmakuṇḍa?

5-10a. The holy bath (even) once in Brahmakuṇḍa is the cause of attainment of Vaikuṇṭha. O Brāhmaṇas, if the Bhasma from Brahmakuṇḍa is held (i.e. smeared) by anyone, the three gods Brahmā, Viṣṇu and Maheśvara become his followers.

If anyone makes Tripuṇḍra mark (on his forehead) with the Bhasma (holy ash) originating from Brahmakuṇḍa, salvation is (as if) within his hand (grasp). There is no doubt about it.

If a man applies that Bhasma all over his body, it is doubtful whether Śaṅkara himself is able to recount his merits.

One who never applies the Bhasma from Brahmakuṇḍa will fall

into Raurava hell and remain there till the moon and the stars exist.

10b-16a. If a base man does not apply the Bhasma from Brahmakuṇḍa all over his body or at least mark Tripuṇḍra with it on his forehead, he will never have happiness.

If a person is engaged in censuring the Bhasma originating from Brahmakuṇḍa, he should be deemed as a product of a mixture of castes by a learned man.

This Bhasma originating from Brahmakuṇḍa is sanctifying to all the worlds.

If a man says that it is equal to or inferior to other (kinds of holy ash) he should he deemed as a product of a mixture of castes by a learned man. Even while this Bhasma originating from Brahmakuṇḍa is available, if a man marks Tripuṇḍra with any other Bhasma, he should be deemed as a product of a mixture of castes by a learned man.

If a man never applies this Bhasma, he should be deemed as a product of a mixture of castes by a learned man.

16b-22. If anyone gives to a Brāhmaṇa the Bhasma originating from Brahmakuṇḍa, it is as beneficial as though the entire earth girdled by the four oceans has been gifted by him. No doubt should be entertained in this regard. I shall say this on oath three times. This is true. It is declared (to be true) with the hand lifted up.

O excellent Brāhmaṇas, apply the Bhasma originating from Brahmakuṇḍa. Indeed this is the Bhasma that came into existence from Brahmā's sacrifice.

Formerly for the redemption from the curse of Śiva, Lord Brahmā, the grandfather of all the worlds, performed all the *Kratus* (sacrifices) on the Gandhamādana mountain in the presence of all the Devas. After duly performing all the Yajñas with plenty of monetary gifts, O excellent Brāhmaṇas, Brahmā was immediately redeemed from the curse of Śaṁbhu.

So, those men who come to this Tīrtha and take their holy bath, undoubtedly attain *Sāyujya* with Mahādeva.

The sages said:

23-24. O disciple of Vyāsa, O highly intelligent one, expert in the topics of the Purāṇas, what was the offence for which Śaṁbhu cursed the Four-faced Lord of Sarasvatī, the creator of the fourteen worlds? Of what nature was the curse that Hara gave him formerly? O sage, narrate all this to us truthfully and earnestly.

Śrī Sūta said:

25-27. Formerly there was a quarrel between Brahmā and Viṣṇu. For some reason they had mutual rivalry and they boasted about themselves: "I am the maker (of the world). There is no other maker on the surface of the earth." So said Brahmā to Hari and Hari said the same to Brahmā. Thus a great dispute arose between them formerly.

28-33. In the meantime, O Brāhmaṇas, for destroying their pride and for enlightening those two lords, a self-luminous Liṅga in a sound condition appeared in their middle.[1]

On seeing the Liṅga Brahmā and Viṣṇu became surprised. They arrived at a mutual agreement in the presence of the Devas, O Brāhmaṇas: "A great Liṅga with no beginning or end is seen before us. It resembles infinite number of suns in brilliance. It has the refulgence of infinite number of fires. Between us, the person who sees the beginning or the end of this Liṅga, shall be superior to the other in the world. He is the lord and maker of the worlds. I shall go up searching for the top of the Liṅga. O Hari, you go down in search of its root."

On hearing his words, the Lord of Ramā said, "So it will be".

34. Thus they entered into an agreement and set out in search. Viṣṇu went in search below, assuming the form of a boar.

35. The Husband of Sarasvatī adopted the form of a swan and flew up. Viṣṇu searched the nether worlds for many many years. He returned to the original place and spoke in the presence of the Devas:

Viṣṇu said:

36-37. I did not see the beginning of this Liṅga.

He was truthful in his speech.

After searching the regions above, Brahmā too came there. On arrival, the Four-faced Lord uttered these false words:

1. The story of appearance of Śiva in a Liṅga form to show that neither Brahmā nor Viṣṇu was superior but he himself is superior to them, etc. is repeated in many Purāṇas, e.g. *Liṅga* Ch. 17, *Kūrma* I.26.66-99.

Brahmā said:

38-43. I have seen the top of this Liṅga.

He repeated the false statement. After hearing the words of Brahmā and Viṣṇu, Maheśvara laughingly spoke these words to the Four-faced Lord who had uttered a lie:

Īśvara said:

Since you spoke an untruth before me, O Four-faced One, you shall not be worshipped at all in the world anywhere at any time.

Then Lord Parameśvara spoke again to Viṣṇu: "O Hari, O Lord of Kamalā, since you spoke the truth, your worship shall be on a par with that of mine. There shall be no doubt about it."

Thereupon the dejected Brahmā spoke to Śaṅkara: "O lord, O storehouse of mercy, forgive my offence. One offence should be forgiven by masters and the lords of the universe."

Then pacifying Brahmā, Maheśvara spoke:

Īśvara said:

44-47. O Brahmā, my words shall not be false. I shall tell you something. Listen. O dear one, immediately go to the Gandhamādana mountain. In order to suppress the sin of false speech, perform *Kratus* there. Thereby you will undoubtedly be rid of your sin. Therefore, O Brahmā, your worship shall always be in the holy rites laid down in Śrutis and Smṛtis. You will not be worshipped in idols.

After saying thus Lord Īśvara vanished there itself. Then, O Brāhmaṇas, Brahmā went to the Gandhamādana mountain.

48-49. He worshipped the Lord of Pārvatī, the maker of Kratus, by means of Kratus. O eminent sages, he performed the sacrifices such as Pauṇḍarīka, etc. for eighty-eight thousand years. All the sacrifices were performed with plenty of monetary gifts. He performed the sacrifices unto Śiva in the presence of all the Devas including Indra. Thereby Śaṁbhu was delighted and satisfied. He granted him boons.

Īśvara said:

50-55. As these Yajñas have been performed, your sin of false utterence has perished, O Four-faced One. Your worship shall be free from impurities and be confined to the holy rites laid down in Śrutis and Smṛtis.

O Brahmā, there shall be no worship of yours in the idols. The place of your sacrifices shall become renowned as Brahmakuṇḍa in all the three worlds. It shall be meritorious and destructive of sins.

O Brahmā, if anyone takes his holy bath at least once in the Tīrtha named Brahmakuṇḍa, the bolt in the doorway to salvation shall instantaneously be broken in his case.

One who applies the Bhasma originating from Brahmakuṇḍa, to his forehead, shall break open the door in the form of Māyā and enter the doorway to salvation.

The person who does not apply to his forehead the Bhasma originating from Brahmakuṇḍa is not born of the semen virile of his father in his mother (i.e. he is a bastard).

56-61. O Brahmā, by applying the Bhasma originating from Brahmakuṇḍa, ten thousand sins of Brāhmaṇa-slaughter shall perish. So also ten thousand sins of drinking liquor, ten thousand sins of defiling the preceptor's bed shall perish. So also ten thousand sins of stealing gold and ten thousand sins of associating with these will be nullified. O Brahmā, the truth has been spoken by me.

Due to the power of applying the Bhasma coming out from Brahmakuṇḍa, evil spirits, ghosts and vampires are destroyed instantaneously.

After saying this, Lord Īśvara vanished there itself.

When the Yajñas were concluded, the sages who had controlled their passions and sense-organs, Indra and other Devas, Siddhas, Cāraṇas and Kinnaras and other groups of divine beings continued to stay permanently on the Gandhamādana mountain. They resorted to the sacrificial site visited by Rudra himself, because they had realized its efficacy.

62. After duly concluding the Yajñas with plenty of monetary gifts, Brahmā who acquired what he desired from Śiva, went to Satyaloka.

63-65. Ever since then, O excellent Brāhmaṇas, the Devas and the Sages resorted to Brahmakuṇḍa and performed Yāgas in accordance with the injunctions.

Hence men who are desirous of performing Yajñas shall do so here itself.

O Brāhmaṇas, this Brahmakuṇḍa[1] is honoured by men, Devas and great sages. It causes destruction of the chain of births and deaths. It is auspicious and destructive of all sins. It bestows all riches.

CHAPTER FIFTEEN

The Glory of Hanmatkuṇḍa:[2] *Dharmasakha Blessed with a Hundred Sons*

Śrī Sūta said:

1. After taking the holy bath in the exceedingly meritorious Brahmakuṇḍa, O excellent Brāhmaṇas, one should, with a pure and composed mind, go to the Kuṇḍa of Hanumān.

2-6. Formerly, when the Rākṣasas had been killed and the war (with Rāvaṇa) was over, and Rāma and others had returned, Hanumān, the son of Wind-god, created this excellent Tīrtha on mount Gandhamādana for the sake of helping all the people. It is the most excellent of all the Tīrthas. He named it after himself.

After realizing its glory, Rudra himself resorts to it. A Tīrtha on a par with it has never existed before nor will there ever be. The men who take their holy bath there, go to the eternal world of Śiva. When this Tīrtha which has great merits and which is destructive of great sins was created by the son of Wind-god for the sake of helping all the world, all the hells (Narakas) became empty for a long time.

7-8. It is doubtful whether (god) Śaṅkara himself knows its glory (fully) or not. Formerly a king named Dharmasakha,[3] born of Kekaya family, devoutly took his holy bath there and obtained a hundred sons.

1. Probably the same as Brahma Tīrtha near Bhadrakālī Amman Temple.
2. This Tīrtha is to the north of Rameswaram Temple.
3. The story of Dharmasakha to illustrate the greatness of Hanumat Kuṇḍa is a contribution of this Purāṇa.

The sages said:

O Sūta, it behoves you to recount now the story of Dharmasakha who obtained a hundred sons by taking his holy bath in the Tīrtha called Hanumatkuṇḍa.

Śrī Sūta said:

9-12. Listen, ye sages, to the story of that king. I shall now briefly recount the story of Dharmasakha. Formerly, there was a just and virtuous king named Dharmasakha. He had conquered his enemies. He was much devoted to the task of protecting the subjects. O Brāhmaṇas, he had a hundred wives, all of whom regarded their husband as their deity. That king ruled the earth consisting of mountains, parks and forests. He did not get any son of them, who would have perpetuated his line.

13. The king made great efforts in order to get a son. He made great charitable gifts for the sake of a son.

14. He performed horse-sacrifices and other Yajñas and worshipped Suras. He made plenty of charitable gifts, the chief of which was *Tulāpuruṣa-dāna* (wherein gold, jewels or other valuable things equal to the donor's weight are given as gift to Brāhmaṇas).

15. The king distributed liberally foodstuffs to everyone till midnight, along with plenty of pulses and vegetable dishes.

16. With the Pitṛs in view, he performed Śrāddhas in accordance with the injunctions. With his passions and senses under perfect control, he performed the Japa of those Mantras having the efficacy of bestowing progeny.

17-21. The king performed these and many other religious rites for the sake of a son. Thus while engaged in the performance of various excellent holy rites continuously for a long time, the king became aged. In spite of his old age, the king continued his effort and he begot of his chief queen a handsome son named Sucandra.

All the excellent mothers impartially nurtured the son thus born, with milk, etc. This son gave delight to the minds and the eyes of the king, of all the mothers, of the citizens and of the ministers. Fondling his son, the king obtained the greatest joy.

22. Once, while the child was lying in the cradle a certain scorpion stung with its tail the foot of the child emitting the fire of poison as it were.

23. On being stung, the child cried very much. All the mothers

too became grief-stricken and frightened. They also lamented.

24-29. All of them stood around the child, O Brāhmaṇas, and lamented. That mingled sound of their cries was intense and confused. King Dharmasakha who was seated in the Assembly along with his ministers and the priest heard the sound of agony. The king sent the *Sauvidalla* (attendant in the inner apartment) in order to find out what the matter was. The *Sauvidalla* went to the exit of the inner apartment, called the elderly eunuchs and spoke these words:

"O eunuchs, why do the ladies lament now? Go there and find out the reason thereof. It is for this purpose that the king has deputed me from the assembly."

On being told thus, they enquired about the reason for the lamentation. Having found it out they came out of the inner apartment and reported to him everything as it had happened. On hearing the words of the eunuchs, the *Sauvidalla* returned to the assembly.

30-34. He intimated to the king that his son had been stung by a scorpion. On hearing this, King Dharmasakha got up hurriedly. He entered the inner apartment along with the ministers, the (family) priest, those well-versed in Mantras and physicians expert in eradicating poison. He got his son treated with various kinds of medicines and other things. When the child regained his normal state of health, the king fondled him. He duly honoured the knowers of spells with jewels, gold and pearls. Then the king came out exceedingly worried. Accompanied by the Ṛtviks, the priest and the ministers he entered the court and sat there.

Seated on an excellent throne, King Dharmasakha spoke these appropriate words to the Ṛtviks and the priest.

Dharmasakha said:

35-40. O excellent Brāhmaṇas, if one has only one son this is conducive only to misery. It is better to have no son at all rather than have a single son, because it involves many risks. Having no son at all is far better. O Brāhmaṇas, it was only after deep thought that I have married a hundred wives. But my age is advancing though I have married thus, O Brāhmaṇas. My vital airs as well as those of my wives are centered round this son. If any danger were to befall him, the death of all my wives is certain. If this single son dies, I too will die (of grief). So what means can I adopt to have many sons? O Brāhmaṇas, the most excellent ones among those conversant with the Vedas, tell that means to me. I must have a son of good qualities of each one of these hundred wives. All of you go through the scriptures and tell me that holy rite which may be conducive to the same.

41. If the fruit (i.e. birth of sons) is attainable by means of any holy rite, great, small or difficult to be performed, I will undoubtedly perform it.

42. There is no doubt about it that I shall perform the holy rite advised by you; know that that holy rite is (as good as) done. I state this on oath, staking my merit.

43. If there is a rite whereby a hundred sons can be got, where should that rite be performed by me? Tell me now.

44. On being asked by the king thus, all the Ṛtviks and the priests joined together and gave to the king their decisive opinion.

The Ṛtviks said:

45. O king, we shall explain to you that there is a means whereby you will beget hundred sons of your hundred wives, through a great holy rite, O king of Kekayas[1].

46. There is a highly meritorious mountain named Gandhamādana in the middle of the Southern Sea. It is there in the form of a Setu.

47-51. It is full of multitudes of Siddhas, Cāraṇas, Gandharvas, Devas and sages. By visiting it and getting contact with it, it destroys great sins.

There is a Tīrtha there, well-known in the worlds as Hanumatkuṇḍa. It suppresses all great miseries. It yields the benefit of heavenly pleasures and salvation. It subdues the suffering in hells (*Narakas*). It liberates (people) from poverty. It bestows sons on those who are sonless and wives on those who have no wives.

There you take your holy bath with purity. Perform the sacrifice Putrīyeṣṭi that bestows all desired objectives on its banks with great concentration. Thereby O king, you will immediately have a son from each of your one hundred wives. Do not have any doubt about this.

52-57. On being told thus by the Brāhmaṇas, Ṛtviks and priests, the king immediately went to the Gandhamādana mountain on the

1. Kekaya is the country between Beas and Sutlej (De 98).

Southern Sea. He was accompanied by his wives, servants, priest, ministers and Ṛtviks. He had taken with him all the requisites for the sacrifices.

After arriving at Hanumatkuṇḍa, he took his holy bath there along with his army and retinue. He stayed there for a month on its banks and regularly performed the holy bath.

Then, in the month of Caitra, at the advent of spring, the excellent king began the Putrīya sacrifice[1] along with the preceptor. The Ṛtviks and the priest performed the holy rites perfectly on behalf of the saintly King Dharmasakha and his wives. When his sacrifice was completed on the banks of Hanumatkuṇḍa, the priest made the wives of the king eat the remnants of the Homa offerings.

58-61. Then, accompanied by his hundred wives, King Dharmasakha duly performed the Avabhṛtha bath in the waters of Hanumatkuṇḍa. He gave innumerable monetary gifts to the Ṛtviks, O excellent Brāhmaṇas. The king granted villages too to the Brāhmaṇas. Then that virtuous king returned to his city with great delight along with his ministers, retinue and his wives. After a lapse of some time, in the tenth month, the hundred wives gave birth to hundred sons of superior qualities.

62. Then the great Dharmasakha, the heroic king who was much delighted in his mind, took his bath. With great purity, he performed the Saṁkalpa rite and performed the post-natal holy rite.

63-65. He gave plenty of cows, plots of lands, gingelly seeds, gold, etc. to the Brāhmaṇas. The chief queen had thus two sons, one elder and one younger. O Brāhmaṇas, all the one hundred and one sons grew up. When they came of age, the king divided the kingdom among them and went to the Gandhamādana mountain, the Setu, along with his wives. After reaching Hanumatkuṇḍa he performed penance on its banks.

66-67. The king performed the penance for a long time. King Dharmasakha meditated on the Trident-bearing Lord. After lapse of a great deal of time, King Dharmasakha, the virtuous king of quiescent mind, passed away.

68-69. The wives of that saintly king followed their husband. The eldest son Sucandra performed the obsequies of his father after the cremation. He performed all the rites up to the Śrāddha

1. i.e. Putrakāmeṣṭi.

rite with great faith. Since the king died here, he and his wives went to Vaikuṇṭha.

70. All those brothers, the princes of great prowess, the chief of whom was Sucandra, enjoyed their respective kingdoms eschewing all rivalry.

71. Thus, O Brāhmaṇas, the glory of Hanumatkuṇḍa has been recounted to you all. The exceedingly wonderful story of King Dharmasakha also has been recounted.

72-73. Hence everyone should take his holy bath (with due rites) in the Kuṇḍa of Hanumān for the sake of achieving all desires.

One who reads this chapter or listens to this with great concentration and mental purity, O Brāhmaṇas, attains infinite happiness hereafter. He shall sport about in heaven along with groups of Devas.

CHAPTER SIXTEEN

The Glory of Agasti Tīrtha[1]*: The Story of Kakṣīvān*

Sūta said:

1. After taking the holy bath in the Kuṇḍa of Hanumān, which is resorted to by Rudra himself, (the pilgrim) with great concentration and purity shall, O eminent Brāhmaṇas, go to Agasti Tīrtha.

2-5. This Tīrtha was created by the Pot-born Sage himself.

Formerly there was a quarrel between Meru and Vindhya mountains.[2] At that time, Vindhya grew up and obstructed (by covering) the entire expanse of the universe. All the living beings became suffocated and unable to breathe. Devas went to Kailāsa and intimated it to

---

1. This Tīrtha is to the north-east of Rameswaram.

2. Agastya seems to be the first explorer of Peninsular India to the south of Vindhya. Purāṇas called it 'subjugation of the Vindhya'. The story is found in Mbh, *Vana* 104.12-13. At the time of Rāma, he was already settled in Daṇḍakāraṇya (VR I.1-42).

But he finally seems to have settled in the South near the source of the river Tāmraparṇī where a mount is named after him as 'Agastya Kūṭa' in Tinnevilly (De 2).

But Vedāraṇya where Śiva promised to manifest himself in his marriage (vv. 6-8), is near Tanjore, five miles from the point Calimere (De 28).

Śaṁbhu. At that time, the Lord was eager to marry Pārvatī. He sent Vasiṣṭha and other sages to request for the hand of Pārvatī (on his behalf). Then he commanded Agastya saying, "O Pot-born One, restrain the Vindhya mountain."

6-8. Then the Pot-born Sage said to the Pināka-bearing Lord: "O Lord, how is it possible for me not to see you in your marriage apparel and pose?"

On being requested thus, Śaṁbhu spoke to the Pot-born One again: "O Pot-born One, accompanied by Pārvatī, I shall reveal unto you, my marriage apparel and pose in the highly meritorious holy spot Vedāraṇya. There is no doubt about it. Therefore, O great sage, go quickly to restrain (the growth of) the Vindhya mountain."

9-13. On being told thus, Agastya restrained the Vindhya mountain. Merely by setting his foot on it he reduced it to the level of the plain ground. He traversed the Southern territories and went to Gandhamādana. Having known the glory of Gandhamādana, the great sage created a Tīrtha of great merit named after him. Even now the Pot-born Sage is present there in the company of Lopāmudrā. If one takes the holy bath there and drinks the water, one shall never have rebirth. O Brāhmaṇas, a Tīrtha, bestower of worldly pleasures and salvation and on a par with it, has never existed in all the three divisions of time (past, present and future) in this world. It bestows everything desired by men, due to the power of holy bath in the Tīrtha.

14. Due to the power of holy bath therein, the son of Sudīrghatamas named Kakṣīvān[1] obtained Manoramā, the daughter of Svanaya, as his wife.

15. This story of Kakṣīvān is meritorious and destructive of sins. I shall recount that story to you all. O eminent sages, listen.

16. These is an extremely virtuous sage named Dīrghatamas. He had a famous son named Kakṣīvān.

17. After being invested with the sacred thread, Kakṣīvān led the life of a celibate religious student. He conquered all his senses

---

1. This Kakṣīvān is different from the sage of the same name in Mbh, *Śānti* 208.27-28. That Kakṣīvān was the son of Aṅgiras and was a famous spiritually powerful sage. This was the legitimate son of Sudīrghatamas. There is a third Kakṣīvān born of Dīrghatamas from a slave girl of Bali (PI 296-297). The author has used a famous old name to describe the glory of this Tīrtha.

and passions. For the study of the Vedas, he stayed in the abode of a preceptor.

18. Staying in the home of Udaṅka, the son of Dīrghatamas learned all the four Vedas along with their ancillary subjects and the six Śāstras (systems of philosophy).

19-20. He learned Itihāsas, Purāṇas and Upaniṣads. Kakṣīvān thus stayed with his preceptor for sixty years. Desirous of returning to his own abode, O Brāhmaṇas, he gave the fee to the preceptor. The learned Kakṣīvān, the most excellent one among those who knew Brahman, spoke to his preceptor:

Kakṣīvān said:

21. I shall go home, O great sage. Permit me. O Udaṅka, look at me with your merciful glance and save me now.

On being addressed thus, Udaṅka spoke to Kakṣīvān:

Udaṅka said:

22-27. O Kakṣīvān, I permit you. Go home. I shall tell you the means for your marriage. O dear one, listen. Go to Rāmasetu (and) the Gandhamādana mountain. There is a Tīrtha there made by Agastya. It fulfils all desires. It yields worldly pleasures and salvation to men. It is destructive of all sins. Take your holy bath in it which is the means of achievement of all auspiciousness. Stay there for three years, strictly adhering to the holy observances and good behaviour. After three years have passed by, in the course of the fourth year, a certain elephant will come out of that excellent Tīrtha. He will have a huge body and four tusks. He will have the refulgence of an autumnal cloud. After taking your holy bath, mount that elephant resembling a mountain.

28-33. O dear one, riding on that elephant, go to the city of Svanaya. On seeing you seated on an elephant that has four tusks, sitting like another Indra, the saintly and intelligent King Svanaya will have his eyes brightened due to delight. He shall certainly get rid of his anxiety over his daughter.

Formerly his daughter Manoramā had made this solemn declaration: "My husband shall be that person who comes here riding on an elephant that has a huge body and four tusks and is white in colour all over its body." On hearing that declaration of his daughter, the king had become excessively agitated in his mind. He pondered over it continuously. While Svanaya was thus anxious, Nārada came there. On seeing the sage arrived, that exceedingly virtuous and saintly king joyously welcomed him and worshipped him with *Pādya, Arghya,* etc.

34. After bowing down to Nārada, the king spoke these words: "This daughter of mine, O celestial sage, has taken this vow previously:

35. 'My husband shall be that person who comes here riding on an elephant that has a huge body and four tusks. It must be white in colour all over its body.'

36. A huge-bodied elephant, white in colour all over its body, having four tusks may exist in the abode of Indra, but it does not exist on the earth.

37. In her childishness, this girl has already made this declaration which is very difficult to fulfil. It is this vow that continuously worries me very much.

38. Indeed an unmarried daughter shall always cause grief to her father."

On hearing these words of his, Nārada spoke to Svanaya:

Nārada said:

39-40. Do not feel sad, O saintly king. Ere long she will have a husband of this sort on the earth itself. He will be an excellent Brāhmaṇa well-known as Kakṣīvān. He shall be your son-in-law.

After saying this, Sage Nārada went along the aerial path.

41. Ever since he heard the words spoken by Nārada, Svanaya began to expect such an arrival day and night.

42. Hence, O gentle, highly fortunate Kakṣīvān, O young ascetic, go quickly to Agastyatīrtha now itself in order to take your holy bath.

43-44. You will achieve all auspicious results.
There is no doubt about it.

On being told thus by Udaṅka, Kakṣīvān, the prominent Brāhmaṇa who had been permitted by his preceptor, went to Gandhamādana. After reaching Agastyatīrtha he who had subdued his passions took his bath there.

45. The eminent sage observed sacred fast in the holy spot for a day. The next day, he took his holy bath once again and per-

formed the Pāraṇā rite (breaking the fast).

46-49. Kakṣīvān who was engaged in holy rites slept there itself during the night. As Sage Kakṣīvān continued his observance thus, a period of three years short by one day passed off. At the end of the three years, on that very day the sage offered the Sandhyā prayers at dusk and then slept soundly on its banks. When there remained only three hours (a *yāma*) in the night, a loud sound rose up. It was comparable to the tumultuous rumbling sound of the waves of the ocean at the time of the final deluge. On account of that loud sound, Kakṣīvān woke up.

50. Then the powerful king named Svanaya who was the king of Madhurā and was interested in hunting, came there along with his followers.

51-52. He killed elephants, lions, boars, buffaloes and deer. That king killed other animals too with arrows.

The king who was very much fond of hunting, was accompanied by his ministers and soldiers. He was equipped with chariots, horses and elephants. He reached the vicinity of Agastyatīrtha.

53. The king was fatigued after a great deal of hunting. Surrounded by the tired soldiers, the king sat on the ground bordering that Tīrtha.

54-56. When the day dawned brightly, the excellent sage Kakṣīvān took his holy bath in Agastyatīrtha and performed the Sandhyā prayers of the morning. Strictly adhering to the observances and repeating the Mantras, he sat on its bank.

In the meantime an elephant came up from the excellent Tīrtha. He had a huge body and four tusks. He appeared to be an embodied form of mount Kailāsa. Coming up from the Tīrtha he approached Kakṣīvān.

57. On seeing that elephant marked by all the characteristics mentioned by Udaṅka arrived, Kakṣīvān took the holy bath in order to mount him.

58. He bowed down to that Tīrtha and praised it repeatedly. Then Kakṣīvān mounted the great elephant with four tusks.

59. After mounting the elephant with four tusks, that resembled a silver mountain, Kakṣīvān desired to go to the city of Svanaya.

60. On seeing him riding on the excellent white elephant with four tusks, the king came to the conclusion that it must be Kakṣīvān.

61. With his heart extremely delighted, the king came near him. After approaching Kakṣīvān, the king spoke these words:

Svanaya said:

62. O Brāhmaṇa, whose son are you? What is your name? Tell me. Where do you wish to go, riding on this elephant?

On being asked by Svanaya thus, Kakṣīvān spoke these words:

Kakṣīvān said:

63-66. I am the son of Dīrghatamas, well-known as Kakṣīvān. I am going to the city of the saintly King Svanaya. I wish to marry his daughter Manoramā. I am seated on an elephant with four tusks in order to fulfil her declared vow. Then, O king, I will take hold of the hand of (i.e. marry) the daughter of Svanaya.

On hearing his statement which was like a shower of nectar to his ears, Svanaya became delighted. His eyes beamed with pleasure. Then Svanaya spoke these words:

Svanaya said:

67-69. O Kakṣīvān, I am satisfied. My task is fulfilled. I am that very Svanaya whose daughter Manoramā you wish to marry. Welcome to you, O excellent sage, O Kakṣīvān, O young ascetic, accept my daughter Manoramā. Perform the holy rites along with her. Carry on your householder's life.

On being told thus by the king, Kakṣīvān who was alert in observance of holy rites, spoke to the delighted King Svanaya, the resident of the city of Madhurā:

Kakṣīvān said:

70-75. O lord, my father named Dīrghatamas is engaged in penance in Vedāraṇya. He is gentle. He is devoted to holy observances and good conduct. Send a Brāhmaṇa to him (to invite him), O king.

On being told thus, King Svanaya became delighted in his mind. With a big army he sent his priest, a Brāhmaṇa named Sudarśana, to the place Vedāraṇya.

Commanded by King Svanaya, Sudarśana went to Vedāraṇya with a great army.

There, in his hut, the priest saw Dīrghatamas, the sage sitting in meditation. He was performing penance and meditating on the lord of Vedāraṇya. He was engaged in the Japa of the excellent Mantra.

76. Sudarśana made obeisance to that sage. Delighting the sage Dīrghatamas, he spoke thus:

Sudarśana said:

77-78. I hope you are quite well, O Brāhmaṇa, and your penance goes on increasing. I hope everyone in the hermitage is happy. I trust you are happy in performing holy rites. Tell me.

On being enquired thus by Sudarśana, sage Dīrghatamas said to Sudarśạna after duly honouring him with *Arghya,* etc.:

Dīrghatamas said:

79-84. I am happy in every respect, O Brāhmaṇa, O Sudarśana of great intelligence. Thanks to the favour of the Lord of Vedāraṇya. I have nothing inauspicious anywhere. I hope you are also happy, O Brāhmaṇa. I hope you had a happy journey. O Sudarśana, what may be the purpose of your visit to my hermitage? Indeed you are the priest of Svanaya. You are the most excellent one among those conversant with the Vedas. Why did you leave that great king, the resident of Madhurāpura, and come here with a great army?

On being asked thus by Dīrghatamas, Sudarśana then spoke to the noble-souled sage of burning refulgence:

"O Brāhmaṇa, thanks to your kindness, I am always happy in every respect. O holy lord, King Svanaya prostrates in front of you and tells you these humble words through me. Listen.

Svanaya said:

85. O Brāhmaṇa, your son Kakṣīvān is now present on the Gandhamādana mountain. He is engaged in taking holy bath in the Tīrtha of Agastya.

86-87. I have come to know that these qualities of him are of the highest order: good features, power of penance, holy rites, good conduct conforming to the injunctions of the Vedas, mastery of the Vedas and scriptures, and nobility of birth. O sage, I wish to give my daughter Manoramā in marriage to your son.

88. O tiger among sages, enthusiastically engaged in hunting,

I have come to the Gandhamādana mountain. I now stay near your son.

89. O excellent sage, your son Kakṣīvān says that without his father's consent he would not marry my daughter.

90. I have now sent Sudarśana along with my army to your presence. Bless me to give my daughter to him (your son) because she is already emotionally attached to him.

Sudarśana said:

91. O holy sage, the king has thus sent me to your presence. So, kindly permit the king to do what he wishes to do.

Śrī Sūta said:

92. After saying this, the priest of Svanaya ceased (to speak). Thereupon, Dīrghatamas said to the priest of Svanaya:

Dīrghatamas said:

93-97. O Sudarśana, let it be as said by Svanaya. This auspicious wedding has my approval. O Brāhmaṇa, I am coming to the Gandhamādana mountain.

After saying this, O Brāhmaṇas, the great sage Dīrghatamas, bowed down to the Lord of Vedāraṇya with great devotion in his mind. Accompanied by Sudarśana, he set out for Setu. Within six days the sage reached the meritorious Gandhamādana. After going to the banks of Agastyatīrtha, Sage Dīrghatamas saw his son Kakṣīvān in front of him. On seeing his father, Kakṣīvān bowed down to him uttering his own name.

98-100. Then Yogī Dīrghatamas placed his son on his lap. He sniffed his head with affection. He embraced him with great horripilation of joy. Then Sage Dīrghatamas enquired after his well-being: "O Kakṣīvān, have you learned all the Vedas? O dear one, have you read all the scriptures? O dear boy, tell me everything." On being asked thus by his own father he told him everything.

CHAPTER SEVENTEEN

The Glory of Agastyakuṇḍa: The Marriage of Kakṣīvān

Śrī Sūta said:

1-5. Again, O eminent sages, Kakṣīvān spoke to his father thus: "I have been sent here by my preceptor Udaṅka. I have come to this Tīrtha, O excellent sage, because I have been directed by my preceptor to accomplish marriage with the daughter of Svanaya. I stayed here continuously practising the means suggested by him. At the end of three years, when I got fully equipped with the requisite means, Svanaya met me here casually staying here itself. He approached me and said, "I shall give my daughter in marriage to you." Thereupon, at my request, the king has called you here."

After saying this to his father Kakṣīvān stopped speaking.

6. Then Sudarśana, the eminent Brāhmaṇa, the priest of Svanaya, went to the presence of the king in order to report everything to him.

7. After approaching King Svanaya, Sudarśana intimated that Sage Dīrghatamas had arrived.

8. Thereupon, having heard from his preceptor that the sage had arrived, Svanaya immediately started from his tent.

9. On the banks of Agastyatīrtha, King Svanaya saw the excellent sage along with his son, like the Lord of Devas visiting Brahmā.

10-13. The king saluted the feet of Dīrghatamas that were conducive to the felicity of all the worlds. Then, O Brāhmaṇas, sage Dīrghatamas made the king rise up. He blessed King Svanaya. In the meantime, the great Sage Udaṅka too came there accompanied by the groups of his disciples, in order to take the holy bath in Rāmasetu in Dhanuṣkoṭi.

O eminent sages, the multitude of sages along with him numbered a hundred thousand. Sage Udaṅka came to this Agastyatīrtha in order to take the holy bath. On seeing Udaṅka arrived Kakṣīvān bowed down to him.

14-21. The Brāhmaṇa, the preceptor, blessed the disciple. Then Dīrghatamas, the Brāhmaṇa, enquired about the health of the great Sage Udaṅka. He too enquired after the health of the great sage. Both the sages were well-known in all the world. There they recounted stories destructive of sins.

The king too bowed down to the eminent sage. Udaṅka granted Svanaya his blessings. There, the delighted King Svanaya spoke to Sage Dīrghatamas, "Let the marriage be celebrated."

Sage Dīrghatamas said "So be it, O king of great intelligence; let it be performed tomorrow itself at an auspicious hour. Let the wedding be celebrated here itself on Gandhamādana. Hence bring here immediately the girl and the inmates of your female apartment."

On being told thus, King Svanaya went to his camp. He called a hundred of old eunuchs and despatched them to bring the princess and the inmates of the Antaḥpura.

22. On being directed by Svanaya, those chief eunuchs mounted very swift horses and went to Madhurā.

23. They went to the Antaḥpura immediately and explained everything to them. Along with the princess and the members of the Antaḥpura, they returned (to Gandhamādana).

24. On the next day, at an auspicious hour, Sage Dīrghatamas duly performed the Godāna (Tonsure) and other holy rites on behalf of his son.

25-28. Godāna and others were completed. Afterwards in order to marry the princess he, accompanied by his father and preceptor, joyously mounted the huge-bodied elephant with four tusks and white complexion all over the body, like another king of Devas. He thereby fulfilled the desire of Princess Manoramā. He was accompanied by thousands of Brāhmaṇas who were uttering benedictory Mantras and verses.

Kakṣīvān, in regard to whom all auspicious rites had been completed delightfully, went to the pavilion of the saintly king, the entrance to which was decorated with an ornamental arched gateway.

29-30. On seeing Kakṣīvān seated on the huge-bodied white elephant with four tusks, arrived with an eagerness to marry her, the daughter of Svanaya who had worn all auspicious ornaments became glad that the solemn declaration she had made, had been fulfilled.

31. Accompanied by Dīrghatamas as well as Udaṅka, Kakṣīvān slowly proceeded towards the outer door of the tent of the king.

32. On seeing Kakṣīvān arrived, Svanaya received him along with his preceptor Sudarśana.

33. The female attendants of the princess performed the Nīrājana

rite to the bridegroom Kakṣīvān by means of golden and silver vessels.

34. Invited by Svanaya, Kakṣīvān, the fortunate one, entered the apartment of the king, surrounded by Brāhmaṇas.

35. Thereupon, with great modesty the king took Sage Dīrghatamas to his abode along with the bridegroom and (the preceptor) Udaṅka.

36-37. Near the decorated well, the king offered *Arghya* to Udaṅka and Dīrghatamas along with garments, chowries and festoons. The bridegroom as well as Dīrghatamas and other sages along with Udaṅka sat there. King Svanaya too sat there along with his ministers and the priest.

38-39. Then they took the bride Manoramā, his daughter, whose tresses had been well arranged, who had been adorned with ornaments and divine clothes on her body. Her lips resembled the Biṁba fruit (*Momordica monadelpha*—a plant with bright red gourd). She was charming in all her limbs with plump protruding breasts. They brought the bride to the spot near the well at which eminent people had assembled.

40. Then, that splendid Princess Manoramā put the garland wreathed with Campaka flowers round the neck of the bridegroom in the midst of the people.

41-44. Then Udaṅka came there and installed the sacred fire on the holy ground. He performed all the rites beginning with *Lājāhoma* (offering fried grain to the fire) and ending with *Agnimukha* sacrifice. He made the bridegroom hold the bride by hand. Udaṅka thus performed all the holy rites there. O Brāhmaṇas, he gave blessings to the bride and the bridegroom. Then King Svanaya fed with cooked foodstuffs of six tastes, three hundred thousand Brāhmaṇas along with the bridegroom, Sage Dīrghatamas, Udaṅka, persons belonging to the bridegroom's party and persons from his own side, O Brāhmaṇas.

45-49. Then he honoured them in various ways with betel leaves and other things.

Then Udaṅka took leave of the excellent sage (Dīrghatamas) and went to his own hermitage. All the other Brāhmaṇas went to their respective places.

Thus, when the marriage celebration of Kakṣīvān and the princess was concluded, that excellent elephant entered Agastyatīrtha and vanished.

Then, O Brāhmaṇas, Dīrghatamas along with his son and daughter-in-law took his holy bath in Agastyatīrtha that had bestowed what they wished. He praised that Tīrtha which was well-known in all the worlds. Then he decided to go to his meritorious hermitage at Vedāraṇya. The excellent sage then took leave of the king and requested him to go over to his place.

50-52. With great joy, King Svanaya gave his daughter a hundred thousand gold pieces as dowry. He gave a thousand cows, thousands of maidens-in-waiting and five hundred villages too. Fond of his daughter, the king gave ten thousand divine garments and a hundred jewel boxes. With great affection for his daughter, he gave her a thousand garlands and necklaces.

53. Taking all these things the sage took leave of the king. Accompanied by his son and daughter-in-law, he went to Vedāraṇya.

54-60. After reaching Vedāraṇya, O Brāhmaṇas, Sage Dīrghatamas lived happily with his son and daughter-in-law. With his wife Kakṣīvān stayed there for a long time serving the Lord of Vedāraṇya who bestows worldly pleasures and salvation.

The saintly King Svanaya too took his holy bath in the highly meritorious Tīrtha created by the Pot-born Sage and then accompanied by all his soldiers, he joyously went back to his city taking the Antaḥpura with him. Thus, O Brāhmaṇas, it was due to the efficacious glory of Agastyatīrtha that the marriage of Sage Kakṣīvān took place—a marriage not easy for others.

Śrī Sūta said:

This legend is meritorious and is found in the Vedas, O leading sages. It is conducive to wealth, fame and longevity. It increases renown and good fortune. O Brāhmaṇas, this should always be listened to and be read by all means by men. Those men who read or listen to this ancient legendary story, do not suffer here or hereafter. They will never have poverty.

CHAPTER EIGHTEEN

The Glory of Rāmakuṇḍa: Dharmaputra's Atonement for False Speech

Śrī Sūta said:

1. After taking the holy bath in Agastyatīrtha, one (pilgrim) should go to the meritorious Rāmakuṇḍa for liberation from sins.

2-6. O Brāhmaṇas, the lake Raghunāthasaras is meritorious and destructive of sins. A Yajña performed on the banks of Raghunāthasaras bestows full benefit even if the monetary gifts be meagre. Similarly study of the Vedas and *Japa* (of Mantras) shall also bestow merit.

O Brāhmaṇas, even if only a handful is offered to a Brāhmaṇa well-versed in the Vedas on the banks of Raghunāthasaras, it shall have infinite benefit. O eminent sages, I shall recount to you an extremely meritorious story about Rāmatīrtha. It is destructive of all sins.

There was a great Brāhmaṇa named Sutīkṣṇa.[1] He was a sage who had restrained his mind. He was a disciple of Agastya. He always meditated upon the lotus-like feet of Rāma. He performed a very severe penance on the banks of the lake called Rāmacandrasaras.

7-9. He performed Japa of the six-syllabled Mantra with Rāmacandra as its presiding deity. He repeated this excellent Mantra with full concentration five thousand times everyday. He regularly bathed in the waters of Raghunāthasaras. He ate only what he got as alms after begging. He had restricted his diet very much. He had conquered anger and his passions. Thus Sutīkṣṇa continued for a long time, O eminent Brāhmaṇas. He always meditated upon Rāma in his heart. With great devotion, he eulogized Rāmacandra accompanied by Sītā.

Sutīkṣṇa said:

10-14. Obeisance to you, O Lord of Jānakī; salute to you, O Lord fond of Hanumān. Bow to you, O Lord actively engaged in

---

1. According to VR this sage was a kind host of Rāma during his sojourn in Daṇḍakāraṇya (VR III.7). He guided Rāma to the hermitage of Agastya (VR III.11). This Purāṇa represents him to be a devotee of Rāma staying near Rāmakuṇḍa on Gandhamādana.

guarding the sacrifice of sage Kauśika (Viśvāmitra). Hail to you, O son of Kausalyā; to the prince dear to Viśvāmitra. Obeisance to the Lord who broke the bow of Hara, O Lord served by the immortal ones. O great king, O slayer of Mārīca. O destroyer of the life of Tāḍakā. O enemy of (demon) Kabandha, O Hari, O son of Daśaratha, obeisance to you. Hail to you, to the conqueror of the son of Jamadagni. Salute to the destroyer of Khara. Obeisance to the lord of Sugrīva. Bow to you, the slayer of Vāli; to the lord who removed the fear and the distress of Vibhīṣaṇa and the destroyer of sins.

15-20a. Obeisance to you, to the destroyer of the misery of Ahalyā, O elder brother of Bharata. Hail to the dispeller of the pride of the Ocean; salute to the builder of Setu thereon.

Obeisance to the Brahman that redeems; to you, O elder brother of Lakṣmaṇa. Hail to you, the destroyer of the Rākṣasas; obeisance to the suppressor of Rāvaṇa; salute to you, the wielder of a bow; to the lord who accords protection to all.

Thus the sage Sutīkṣṇa eulogized Rāma everyday. With his mind fixed on Rāmacandra he always spent his time (joyously). As he repeatedly performed Japa of the six-syllabled Mantra of Rāma, as he eulogized Rāmacandra by means of this prayer, as he took his daily bath in the lake Raghunāthasaras, O sages of righteous conduct, his devotion to Rāmacandra became steady and free from impurities.

20b-26. He had perfect knowledge of non-duality characterised by the one-ness of soul. Without study he had the knowledge of the Vedas; he could understand even that which was not heard. O Brāhmaṇas, he had the ability to enter the body of another person, ability to go through the sky, skill in the arts; without a preceptor he could understand the scriptures not heard before. He could go to all the worlds without any obstacle. He could see those objects which are beyond the ken of the sense-organs. He could converse with Devas. He had the knowledge of the activities of ants and other creatures, O Brāhmaṇas. He could travel to the worlds of Brahmā, Viṣṇu and Mahādeva. He had the ability to traverse at his will to all the fourteen worlds. These and all other skilful activities usually attributed to Yogins alone, O excellent Brāhmaṇas, Sutīkṣṇa achieved by resorting to Rāmatīrtha.

That Tīrtha has such a power. It is destructive of great sins.

27-30. It confers great Siddhis. It is meritorious. It prevents premature and accidental deaths. It gives worldly pleasures and salvation to men. It destroys the tortures of hells. It grants constant devotion to Rāma. It causes destruction of worldly existence. The scion of the family of Raghu installed the great Liṅga on its banks and worshipped it with a desire to bless the worlds. By taking holy bath in the extremely meritorious Rāmatīrtha and by visiting that Liṅga, men will achieve even liberation. What to speak about other achievements! Formerly, O Brāhmaṇas, Dharmaputra (Yudhiṣṭhira) took his bath there and visited Śiva. Instantaneously he became liberated from the evils arising from the utterance of falsehood.

The sages said:

31. O son of Sūta, why was a lie uttered by Dharmaputra? (What was that lie) to suppress the evils of which he took his holy bath in the extremely sacred Rāmatīrtha?

Śrī Sūta said:

32. O sages, I shall recount to you how a lie was fraudulently uttered by Dharmaputra and how it perished (by bath) in Rāmatīrtha.

33-35. Formerly, O Brāhmaṇas, the sons of Pāṇḍu including Dharmaputra and the sons of Dhṛtarāṣṭra headed by Duryodhana, had great enmity mutually on account of the kingdom.[1] O excellent Brāhmaṇas, they gathered together at Kurukṣetra with a vast army. They were great warriors who never retreated from battles. They fought with one another. After fighting for ten days the son of Gaṅgā (i.e. Bhīṣma) fell down on the ground.

36. Then for five days, the preceptor Droṇa of great strength and valour, fought with Dhṛṣṭadyumna.

37. Discharging many missiles and weapons, the exceedingly powerful Droṇācārya harassed the army of Pāṇḍavas.

38. The highly powerful Dhṛṣṭadyumna who was a hero expert in the use of divine weapons harassed the army of Droṇa in diverse ways by means of volleys of arrows.

39-40. At that time, Droṇa showered Dhṛṣṭadyumna by means of many arrows. Then the army of the sons of Kuntī became excessively afflicted by Droṇa's arrows. In their great fight, O

1. VV 35-83 give a summary of the Bhārata War up to Droṇa's death.

excellent Brāhmaṇas, they fled in all direction. Thereupon, Arjuna, the most excellent one among great fighters in chariots, fought with Droṇa.

41. The sky was completely filled with the Devas who had come to witness the battle between Arjuna and Droṇa who were equally efficient in fighting.

42. There is nothing on the earth, O Brāhmaṇas, with which the fight between Droṇa and Arjuna could be compared. At that time the fight was between a preceptor and his disciple who were equally furious.

43. The fight between Droṇa and Arjuna was comparable (only) to the fight between Droṇa and Arjuna.[1] Droṇa appreciated and honoured mentally the great valour of Arjuna.

44. Thereupon Droṇa avoided Arjuna, his dear disciple of great vigour, and fought with Pāñcāla's army.

45. There in the battle, Droṇācārya killed two lacs and ten thousands of kings along with their elephants and horses.

46. Dhṛṣṭadyumna became furious and struck Droṇa with arrows. Droṇa seized a sharp-edged spear and hit Dhṛṣṭadyumna.

47. With sharp arrows comparable to the flames of fire, he pierced him in the course of that fight. Struck with the arrows, Dhṛṣṭadyumna began to retreat.

48-53. Then Bhīma approached Dhṛṣṭadyumna who was without a chariot. He placed him in his own chariot and spoke thus to Droṇācārya:

"There are some base Brāhmaṇas. They are not contented with their own duties (specific to their caste) and they have trained themselves in the use of weapons. If those ruthless ones had not fought, many kings would not have been killed in the battle. It has been declared in Smṛtis that non-violence is the greatest virtue of Brāhmaṇas. It is the tribes like hunters who protect (i.e. maintain) their wives and children by means of violence and injuries to others. For the sake of your only son you stood firm in the battlefield and killed many kings. O Brāhmaṇa, that son of yours too is lying killed in the battlefield. Still you are not ashamed, nor are you grief-stricken."

Hearing from Yudhiṣṭhira that these words of Bhīma were true, he cast off his weapons and fell down in his chariot. Then, O

1. An example of a figure of speech *Ananvaya*.

Brāhmaṇas, Droṇācārya who was conversant with Yoga, resorted to fast unto death.

54-56. Having understood that it was a good opportunity (Dhṛṣṭadyumna) who had a sword in his hand, came to the side of Droṇācārya and rushed at him in order to cut off his head. Though he was prevented from it by Arjuna and others, he rushed to cut off his head. Because he (Droṇa) was conversant with Yoga, a fiery flame went up to heaven through the head of Droṇa. It was seen by Kṛṣṇa, Arjuna, Kṛpa, Dharmaputra and others in the battlefield. (He) cut off the head from the body of Droṇa which was thus bereft of life.

57. When Bhāradvāja (i.e. Droṇa) was killed in the battle, Kauravas fled out of fear, O Brāhmaṇas, and Pāṇḍavas, Dhṛṣṭadyumna and others became delighted.

58-59. On seeing the army fleeing, the son of Droṇa asked Suyodhana, "O king, why does the army flee thus? Why has it cast off the weapons?"

Then King Duryodhana was unable to tell it himself. He urged Kṛpācārya to announce the death of Droṇa in the battle. At that time Kṛpācārya intimated the death of his preceptor to the son of Droṇa.

Kṛpa said:

60-64. O Aśvatthāman, your powerful father despatched to the abode of Yama hundreds of the enemies in the battlefield killing them by means of his Brāhma missile.

On seeing his valour unassailable, O great Brāhmaṇa, Keśava, an expert in (logical) speech, spoke these words to Pāṇḍavas:

Keśava said:

O Pāṇḍavas, there is an expedient to defeat the invincible Droṇa in the battle. If an authoritative and truthful person were to say thus, "O Droṇa, your son Aśvatthāmā has been killed in the battle", Droṇa may instantaneously cast off his weapons ana desist from fighting. Hence Dharmarāja should make now this false announcement.

65-67. Otherwise Droṇa, an expert in battle, cannot be defeated. If it is not possible to vanquish an enemy by righteous means, one may resort even to non-righteous means and conquer the enemy.

* * *

On hearing these words of Keśava, Bhīma, the son of Kuntī, approached your father and uttered these false words. "O Droṇa, Aśvatthāmā has been killed in this battle. He has fallen down now."

Droṇācārya thought these words to be truthful.

68-73. Not being convinced, he came to Dharmaputra and spoke thus: "O son of Dharma, is my son Aśvatthāmā killed in the battle? You do tell me. You are considered to be truthful in speech." Dharmaputra was afraid of speaking a lie. (At the same time) he was eager to have victory over the enemy. His mind began to waver 'What should be done by me now?' (He thought.) On seeing an elephant named Aśvatthāman, killed by Bhīma, Dharmaputra spoke these deceitful words to Droṇa: "The great Aśvatthāman was killed today in the battle by Bhīma." On hearing it, your father cast off his weapon and desisted from fighting. Of course thereafter Dharmaputra had said the word "elephant" too.[1] But, O dear one, Droṇa, your powerful father again declared, "I will not again take up in the (same) battle the weapon that had been set aside once."

74-77. Hence he did not take up the weapon again, because he was afraid of breaking his vow. On seeing Dhṛṣṭadyumna your father thought about his death (to be brought about) by fasting unto Death. He was conversant with Yogic exercises. He stayed within the chariot and entered into ecstatic meditation. He restrained his breath and controlled his speech. Then instantaneously his vital airs came out piercing the crown of his head. After Droṇa had died thus in the battlefield, O dear one, Dhṛṣṭadyumna caught hold of his hair with his hand and cut off his head with his sword. All the sons of Kuntī and other warriors cried out to him, "Do not strike." Though he was prevented by all of them he struck (your father thus from the sides).

Śrī Sūta said:

78-83. On hearing that his father had been killed, O Brāhmaṇas, the son of Droṇa lamented for a long time. He blazed with great fury and spoke these words: "Ere long I will kill that son of Kuntī who made my father set aside the weapons by telling him a lie.

1. This refers to an equivocation on the part of Yudhiṣṭhira: "Aśvatthāmā, a man or an elephant, is killed" (Mbh, *Droṇa* 190.55).

I will kill the other Pāṇḍavas also. I will kill Dhṛṣṭadyumna too who caught hold of the hair (of my father) and by deceitful means cut off his head after he had cast off his weapons. Let the Pāṇḍavas along with Kṛṣṇa see my valour." Thus, O Brāhmaṇas, the son of Droṇa took a dreadful vow. Then the sun set. All the kings of both the sides entered their respective tents after the death of Droṇa. Thus in eighteen days the battle came to a close.

84-85. After killing Śalya, Karṇa and sons of Dhṛtarāṣṭra of whom Duryodhana was prominent (or the eldest), Dharmarāja Yudhiṣṭhira performed as per injunctions the obsequies of the dead of his own and the enemy side, along with (his family preceptor) Dhaumya and other Brāhmaṇas, O Brāhmaṇas.

86-88. All the sons of Pāṇḍu joined together and paid their respects to Dhṛtarāṣṭra. After being permitted by him they all went to Hastināpura accompanied by the people who had survived. They entered their palace.

It is reported that after a few days had passed by, O eminent sages, the citizens along with Dhaumya and other sages, began the preparations for the coronation of the noble-souled Dharmaputra.

89-93. When the rites of coronation of Dharmaputra started, an unembodied speech addressed Dharmaputra.[1]

"O illustrious Dharmaputra who are kind even to the enemies, do not celebrate your coronation. You do not deserve to take up the administration of the kingdom because you told a lie to the preceptor, an excellent Brāhmaṇa, and deceitfully made him cast off his weapons and shamelessly brought about his death, O king. Hence, O Dharmaputra, you have incurred plenty of sins. You shall not be entitled to take up the administration of the kingdom without the requisite expiation. Hence perform the expiatory rites."

After saying this, that unembodied speech ceased.

94-99. At that utterance, King Dharmaputra became extremely frightened. He thought: 'I have been deluded. I have been ruthlessly foolhardy. I have been harsh and treacherous. I have been deluded by greed. I have committed such a sin on account of my desire for a worthless kingdom. What shall I do for purification from this sin? What is my wayout? What charitable gift shall I make? Where shall I go?'

---

1. This onwards is the continuation of SkP glorifying Rāmatīrtha.

While King Dharmaputra was grief-stricken thus, Kṛṣṇa Dvaipāyana Vyāsa came to him. He saluted Vyāsa and received him duly with palms joined in reverence. With the mind full of devotion, O Brāhmaṇas, he honoured him with *Arghya,* etc. Extremely dejected in spirit, Dharmaputra recounted to Vyāsa everything that had been declared by the unembodied speech. After hearing the whole of the speech of Dharmaputra, the sage meditated for a long time and began to speak thus:

Vyāsa said:

100. O king, do not be afraid. I shall tell you the proper means for suppressing this sin. Let it be listened to and acted upon by you.

Yudhiṣṭhira said:

101. Tell me, what is that, O son of Parāśara, O great Yogin, O storehouse of mercy. What is that whereby my sin can perish in no time? Tell it to me.

Vyāsa said:

102-107. In the southern ocean, on Rāmasetu, on the Gandhamādana mountain, O great king, there is a meritorious lake well-known as Rāmatīrtha. It has been proved to be destructive of great sins. Merely by viewing it crores of great sins perish immediately like darkness at sunrise.

When one sees Rāmatīrtha created by Rāma himself, one is absolved of Brahmahatyā (sin of Brāhmaṇa's slaughter). There is no doubt about it.

After going to Rāmatīrtha which bestows salvation, O great king, take your holy bath; you will get purified of the sin and you will become entitled to protect the kingdom (as a king).

Make charitable gifts on its banks, of cows, plots of lands, gingelly seeds and clothes. O Yudhiṣṭhira, make gifts of gold and silver; certainly before long, all your sins will be purified.

Śrī Sūta said:

108-110. On being told thus by Vyāsa, O excellent Brāhmaṇas, Dharmaputra installed Sahadeva on the kingdom and immediately started for Rāmasetu, accompanied by his brothers and Dhaumya. He did not use any vehicle for the journey. Within a few days he reached Rāmasetu.

111-114a. The son of Pāṇḍu reached Rāmatīrtha along with Dhaumya. He duly performed the Saṁkalpa rite in the manner laid down by the priest. He took his holy bath in the Tīrtha called Rāmasaras, which is meritorious and destructive of sins. Having become pure after the bath, he offered the Kṣetra Piṇḍa. Yudhiṣṭhira made all the gifts as suggested by Vyāsa. Dharmaputra observed fast for a full month and took his holy baths. O Brāhmaṇas, without any covetousness for money, he made charitable gifts everyday.

114b-120a. When a month elapsed, one day, the unembodied voice said once again to Dharmaputra on a certain day:

"O king, O Yudhiṣṭhira, all your sins have perished. The sin that you committed formerly by speaking deceitful words causing the death of the preceptor has perished, O scorcher of enemies. Go back to your city, O king, and protect the earth. Get yourself crowned. There is no doubt about it that you are now entitled to the kingdom."

After saying thus the unembodied voice ceased. Dharmaputra became delighted and bowed down to that direction from where the unembodied speech had come. With his mind fully delighted, he went to Hastināpura along with his younger brothers.

120b-123. Having been coronated in the kingdom he ruled the earth. Thus Dharmaputra became rid of sins, O Brāhmaṇas, by resorting to Rāmatīrtha and taking his holy bath therein. He became purified in his soul. He became entitled to rule the kingdom.

Thus the wonderful glory of Rāmatīrtha has been recounted to you all. It is destructive of all sins. It bestows devotion, worldly pleasures and salvation. It is by taking his holy bath there that Dharmaputra became absolved of the sin of uttering a lie.

O excellent Brāhmaṇas, those who read this chapter, the men who listen to this become rid of sins. They will go to Kailāsa which cannot be attained by anyone else. After going there, they do not have to undergo rebirth.

CHAPTER NINETEEN

The Glory of Lakṣmaṇatīrtha: Balabhadra's Redemption from the Sin of Brāhmaṇa-Slaughter

Śrī Sūta said:

1-6. After taking the holy bath in that Tīrtha of Tārakabrahman (i.e. Rāmatīrtha), O excellent Brāhmaṇas, one should then proceed to Lakṣmaṇatīrtha with great concentration and mental purity.

By taking the holy bath in the Tīrtha of Śrī Lakṣmaṇa, they shall be liberated from all sins. They will attain salvation free from impurities which is characterized by not getting any rebirth. By taking the holy bath in Lakṣmaṇatīrtha poverty will be entirely removed. A learned son endowed with long life and good qualities will be born to him.

He who recites Lakṣmaṇa's Mantra on the banks of Lakṣmaṇatīrtha shall become a master of all scriptures. He shall become conversant with all the four Vedas.

Lakṣmaṇa installed a great Liṅga on its banks. He who takes his holy bath in the Tīrtha and worships Lakṣmaṇeśvara is liberated from poverty and sickness in this world and (after death) is liberated from worldly existence.

By taking his holy bath in Lakṣmaṇatīrtha and witnessing Lakṣmaṇeśvara, O Brāhmaṇas, Balabhadra of yore became rid of the sin of slaying a Brāhmaṇa.

The sages said:

7. O Sūtaja, how did the son of Rohiṇī incur the sin of killing a Brāhmaṇa? How was it destroyed here? Narrate this, O great sage.

Śrī Sūta said:

8-13. Lord Balabhadra is an incarnation of Śeṣa, O Brāhmaṇas. Formerly on seeing the preparations for a war by Kurus and Pāṇḍavas, the lord with the plough for a weapon was unable to brook the (imminent) mutual slaughter by relatives. Balabhadra of great intellect thought thus: 'If I were to render help to the Kuru king, the sons of Pāṇḍu will inevitably be furious with me. If I help Pāṇḍavas, Duryodhana will be angry.' Having understood (the consequences) of both, Balabhadra (wanted to be) neutral. He, therefore, left the place under the pretext of a pilgrimage.

He went to Prabhāsa and took his holy bath along with the requisite Saṁkalpa. With the holy water he offered libations to Devas, sages and groups of Pitṛs.

14-18. Then he went to Sarasvatī flowing to the West. Balabhadra then went to Bindusaras with plenty of water (or to the Tīrtha called Pṛthūdaka—modern Pehoa) and to Brahmatīrtha that bestows salvation. He went to various Tīrthas such as Gaṅgā, Yamunā, Sindhu, Śatadru and Sudarśana. After going to different Tīrthas, he took his holy bath in them devoutly. Then he went to Naimiṣa forest frequented by eminent sages.

On seeing him come there, the sages belonging to Naimiṣa who had been engaged in a long *Sattra*, who had maintained strict observances and were absorbed in holy activities, stood up to receive the great scion of the family of Yadus. After getting up from their respective seats they bowed down to him. They honoured him by offering seat, etc. and roots, fruits and bulbous roots and other things. After being received thus and honoured he took up his seat.

19-26. He saw Sūta, the disciple of Vyāsa, seated on a lofty seat.[1] He did not bow down to him. He did not get up. He did not join the palms in reverence. He continued to be seated. But on seeing him the Brāhmaṇas had bowed down their heads. Observing this, the son of Rohiṇī, became furious with Sūta, the most excellent one conversant with the Purāṇas. (Then he said thus:) "Why does this *Anuloma* born (i.e. born of a woman inferior in caste to the father) censurable Sūta occupy a lofty seat in the middle of the sages. This is not at all proper. We are the protectors of Dharma. But he has insulted us very much. He does not get up. He dares to be seated continuously. He does not pay respect to us. He has read the Purāṇas under the supervision of Dvaipāyana. He has learned many scriptures on Dharmaśāstra along with the legendary narratives. Still he does not make obeisance to me even after seeing me, nor does he leave his seat. Dvaipāyana has many great disciples, the Brāhmaṇas Paila and others. They will not commit such an offence as this fellow does. Hence I shall kill this wicked and senseless fellow. Indeed it is to restrain wicked ones

1. The incident mentioned in vv 19-32 is based on BhP X.78.

that I have come down to the terrestrial world. Undoubtedly this vicious one will attain purity on being killed by me."

27-32. After saying thus, the powerful Lord Rāma, the wielder of mace and plough, furiously cut off his head with the tip of the Kuśa grass that was in his hand. All the sages present there shouted, "Oh what a pity! Alas! What a pity!" Then the sages, the expounders of Brahman, spoke to Rāma: "O Rāma, O Lord Saṅkarṣaṇa, a grievous offence has been committed by you. The great *Brahmāsana* (the honourable seat of the presiding officer) was offered by us to this Sūta. O Plough-wielding Lord, never-ending life too has been given to him by us. Unwittingly a culpable murder of a Brāhmaṇa has been committed by you today.[1] Since you are the lord of Yoga, there is no one to restrain you. Ponder over what should be done in regard to this Brāhmaṇa's slaughter. For the sake of the welfare of the world, O Lord Rāma, you yourself perform some expiatory rites. You need not do so on being directed by another person.

On being told thus, Lord Rāma said to those sages.

Rāma said:

33-39. O pious believers (in Śāstras), I shall perform expiatory rites in order to dispel the sins. I shall do so for the sake of the welfare of the world now, and not out of any other desire.

Ye all be pleased to tell us the various observances that should be practised by us for expiating the sins. Since never-ending life has been granted to this Sūta by you all, I shall by means of my Yogic Māyā restore his sense-organs and life.

The sages said:

O Lord Rāma, it behoves you to do what is befitting to your valour, to your weapon, and to the (lord of) Death. See that our words too remain true.

Rāma said:

The Vedas always proclaim that one is reborn in the form of a son, O eminent Brāhmaṇas. So, let a long-lived son be born from

1. Romaharṣaṇa was a Sūta (born of a Brāhmaṇa father and Kṣatriya mother). But SkP regards him as a Brāhmaṇa and Balarāma is advised to go to Lakṣmaṇa-tīrtha to get absolved of the sin of Brāhmaṇa-slaughter.

the body of this Sūta. He shall be powerful with intrinsic strength and vigour of his sense-organs. He will recount to you everyday the Purāṇas, etc. By the power of my Yogic Māyā he will become omniscient.

40-41. After saying this, the son of Rohiṇī spoke to them in an humble way:

"Whatever you may desire, I shall do. Tell me what desire of yours I am to carry out. I shall undoubtedly do it, O sages. You should tell me the expiatory rite for the sin that I have committed unknowingly, O excellent sages."

The sages said:

42-46. A certain Dānava named Balvala, the son of Ilvala, defiles our sacrifice on Parvan days. Do kill that wicked sinful Dānava, a thorn unto the worlds. By means of this a great honour would have been done by you to us. That Dānava comes here and always showers bones, faeces, urine, blood, liquor and flesh on the sacrificial fire.

With great concentration and mental purity take the holy baths for a year in all the Tīrthas that exist in Bhārata. Thereby your sins will be expiated. No doubt need be entertained in this regard.

Śrī Sūta said:

47-51. At the time of a Parvan, O eminent Brāhmaṇas, when the sacrifice of the sages was begun, there appeared an exceedingly dreadful shower of dust particles and a dreadfully violent stormy wind. There was a shower of pus and blood. Thereafter a shower of faecal matter was made by Balvala. Instantly Balabhadra saw the Asura of great strength within the sacrificial hall. He was armed with a spear. On seeing that huge-bodied Asura who resembled a burning mountain and whose face was hideous on account of the moustaches and beards resembling red-hot copper and the curved teeth, Rāma remembered his threshing rod that tore off enemies, the ploughshare that destroyed Dānavas and the club that struck down Daityas.

52-59a. The weapons thought of by him approached Rāma. While Balvala passed through the sky, the infuriated Balarāma dragged him with the tip of his plough and killed him with the threshing rod by hitting his head forcefully. With the forehead broken he fell on the ground and vomited blood. Crying piteously, Balvala, the Asura, fell down like a mountain struck down by the thunderbolt.

The sages eulogized Rāma and offered him pure (auspicious) blessings. Just as the Suras showered Indra after Vṛtra had been killed, so also they showered him with holy and auspicious waters. They gave him the Vaijayantī garland rendered splendid by the refulgent lotuses. To Mādhava they gave two splendid clothes and splendid ornaments. Wearing all those things, the exceedingly powerful son of Rohiṇī appeared like the Kailāsa mountain covered with trees in full bloom. Permitted by the sages, O Brāhmaṇas, he travelled to all the Tīrthas in the course of a year and took his holy baths in them. He maintained all holy observances and good conduct. Then, the breaker of Kālindī concluded his pilgrimage and began his return journey.

59b-65. Then Baladeva saw a lean dark shadow closely following him. It was shouting loudly. Then he heard these words issuing from the sky:

"O Rāma, O Rāma, O extremely mighty son of Rohiṇī, having white lustre, O sinless one, the sin of Brāhmaṇa's slaughter has not yet been expunged, though you have concluded your pilgrimage. O son of Rohiṇī, that sin has not been completely eradicated."

On hearing these words, Bala began to ponder: 'The expiatory rite has been performed by me through the visits to the Tīrthas for the period of a year. Still I hear these words saying that the sin of Brāhmaṇa's slaughter has not perished. What shall we do?'

Thinking thus he went to Naimiṣa forest. After going there the suppressor of the enemies intimated to the sages what he had heard from the sky and the dark shadow that he had seen. The son of Rohiṇī stated everything to the sages. On hearing it, all the sages spoke these words to Rāma:

The sages said:

66-69. If, O Rāma, your sin of Brāhmaṇa's slaughter has not been completely eradicated, O illustrious one, go to the Gandhamādana mountain which puts an end to great miseries and destroys (cures) great ailments. On the Gandhamādana mountain, on Rāmasetu of great merit, there is a lake named Lakṣmaṇatīrtha. It is destructive of sins. Do take your holy bath there and bow down to that Liṅga. Thereby your sin of Brāhmaṇa's slaughter will be completely eradicated. There is no doubt about it.

Śrī Sūta said:

70-73. On being told thus, Rāma went to the Gandhamādana mountain, O eminent sages, and reached Lakṣmaṇatīrtha. The lord with ploughshare for his weapon took his holy bath in that Tīrtha along with the requisite *Saṁkalpa* rites. Then he gave away monetary gifts, foodgrains, cows and plots of land.

At that time an unembodied speech said to Rāma: "Now, your sin of Brāhmaṇa's slaughter has been eradicated completely, O Rāma. You need not have any doubt about this. Go happily to your city." On hearing it, Balabhadra praised that Tīrtha.

74-76. Thereafter Mādhava (i.e. Bala) took his bath in all the local Tīrthas. He then bathed in Dhanuṣkoṭi and worshipped Rāmanātha. Having got rid of all his sins, he went to his city Dvārakā.

Śrī Sūta said:

Thus, O Brāhmaṇas, Śrīlakṣmaṇasaras devoid of impurities has been recounted to you. It is meritorious, sacred and destructive of sins. It dispels sins such as that of Brāhmaṇa's slaughter.

77. He who reads this chapter or listens to it with great concentration and mental purity attains salvation, O eminent Brāhmaṇas, without ever returning (to the earth).

CHAPTER TWENTY

The Glory of Jaṭātīrtha: Śuka Attains Purity of Mind*

Śrī Sūta said:

1. After taking the holy bath in the great Tīrtha of Lakṣmaṇa which is destructive of the sin of Brāhmaṇa's slaughter, the pilgrim should go to Jaṭātīrtha for the sake of gaining purity of mind.

2. Excepting Jaṭātīrtha there is nothing that can remove the ignorance of those people whose minds are afflicted on account of the worldly existence which is full of births, deaths and old age.

---

* This Tīrtha is about two miles or so from Rāmeśvaram on the Rāmeśvaram-Dhanuṣkoṭi Road. It is opposite to Pāpahareśvara temple. The Tīrtha is about 300 sq. ft. in area.

3. There are certain persons in the world who desire salvation and so wish to gain purity of mind. They read Upaniṣads but do not meditate on them in silence.

4. Those who have fallen in the ocean of Vedānta where the *Pūrvapakṣa* (the *prima facie* view) is like a great crocodile, and *Siddhānta* (the final view) is a fish that makes it agitated, become deluded till perfect knowledge is attained. O Brāhmaṇas.

5. Those who seriously study the Upaniṣads for the sake of attaining purity of mind, begin to argue after studying (a little) and indulge in a quarrel.

6. Purity of mind cannot be attained through Vedānta which is the cause of great delusion and confusion. Hence, O eminent sages, we do not highly esteem Vedānta.

7. It you wish for purity of mind by an easy means, O ascetics, I loudly proclaim unto you all: "Do resort to Jaṭātīrtha."

8. Formerly for helping everyone, this Tīrtha which is destructive of ignorance was created by Śaṁbhu himself on the Gandhamādana mountain.

9. The water in which the virtuous Rāma washed his matted hair after Rāvaṇa had been killed, O Brāhmaṇas, is called Jaṭātīrtha.

10-11. Taking holy plunge in the waters of Gaṅgā for sixty thousand years is on a par with taking the holy bath in Godāvarī once when the planet Jupiter is in the Zodiac Leo. The benefit of a thousand such baths when Jupiter is in Leo, and of (taking baths in) Gomatī in the course of years is obtained by a visit to Jaṭātīrtha.

12. If, O eminent Brāhmaṇas, men take a holy bath in Jaṭātīrtha, their minds shall become pure and their ignorance shall perish.

13. If ignorance is dispelled, one shall obtain perfect knowledge. Thereafter one will obtain salvation. Further, he shall be saturated with (the divine qualities of) existence, knowledge and bliss.

14. In this connection they cite the following ancient conversation between father Vyāsa and son Śuka.

15. Formerly, O Brāhmaṇas, Śuka bowed down his head to and asked Vyāsa who is called Kṛṣṇa too. He was an excellent sage, who had purified his soul. He never swerved (from the path of piety) and was specially conversant with traditions and was an expert in all the Śāstras.

Śrī Śuka said:

16-20. O holy lord, O father, O omniscient one, tell me this excellent secret. What is it whereby I shall gain purity of the mind? What is that which destroys ignorance? What is that whereby knowledge is dawned (in the mind)? What is that whereby ultimately I shall get perpetual salvation too? Tell me that means out of affection for me.

Upaniṣads, Itihāsas, Purāṇas, etc. have been completely learned by me from you. But they have not purified my mind. Hence how shall I obtain purity of mind? O father, tell me how to gain purity of mind.

On being asked thus by Śuka, O excellent sages, Vyāsa mentioned to him the secret whereby *Avidyā* (Ignorance) is destroyed.

Vyāsa said:

21. O Śuka, I shall tell you the secret means of cutting the knot of *Avidyā*. It bestows purity of intellect on men and is destructive of the fear of birth, etc.

22. There is a Tīrtha well-known as Jaṭātīrtha on Rāmasetu on the highly meritorious Gandhamādana mountain. It destroys sins.

23. It was there that Rāma, Hari himself, cleaned his matted hair. Rāma, the glorious son of Daśaratha, granted a boon unto the Tīrtha.

24. "Those who come here and take their holy bath in the extremely sacred Jaṭātīrtha shall obtain purity of mind." Thus he spoke.

25. By a mere holy bath in Jaṭātīrtha, men will obtain purity of intellect without Yajña, without perfect knowledge, without any Mantra to be recited, without observing fast.

26. By taking the holy bath here one will attain merit that is on a par with that of the gift of everything (or all kinds of *Dānas*). By means of this, one surmounts difficulties and attains meritorious worlds.

27. By taking the holy bath in Jaṭātīrtha of auspicious waters, one attains greatness. There is no other means of purification of the inner faculties (*antaḥkaraṇa*) than (bath in) Jaṭātīrtha.

28. No observance, no Japa, and no (propitiation of any other) deity will achieve that. It is conducive to wealth, fame and longevity, as is well-known in all the worlds.

29. It is the most sacred of all sacred things now, O Śuka. Jaṭātīrtha suppresses all sins. It is the most auspicious of all

auspicious things.

30. Formerly, O Śuka, Bhṛgu, the son of Varuṇa, asked his father Varuṇa about a splendid and sacred means to attain purity of intellect. Varuṇa told him the means that is auspicious as well as yielding the purity of intellect.[1]

Varuṇa said:

31-34. If one takes the holy bath in Jaṭātīrtha on Rāmasetu on the meritorious Gandhamādana mountain, one shall certainly attain purity of intellect.

At the instance of his father, Bhṛgu, the son of Varuṇa, immediately went to Jaṭātīrtha, took his holy bath and obtained purity of intellect. On account of that purity, the persistence of ignorance stopped and Bhṛgu had perfect knowledge of non-duality from his father Varuṇa. O Śuka, he thus became one saturated with (the divine qualities of) uninterrupted existence, knowledge and bliss.

35. Durvāsas, a part of Śaṅkara, obtained purity of mind through holy ablution in Jaṭātīrtha. He too became saturated with the bliss of Brahman.

36. Dattātreya too, a part of Viṣṇu, took his holy bath in this Tīrtha. Thereby his mind became pure, O Śuka, and he became one with the form of (i.e. identical with) Brahman.

37. One who wishes for destruction of ignorance should certainly take the holy bath in the purest and the holiest Tīrtha named Jaṭātīrtha which is destructive of all sins.

38. Therefore, O Śuka, you too go to Jaṭātīrtha. O highly intelligent one, take your holy bath in that Tīrtha which bestows purity of mind and great merit.

39-41. On being told thus by his father Vyāsa, O Brāhmaṇas, the son Śuka went to Rāmasetu and the highly meritorious Gandhamādana mountain. He was desirous of taking his holy bath in Jaṭātīrtha which bestows purity. After taking the holy bath along

1. We meet with Bhṛgu, the son of Varuṇa, in *Taittirīya Up.* 3.1.1. but no Jaṭātīrtha is mentioned there, nor in Mbh where Bhṛgu is shown to have enlightened Bharadvāja in philosophy (Mbh, *Śānti*, Chs. 182-192). The names of Bhṛgu, Durvāsas, Dattātreya, Śuka are used to highlight the importance of the Tīrtha.

with the requisite Saṁkalpa rite in Jaṭātīrtha sage Śuka obtained purity of mind. As the *Ajñāna* (ignorance) perished thereby, he attained his own real form, the form of the greatest bliss.

42. Those others too who are desirous of purity of mind, O excellent Brāhmaṇas, should take their bath in Jaṭātīrtha with great devotion.

43. Alas, even when the splendid Jaṭātīrtha which is like the wish-yielding cow (*Kāmadhenu*) is present, why do deluded people take delight elsewhere?

44. Merely by taking holy bath here, he who is desirous of worldly pleasures shall obtain worldly pleasures and he who is desirous of salvation shall obtain that. They will attain the same merely by taking their holy bath in Jaṭātīrtha. O Brāhmaṇas, the truth has been spoken by me.

45. It is possible that men will attain purity of mind through the merit of reciting the Vedas, through Yajña, through charitable gift, through penance, through holy rites, through the observance of fasts, through Japa and through Yoga.

46. But without all these things, O eminent Brāhmaṇas, merely by taking bath in the highly sacred Jaṭātīrtha, Brāhmaṇas will certainly obtain purity of mind.

47. It is not possible for me to recount the greatness of Jaṭātīrtha. Śaṅkara understands that Tīrtha. Hari knows it and so also does Brahmā.

48-49. A Tīrtha on a par with Jaṭātīrtha has never existed before. Nor will there be one in the future. If one offers Kṣetra Piṇḍa on the banks of Jaṭātīrtha, one will certainly obtain merit on a par with that of Gayāśrāddha. There is no doubt about it. If a man takes his holy bath in Jaṭātīrtha, he is never defiled by sins. He never suffers on account of poverty. He never falls into the ocean of Naraka.

Śrī Sūta said:

50-51. Thus, O Brāhmaṇas, the power of Jaṭātīrtha has been recounted to you all. It was there that the Yogin, the son of Vyāsa, obtained purity of mind by taking the holy bath in the Tīrtha that rids one of sins. He obtained purity of mind that is the means of achieving perfect knowledge of non-duality (i.e. identity with Brahman).

52. He who reads this chapter and listens to it with concentration and mental purity, shall get rid of all sins. He will obtain the region of Viṣṇu.

CHAPTER TWENTYONE

The Glory of Lakṣmītīrtha: Dharmaputra Obtains Unlimited Wealth

Śrī Sūta said:

1. After taking the holy bath in the Tīrtha named Jaṭātīrtha that is destructive of all sins and the means of getting the soul purified, a pilgrim should go to Lakṣmītīrtha.

2. With whatever desire in view a man takes his bath in Lakṣmītīrtha he attains the desired object, O excellent Brāhmaṇas.

3. It destroys great poverty. It bestows plenty of foodgrains. It subdues great miseries and it increases vast wealth and fortune.

4. Formerly directed by Śrīkṛṣṇa while he was in Indrapraṣtha, Dharmaputra took his holy bath here and attained great prosperity.

The sages asked:

5. O great sage, tell us how, by taking his holy plunge in Lakṣmītīrtha at the instance of Kṛṣṇa, Dharmaputra obtained prosperity.

Śri Sūta replied:

6. Directed by Dhṛtarāṣṭra, O Brāhmaṇas, formerly the five Pāṇḍavas of great strength and valour went to Indraprastha and stayed there.

7-8. Once Kṛṣṇa went to Indraprastha on a visit to them. On seeing him arrived, those Pāṇḍavas eagerly received him with great joy and took him to their abode. Kṛṣṇa stayed in that excellent city for some time.

9. Once Yudhiṣṭhira invited the lotus-eyed Kṛṣṇa, the lord of the universe, the son of Vasudeva, honoured him and then asked him.

Yudhiṣṭhira said:

10. O Kṛṣṇa, O Kṛṣṇa of great intellect, tell me, O highly intelligent one, by what holy rite do men obtain great prosperity.

On being enquired thus by Dharmaputra, Kṛṣṇa told Yudhiṣṭhira:

Śrīkṛṣṇa said:

11-15a. O illustrious Dharmaputra, there is a Tīrtha on the Gandhamādana mountain, well-known by the name Lakṣmītīrtha. It is the sole cause of prosperity. Do take your holy bath there. You will become prosperous. By taking the holy bath there, riches increase and foodgrains flourish in plenty. All enemies perish. The valour of the (devotees) increases.

Formerly Devas took their holy bath in the meritorious Tīrtha named Lakṣmītīrtha. By the merit thereof, O Dharmaputra, they obtained all prosperity.

15b-18. Men who regularly take their holy bath in that Tīrtha, will get before long, earth, wealth and virtue. Do not have any doubt in this regard. O son of Pāṇḍu, by taking the holy plunge in Lakṣmītīrtha wealth is obtained in the same manner as (it is got) through austerities, sacrifices, charitable gifts and blessings. All sins perish and all obstacles disappear always. By resorting to Lakṣmītīrtha, all ailments are cured completely and abundant welfare is obtained in the world. There is no doubt about this.

19. O Dharmaputra, merely by taking his holy bath in this Tīrtha of Lakṣmī, King Avadha[1] obtained Rambhā, the most excellent one among the celestial women.

20. By taking his holy bath in this meritorious Tīrtha, Kubera Naravāhana became owner of the Treasures (*Nidhis*), the chief of which is Mahāpadma.

21-22. Hence, O prominent king, you too, in the company of your younger brothers, the chief of whom is Bhīma, take your holy bath in Lakṣmītīrtha that bestows auspiciousness and welfare. You will (thereby) acquire great fortune and conquer enemies. No doubt need be entertained in this matter, O my father's sister's son, O Dharmaputra.

* * *

---

1. Untraced in Mbh, VR, PE & PI.

23. On being told thus by Kṛṣṇa, Dharmaputra of a wonderful appearance, immediately went to the Gandhamādana mountain along with his younger brothers.

24. Then he went to Lakṣmītīrtha, the cause of great prosperity. There, along with his younger brothers Yudhiṣṭhira observed all the requisite rites and took his holy bath.

25. Along with his younger brothers and strictly adhering to all holy observances, he took his baths for the period of a month in the waters of Lakṣmītīrtha destructive of all sins.

26. He gave plenty of cows, plots of lands, gingelly seeds, gold and other things to Brāhmaṇas. Thereafter Dharmaputra returned to Indraprastha along with his younger brothers.

27-33. Then Yudhiṣṭhira wished to perform Rājasūya sacrifice. Dharmaputra who was desirous of performing the sacrifice invited Kṛṣṇa.

On being invited through a messenger of Dharmaputra, Kṛṣṇa hurriedly came to Indraprastha accompanied by Satyabhāmā riding in a swift chariot yoked with four horses.

On seeing him arrived, Dharmaputra joyously mentioned to Kṛṣṇa about his preparations for Rājasūya. Kṛṣṇa permitted him by saying, "Let it be done so".

He then spoke to Dharmaputra these words with cogent arguments: "O virtuous nephew of my father, listen to my beneficial words. This Rājasūya sacrifice cannot be easily performed by all kings. Only a king who has many hundreds of foot-soldiers, chariots, elephants and horses deserves to perform this Yajña. No one else. At the outset all the ten quarters should be conquered by you with your own might.

34. Excellent tribute must be levied (and collected) from the defeated enemies. This excellent sacrifice should be performed by means of that collection of gold.

35. I am encouraging you. I am not frightening or warning you because I know cogent reasons. Hence before beginning the sacrifice, begin the conquest of the quarters."

36. On hearing the wholesome advice of Kṛṣṇa, Dharmaputra praised the son of Devakī and called his younger brothers.

37-40. After calling all his four brothers, Dharmaputra spoke to them making them glad: "O Bhīma, O mighty one, O Dhanañjaya of great heroism, O twin brothers of tender limbs always ready to destroy the enemies, I wish to perform the great Yajña called

Rājasūya. That (sacrifice) should be performed after conquering all the kings in battle. Hence all the four of you along with your vast armies do go to the four quarters to conquer the kings. All of you are valourous and heroic. I shall perform the great sacrifice with the riches brought by you all."

41-48. On being told thus with great enthusiasm the younger brothers of Dharmaputra, the chief among whom was Bhīma, became delighted. In order to conquer the kings, Pāṇḍavas started from the city and went in all directions.

All of them conquered those kings present in all the four directions. The sons of Pāṇḍu brought those kings under their control. They took with them vast wealth of various sorts given by them (i.e. kings) and hurriedly reached their city where they had Kṛṣṇa to support them.

Bhīma of great strength and valour came there to the excellent city with gold weighing a hundred Bhāras. Then Arjuna of great strength and power came to Indraprastha taking with him a thousand Bhāras of gold. Similarly Nakula of great refulgence came to the excellent city of Indraprastha taking with him a hundred Bhāras of gold.

Taking with him fourteen golden palmyra trees given by Vibhīṣaṇa as well as the vast collection of wealth of the Southern kings, Sahadeva immediately came to his own city.

49. Kṛṣṇa, (the leader) of the Yādavas, gave Dharmaputra hundreds and thousands and hundred thousands of gold pieces.

50-51. With the unlimited wealth brought by his younger brothers and the innumerable riches (gold pieces) given by Kṛṣṇa, Yudhiṣṭhira who had the support of Kṛṣṇa, O Brāhmaṇas, performed the Rājasūya sacrifice. The son of Pāṇḍu gave monetary gifts to Brāhmaṇas as much as they wished.

52. Yudhiṣṭhira gave foodstuffs to the Brāhmaṇas. Similarly he gave them clothes, cows, plots of land as well as ornaments.

53. Dharmaputra gave the suppliants the quantity of gold, etc. twice as much again as they would be ordinarily contented with.

54. Even crores of Brahmās could not keep an account of the unlimited wealth thus distributed and could not say that this much of gold and wealth of diverse kinds has been given to the seekers of wealth.

55. On seeing the riches being given to the seekers, the people said that everything he possessed was given away by the king.

56-60. On seeing the inexhaustible treasures with infinite number of jewels and gold pieces, the people said that only a little fraction had been given to the suppliants.

After performing the Rājasūya sacrifice thus, Dharmaputra and his younger brothers rejoiced in that excellent city with flourishing wealth.

It was due to the power of Lakṣmītīrtha that Yudhiṣṭhira, the son of Dharma, got everything, O Brāhmaṇas.

Oh, what a glory of the Tīrtha! This Tīrtha is of great merit. It suppresses great poverty. It yields wealth and foodgrains to men. It destroys great sins. It dispels (the fear of) the great Narakas. It causes great miseries to recede.

61-64. It yields salvation and heavenly pleasures perpetually. It grants excellent wives and good sons to men. It relieves men of their indebtedness. A Tīrtha on a par with this has never existed before, nor will there ever exist.

Thus, O Brāhmaṇas, the glory of Lakṣmītīrtha has been described to you. It destroys bad dreams. It is meritorious. It achieves all that the devotees desire.

He who reads this chapter or listens to this with devotion shall be prosperous with wealth and plenty of foodgrains. There is no doubt at all. After enjoying all pleasures here, he shall attain salvation after death.

CHAPTER TWENTYTWO

The Greatness of Agnitīrtha: Duṣpaṇya Relieved of His Ghosthood

Śrī Sūta said:

1. After taking the holy bath in Lakṣmītīrtha which is the sole cause of all riches of men, O excellent Brāhmaṇas, the man should go to Agnitīrtha.

2. Agnitīrtha is highly meritorious. It is destructive of all great sins. It is the most excellent of all Tīrthas. It is the sole means of achieving all desired objectives. The man should devoutly takes his holy bath there for the purification of his own sins.

The sages enquired:

3-4. How did it become famous as Agnitīrtha, O great sage? Where is this Agnitīrtha? Of what nature is its glory? It behoves you to narrate this in detail to us because we have great faith.

Śrī Sūta replied:

5-10a. You have put an apt question, O eminent sages. Listen. Formerly, after killing Rāvaṇa with all his followers, Rāghava installed his (Rāvaṇa's) brother Bibhīṣaṇa (i.e. Vibhīṣaṇa) as the lord of Laṅkā. Accompanied by Sītā and Lakṣmaṇa, Rāma, the son of Daśaratha, came to the Gandhamādana mountain. He was eulogized by Siddhas, Cāraṇas, Gandharvas, Devas, groups of celestial damsels and multitudes of sages. He was of truthful desires and eager to visit Tīrthas. Rāma of irresistible valour held the bow sportingly. He was accompanied by groups of Devas including Indra, by sages, and by Pitṛs, Bibhīṣaṇa and all the monkeys. It was to accomplish his own purification and to purify Sītā that he came there.

10b-12a. Standing on the banks of Lakṣmītīrtha, he invoked Agni (Fire-god) for the purpose of testing Sītā. He invoked Fire-god in the presence of Devas, sages and Pitṛs.

Far away from Lakṣmītīrtha, Fire-god came up from the great ocean. Even as all the people remained watching, Fire licked up the waters.

12b-15. His eyes were copper-coloured. He was yellow in colour. He was clad in yellow robes. He held a bow (in his hand). With his seven tongues he began licking up the ten quarters. Looking at the scion of the family of Raghu, the (divine) hero who had sportingly assumed the form of a man, he spoke these charming words concerning the purity of Jānakī:

"O Rāma, O Rāma, the mighty one who instils fear in Rākṣasas, it was due to the chastity of Sītā that Your Honour killed Rāvaṇa. It is the truth. It is the truth. Again, I repeat, it is the truth. No doubt need be entertained in this respect.

16-22. This is Lakṣmī herself, the mother of the world, who had sportingly assumed a human form. While a human being she has a human body. She adopts her body which is befitting to the form of Viṣṇu.

O Janārdana, O lord of Devas, O lord of the universe, whenever you take up incarnations, she too assists you. When you were Bhārgava Rāma, she had been Dharaṇī (Earth). Now she has become Jānakī and she will be born as Rukmiṇī. In other incarnations too she assists Viṣṇu. Hence, O Rāghava, accept her at my instance."

On hearing these words of Fire-god, Devas, great sages, Vidyādharas, Gandharvas, human beings, serpents and other groups of living beings again and again praised Rāma, the son of Daśaratha, and Jānakī, the daughter of the king of Mithilā. At the instance of Agni Rāma accepted Sītā who was devoid of impurities.

23-29a. Thus, for the sake of the purification of Sītā, Agni was invoked by Rāma of unobstructed activities. O excellent Brāhmaṇas, know that spot as Agnitīrtha, the spot far away from Lakṣmītīrtha, from the spot where Fire came up from the ocean. That is the excellent spot. It is called Agnitīrtha because Fire-god came out through it.

One should devoutly take one's holy bath in the Tīrtha of Agni that bestows salvation. He should observe fast and then feed Brāhmaṇas. He should give them clothes, wealth, plots of land and a well-adorned girl. He shall be rid of all sins and attain *Sāyujya* with Viṣṇu.

Gift of food on the banks of Agnitīrtha is (meritorious) in particular. There has never been before nor will there ever be a Tīrtha on a par with Agnitīrtha. It was by taking his holy bath there, that Duṣpaṇya, a great sinner, abandoned his ghosthood of highly dreadful nature and attained a divine form.

29b-35. Formerly there was a Vaiśya named Paśumān in Pāṭaliputra. He was always devoted to pious activities. He was interested in propitiating Brāhmaṇas. He always carried on agricultural activities and protection of cows. He sold gold and other things in the marketplace righteously.

This excellent merchant named Paśumān had three wives; all of them were devoted to the service of their husband. The eldest wife gave birth to three sons, Supaṇya, Paṇyavān and Cārupaṇya, who were capable of making that Vaiśya family flourish. The second wife gave birth to two sons, Sukośa and Bahukośa. That Vaiśya begot of the third wife three sons known as Mahāpaṇya, Mahākośa and Duṣpaṇya. Thus, O excellent Brāhmaṇas, that Vaiśya Paśumān had eight sons of his three wives.

36-38. All those sons, Supaṇya and others, grew up gradually.

Playing about in the dust they delighted their parents. Those Vaiśya boys gradually became five-year olds. The eminent Vaiśya Paśumān trained those children ever since their childhood in their duties. They were trained step by step in all the activities connected with agriculture, breeding of cattle and business dealings.

39-41. All the seven, the chief of whom was Supaṇya, listened to (obeyed) the instruction of their father. Whatever Paśumān said they immediately carried it out. They obtained great skill in dealings in gold also.

But the eighth son Duṣpaṇya was always engaged in evil ways ever since his childhood. He did not pay heed to the words of his father. Since the day of his playful activities in the dust, he was always engaged in vicious acts.

42-47. Even as a boy that son harassed boys of other people. Though the father Paśumān noticed him engaged in evil activities, he remained indifferent saying that after all he was only a child.

All the eight sons of the Vaiśya became young men. Still the eighth son Duṣpaṇya did not improve. He became the strongest of all. He used to catch hold of the boys in the city and cast them off into wells, lakes and rivers. The people were not at all aware that this was his misdemeanour. (The cruel Vaiśya youth) held the children under water till they died. The fathers and mothers of the dead children used to search for them all over the city. On seeing their sons dead what the people could do was only to weep.

48-50. After finding out the dead bodies in waters the people did everything necessary (to dispose of them). Thus Duṣpaṇya continued to kill children in the city everyday. For a long time he carried on like this without being detected by the people. As the children died thus as a result of the activities of the Vaiśya youth, there was no rise in the population and the city became a void as it were. Thereupon, the citizens gathered together and intimated to the king everything.

51. On hearing their words (complaints) the king called together all the chief village officials and commanded them to investigate into the cause of the deaths of the children.

52. The village officials agreed and established themselves in different places. They looked into all the aspects of the problem of murder of children.

53. In spite of the fact that they probed deep into the matter, they could not find out the murderer of children. They came back

to the king with great fear and reported in these words:

54. "Although we have searched thoroughly, O king, we are unable to find out the person who stays in this very city and goes on murdering the children."

55. Again all the grief-stricken citizens went to the king and complained to him with tearful eyes that there had been further cases of murder among the subjects.

56-58. Unable to understand the reason thereof, the king kept quiet pondering over everything.

Once this Vaiśya youth came near a lake along with five children under the pretext of plucking lotuses. Even as they were crying piteously Duṣpaṇya caught hold of them forcibly. The cruel-hearted Duṣpaṇya drowned them in neck-deep water of the lake. Thinking that they were dead Duṣpaṇya went back to his abode.

59-64. The fathers of those five children began searching for the five children throughout the city. Even as they were searching thus, those five very small children, in spite of the fact that they were kept under the water, did not die. With their heads and hairs drenched in water all those five children came to the banks. As they were very small children, they could not go back to the city. They loitered to and fro (near the lake) there. On hearing their names being called out by their kinsmen from afar, all those five children responded by way of reply. On hearing their shouts in reply, their fathers came to the banks of the lake, saw their children alive and became excessively delighted. "What is this? How did this happen?" The children were enquired by their fathers and others. They related to their kinsmen the misdeeds of Duṣpaṇya. Thereupon the citizens knew all the details. They went over to the king and told him the details of the (cruel) action of Duṣpaṇya as recounted by the five (children).

65. Thereupon the king summoned the excellent merchant Paśumān. Even as the citizens stood hearing, he spoke these words.

The king said:

66-69. O Paśumān, know that this city of many subjects has been practically made a void by your vicious son named Duṣpaṇya. Now he had attempted to drown these extremely small children under water. By chance they have survived and they have come back to the city. As the incident has come up to this stage, tell me now what should be done? I ask you alone now, because you are virtuous and pious.

On being asked thus by the king, Paśumān who was conversant with virtue, replied suitably:

Paśumān said:

70-76. He deserves capital punishment as the entire town has been devastated by him. There is nothing to be asked (of me), O king, in this matter. He is no longer my son. He is definitely my enemy because he has been a great sinner. I do not find any means of redemption for him by whom the city has been entirely crippled. Let him be sentenced to death. He is a wicked-minded one. I am telling you the truth.

On hearing the words of Paśumān all the citizens praised the excellent merchant and spoke to the king thus: "Let not this vicious fellow be put to death. Quietly banish him from the city."

Thereupon, the king summoned Duṣpaṇya and said thus: "O vicious one, now get away from this place immediately. If you continue to linger here, I shall punish you with death sentence."

Thus the king rebuked him and exiled him through his messengers from the city limits. Duṣpaṇya became frightened. He left the land and went away to the forest fully populated by groups of sages.

77-79. There too he killed the son of a sage by drowning him under water. The sons of the other sages who had come there for playing games saw the dead child and informed its father with great distress.

Ugraśravas heard from them about the death of his child under water. By the power of his penance he knew that it was the work of Duṣpaṇya. Ugraśravas then cursed Duṣpaṇya, the son of the Vaiśya.

Ugraśravas said:

80-83. Since you killed my son after drowning him under water your death too will be likewise by sinking under water. After death you will become a Piśāca (evil spirit, ghost). You will remain so for a long time.

On hearing this curse, Duṣpaṇya became dejected in mind. Immediately he left that forest and went to another forest still more dreadful. When he reached that forest full of lions and other beasts of prey, a violent gust of wind blew there showering a great deal of dust and shattering and uprooting many trees. Even the mere touch of the storm was felt to be like the blow of a thunderbolt.

84-86. There was an unbearable downpour that pierced his body with its velocity. On observing it, Duṣpaṇya became excessively dejected. He began to ponder over it. Then he saw a dry, dead body of a huge elephant. Unable to bear the stormy downpour and violent gust of wind he entered the cavity of the belly of the elephant through its mouth. As soon as he entered the body, the rain increased enormously.

87-89. As the rain water gathered a great stream of water began to flow. That stream turned into a big river in the forest. The belly of that dead elephant was filled with rain water. It began to float in the big flood that ensued. All the openings became closed. Hence Duṣpaṇya could not get out of the belly of the elephant as it had been filled with water and there was no opening at all.

90. Then the flood caused by rainwater flowed rapidly and terribly. It carried the carcass of the elephant to the ocean along with Duṣpaṇya who was within its belly.

91. The moment he sank into the water, Duṣpaṇya lost his life. As soon as he died he was transformed into a Piśāca.

92. Afflicted with hunger and thirst, he went into an impassable forest. In the terrible days of summer he shouted and lamented dreadfully (and moved here and there).

93-103. He stayed in the dense forest experiencing much misery for thousands of crores of Kalpas and hundreds of crores of Kalpas. That Piśāca stayed in that dreadful forest in great misery. He ran from forest to forest and country to country. Everywhere he experienced misery. He then gradually came to Daṇḍaka forest. He wandered in the region not very far from the meritorious hermitage of Agastya. He cried in a dreadfully severe voice and spoke these words loudly:

"Oh! O ascetics, ye all listen to my words. Indeed all of you are kind and considerate. You are engaged in activities conducive to the welfare of all living beings. Bless me with your benign glances. I am extremely afflicted with miseries. Formerly I was a Vaiśya in Pāṭaliputra named Duṣpaṇya. I was a son of Paśumān. At that time I killed many children. I was, therefore, exiled by the king from that land. I went to the forest. There I killed the son of Sage Ugraśravas under water. That sage cursed me that I would also die under water. He had said that I would be transformed into a Piśāca with a lot of suffering. I have already experienced the state of a Piśāca in desolate forest regions for thousands of crores of Kalpas and hundreds of crores of Kalpas. I am unable to bear thirst and hunger. Hence ye all do save me kindly. I have suffered much misery. O ascetics, kindly do that whereby I shall be liberated from the state of a Piśāca."

On hearing these words of the Piśāca, the ascetics said to the Pot-born Sage accompanied by Lopāmudrā:

The ascetics said:

104-105. O holy lord, tell the excellent means of redemption for this Piśāca. You are capable of saving sinners like this.

Agastya heard their words and became extremely compassionate. He called Sutīkṣṇa, his favourite disciple, and spoke these words:

Agastya said:

106-110. O Sutīkṣṇa, go quickly to the Gandhamādana mountain. There is a great Tīrtha there named Agnitīrtha. It is destructive of sins. Take your holy bath there, O highly intelligent one, for the liberation of the Piśāca. When you take the holy bath on behalf of that Piśāca there along with the requisite Saṁkalpa rites, he will cast off his Piśāca form and assume a divine form. Except resorting to that Tīrtha, I do not see any other means of redemption for him. Hence, O Sutīkṣṇa, protect this Piśāca.

On being told thus by Agastya, Sutīkṣṇa went to Gandhamādana. For the sake of the Piśāca, he performed the rite of Saṁkalpa. The sage, the storehouse of mercy, took the holy bath for three days there with due observances of the rules and restraints.

111-115a. He visited Rāmanātha and other deities and took with him the holy (water from that) Tīrtha. The excellent Brāhmaṇa Sutīkṣṇa went back to his hermitage and sprinkled the Tīrtha water on the Piśāca. Thereby he discarded the state of Piśāca. By the power of that Tīrtha he attained a divine form immediately. He got into an excellent aerial chariot attended by divine damsels. He bowed down again and again to Sutīkṣṇa, Agastya and other ascetics. With great delight he took leave of them and ascended to heaven quickly. He was honoured by Devas too.

115b-118. Thus, by the power of Agnitīrtha, Duṣpaṇya, the son of a Vaiśya, cast off the form and features of a Piśāca which he had got as a result of a curse and attained a divine form. Thus, O Brāhmaṇas, the glory of Agnitīrtha has been recounted to you.

He who reads this chapter or listens with devotion to this narrative of the liberation of a Piśāca shall be released from all sins. He will enjoy great worldly pleasures here and obtain happiness in the other world too.

CHAPTER TWENTYTHREE

The Glory of Cakratīrtha: Āditya Gets Golden Hands

Śrī Sūta said:

1-5. After taking the holy bath in the Tīrtha named Agnitīrtha that is destructive of all sins, the devotee shall have purified his soul. He should then go to Cakratīrtha.[1]

A man obtains all the desires for the realization of which he may have performed the rite of holy ablution in Cakratīrtha, O excellent Brāhmaṇas.

Formerly a great sage named Ahirbudhnya[2] who had fulfilled his religious vows, performed penance and worshipped Sudarśana on Gandhamādana.

As the sage was engaged in penance, O Brāhmaṇas, Rākṣasas of extremely dreadful forms who were eagerly engaged in creating obstacles in penances, always harassed him.

---

1. This is probably the same as shown within the Temple premises, as one is advised to go from this to Śiva-tīrtha which is in the Temple premises of Rāmanātha.

2. Ahirbudhnya: One Ahirbudhnya is the son of Viśvakarmā, another Ahirbudhnya is the name of a Rudra, the son of Bhūta and Surūpā (Mbh, *Udyoga* 114-4; *Śānti* 208.19-20; BhP VI.6.16; also PI I, p.142). Another Ahirbudhnya is the author of the famous Vaiṣṇavite *Ahirbudhnya-Saṁhitā*. But this sage Ahirbudhnya is a different person.

At that time, the Discus Sudarśana came there with the desire of protecting its devotee. It playfully destroyed all the demons who were harassing him.

6-8. O Brāhmaṇas, at the request of its devotee that Discus is present in the Tīrtha made by Ahirbudhnya ever since and hence that Tīrtha is called Cakratīrtha. With the favour of Sudarśana, if one takes the holy bath therein one will never be afflicted by Rākṣasas, Piśācas, etc.

Formerly, Sun-god whose hands had been cut, obtained golden hands by taking his bath in this holy Tīrtha. He obtained them due to the efficacy of the Tīrtha.

The sages asked:

9. O son of Sūta (Sūtanandana), how did Sun-god get his hands cut and how did he get golden hands? Narrate this to us.

Śrī Sūta replied:

10-14. Formerly, Suras including Indra were continuously being harassed by Daityas. They were in a fix. 'What shall we do?' They thought and had a collective discussion about the matter. They consulted one another for a long time with Bṛhaspati as the presiding officer. Then, with Indra at their head, the Suras went to the abode of the Self-born Lord. They approached Brahmā, met him and devoutly eulogized him. Thereafter, they intimated to him the reason for their arrival.

The Suras said:

O Lord, O Lord of the Goddess of Speech, Daityas, haughty on account of their strength, harass us continuously. O Lord, tell us the means of redress (from the harassment).

On being asked thus by the Suras, Brahmā said to them these words sympathetically:

Brahmā said:

15-20a. O Suras, do not be frightened. I shall tell you the means in that connection. The great Yajña intended for Maheśvara is destructive of Asuras. Begin it, O Suras, along with the sages, the seers of truth. This Yajña was performed by all the Devas without any omission* of the rules of procedure.

Let this great Yajña of Maheśvara be performed on Gandhamādana. If, O great Suras, you were to perform that Yajña elsewhere, the wicked Asuras would cause obstacles to that Yajña. If this Yajña is performed on the Gandhamādana mountain, there will not be any obstacle due to the favour of Sudarśana. Sudarśana is present in that Tīrtha on Gandhamādana for the sake of blessing the great sage named Ahirbudhnya.

20b-24. Hence you do perform that Yajña which destroys Asuras, on Gandhamādana, not very far from Cakratīrtha.

Then at the instance of Brahmā they immediately proceeded to Gandhamādana with Bṛhaspati at their head, with a desire to perform the Yajña. They bowed down to Ahirbudhnya, the noble-souled eminent sage. They constructed the sacrificial hall not far from his hermitage.

Accompanied by the ascetics, expert in the performance of Yajña, the Devas began the sacrifice that is destructive of Asuras. In that holy rite, Bṛhaspati himself was the Hotṛ.

25-31. (The posts of the sixteen assistant priests in the sacrifice were manned by the Devas and the sages.) Jayanta, the son of Indra, became Maitrāvaruṇa. The eighth Vasu became Acchāvāka priest. Parāśara, the son of Śakti, became Grāvastut priest. Aṣṭāvakra of great refulgence took up the duties and responsibilities of Adhvaryu. Viśvāmitra, the great sage, became Pratiprasthātṛ priest. Varuṇa became Neṣṭṛ priest, Dhaneśvara (Kubera) became Unnetṛ. Savitṛ became Brahmā, holding half of the burden (responsibility) of the Yajña. Vasiṣṭha, the excellent Brāhmaṇa, became Brāhmaṇācchaṁsin priest. Śunaḥśepa became Agnīdhra priest. Pāvaka (Fire-god) became Potṛ priest. Vāyu became Udgātṛ priest. Paretarāṭ (Yama) became Prastotṛ priest. The Pot-born Sage Agastya became Pratihartṛ priest. Madhucchandas, the great son of Viśvāmitra, became Subrahmaṇya priest. Purandara, the king of Devas, himself became Yajamāna (the sponsor of the sacrifice). Sage Śuka, the son of Vyāsa, became Upadraṣṭṛ.

32. Then all those Ṛtviks duly initiated Purandara, the king of Devas, in that Kratu pertaining to Maheśvara.

---

* *Lobha* is a misprint for *Lopa*. But the line is out of context.

33-34. In this manner the great Yajña began to be performed there. The Asuras had been afflicted very much by the unbearable prowess of Sudarśana. So they did not get any opportunity (weak point) to enter (the place) where the Yajña was performed. Thus the great sacrifice went on without any hindrance.

35-40. There the sacrificial fire blazed brightly consuming the Havis.* The Adhvaryu performed all the holy rites duly without any mistake. He consigned to the fire the Puroḍāśa sanctified by means of the Mantra. What remained of the Puroḍāśa after the Homa was carefully divided by the Adhvaryu. He gave that which was destructive of sins to the Ṛtviks, the chief among whom were Hotṛs. To Savitṛ who was Brahmā in that sacrifice, he gave an excessively fierce and fiery part of the Puroḍāśa named *Prāśitra*[1]. Savitṛ received that *Prāśitra* with both the hands. The moment when it was touched by Savitṛ that unassailable (Puroḍāśa named) *Prāśitra* cut off his hands even as all the Ṛtviks were watching. With his hands cut off thus by *Prāśitra* of fierce refulgence, Savitṛ became frightened saying "What is this?" He became very dejected.

41-43. Savitṛ called all the Ṛtviks and spoke to them thus:

Savitṛ said:

My share of the Puroḍāśa named *Prāśitra* was given to me. Instantly it cut off my hands even as all of you were watching. Hence all of you Ṛtviks should join together and make me (new) endowed with (new) hands. If not, I will destroy this *Yajña*.

On hearing the words of Savitṛ, all of them began to confer (with each other).

44. Then in the middle of all the Devas and the eminent sages Aṣṭāvakra of great refulgence spoke to those Ṛtviks:

Aṣṭāvakra said:

45-51. Listen ye all Ṛtviks to my statement with attention.

---

* *Hari* in the printed text is a misprint for *Havi*.

1. *Prāśitra* is the portion of the *havis* (oblation) left over after offering into the fire. It is to be given to the Brahmā-priest. It is given from a vessel of Khadira wood shaped like a cow's ear. This vessel is called *Prāśitraharaṇa*.

For the procedure of distribution of *Prāśitra vide* HD II.ii, pp. 1064ff.

A hundred Brahmās have passed away during my life. Crores of Four-faced Ones (Brahmās) are born and they die. I have maintained my life seeing all of them (i.e. I have survived all of them).

During the rule of the present Prajāpati named Lokeśvara, a Brāhmaṇa named Harihara who was a resident of Śyāmalāpura was hit with arrows by a hunter of the forest, who was hitting various targets for sport. He came within (the range of) his aim and his feet were cut off. Directed by sages, he went to Gandhamādana and took his holy bath in this Munitīrtha. Thereby, in those days of yore, he regained his feet. At that time this Tīrtha was called Munitīrtha. Now it has acquired the name of Cakra. It is called Cakratīrtha. Therefore, let Savitṛ whose hands have been cut off by *Prāśitra* take his holy bath in Munitīrtha if it is liked by you all.

52. On being told thus by the great sage Aṣṭāvakra, all the Ṛtviks became delighted and they spoke to Savitṛ:

53. "O Savitṛ, take your holy bath in this Tīrtha. You will have your hands restored. With great concentration do in accordance with Aṣṭāvakra's statement."

54-55. Thereupon Savitṛ went to the great Cakratīrtha. For the sake of regaining the hands, he took his holy bath there which bestows all the desired objectives. After devoutly taking his holy bath, when he rose up, he was seen endowed with two golden hands.

56-60. On seeing him (blessed) with golden hands all the Ṛtviks became delighted. Thereafter Indra and other Suras concluded that Yajña, conquered the multitude of Daityas and went back to heaven with great pleasure.

Hence this Tīrtha should be resorted to by all men perfectly for the achievement of their respective desires.

This Tīrtha which bestows all desires should be resorted to by the blind, crippled persons or persons with crooked arms, the dumb, the deaf, hunch-backed persons, lame people, people with mutilated or amputated legs as well other people wanting in limbs. It must be resorted to by persons with their hands or feet cut and persons with the other limbs also amputated. They must resort to this for regaining their lost limbs.

61-63. Thus, O Brāhmaṇas, the glory of Cakratīrtha has been recounted to you. By taking his holy bath here Sun-god got back his severed hands.

He who reads this chapter or listens to this with concentration and mental purity shall undoubtedly regain lost limbs. He will have his severed limbs made perfect and whole. One who is desirous of salvation will have it. There is no doubt about it.

CHAPTER TWENTYFOUR

The Glory of Śivatīrtha: Bhairava Absolved of the Sin of Brāhmaṇa-Slaughter

Śrī Sūta said:

1-2. After taking the holy bath in Cakratīrtha, the man should go to Śivatīrtha.[1] By taking the holy bath therein crores of great sins and the sins of associating with the great-sinners, perish instantaneously, O ascetics. It was by taking his bath here that Kālabhairava got rid of the sin of Brāhmaṇa-slaughter.

The sages asked:

3. How did Rudra, Kālabhairava, incur the sin of a Brāhmaṇa's slaughter, O great sage, Sūta? It behoves you to recount it to us.

Śrī Sūta narrated:

4. I shall tell ye all, O sages, the ancient legend that yields salvation. One is liberated from all sins by listening to it.

5-7. Formerly, there was a quarrel between Prajāpati (Brahmā) and Viṣṇu[2] in the presence of all the people, for some reason.

Brahmā thought thus: 'I alone am the maker of the universe. No one else is its creator. I am the bestower of blessings and controller of all the worlds. There is no one superior to me or equal to me among the Suras too.' So did Brahmā think (and say)

1. This Tīrtha is in the Temple premises of Rāmanātha. It is close to the Nandi Maṇḍapam.

2. This is another version of the quarrel between Brahmā and Viṣṇu given in Ch. 14, *Supra*.

in the presence of the Devas in the days of yore.

8-11. Then, O eminent Brāhmaṇa, Nārāyaṇa laughingly said thus: "Why do you say thus with pride now? O Brahmā, it does not behove you to make a statement like this again. I alone am the maker of the universe. I am Yajña. I am Lord Nārāyaṇa. Without me the life of this universe will be impossible. It was with my favour that the universe consisting of mobile and immobile beings has been created by you."

Even as Brahmā and Viṣṇu were arguing thus with a desire to have victory over each other before the Devas, the four Vedas came there and spoke the following truth that sheds light on the ultimate reality.

The Vedas said:

12-15. You are not the creator of the universe, O Viṣṇu, nor are you, O Brahmā, O Prajāpati. But Īśvara who is greater than the greatest is the maker of the universe. He is the lord. This universe consisting of mobile and immobile beings is evolved out of his Māyā Śakti. Sāṁba (i.e. Śiva) is worthy of being saluted by all the Devas. He has the characteristics of *Satya* (Truth), etc. He alone is the creator, protector and annihilator of all the worlds. He is the Lord.

On hearing this speech of splendid words uttered by the Vedas, Brahmā and Viṣṇu spoke thus, O eminent Brāhmaṇas:

Brahmā and Viṣṇu said:

16-17. Śaṁbhu is embraced by Pārvatī. He has a physical form. He is the lord of Pramathas. How can he be the supreme Brahman that is devoid of all attachments?

When this was uttered by them, O Brāhmaṇas, *Praṇava* which is devoid of a form assumed a form and spoke to them in a loud tone:

Praṇava said:

18-22. This Śaṁbhu, the great lord, does not sport about with Pārvatī who is apart and different from himself but with her who is of the same form as himself.[1] This Śaṁbhu has no other lord above him. He is self-luminous and unsullied. Mahādeva is transcendental to the universe. He is mentioned in the Vedas as superior and transcendental to the universe. He is the immanent soul of all. He is the maker of all. He is independent and the creator of all. O Brahmā, at the time of the creation, he engages you and directs you with the Rajas Guṇa.

O Keśava, (endowing you) with Sattva Guṇa, Śaṁbhu employs you in the act of protection of the universe. In the act of annihilation, he directs (the deity) called Kālarudra (equipping him with) the Tamas Guṇa.

Hence, O Viṣṇu there is no independence for you both. Nor is Prajāpati independent. But Śaṁbhu (alone) is independent.

23-28. O Brahmā, O Viṣṇu, how is Maheśvara who is the maker of all the worlds not known to you as being superior to the universe. Goddess Umā, that Śakti, is not separate from Śaṅkara at any time. It is well-known that the goddess who is the bliss of Śaṁbhu is no adventitious intruder and different from Śaṁbhu. Hence Rudra who is superior to the universe, who is independent, who is immutable should be worshipped by all the Devas. Śaṅkara is to be worshipped by you two also. Rudra has no maker nor anyone superior to him. There is no one on a par with him too in any of the hundreds of the worlds. Hence, O Brahmā, O Viṣṇu, do not get deluded.

Even after hearing these words uttered by Praṇava, Brahmā and Keśava, deluded by Māyā, did not get rid of their ignorance. In the meantime, Brahmā witnessed a great miracle.

29. A fiery column of great refulgence resembling infinite number of suns appeared in the middle of the sky. It spread through the sky and had faces in all directions.

30-32. Brahmā lifted up his face in order to survey it. With a fifth face created by means of the power of penance, the lord looked frequently at the column of refulgence. By surveying the brilliant splendour, the face blazed with fury. The refulgence resembling infinite number of suns was (as if) desirous of burning that fifth head. It shone like the submarine fire that is desirous of burning the worlds at the time of the deluge.

---

1. This identification between Śiva and Pārvatī is probably due to the influence of Kashmir Śaivism. See vv 23-28 below.

33. Then that refulgence appeared as Nīlalohita (i.e. Śiva). On seeing him Brahmā, the creator, spoke to Parameśvara:

34. "O Mahādeva, I know you. O Śaṁbhu, you came out of my forehead in days gone by. You are my son named Rudra."

35. On hearing these words full of pride, Maheśvara sent a Puruṣa named Kālabhairava.

36-37. Kālabhairava fought with Brahmā for a long time. Kālabhairava who was born of a part of Mahādeva and who held a trident, an axe and an iron-club fought with Brahmā for a long time and then looked at the splendid fifth face of Brahmā.

38. After looking at the fifth face of the Lord of the Goddess of Speech, that had been above and was full of pride, he became infuriated and blazed (as it were).

39. Then with great fury, Bhairava cut off that fifth face. On being struck by Kālabhairava, Brahmā then died.

40-42. With the favour of Īśvara, he regained his life. Then he looked at Śaṅkara who was adorned with the moon and the eight prominent serpents including Vāsuki. On seeing Śaṅkara, the great lord accompanied by Pārvatī, he obtained the perfect knowledge pertaining to Maheśvara due to the favour of Mahādeva. Then he eulogized the excellent Lord Giriśa, Śiva, the bestower of boons.

Brahmā said:

43-45. O Giriśa, be pleased with me, O lord with the moon for your crest. O storehouse of kindness, forgive the offence committed by me. Forgive me for my pride, O Śaṅkara.

Saying thus again and again, he bowed down to the Crescent-moon-crested Lord accompanied by Umā.

Then the lord became pleased with Brahmā who was born of a part of himself. Śaṁbhu said: "Do not be afraid" and then spoke to Bhairava:

46-51. "This eternal Brahmā is worthy of being worshipped by the entire universe. You hold (in your hand) the head of Brahmā who has been killed now. In order to purify the sin of Brāhmaṇa's slaughter and with a desire for the welfare of the world, O Bhairava, go about begging for alms along with the skull at my bidding."

After saying to him thus, O Brāhmaṇas, Śaṅkara, Lord Nīlakaṇṭha, the great lord, vanished there itself with the Daughter of the

Mountain constituting half his body.

O Brāhmaṇas, he made Bhairava hold the skull of Brahmā (and said): "Wander about for the sake of purifying the sin and for the sake of the welfare of the worlds. Let Bhairava beg for alms holding the skull in his hand."

After saying this Giriśa (created) a dreadful girl named Brahmahatyā who was cruel and who resembled the submarine fire. After directing her, Giriśa spoke to Bhairava again.

Īśvara said:

52. O Bhairava, perform this holy rite and observe this vow for a year in order to purify the sin of Brāhmaṇa-slaughter. Take your holy bath in all the Tīrthas for purifying yourself.

53-54. Then you do go to Vārāṇasī for suppressing the sin of Brāhmaṇa-slaughter. By your entry in Vārāṇasī, the base sin of your Brāhmaṇa-slaughter shall perish leaving a quarter of it as remnant. A quarter of the sin will not perish (there). I shall tell you how it can perish. O Bhairava, listen.

55-57. On the shore of the Southern Sea, on the Gandhamādana mountain, a splendid Tīrtha has been created by me for helping all living beings. It is called Śivatīrtha. It is highly meritorious. Go to it with great respect. Merely by entering it, this inauspicious sin of Brāhmaṇa-slaughter of yours shall certainly perish, due to the efficacy of Śivatīrtha. It shall perish completely.

After saying this to Bhairava, Rudra immediately went to Kailāsa.

58. Then Bhairava who had been directed by Śiva wandered in the worlds of Devas, Dānavas, Yakṣas and others with the skull in his hand.

59-62. As he went on, the extremely terrible sin of Brāhmaṇa-slaughter too followed him. After sportingly wandering in all the meritorious shrines and all the Tīrthas, the lord went to Vārāṇasī. When Bhairava, born of a part of Śaṅkara, entered Vārāṇasī, the extremely despicable sin of Brāhmaṇa-slaughter perished except a quarter of it. With the remaining quarter (of itself), she then chased Bhairava. Thereafter at Śiva's bidding, the trident-bearing Lord Bhairava went to the Gandhamādana mountain holding the skull.

63-64. Thereafter, O Brāhmaṇas, Bhairava went to Śivatīrtha and took his holy bath. The moment he took his holy bath in the great Śivatīrtha, the extremely terrible sin of Brāhmaṇa-slaughter completely perished. At that time Śaṁbhu appeared in front of him. Mahādeva who appeared thus in front of him spoke these words to Bhairava:

Īśvara said:

65-68. By your taking the holy plunge in Śivatīrtha, your sin of Brāhmaṇa-slaughter has completely perished. O virtuous one, there is no doubt about it. Keep this skull anywhere in Kāśī.

After saying this, Lord Śaṁbhu vanished there itself.

Having got rid of the sin of Brāhmaṇa-slaughter, O Brāhmaṇas, due to the efficacy of Śivatīrtha, Bhairava went to the city of Vārāṇasī. O Brāhmaṇas, he placed the skull in a certain place. Then that spot acquired the name Kapālatīrtha.

Śrī Sūta said:

69-71. That Śivatīrtha has this much of power. It is meritorious. It bestows salvation. It suppresses all miseries and destroys all sins. It subdues the distress in Narakas. It bestows heaven and salvation.

The glory of Śivatīrtha has been recounted by me. It bestows salvation. One who reads this always is liberated from a multitude of miseries.

CHAPTER TWENTYFIVE

The Glory of Śaṅkhatīrtha: Vatsanābha Freed from the Sin of Ingratitude

Śrī Sūta said:

1. After taking bath in Śivatīrtha that redeems one from the sin of Brāhmaṇa-slaughter, the man should proceed to Śaṅkhatīrtha[1] for the purpose of suppressing the multitude of his own sins.

---

1. Śaṅkhatīrtha is (now a well) in the second east Prākāram of the temple premises. It is named after the sage Śaṅkha who dug it (v 5).

2-3. Merely by taking the holy bath in it, even an ungrateful person becomes liberated. Those deluded persons who do not pay respect to their mothers, fathers and preceptors and others, who are wicked, ungrateful and shameless become pure merely by taking the holy bath in this Śaṅkhatīrtha.

4. Formerly, there was a sage named Śaṅkha on the Gandhamādana mountain. He was engaged in penance. With great concentration and mental purity, he meditated on Viṣṇu.

5. For the sake of taking the holy bath, he made an excellent Tīrtha here. Since it is made by Śaṅkha, it is called Śaṅkhatīrtha.

6-7a. By taking holy bath therein even once, even an ungrateful person is liberated. In this context I shall recount an ancient legend that is destructive of sins. Merely by listening to it a man attains salvation.

7b-10. Formerly there was an eminent Brāhmaṇa, a great sage named Vatsanābha. He was truthful and of good conduct. He was eloquent. He was kind and considerate to all living beings. He was impartial towards enemies as well as friends. He had self-control. He performed penance. He had conquered his passions. He was an expert (in meditating) on the Supreme Brahman. Brahman, the ultimate principle, was his sole support. That sage who had such power, performed penance in his own hermitage. He stood on the ground without moving any limb. He did not move from his place even as much as the extent of an atom.

11. As he performed the penance for many hundreds of years remaining in a single spot, an anthill grew over him and concealed all his limbs by covering them.

12. Although his body was covered up by the anthill, Vatsanābha, the great sage, still carried on his penance. He was not even aware of the anthill.

13. While he was engaged in penance, O eminent sages, Vāsava (Indra) let loose on him clusters of clouds and showered with great velocity.

14-20. Thus he showered continuously for seven days. Although the sage was showered with a great downpour, he received it (unperturbed) with his eyes still closed. Deafening the ears by means of great thunderous sound, a great thunderbolt fell on the anthill. When the cloud continued to shower and it became unbearable on account of chill winds, the top of the anthill was smashed on being struck down by the thunderbolt. When the top of the anthill was thus smashed on being struck down by the thunderbolt, Vatsanābha who was engaged in contemplation continued to endure the unbearable downpour.

When the great sage was afflicted day and night by the torrential downpour, Dharma felt very great sympathy and consideration in his mind. Dharma thought thus: 'Wonderful indeed is Vatsanābha's steadfastness of mind in virtuous activities. When Vatsanābha is engaged in penance, there is a great downpour. (But) even when there is a great downpour, he does not swerve from penance.'

21-24. As he thought thus, an idea struck him. 'I shall assume the form of a very big, attractive buffalo with a very thick skin which can endure the heavy downpour of rain. After adopting the form of a buffalo, I shall stand above the Yogin. Then the downpour of rain will not afflict him, though it may have great velocity.'

After deciding thus, Dharma stood above Vatsanābha covering his body completely and bearing the brunt of the torrential rain. At the end of seven days, the downpour of rain stopped.

25. Thereupon, Dharma in the form of a buffalo, who was extremely kind, left that anthill and stood not very far away from it.

26-30. When the downpour receded, Vatsanābha, the great sage, ceased performing the penance. Glancing all round he thought thus: 'I had been standing in the rain while engaged in the great penance. The whole earth all round is seen drenched in water. The summits of mountains, forests, parks and the hermitages of the great sages are immersed in fresh water.'

Seeing these and other things he became delighted. The righteous-souled great sage Vatsanābha thought again: 'Certainly, during this great downpour, I was protected by someone. Otherwise how could I have lived through this torrential downpour?'

31-32. After thinking thus, the excellent sage looked all round. Thereupon, he saw the blue-coloured buffalo of very huge body standing not very far away, in front of him. Vatsanābha, the ascetic, then thought thus in regard to that buffalo.

33-34. 'How (wonderful is it) that even in lower animals virtuous habit is perceived! I have been saved from the great downpour by this buffalo. Let it be long-lived, since it has saved me here.' After thinking thus, he began to perform the penance once again.

35. On seeing him engaged in penance once again, (Dharma) who had assumed the form of a buffalo, became very much de-

lighted with hair standing all over his body.

36. Sage Vatsanābha who began to perform the penance once again could not concentrate his mind in the Supreme Brahman as before.

37-39. With a dejected mind, Vatsanābha began to ponder thus: 'The mind begins to waver if it is not free from impurities. If there are many sins, the mind never becomes free from impurities. But I have not incurred the least of sins. How then does my mind waver?'

Thus Vatsanābha thought about the cause of sin again and again. After thinking and coming to a decision, he presently began censuring himself:

40-46a. 'Fie upon me! I am a wicked soul. I am extremely deluded. Ingratitude, the greatest of all defects, has beset me today. I have incurred ungratefulness, as I stay here without worshipping this excellent buffalo who had saved me from such a heavy downpour. Ingratitude is a great fault (and sin). There is no means of expiation in regard to an ungrateful one. The ungrateful has no worlds (for refuge). The ungrateful person has no kinsmen. My mind has become dirty on account of the defect of ingratitude. The ungrateful persons fall into hell. So also those who commit breach of trust. I do not see any means of expiation in the case of ungrateful persons except giving up their lives, as is spoken by those conversant with righteousness (Dharma). By not supporting parents, by not giving monetary gifts and fee to preceptor, and by becoming ungrateful (one incurs sins), the expiation for which is only death. Hence I shall cast off my life and expiate for my sins.'

46b-48. After resolving thus in his mind, Vatsanābha, the great sage considered his life insignificant like a blade of grass. His inner soul became detached (from worldly affairs). With a desire to atone for his sins he climbed on the summit of Meru. The sage desired to fall off from the summit. When he finally attempted to leap down, Dharma abandoned the form of buffalo and saying "Do not be in a hurry" he prevented him.

Dharma said:

49-55. O Vatsanābha of great intellect, live for many years. I am pleased with you, welfare unto you. I am pleased with your readiness to cast off your body. As regards your eagerness for virtuous activities, there is no one on a par with you in the world.

Although casting off one's life may be the means of expiation for an ungrateful person, I shall tell you another way of atonement, because of your virtuous conduct.

There is a Tīrtha named Śaṅkhatīrtha on the Gandhamādana mountain. For the purpose of quelling this sin, take your holy bath there with concentration and mental purity. You will obtain purity of mind. Hence you will be rid of your sins. Thereby you will acquire perfect spiritual knowledge and then attain the eternal region.

O great Yogin, I am Dharma, I am speaking the truth to you.

On hearing these words of Dharma, Vatsanābha, the great sage, went to Gandhamādana with a desire to take his holy bath there. After reaching Śaṅkhatīrtha the great sage took his holy bath there.

56. Thereby he was rid of his sins. His mind became pure. Not long after that the sage attained union with Brahman (i.e. Salvation).

57-59. Thus, O Brāhmaṇas, the greatness of Śaṅkhatīrtha has been recounted to you. Merely by taking holy bath there even an ungrateful person is liberated.

One who is antagonistic to one's mother, father or preceptor as well as multitudes of ungrateful persons of various types become liberated by taking holy plunge here. Hence this must always be resorted to by ungrateful persons. Oh! wonderful indeed is the glory of this Tīrtha, because even an ungrateful person is liberated.

60-63. By not supporting parents, by not giving monetary gifts and fee to preceptor, and by becoming ungrateful, (one incurs sins) the expiation for which is nothing short of death. But here, merely by taking holy bath, even an ungrateful person can expiate for his sin. Merely by taking holy bath in that Tīrtha ingratitude perishes. Nothing need be said in regard to other insignificant sins.[1]

One who reads this chapter with devotion shall be rid of one's sins, even if one happens to be an ungrateful person. With his inner soul purified he shall go to Satyaloka becoming equal to Brahmā and attain salvation.

---

1. Vatsanābha: The story how Dharma dissuades Vatsanābha from committing suicide as an expiation for ungratefulness is given in Mbh, *Anuśāsana* Ch. 12 of the Southern Recension.

CHAPTER TWENTYSIX

The Greatness of Gaṅgā, Yamunā and Gayā: Jānaśruti Attains Perfect Knowledge

Śrī Sūta said:

1-5. After taking the holy ablution in Śaṅkhatīrtha, O excellent Brāhmaṇas, the man should proceed to Yumunā, Gaṅgā and Gayā in the due order.[1]

The great Tīrtha named Yamunā, the excellent Gaṅgātīrtha and Gayātīrtha are destructive of great sins. These three Tīrthas are meritorious and well-known in all the worlds. They suppress all obstacles and destroy all ailments. These three Tīrthas are indeed annihilators of all ignorance. When Avidyā (Māyā, ignorance) is (thus) destroyed, they bestow perfect knowledge on men.

Jānaśruti[2], a great king, took his holy bath in all these Tīrthas formerly and obtained excellent and perfect knowledge from Raikva, an excellent Brāhmaṇa.

The sages asked:

6-7. O Sūta conversant with all topics, O disciple of Vyāsa, O highly intelligent one, how (and why) did the three Tīrthas famous as Gaṅgā, Yamunā and Gayā come to Mount Gandhamādana? How did Jānaśruti, the saintly king, attain perfect knowledge by taking the holy bath in all the three Tīrthas? How did he get the knowledge from Raikva? O Sūta, narrate this to us.

---

1. These three Tīrthas are three wells in the second north Prākāram in the temple premises.

2. Jānaśruti Pautrāyṇa is an ancient king mentioned in *Chāndogya Up* 4.1.1, 5; 4.2.1, 3. The king offered to Sayugvā Raikva 600 and 1000 cows for imparting spiritual knowledge (*Ibid.* 4.2.2 and 4). It is doubtful whether the Upaniṣadic Raikva was a Brāhmaṇa at all. This Purāṇa states that he was a lame Brāhmaṇa sage who had to use a cart for movement from place to place. He is called *Sayugvan* due to his dependence on a cart for movement (vv 8-14). The Upaniṣadic reference to Raikva's being afflicted with scabs and scratching them also is used here to confirm his identity with the Raikva of this Purāṇa.

The only difference is the non-mention of his stay at Gandhamādana and the appearance of these three Tīrthas for him in the Upaniṣad.

Śrī Sūta said:

8-14. Formerly there lived on Gandhamādana a great sage named Raikva. He was a storehouse of penance. He lived there engaged in very severe penance. That great sage Raikva continued the penance for a long time. By the great power of penance, he obtained a long life.

The great sage named Raikva was lame ever since his birth. Since he was lame, he was incapable of going to Tīrthas. This sage used to move about by means of a cart to all those Tīrthas which were on Gandhamādana, because of their proximity.

Since Raikva, the excellent sage, had a *Yugvā* (a cart) always, that ascetic came to be called *Sayugvā* by Vedic scholars in the world. A cart is spoken of by the word *Yugvā*. He was always (seen) with a cart. It was thus that the excellent sage came to be named Sayugvā. Endowed with full knowledge, the sage performed penance of the Gandhamādana mountain.

15. During summer he remained in the midst of five fires and performed the great penance. During rainy season he stayed under neck-deep water.

16. As his body was dried up due to the penance, he had (developed) scabies on the skin which the eminent sage used to scratch day and night.

17-21. Even as he continued to scratch the scab, the sage did not cease to perform his penance. It once occurred to the mind of the sage Sayugvā: 'Now itself I must have my holy bath in the three Tīrthas of great merit, namely Yamunā, Gaṅgā and Gayā.'

After thinking thus the sage had another worry: 'I am lame from the very birth. Hence the holy bath (in them) will be impossible to have. It is impossible for me to go very far in my cart. What shall I do then?'

Having pondered thus, that highly intelligent sage decided what he should do in order to take the holy bath in all the three Tīrthas: 'I have unbearable and unassailable power of penance. Thereby I shall invoke those three Tīrthas to this spot.'

22-25. After resolving thus mentally, he sat facing the East. With all the organs under control, he performed the *Ācamana* rite thrice. Then *Sayugvā* earnestly meditated for a short while. By the power of his Mantras, Yamunā, the great river, Gaṅgā, the daughter of Jahnu, and Gayā, the destroyer of sins—all the three broke the ground and rose up suddenly from the nether worlds. Assuming human forms, they joyously approached Sayugvā and spoke to the sage giving delight to him:

26-28. "O Sayugvā Raikva, welfare unto you. Desist from this meditation. Drawn by your Mantra, we have come here. What should be done by us for you? O eminent sage, speak it out to us."

On hearing their words, Sayugvā, the great sage, refrained from his meditation. He saw them standing in front of him. After honouring them duly, Raikva spoke these words:

29-36a. "O Goddess Yamunā, O Goddess Gaṅgā, O Gayā, the destroyer of sins, always be present near me on the Gandhamādana mountain. The places from where you emerged should be meritorious Tīrthas known after your names."

They said "So be it" and vanished suddenly. The places where they vanished thus, have become three holy Tīrthas. They are always praised by the people and addressed by their respective names.

The place where Yamunā pierced the ground and came out then is called *Yamunā Tīrtha* by the people. The chasm in the earth through which Gaṅgā gushed out suddenly, is well-known in the world as *Gaṅgā Tīrtha*. It is destructive of sins. The cavity in the ground through which Gayā came out in human guise, is called *Gayā Tīrtha*. Thus these three excellent Tīrthas are excessively meritorious.

They suddenly rose out of the earth, due to the power of the Mantra of Raikva.

36b-42. The excellent men who take holy bath in all these three Tīrthas shall get their *Ajñāna* (Ignorance) destroyed. Their perfect knowledge will increase.

The sage spent his time regularly taking his holy bath in the three Tīrthas invoked through his own Mantra.

At the time, there was a great king named Jānaśruti. He was the grandson of a saintly king named Putra. He was very much devoted to holy rites and pious activities. He gave foodstuffs and other things to suppliants with great faith and sincerity. Hence people in the world called him Śraddhādeya.

Since the king had ample *Vākya* (instructions?) in the abode for the propitiation of hungry people who sought food, he was called by all those suppliants *Bahuvākya*.

That king was Pautrāyaṇa (belonging to the family of Putra).

He was powerful. He was the son of Janaśruta. He was *Priyātithi* ('fond of guests'). He was also *Bahudāyī* ('one who gives liberally').

43-45. In all the cities, countries, villages, parks, all the quadrangles and in the highways, he made arrangements for various articles of hospitality along with much foodstuff and many kinds of beverages, pulses, vegetables, etc. for propitiating the people who sought the same. In the different places where the people gathered together, he announced thus: "O suppliants, make use of the foodstuffs and beverages."

46. The king's good qualities became well-known everywhere as he was fond of guests, as he gave much to the suppliants and was fond of making gifts.

47. When the king belonging to the family of Putra stayed thus with his good qualities, Devas and sages of great fortune desired for his blessings.

48-49. During the night in summer season they assumed the forms of swans, formed beautiful rows and flew swiftly along the ethereal path above the king who was seated at a window of his mansion.

50-54. As those swans flew swiftly a certain swan that had been flying in the rear of them all, addressed the swan that was at the head. Even as the king heard everything, he (the swan) spoke these words sarcastically: "O Bhallākṣa, O Bhallākṣa, O swan that goes at the head of all, the king, the son of Janaśruta, is seated in front of you in his mansion. He is worthy of being worshipped. Don't you see like a blind one? His refulgence is inviolable (and hence dreadful). It resembles infinite number of Suns. It blazes in front everywhere right from the abode of Brahmā. Do not fly so swiftly away from and above that saintly king bypassing him thus. If you do so, his refulgence will burn you up."

55-58a. As the swan spoke thus, the swan at the head replied: "Oh! You have great understanding and are worthy of being praised by poets.

Why then do you praise this cheat who is not at all worthy of being praised? Why do you praise this worthless person?

He merely breathes like an animal or like a bellows. This king does not know the secret of Dharma as the excellent Brāhmaṇa Sayugvā Raikva, the knower of truth, knows.

58b-63. The secret of the great splendour of Raikva (cannot be comprehended) even by Devas. No other living being has such a brilliance as his. No limit can be set to the mass of the merits of Raikva.

The dust particles on the ground can be counted. The stars in the firmament can also be counted. But the mass of the merits of Raikva as huge as Meru, cannot be estimated. Further let these transient Dharmas of that sage be (kept aside). The knowledge of Brahman that the sage possesses makes him praiseworthy. Jānaśruti has no such Dharma. How great is the glory of that knowledge which is difficult to be obtained by even leading Yogins! Why do you leave him off (i.e. ignore him) and praise this wretched man of evil soul? Let that sage, Sayugvā Raikva, alone be praised by you.

64-68a. That eminent sage is congenitally lame. He was desirous of taking his holy bath. Hence with his Mantra he invoked Gaṅgā, Yamunā and Gayā and brought them to the vicinity of his hermitage. In the mass of Dharmas of that great sage Raikva (which is so great) all the Dharmas of the beings present within the three worlds get included. But the extensive Dharmas of Raikva cannot come within the fold of the Dharmas of the living beings present in all the three worlds."

When the swan going in front stopped after speaking thus the prominent sages in the form of swans proceeded towards the world of Brahmā.

68b-75a. On hearing Raikva (praised) to the highest level and to the greatest extent, King Jānaśruti, the grandson of Putra, the suppressor of enemies, became excessively distressed like a pitiable wretch defeated at a game of dice. Heaving deep sighs repeatedly the king began to think thus: 'That swan who lauded (the superiority of) Raikva said that I am mean and lowly. Wonderful indeed is the greatness of Raikva whom even the birds praise. So I shall renounce the worldly affairs and the entire kingdom now and seek refuge in that noble-souled Sayugvā. Raikva is a storehouse of mercy. He will accept me when I seek refuge in him and will instruct me in the spiritual knowledge of the Ātman.'

Thinking thus, O Brāhmaṇas, and remaining awake, he spent (the remaining part of) that terrible night with great difficulty. When the night came to a close, he heard the auspicious sounds of the songs sung by the bards and the musical instruments played by them.

75b-80. On hearing it, the great king summoned his charioteer before leaving his bed. To him he spoke these words in all earnestness: "O my charioteer, take the chariot and hasten to search for the eminent Yogin named Raikva. He is lame and is (always) seated in a cart. He is the sole refuge of all holy Dharmas. Search for him in the hermitages of great sages, in holy forests, in desolate regions, in the residential areas of good noble men, on the shores and banks of the Tīrthas and rivers and in all other places where great sages are (usually) present. Search for Sayugvā, the abode of the perfect knowledge of Brahman. After searching for him, O charioteer, come back to me as quickly as possible (after knowing his whereabouts) to delight me."

81-86. He said, "So it shall be", and set out seated in a very fast chariot. He searched for Sage Raikva, the knower of Brahman, everywhere.

He searched for him in the caves of mountains and the hermitages of sages. In the course of his search, he wandered over the entire earth. After searching in different countries with great haste, he, in due course, came to Gandhamādana where many great sages had gathered together. He searched for him there too and saw the great sage scratching his scabies seated in his cart. He was in continuous meditation of the non-dual Brahman without divisions and parts. On seeing the great sage Sayugvā, he thought, 'This must be Raikva', and approached him. He humbly bowed down to the sage, sat near him and asked him:

87-91. "O holy lord, are you (the Sage) Sayugvā named Raikva?"[1] On hearing his words the sage replied: "I surely am Sayugvā named Raikva." He heard the words of the sage. Through various gestures, he understood that the sage wished for some money to meet the expenses of maintaining the family. After returning from Gandhamādana, he intimated everything to the king.

After hearing the words of the charioteer with great respect, the king took with him six hundred cows, a *Bhāra* of gold coins and a chariot fitted with a mule. Taking all these with him, King Jānaśruti, the saintly king belonging to the family of Putra, proceeded towards (the abode of) Raikva. After going there, that king spoke these words to Raikva:

---

1. The episode and the conversation recorded in the *Chāndogya Up*. 4.1.8, etc. is echoed here, the only difference is that the spiritual knowledge imparted in the *Upaniṣad* is not reproduced here.

92-95. "O holy lord Raikva, O Sayugvā, let what is offered by me be accepted. Accept from me six hundred cows, a *Bhāra* of gold coins and a chariot fitted with a mule. After accepting these, O holy Brāhmaṇa, train and instruct me. Let the perfect knowledge of the non-dual Brahman be imparted to me."

On hearing these enthusiastic and excited words of his, Sayugvā Raikva replied to Jānaśruti, the suppressor of foes:

Raikva said:

96-98. Let these cows be with you alone. So also the *Bhāra* of gold coins and the chariot. Of what avail to me is this small quantity (of wealth, etc.), for I am one who remains alive for many Kalpas? This is not adequate for me to maintain the family. Even if you were to give me hundred times this present, O eminent king, that will not be enough for the maintenance of my family.

On hearing, these words of Raikva, Jānaśruti replied:

Jānaśruti said:

99-100. These cows, ready cash and the chariot are not intended to be the price of the perfect knowledge of Brahman, O sage, to be imparted by you. You may or may not accept these cows, etc. from me. But, O Brāhmaṇa, do impart to me the perfect knowledge of the undivided (indivisible) non-dual Brahman.

On hearing these words of his Sayugvā spoke these words:

Raikva said:

101-105a. Only that person is fit to have the instruction (in spiritual knowledge) who is completely detached from worldly affairs and whose merits and demerits that began to yield results have exhausted. Although you are completely indifferent to worldly affairs, the merits and sins have not completely ceased. The mass of merits and sins is the cause of rebirth. Usually they are not destroyed, O king, unless their results are experienced. Still, I shall tell you the means of destroying them, since you have sought refuge in me. Listen with concentration and mental purity.

105b-109. There are three Tīrthas here that bestow what is desired. They are destructive of all *Prārabdhas* (i.e. merits and sins that have begun to yield results) of all those who are desirous of salvation. This is Yamunā-tīrtha; this is Gaṅgā-tīrtha, and this is Gayā-tīrtha. So take your holy bath in these. Do not delay. All the *Prārabdhas* will perish. There is no doubt about it. Thereby, you shall become pure in mind and I shall impart knowledge unto you.

When this was spoken by sage Raikva, the king was delighted very much. His eyes beamed with pleasure like lotuses in full bloom. He entered the three Tīrthas with great excitement and took his holy bath in them. Merely by taking his holy bath in those Tīrthas, the king obtained the purity of mind.

110-113. That king served Sayugvā as his preceptor. Raikva, the sage Sayugvā, mercifully imparted perfect knowledge to Jānaśruti, the perfect knowledge that is difficult to have even by eminent sages.

The moment the perfect knowledge in the form of Brahman was imparted by him, the excellent king had uncontradicted experience (of Brahman). With the favour of Raikva, the Yogin, he attained the form of Brahman. The whole world in (the form of various objects) such as pot, wall, granary, etc. did not appear before him. He pierced through (the veil of) Māyā and became the Sole Brahman.

114-116. It is wonderful that King Jānaśruti attained the form of Brahman difficult of access even unto great Yogins by taking his holy bath in the three Tīrthas.

Thus, O Brāhmaṇas, the glory of those three Tīrthas has been recounted to you all.

He who reads this chapter on the glory of the three Tīrthas, shall pierce through the darkness of ignorance and attain Brahman.

CHAPTER TWENTYSEVEN

The Glory of Koṭitīrtha: Kṛṣṇa Atones for His Sin of Killing His Uncle

Śrī Sūta said:

1. After joyously taking the holy bath in Yamunā, Gaṅgā and Gayātīrtha in accordance with the injunctions, the man should go to Koṭitīrtha.[1]

2. Koṭitīrtha is extremely meritorious. It is well-known in all the worlds. It is pure. It causes (confers) all fortune. It is destructive of all sins.

3. It dispels (the effect of) evil dreams. It is destructive of great sins. It suppresses great obstacles. It accords great peace to men.

4. Merely by remembering it one can get rid of all sins. It was created by Rāma himself sportingly with the tip of his bow.

5-11. Formerly, after killing Rāvaṇa in battle, Rāma, the son of Daśaratha, installed a Liṅga on the Gandhamādana mountain to get rid of the sin of Brāhmaṇa-slaughter and with a desire for the welfare of all the people. He searched for fresh and pure water for the ablution of the Liṅga.[2] The son of Daśaratha did not get water nearby. He thought thus, 'Where is the water fit for the ablution of the Liṅga? I must bathe the Liṅga with fresh water.'

After deciding thus, remembering Gaṅgā, the scion of the family of Raghu pierced the earth with the tip of his bow immediately. At that time the tip of the bow of Rāma reached nether worlds. Thereafter, the most excellent one among the wielders of bow drew up the bow. While the bow was being lifted up by Rāghava, Gaṅgā who had been remembered by Kākutstha, came out of that hole. The scion of the family of Raghu bathed that Liṅga with that water.

12. Since it was formerly created by the tip (Koṭi) of the bow of Rāma, that Tīrtha has become well-known in all the three worlds as Koṭitīrtha.

---

1. Koṭitīrtha (Kodi Teertham) is within the temple premises. It is between Viśālākṣī and Vibhīṣaṇa Liṅgam and Jyoti Liṅgam.

2. VV 5-12 narrate why and how Koṭitīrtha came to be created by Rāma. The Tīrtha is called Koṭitīrtha as it was created by the tip (*Koṭi*) of Rāma's bow.

13-16. The devotee should at the outset take his holy baths in all theTīrthas on the Gandhamādana mountain and get his sins dispelled. The man should then take his holy bath in Koṭitīrtha to get rid of the remaining sins.

The mass of sins that cannot be destroyed by means of the holy baths in the other Tīrthas and the sins clinging to the bones having been acquired in the course of many crores of births—all these perish, if the devotee takes his holy bath in Koṭitīrtha. There is no doubt about this.

If, O Brāhmaṇas, a man takes his holy bath here in Koṭitīrtha at the outset, he becomes liberated and all the other Tīrthas cease to be of use to him.

The sages said:

17-19. O Sūta, the knower of all topics and principles, O disciple of Vyāsa, O great sage, dispel a doubt of ours, O most excellent one among people conversant with the Purāṇas. If bath in other Tīrthas does not serve any purpose of the person who has taken his holy bath in Koṭitīrtha, why do men take their holy baths in the Tīrthas such as Dharmatīrtha? Why do they not bypass all those Tīrthas and take their holy bath here in this Koṭitīrtha itself? Tell us.

Śrī Sūta said:

20-21a. O eminent sages, a great secret has been asked by you all. Formerly, Śaṁbhu spoke this to Nārada when he asked him about it. I shall tell it, O excellent sages. Listen to it, with great faith.

21b-25. Going along the path casually or engaged in a pilgrimage, O excellent Brāhmaṇas, if a man sees on the way a Tīrtha or a temple or hears about it (he must visit it). If, out of delusion, the base man does not resort to it, there is no redemption from sin for him. So say the great sages.

If a man who is on his way to Setu, does not take his holy bath in the other Tīrthas too, he will be defiled by the defects of transgressing a Tīrtha. He must be excommunicated by Brāhmaṇas.

Hence, O Brāhmaṇas, one must necessarily take the holy bath in Cakratīrtha and others. After taking the holy bath in these Tīrthas, men should, with great purity, take their bath in Koṭitīrtha for getting rid of the lingering sins.

26. After taking the holy bath in Koṭitīrtha, the pilgrim should not stay on Gandhamādana any longer.[1] After getting rid of the sins, he should return from Gandhamādana immediately.

27-28. Formerly, after bathing Rāmanātha with the waters of Koṭitīrtha, Rāma himself took his holy bath there and became liberated from the sin of Brāhmaṇa-slaughter (i.e. killing of Rāvaṇa). At the same instant, Rāma got into the aerial chariot Puṣpaka accompanied by his younger brother and the monkeys.

29. Therefore, like Rāma, the son of Daśaratha, the man who has taken his holy bath in Koṭitīrtha and who has got rid of the lingering sins, should return immediately.

30. Indeed this is the most excellent of all Tīrthas, well-known in all the worlds. It was created by Rāghava for the sake of the ablution of Rāmanātha.

31. It is the place where Goddess Gaṅgā is present. It is the place where Rāma, the Tārakabrahman (identical with Brahman that redeems) had taken his holy bath with great respect.

32-33. By whom can the glory of that Koṭitīrtha be recounted? It is the spot where formerly Kṛṣṇa took his bath for the welfare of the world. He was liberated from the sin of killing Kaṁsa, his (maternal) uncle.[2] By whom can the greatness of Koṭitīrtha be described?

The sages said:

34. Why did the scion of the family of Yadu kill Kaṁsa, his uncle? (Why did he commit this sin) for quelling which, O Sūta, the noble-minded lord, took his bath in Koṭitīrtha?

Śrī Sūta said:

35-39. In the family of Yadu, there was a son of Śūra, well-known as Vasudeva. He married the daughter of Devaka, renowned as Devakī. After marriage, he got into a chariot and set out for his city. Kaṁsa was the charioteer of Ānakadundubhi (i.e. Vasudeva).

---

1. Bath in Koṭitīrtha is the last bath in this pilgrimage. After this bath the pilgrim should leave and go back from Gandhamādana.

2. The story up to Kaṁsa's killing is based on BhP but Kṛṣṇa's pilgrimage to Koṭitīrtha for expiation of Kaṁsa's killing has no basis in BhP and Mbh. It is contributed by the Purāṇa to glorify Koṭitīrtha.

At that time, an unembodied voice spoke to Kaṁsa who acted as the charioteer and took his sister and her husband in his excellent chariot and drove it: "There is no doubt in this that the eighth child from the womb of this (lady) whom you are driving in your chariot, is going to kill you, O suppressor of enemies."

On hearing this celestial voice, O eminent Brāhmaṇas, Kaṁsa took out his sword and attempted to kill his sister.

40-41. Thereupon Vasudeva pacified Kaṁsa and said:

Vasudeva said:

O Kaṁsa, I shall give away the sons born of this (lady) to you. Do not harm or injure this sister of yours. Indeed there is nothing to fear from her.

On hearing his words, Kaṁsa refrained from killing her.

42-44. He went to his own city along with Devakī and Vasudeva. Kaṁsa, the vicious one, placed Devakī and Vasudeva in prison with their feet fettered. After a long time, O eminent sages, Devakī bore to Vasudeva six sons in succession. As soon as they were born, they were handed over to Kaṁsa by Vasudeva and he (Kaṁsa) killed them all.

45-48. After all these six sons born of Devakī had been killed, O excellent Brāhmaṇas, by the ruthless, cruel-hearted Kaṁsa, Śeṣa became the seventh child in the womb of Devakī. Urged by Viṣṇu, Goddess Māyā transferred that child in the womb of Devakī to that of Rohiṇī in the abode of Nandagopa.

By the grace of Viṣṇu a rumour gained currency in the world that the seventh child in the womb of Devakī was aborted. Afterwards, Viṣṇu came into the womb of Devakī.

49-51. When ten months elapsed, the immutable Hari was born of Devakī. He became well-known as Kṛṣṇa.

He manifested himself in his divine form with the conchshell, discus, iron-club and sword shining in his four arms. He had a crown on his head. He wore the garland of sylvan flowers. He dispelled the grief of his parents. On seeing Lord Hari, Ānakadundubhi eulogized him (thus):

Vasudeva said:

52-54. You are the universe. You alone are the lord of the

universe. You are the source of origin of the universe. The universe rests in you. You are the great Pradhāna. You are *Virāṭ* (cosmic-formed). You are *Svarāṭ* (Supreme Being). You are *Samrāṭ* (universal Ruler). O Lord, you are everything.

Obeisance, obeisance to Nārāyaṇa, the splendour that is the cause of the universe, to the Lord of boundless valour, to the Lord holding the conchshell, discus, sword and iron club. Obeisance to the Lord who has assumed the form of a human being.

As Vasudeva, the son of Śūra, eulogized thus, O excellent Brāhmaṇas, Hari spoke thus, delighting him and Devakī:

Hari said:

55-56. I shall kill Kaṁsa, O my parents, do not be afraid. Yaśodā, the wife of Nandagopa, has given birth last night to my Māyā who enchants all the worlds.

Place me on her bed. Take that daughter of Yaśodā, O excellent scion of the family of Yadu, and place her on the bed of Devakī.

57-59. On being told thus by Kṛṣṇa, O Brāhmaṇas, he did the same. The daughter lying on the bed of Devakī, who was Māyā herself, began to cry.

On hearing the cry of a child, Kaṁsa became excited in his mind. He came into the lying-in-chamber and took up that girl. The shameless and ruthless fellow then smashed the child on a rock.[1] (The child) got out of his hand forcibly (and appeared in the sky as) the great goddess with eight well-armed hands of great power. She furiously challenged Kaṁsa and spoke these words:

Māyā said:

60-62. O sinful, vicious Kaṁsa, of deluded mind, your enemy, the destroyer of your life, is present somewhere else. The destroyer of your life has appeared. Search for that enemy, O Kaṁsa. Do not delay. He is the death unto you.

After saying thus the goddess went back to the divine abodes.

1. There is another version in VāP II.134.212-15. As the child was a girl, Kaṁsa spared her and she grew up as a Goddess among the Yādavas. BdP 2.3.72.220 supports this version.

If she was adored by human beings, she became the bestower of everything desired (by them).

63-66. On hearing the words of the goddess, Kaṁsa became extremely perplexed and excited. He despatched Pūtanā and many other evil spirits to attack his enemy as well as other children in different parts of the land. All those evil spirits, child-catchers, went to the cowherd colony of Nanda. They were killed and despatched to the abode of Yama by Kṛṣṇa.

After the lapse of some days, O eminent Brāhmaṇas, the boys Rāma and Kṛṣṇa grew up in the cowherd colony. The suppressors of the enemies sported about with many games and plays befitting children.

67-71. For some time they tended the calves and played on their flutes. For some time they tended cows embellishing themselves with Guñjā and Tāpiccha, i.e. red and black berries and the flowers of Tamāla plant, a dark-barked and white-blossomed tree. Rāma and Keśava sported about in the cowherd colony for a long time.

Once, Kaṁsa sent Akrūra to the cowherd colony, O eminent Brāhmaṇas, to take Rāma and Keśava from the cowherd colony (to Mathurā). Akrūra took Rāma and Kṛṣṇa from the cowherd colony, at the bidding of Kaṁsa, to Mathurā which shone with gold festoons and ornamental geteways.

After bringing Rāma and Keśava, the son of Gāndinī (i.e. Akrūra) went ahead to the city. He met Kaṁsa and intimated everything to him. Afterwards he went home.

72. In the afternoon, the next day, the sons of Vasudeva went to the city of Mathurā along with their dear friends, the cowherd boys. They went to the city of Mathurā which had tall towers and minarets and where tall stakes had been fixed on the ground.

73. Listening to the songs of praise of the young damsels of the city, Kṛṣṇa and Rāma went ahead and entered the hall of bows. There they saw a huge bow with the string tied firmly.

74. They drove away all the guards of the bow. Kṛṣṇa sportingly took up the bow. In order to fix the string to it, he bent it. But it broke into two in the meantime.

75. On hearing the sound that rose when the bow broken into two, the guards rushed at them in order to kill them.

76-77. Then, in an instant, Rāma and Kṛṣṇa of great power and valour killed Kuvalayāpīḍa, the elephant that stood at the entrance. They extracted its tusks and held them in their hands.

Presently they placed the tusks on their shoulders and entered the arena.

78. They struck the wrestlers Cāṇūra, Muṣṭika, Tośala and others and despatched them to the abode of Yama.

79. They swiftly climbed on the lofty platform. They went near Kaṁsa who was seated on the lofty seat and stood there treating him with contempt like lions that ignore an insignificant animal.

80. Kṛṣṇa dragged Kaṁsa who was seated on a raised seat. Catching hold of his feet, he whirled him in the sky.

81. He thrashed him on the ground and left him on the ground bereft of life. O Brāhmaṇas, with his fist, Balarāma slew the eight brothers of Kaṁsa.

82. After slaying Kaṁsa, Kṛṣṇa, the suppressor of the army of the enemies, released his parents who were extremely sad and miserable, from their fetters.

83-84. Accompanied by Balarāma, Mādhava established all of them (in their respective places). On hearing that Kaṁsa had been killed by Śrīkṛṣṇa all those kinsmen who had been formerly harassed by Kaṁsa at Mathurā, returned to that city. Further, Keśava re-established Ugrasena in the kingdom.

85. Unable to hear the heinous sin committed by Kaṁsa against his parents, he slew his maternal uncle Kaṁsa who was a thorn to Devas and Brāhmaṇas.

86. Once thereafter when Nārada and other sages came to see him, Kṛṣṇa the excellent (lord), asked all of them thus:

Śrīkṛṣṇa said:

87-88. My maternal uncle Kaṁsa who had committed many sins was killed by me, O Brāhmaṇas. If the uncle is killed one incurs sin. This has been said by those excellent persons who are conversant with the scriptural texts. Hence tell me the means of expiation for dispelling this sin.

Thereupon, O Brāhmaṇas, Nārada spoke in sweet voice, with devotion and affection to Kṛṣṇa of wonderful exploits.

Nārada said:

89-95. You are always pure. You are ever liberated. You are

ever good. You are the eternal Supreme Soul of the form of Existence, Knowledge and Bliss. O Kṛṣṇa, the scion of the family of Yadu, you have neither sin nor merit. Still in order to guide and instruct the common people, O Garuḍa-emblemed Mādhava, the rites of expiation must be performed by you in accordance with the following injunctions. You must perform what is conducive to the welfare of the world now.

Formerly the Liṅga named Rāmanātha was installed by Rāma on Rāmasetu on the Gandhamādana mountain. For the sake of the water for its ablution, the scion of the family of Raghu, created the Tīrtha well-known as Koṭitīrtha by piercing the ground with the tip of his bow. It is the Tīrtha made by Rāma himself, your previous incarnation[1], of unimpaired activities for the sake of the purification of the sin of Brāhmaṇa-slaughter. You do take your holy bath there in that sanctifying Tīrtha, destructive of sins.

96-98. Thereby your sin due to the slaying of your uncle will perish quickly. O Hari, the holy bath of Koṭitīrtha dispels the sin of Brāhmaṇa-slaughter, etc. It bestows heavenly pleasures and salvation on all men. It increases longevity and good health.

On hearing these words of Sage Nārada, Mādhava bade farewell to all those sages. At the very same instance, O Brāhmaṇas, he hurried to Rāmasetu for the sake of dispelling his own sins.

99-100. The scion of the family of Yadu went to Koṭitīrtha in a few days. He took his holy bath there along with the requisite *Saṁkalpa* rite and made many charitable gifts. Instantaneously, he was liberated from the sins arising from slaying his own uncle. After serving Rāmanātha he went to his own city Mathurā.

Śrī Sūta said:

101. Koṭītīrtha has such power. It is meritorious, O great sages. A man is immediately released from Brāhmaṇa-slaughter and other sins. There is no other Tīrtha on the earth on a par with this.

102-104. If one takes the holy bath here, O Brāhmaṇas, the three Devas, Brahmā, Viṣṇu and Śiva, as well as the other Devas become delighted. There is no doubt about it.

---

1. The author's mention of Rāma being Kṛṣṇa's previous incarnation shows that the present belief in the ten incarnations of Viṣṇu was prevalent at the time of the Purāṇa.

Thus the wonderful glory of Koṭitīrtha has been recounted to you all. On hearing this a man on the earth is liberated from all sins.

By listening to this meritorious chapter, O eminent sages, and by reading this, a man is really liberated from Brāhmaṇa-slaughter and other sins.

CHAPTER TWENTYEIGHT

The Glory of Sādhyāmṛtatīrtha: Purūravas Liberated from a Curse

Śrī Sūta said:

1. After resorting to the highly meritorious Koṭitīrtha the man who has conquered his passions, should surely go to Sādhyāmṛta[1] (Tīrtha) to take his holy bath.

2-3. The great Tīrtha Sādhyāmṛta is on the Gandhamādana mountain. It bestows great merits. It subdues great miseries. It dispels the sins of men. It yields all desired objects. By taking his holy bath devoutly here, the man shall attain all desires.

4. Neither by penance nor by the vow of celibacy, neither by Yajñas nor by charitable gifts, does a man obtain that goal which one obtains by taking the holy plunge in Sādhyāmṛta.

5. Those whose limbs are touched by the auspicious waters of Sādhyāmṛta, all the sins in their bodies perish instantaneously.

6. The man who performs the holy rite of Aghamarṣaṇa in the holy waters of Sādhyāmṛta, gets rid of all his sins and is honoured in the world of Viṣṇu.

7-8. If a man commits sins in the early days of his life but repents for them in the later days and resorts to Sādhyāmṛta, he shall undoubtedly become liberated. By taking his holy bath in Sādhyāmṛta one becomes liberated from the bondage of the body.

9. Men of evil deeds who take their holy bath in the waters of Sādhyāmṛta never fall into Narakas that are terrible due to manifold distress.

---

1. If what is presently called 'Satyāmṛta Teertham' be the same as 'Sādhyāmṛta Tīrtha', it is near the Navaśakti Maṇḍapam.

10. The goal that men attain by taking the holy bath in the waters of Sādhyāmṛta, O Brāhmaṇas, cannot be obtained by means of Yajñas, Vedas and meritorious deeds.

11. Men stay in the world of Śiva and are honoured there very well for as many years as the number of bones of theirs remain deposited in the waters of Sādhyāmṛta.

12. Just as the sun at the time of rising, dispels the dreadful darkness and shines, so also the person who regularly takes his holy bath in Sādhyāmṛta breaks through sins and shines.

13. The man who takes his holy bath here always acquires all his desired objectives. By taking his holy bath in this highly meritorious Tīrtha formerly King Purūravas got rid of the separation from Urvaśī resulting from Tuṁburu's curse.

The sages said:

14-16. O illustrious Sūta, how did the mortal king Purūravas at the outset come into contact with Urvaśī, the celestial damsel? How did he get rid of the separation from Urvaśī resulting from the curse of Tuṁburu? For what reason did Sage Tuṁburu curse the king? Describe all this in detail, O eminent sage.

Sūta said:

17-22. Formerly there was a king named Purūravas. In valour he was on a par with Indra. He was equal to Kubera (in affluence). He was honoured by the immortal beings. That excellent king ruled the earth righteously. He performed many Yajñas and always made charitable gifts.

While that king of great intellect was reigning over the entire earth, O Brāhmaṇas, Urvaśī came to the earth as a result of the curse of Mitrāvaruṇa. Urvaśī wandered here and there near the city of that king. She sang in a garden with a sweet lute and in a voice as sweet as the chirping of a cuckoo.

Once the king rode on a horse and went to that garden accompanied by a hundred young women, as he was eager to sport about therein. He saw the slender-waisted Urvaśī of such a beauty there. The king proposed to her, "Be my wife."

23-27. She too was afflicted with love and replied to the king thus: "Let it be so, O excellent one among men. If you agree to my stipulations, I will live with you with all eagerness and enthusiasm."

He replied, "O lady of beautiful eyebrows, I shall abide by your conditions."

Thereupon Urvaśī said to Purūravā enthusiastically: "If you protect the pair of rams I keep like my pet sons, if, O king, you are never seen naked (by me), if you never give me the remnants of your food, I shall stay with you. O excellent king, ghee alone shall be my food."

The king said, "It will be so." After saying so, the king took her to his abode.

28-31. The king sported with her in Caitraratha park in Alakā (Kubera's city) on the banks of Sarasvatī charming on account of clusters of lotuses.

The king spent sixty-one years sporting with her. Therefore the love of Urvaśī increased day by day. The slender-waisted lady had no desire (to go back to) the world of Devas. Without her the world of Devas ceased to be all (that) charming.

So, O Brāhmaṇas, Viśvāvasu thought thus, 'I shall bring her back to the world of the Devas.' Thinking thus he went to the terrestrial world in a trice.

32-37. Viśvāvasu had known the agreement of the king with Urvaśī. Accompanied by Gandharvas, he came in the middle of the night and swiftly seized one of the rams from the vicinity of the bed of Urvaśī.

While it was being carried through the sky, Urvaśī heard its bleat and so spoke to her husband: "By whom is my son being taken away? Let him be protected. I am helpless. I have lost consciousness. Whom shall I seek refuge in? Which man shall I look up to for shelter?"

Purūravas did hear her words during the middle of the night, but he did not stir out of his bed, lest he should be seen naked by her.

Then the Gandharvas seized the other ram too and went away. Urvaśī heard the bleating sound of that ram too. Then the gentle lady lamented loudly: "Helpless that I am, my son is being taken away by thieves. Which man shall I turn to for succour?"

38-40. On hearing her words, the king became very furious. Thinking that the whole place was plunged in darkness, the king seized a sword and rushed out saying, "O wicked one, O wicked one, where can you go?" In the meantime the lightning flash caused by the Gandharvas shone brilliantly. By the sparkling lustre of the same the queen saw the king bereft of clothes. As the agreement was broken she set off at that very moment.

41-42. The Gandharvas too abandoned those rams there and went away. The king came back to his bed taking the rams with him with very great pleasure. But he did not see the large-eyed beautiful Urvaśī there. Unable to see her he wandered over the earth still naked like a mad man.

43. The king went to Kurukṣetra and saw her sporting about along with four celestial damsels in a lake full of lotuses.

44. "O my wife of a cruel mind, wait." He spoke thus very often. The king made very many utterances of this kind.

45-47. Sporting about in the company of the groups of celestial damsels, Urvaśī spoke: "O great king, O sinless one, no longer should you indulge in these (restless) activities. I have already conceived from you. You should come here at the end of the year. A son of great virtues will be born to you. Then I will stay with you for one night."

On being told thus, O Brāhmaṇas, the king became delighted. He entered his city (i.e he returned to the city).

48-51. To those celestial damsels she spoke about the king: "This is that excellent man who has the handsome features of Kāma. I had been overwhelmed with love and had been living with this king for a very long time till recently."

On being told thus the companions said to her: "Well done! Well done! O friend, we, on the other hand, would have remained with him forever." So said the celestial damsels to Urvaśī, their friend then. When the year was complete, the king too came to the lake.

52. On seeing King Purūravas come there, Urvaśī became delighted in her mind. She presented her son Āyus to him.

53. With great love, she spent a night with him. In this manner Urvaśī bore to him five sons (lit. a foetus, giving birth to five sons).

54-55. Urvaśī, the excellent lady, said to the king: "Out of affection for me, O king, the Gandharvas will grant you boons. O excellent king of saintly features, let (the proper) boon be requested for by you."

On being told by her thus, the king spoke to the excellent Gandharvas:

56-57. "My treasury is full. I have conquered the hosts of my enemies. I have nothing to be obtained except *Salokatā* (residence in the same world) with Urvaśī. Hence I choose a boon so that I can spend my time along with Urvaśī."

When this was spoken by the king, the Gandharvas became delighted in their minds. They gave him an *Agnisthālī* (i.e. a pot or pan for sacred fire) and said to the king:

58-59. "O excellent king, following the injunctions of the Vedas divide the sacred fire into three. By performing a Yajña, O king, do attain Sālokya with Urvaśī."

On being told thus, the king received the *Sthālī* for fire and went (to his city).

60-63. In the middle of the forest, he thought thus: 'Alas! What a fool had I been! Urvaśī has not been obtained by me. Of what avail is this *Agnisthālī* for me?' Then the king dropped the *Agnisthālī* in the forest and went to his own city. When the midnight was past he woke up from his sleep and thought thus: 'It is for the purpose of achieving the world of Urvaśī that the *Agnisthālī* was given to me by the eminent Gandharvas. But it has been dropped in the forest by me. I shall get it back.' Thinking thus, he got up and went to the forest. But Purūravas was not able to see the *Agnisthālī* there.

64-66. In the place of the *Agnisthālī*, he saw an Aśvattha tree with latent fire. Then he thought: 'The Sthālī was dropped here in the forest earlier by me. But it has now become Aśvattha with the fire latent within it. Hence I shall take this to the city with me. It has the form of fire. I shall make an *Araṇi* (wood for the sake of creating fire by attrition). I shall respectfully worship the fire generated from it.' Resolving thus the king went to his city.

67-70. He made a beautiful *Araṇi* measured with his own fingers. At the time of making it, O Brāhmaṇas, the king repeated the Gāyatrī Mantra. The king made the Araṇi as many Aṅgulas long as there are syllables in the Gāyatrī Mantra he recited. The king then churned it and generated three fires. With the desire for the benefit of attaining the world of Urvaśī, the king joyously performed Homa in all the three fires in accordance with the injunctions in the Vedas. By the same procedure he performed many Yajñas.

71. Thereby the lord of the universe attained the world of Gandharvas, O excellent Brāhmaṇas. In the company of Urvaśī, he sported for a long time in the world of Devas.

72. Once, accompanied by all the immortal ones, the Slayer of Bala and Vṛtra (i.e. Indra) was engaged in witnessing the dance of the celestial damsels in his court.

73-76. King Purūravas too had come then to the court of Devas in order to witness the dance of the womenfolk of Suras, the heavan-dwellers.

One by one, those ladies came before Indra and danced. Then Urvaśī came and danced before Hari (Indra). Urvaśī who was proud of her skill in dancing and symbolic gesticulations, looked at Purūravas and smiled fascinatingly. On seeing Urvaśī the king too smiled. Tuṁburu, the dance-instructor, was furious on account of this smiling (of mutual admiration). In his anger, he cursed both of them, Urvaśī and the excellent king.

Tuṁburu said:

77-81. Since (a mean thing) has been committed by both of you here in this assembly filled with many Devas, since you smiled for no reason at all in the midst of the dance programme, O eminent king, both of you will be separated presently.[1]

Thus he cursed him in the presence of all the Devas. On being cursed by the Dance Instructor, the king became extremely sad. He sought refuge in Indra saying, "Save me; save me" Purūravas spoke to Indra in a piteous tone: "It was for the purpose of obtaining Sālokya with Urvaśī that I performed Yajñas. Hence, O Indra, separation from her is unbearable to me."

82-87. As the king said thus, the Thousand-eyed Lord of Śacī said to him:[2] "O excellent king, do not be afraid. I shall tell you

---

1. The legend of Purūravas and Urvaśī, their love and separation, forms the background of the famous Saṁvāda Sūkta in RV. In the transmission of the story during the Purāṇic period the curse motif was used to explain the separation; the person giving the curse is Brahmā, Mitrāvaruṇa; and here he is the dance-teacher, Sage Tuṁbaru.

The story is used to explain how the institution of sacrifice began in Purūravas' times, the use of Agnisthālī and finally the method of producing fire by attrition of Aśvattha wood. PI gives a number of references to this story in different Purāṇas. See PI I, p. 243.

2. As expected of a Sthala-Purāṇa, the curse of Purūravas is shown to be removed by a bath in Sādhyāmṛtatīrtha.

the means of redemption from the curse. In the Southern Ocean on the meritorious Gandhamādana mountain there is an excessively great Tīrtha well-known as Sādhyāmṛta. It is resorted to by all Devas, Siddhas, Cāraṇas and Kinnaras; it is resorted to by groups of many Yogins and sages including Sanaka. It yields worldly pleasures and salvation to men. It bestows release from all curses. O king, do go to that Tīrtha immediately. By taking the holy bath there everyone can obtain Amṛta. Hence it is well-known in all the worlds as Sādhyāmṛta. By taking the holy bath there, you will have reunion with Urvaśī. You can have your residence in my world too. There is no doubt about it."

88. On being directed thus, the king became delighted in his mind. He immediately started to the great Tīrtha Sādhyāmṛta.

89. He took his holy bath there in Sādhyāmṛta that is destructive of all sins. By taking his holy bath there, O Brāhmaṇas, the king was immediately released from the curse.

90. Immediately after the holy bath he was joined by Urvaśī. Seated in an aerial chariot along with her, he went to Amarāvatī.

91-96. Again he continued to sport with her in the divine abode like a Deva. That Tīrtha Sādhyāmṛta has such power. It is excellent. By taking his holy bath there, Purūravas became united with Urvaśī. Hence he who takes his holy bath in this Tīrtha which is destructive of all great sins, obtains everything he desires. He goes to the excellent heaven. If a man devoid of any desires bathes there, he will attain salvation.

He who reads this holy chapter that destroys sins and the man who listens to this attains the stay in Vaikuṇṭha.

Thus, O Brāhmaṇas, the glory of the Tīrtha Sādhyāmṛta has been recounted to you. It is destructive of sins. It has been faithfully recounted by me in detail. The same was previously narrated to Sanaka and others by the Four-faced Lord.

CHAPTER TWENTYNINE

The Glory of Sarvatīrtha: Sucarita Attains Sāyujya

Śrī Sūta said:

1. After taking the holy bath in Sādhyāmṛtatīrtha which redeemed the king from a curse, the man observing restraints should go to Sarvatīrtha.[1]

2-8. Sarvatīrtha is extremely meritorious. It is destructive of great sins. One who is defiled by great sins or all sorts of sins, shall becomes pure instantaneously by taking the holy plunge in Sarvatīrtha. O sages of good holy rites, all the sins stay in the body only until the sinning man takes his holy bath in this Sarvatīrtha. On seeing a man going to Sarvatīrtha for the sake of taking the holy bath in it, O Brāhmaṇas, all the sins begin to tremble thinking, 'Our ruin is certain.'

A man suffers from the miseries of staying in the womb and the like as long as he does not take his holy bath in this Sarvatīrtha, O eminent Brāhmaṇas. By taking his holy bath here a man obtains the benefit that is usually obtained by performing great sacrifices, by resorting to Tīrthas, by performing the Japa of Gāyatrī and of other great Mantras, by observance of all restraints, by recitation of all the Vedas a hundred times, by the devout worship of the deities (like Śiva, Viṣṇu and others), and by observing fast on Ekādaśī (eleventh) and other Tithis.

The sages said:

9. O Sūta, how did this Tīrtha come to be famous by the name Sarvatīrtha? Describe this meritorious thing in detail to us who are listening to it (eagerly).

Śrī Sūta said:

10-16. Formerly a sage called Sucarita,[2] born in the family of Bhṛgu, was congenitally blind and was distressed due to old age.

1. Sarvatīrtha: It is in the inner courtyard of Rameswaram shrine.
2. The story of Sucarita is the special contribution of this Purāṇa for the glorification of this Tīrtha.

He strictly adhered to the observance of restraints. Due to his blindness he was unable to go on a pilgrimage, O Brāhmaṇas.

The great sage who was desirous of taking bath in all holy Tīrthas went to the sacred mountain Gandhamādana on the shore of the southern ocean. Reaching there he performed a difficult penance with God Śiva in view (hoping thereby to realize his desire to take bath in all holy Tīrthas). He controlled his passions and observed fasts. He worshipped Śaṁbhu thrice (everyday). He took the holy plunge three times everyday. He honoured the guests. He stayed in water during winter and stood amidst five fires in summer. During rainy season he used to endure torrential downpour. (Sometimes) he had only water or wind as diet. He always applied *Bhasma* all over his body or applied *Tripuṇḍra* marks on his forehead as per instructions mentioned in *Jābāla Upaniṣad*. He regularly wore Rudrākṣa rosaries. Thus that Brāhmaṇa performed a severe penance for ten years.

17. Being pleased with the penance of that Sage Sucarita, O Brāhmaṇas, that moon-crested Lord Śaṅkara appeared before the sage.

18. The Lord was riding on his great Bull. He was attended upon by multitudes of Bhūtas (goblins and spirits). Half of his body was that of the Daughter of the Mountain. The Trident-bearing Lord had the lustre of a crore of Suns.

19-21. With his refulgence he brightened all the quarters and made them free from darkness. All his limbs were grey on account of the application of the holy ash (*Bhasma*). He was embellished with clusters of matted hair. He was adorned with ornaments in the form of Ananta and other great serpents.

Appearing before him, Śaṁbhu, Śaṅkara, the consort of Pārvatī (Daughter of the Mountain) granted him two eyes, the power of vision, so that he could see him (God Śaṁbhu). On seeing the great Īśāna (Śiva), O Brāhmaṇas, Sucarita, to whom a pair of eyes had been given by Śaṁbhu, eulogized the Lord with delighted mind.

Sucarita said:

22-28. Be victorious, O Lord Maheśāna, be victorious. O Śaṅkara, O Dhūrjaṭi, be victorious, O lord, worthy of being worshipped by Brahmā and others, O slayer of the three Puras, O annihilator of Yama; be victorious, O lord of Umā, O Mahādeva, O slayer of Kāma; be victorious, O lord devoid of impurities. Be victorious, O physician (who cures people of the disease) of worldly existence, O protector of the Bhūtas, O immutable Śiva. Obeisance to you, O three-eyed one, O lord always readily engaged in protecting the devotees. Bow to you, O sky-tressed one. Be victorious, O lord, O mercy incarnate. Obeisance to you, O blue-throated lord. Be victorious, O lord releasing the devotee from worldly chaos. Hail to you, O Maheśvara, O personification of the greatest bliss. Obeisance to you, O holder of Gaṅgā, O lord of the universe, O Mṛḍa. O immutable one, obeisance to Lord Vāsudeva, to Saṁbhu. Bow to Śarva, Ugra, Garbha. Obeisance to the lord of Kailāsa. Protect me, O ocean of mercy, with your benign glance. Do not mind my conduct. Kindly protect me, O Hara.

Śrī Sūta said:

29. On being eulogized thus, Mahādeva, the ocean of mercy, the lord of Umā, said thus to Sage Sucarita, O Brāhmaṇas.

Mahādeva said:

30. O Sage Sucarita, choose whatever you desire as your boon. It is to grant you the boon that I have come to this splendid and meritorious hermitage.

On being told thus, the sage spoke to Mahādeva, the storehouse of mercy:

Sucarita said:

31-33. O Moon-crested Lord, if you are pleased with me, I shall choose as boon what I desire. My body has been afflicted with old age. I am unable to go anywhere. I eagerly desire to take my holy bath in all the Tīrthas. Hence tell me the means of attaining that merit which a man obtains by taking the holy bath in all the Tīrthas.

Mahādeva said:

34-41. I shall invoke all the Tīrthas here on this Gandhamādana mountain that has been sanctified by Rāma's Setu.

After saying this, the excellent Lord Mahādeva invoked the Tīrthas on Mountain Gandhamādana to please the sage. Thereafter

Śaṅkara, the storehouse of mercifulness, said to Sucarita:

"O Sage Sucarita, this Tīrtha is destructive of all great sins. Since all the Tīrthas are present herein, it is remembered by the name Sarvatīrtha. Since all the Tīrthas have been drawn by me mentally, this Tīrtha will get the name *Mānasatīrtha*. It bestows worldly pleasures and salvation. Hence, O Sucarita, bathe here for the sake of immediate salvation. It has the refulgence on a par with a forest-fire to burn down all the masses of great sins. It is destructive of lust, delusion, fear, anger, greed, ailment, etc. It is the cause of immediate salvation without a perfect knowledge of Vedānta. It takes (the devotee) across the ocean of worldly existence full of crocodiles in the form of birth, death, etc. It is destructive of all the hells such as Kumbhīpāka, etc."

42. On being told thus by Śambhu, the enemy of Madana, O Brāhmaṇas, Sucarita took his holy bath in Sarvatīrtha in the presence of Mahādeva.

43. When Sucarita took his holy plunge and came out, he appeared to all the men extremely handsome and free from old age and grey hair.

44. On observing the handsome features of his own body, Sage Sucarita praised that Tīrtha. The other ascetics too praised it in diverse ways.

45-47. Thereafter, Mahādeva spoke to Sucarita: "O Brāhmaṇa Sucarita, stay on the banks of this Tīrtha. Take the holy bath regularly remembering me, the bestower of salvation. O excellent Brāhmaṇa, do not go to the Tīrthas in the other lands. Thanks to the glory of this Tīrtha, you will certainly attain me in the end. Others too, O Brāhmaṇa, who will take their bath here will attain me."

48-50. After saying this, Lord Īśa vanished there itself. After Rudra had vanished, Sage Sucarita lived for a long time on the banks of Sarvatīrtha. Strictly adhering to the observance of restraints, he regularly took his holy bath in the Tīrtha (named) Mānasa. At the end of the body (on death) he was liberated from all bondage. He attained Śaṅkara. By the power of Sarvatīrtha he attained Sāyujya.

51. Thus, O Brāhmaṇas, the glory and power of Sarvatīrtha has been recounted to you. He who reads this or listens to this, is liberated from all sins.

CHAPTER THIRTY

The Glory of Dhanuṣkoṭi

Śrī Sūta said:

1-3a. After taking the holy bath in the extremely sacred Sarvatīrtha, the man should go to Dhanuṣkoṭi[1] that is destructive of the sins of Brāhmaṇa-slaughter, etc.

Merely by remembering it, a man on the earth shall become liberated. Those who visit Dhanuṣkoṭi, take their bath in it and speak about it, never experience the tortures in the twenty-eight different Narakas (hells).

3b-8. The following are the twenty-eight Narakas:[2] Tāmisra, Andhatāmisra, Mahāraurava, Raurava, Kuṁbhīpāka, Kālasūtra, Asipatravana, Kṛmibhakṣa, Andhakūpa, Sandaṁśa, Śālmalī, Sūrmi, Vaitaraṇī, Prāṇarodha, Viśasana, Lālābhakṣa, Avīci, Sārameyādana, Vajrakaṇaka, Kṣārakardamapātana, Rakṣogaṇāśana, Śūlaprota, Vitodana, Dandaśūkāśana, one called Paryāvartana, Tirodhāna, Sūcīmukha, Pūyaśoṇitabhakṣa and Viṣāgniparipīḍana. O Brāhmaṇas, these are the group of hells twenty-eight in number.

9-11a. By taking the holy plunge in Dhanuṣkoṭi, O Brāhmaṇas, a man can avoid falling into these Narakas.

If anyone steals others' wealth or abducts their children or wives, he will be firmly bound by the noose of Kāla. He is cast into the dreadful Tāmisra Naraka and confined there for many years by terrible messengers of Yama.

If he takes his holy bath in Dhanuṣkoṭi, he is spared from being thrown into this hell.

11b-12. He who kills his master and enjoys his wealth, etc. is thrown into the hell Andhatāmisra, full of great miseries and sufferings. If he takes his holy bath in Dhanuṣkoṭi, he is not thrown into this hell.

---

1. Dhanuṣkoṭi: The place where Rāma destroyed his Setu with the tip of his bow at the request of Vibhīṣaṇa. The whole story of how and why Rāma destroyed his Setu is given in vv 69-78. Bath in Dhanuṣkoṭi saves a sinner from all hells (v. 9).

2. The number of hells varies in different Purāṇas. It is 28 here, 22 in BP 214.14. But the 28 is confirmed in this text elsewhere and also in AP 371.13, SP V.8.18. The names vary.

VV 9-49 give the list of the types of sins committed and the particular hell into which the sinner is thrown.

13-14. One who maintains his family members by harassing all living beings, leaves them here, and is certainly thrown into Raurava, full of great poisonous serpents, by the attendants of Yama. If he takes his holy bath in Dhanuṣkoṭi, he is spared from being thrown into that hell.

15-20. One who maintains only his body without (caring for) wives, children and others, is thrown into the dreadful hell Mahāraurava where he eats his own flesh. If he takes his holy bath in Dhanuṣkoṭi he is not thrown into that hell.

He who confines (encages) birds and other living beings is worthy of being censured more than Rākṣasas, because he is devoid of the least possible compassion. The followers of Yama throw him into hot boiling oil in Kuṁbhīpāka. If he takes his holy bath in Dhanuṣkoṭi, he is not thrown into that hell.

A mean man who harasses his mother, father and Brāhmaṇas, is thrown into Kālasūtra hell that extends to ten thousand Yojanas. O Brāhmaṇas, he is put in copper cauldrons heated by fire from below and the sun's rays from above. He is left there afflicted with hunger. If he takes his holy bath in Dhanuṣkoṭi, he is not thrown into that hell.

21-26. A man who transgresses the Vedic path and goes along a despicable path is cast into Asipatravana by the servants of Yama. But if he takes his holy bath in Dhanuṣkoṭi, he is not thrown therein.

If a king or a king's servant punishes anyone who should not be punished or if he gives corporal punishment to a Brāhmaṇa, O Brāhmaṇas, he is thrown into the dreadful hell Śūkaramukha. Like a sugarcane stem he is crushed in a machine. But if he takes his holy bath in Dhanuṣkoṭi, he is not cast into it.

A person who violently injures living beings who dedicate all their activities to God is thrown by the servants of Yama into the highly terrible (Naraka) named Andhakūpa. He is now tormented by those creatures that were previously tormented by him. In that hell with excessive darkness, he remains awake and wanders about without any pleasure. But if he takes his holy bath in Dhanuṣkoṭi, he is not cast into it.

27-29. If a person sits in a different row and eats vegetable dish, pulses, etc. or if a person deludedly takes food without performing the five great Yajñas, O Brāhmaṇas, he is thrown into the hell named Kṛmibhojana by the soldiers of Yama. He will be eaten by hundreds of worms. He will himself eat masses of worms. Then he will be transformed into a worm and stay there till all the sins are destroyed. But if he takes his holy bath in Dhanuṣkoṭi, he is not thrown into it.

30-35a. If any one takes away the wealth of a Brāhmaṇa either by way of stealth or by force, if a king or his officer takes away the wealth of others, he is put in the iron containers of fire and is extremely tortured by means of pincers. He is thrown into the terrible Naraka named Sandaṁśa. But if he takes the holy bath in Dhanuṣkoṭi, he is exempted from being thrown into it.

If a base man carnally approaches a forbidden woman, O Brāhmaṇas, or if a woman carnally approaches a forbidden man, he or she has to embrace a red-hot iron statue of the woman or the man (as the case may be) and remains like that as long as the stars and the moon (shine). They are thrown into the dreadful Naraka with plenty of thorns. If he (or she) takes his (or her) bath in Dhanuṣkoṭi, he (or she) is not thrown therein.

35b-36. A man who harasses all creatures with different kinds of torturing devices, is thrown into the dreadful Śālmalī hell full of thorns. If he takes his holy bath in Dhanuṣkoṭi, he is not thrown therein.

37-40. If a king or his attendant with heretic leanings were to break the bounds of morality, he is thrown into Vaitaraṇī. But if he takes his holy bath in Dhanuṣkoṭi he is not thrown therein.

A person who is defiled by contact with a Śūdra woman, who is devoid of cleanliness and the conduct leading to it, who is shameless, who has forsaken the Vedas and who is devoted to brutish activities, is cast into the highly despicable and hideous Naraka filled with putrefying faeces, urine, blood, phlegm, bile, etc. by the servants of Yama. If he takes his holy bath in Dhanuṣkoṭi, he is not thrown into it.

41-42. If a hunter were to kill or harass deer by means of stones or arrows, he will be hit and pierced in the other world by the servants of Yama with volleys of arrows. He is thrown into the Naraka named Prāṇarodha by the attendants of Yama. But if he takes his holy bath in Dhanuṣkoṭi, he is spared from being thrown therein.

43-44. A hypocrite who kills animals in Yajña ignoring the prescribed procedure, O Brāhmaṇas, is thrown into the Naraka Vaiśasa in the other worlds by the servants of Yama. He is pierced and torn by the soldiers of Yama after being thrown into the Naraka full of misery. But if he takes his holy bath in Dhanuṣkoṭi, he is not thrown therein.

45-49. A person who makes his own wife of the same (his own) caste drink semen is thrown into the Retaḥkuṇḍa ('pit of semen') and is compelled to drink semen. If he takes his holy bath in Dhanuṣkoṭi, he is not thrown therein.

A person who follows the path of robbers, administers poison and burns villages and one who takes away the wealth of a merchant, O excellent Brāhmaṇas, is thrown into the Naraka called Vajradaṁṣṭrāhika and kept there for a long time. But if he takes his holy bath in Dhanuṣkoṭi, he is exempted from being therein. If a man takes the holy plunge in Dhanuṣkoṭi, he can prevent his own fall into the other Narakas too in the other world. By taking the holy bath in Dhanuṣkoṭi, one gets the benefit of a horse-sacrifice.

50. He will acquire the knowledge of soul. He will directly attain the four varieties of salvation. His intellect never indulges in sinful activities. He will never have any misery.

51-55a. By taking the holy plunge in Dhanuṣkoṭi, the intellect becomes happy and perfect. By taking the holy plunge in Dhanuṣkoṭi, persons attain that benefit which is obtained by men by means of the gift of *Tulāpuruṣa*.

By taking the holy bath in Dhanuṣkoṭi a man obtains that merit which men acquire through the charitable gift of a thousand cows.

By taking the holy plunge in Dhanuṣkoṭi, a man instantaneously obtains whatever out of virtue, wealth, pleasure and salvation he wishes to have. Whether a person is defiled by the great sins or all the sins, O Brāhmaṇas, he is instantaneously purified by taking the holy plunge in Dhanuṣkoṭi.

55b-61. By taking the holy plunge in Dhanuṣkoṭi, men obtain wisdom, fortune, renown, riches, perfect knowledge, virtue, detachment and mental purity.

Ten thousand sins of Brāhmaṇa-slaughter, ten thousand sins of imbibing liquor, ten thousand sins of carnally approaching the wife of the preceptor, ten thousand sins of theft of gold and crores of the sins of having an association with these sinners—all these perish by taking the holy bath in Dhanuṣkoṭi.

O believers in Vedas, all the sins on a par with Brāhmaṇa-slaughter, with drinking of liquor, those that are on a par with the sin of carnally approaching the wife of the preceptor, those that are on a par with the theft of gold and the sins similar to the sin of associating with the sinners committing such sins—all these perish by taking the holy plunge in Dhanuṣkoṭi. No doubt should be entertained in what has been said before. I will place a red-hot axe at the tip of the tongue. There is no doubt about it. One who says that this is only *Arthavāda* (i.e. exaggerated expression of praise) will become a dweller in Naraka.

62-65a. He should be known as one of a mixture of castes. He is excluded from all holy rites. Alas, the foolishness of the people, O excellent Brāhmaṇas! Alas, the stupidity! Alas, the mental deficiency! Even when the Tīrtha named Dhanuṣkoṭi, which is destructive of all sins, which bestows non-dualistic knowledge on men, which yields worldly pleasures and salvation, which grants desired and desirable objectives always and which is destructive of ignorance, exists, people leave it off and resort to other places. Alas, the immensity of their delusion cannot be described by me!

65b-66. One who has taken the holy bath in Dhanuṣkoṭi need not be afraid of the god of Death. Those men who visit Dhanuṣkoṭi, those who take their holy bath there, those who eulogize, those who adore, touch and bow down to it, O eminent Brāhmaṇas, do not drink the breast milk of mothers (i.e. are liberated).

The sages said:

67-68. How did it (Tīrtha) acquire the name Dhanuṣkoṭi, O Sūta? Describe everything truthfully and in detail, O great sage.

On being asked thus by the residents of Naimiṣa, Sūta spoke to them again:

Śrī Sūta said:

69-72. After Rāvaṇa, the oppressor of the worlds, was killed in battle by Rāma, and Vibhīṣaṇa was installed as the king in Laṅkā, Rāma, the son of Daśaratha, went to Gandhamādana accompanied by Sītā and Lakṣmaṇa and surrounded by heroic monkeys, the chief of whom was Sugrīva. His wonderful feats were eulogized by Siddhas, Cāraṇas, Gandharvas, Devas, Vidyādharas, sages and celestial damsels continuously. With his bow gracefully held aloft, he resembled Śiva who destroyed the three Puras.

73. With the palms joined in reverence, Vibhīṣaṇa who was conversant with Dharma, requested the noble-souled Rāghava, the slayer of Rāvaṇa who was staying there:

74-75a."By this Setu of yours, O Rāma, all the kings superior in power may come to my city and harass me. Hence, O scion of the family of Raghu, break this Setu with the tip of your bow."

75b-76.On being requested thus by the descendant of Pulastya, Rāghava, the delighter of the members of the family of Raghu, destroyed his own Setu with the tip of his bow. Hence, O Brāhmaṇas, that Tīrtha became well-known thereafter as Dhanuṣkoṭi.

77. He who sees the line drawn with the tip of the bow of Śrīrāma never experiences the stay in the womb that involves a lot of strain and pain.

78. A line was drawn in the briny sea by Rāma with the tip of his bow. By seeing it one shall attain salvation. I do not know the (greatness of the) benefit of the holy bath.

79-81. Performing penance on the banks of Narmadā is destructive of great sins. Death on the banks of Gaṅgā is conducive to salvation. Charitable gift in Kurukṣetra purifies the sins of Brāhmaṇa-slaughter, etc., O Brāhmaṇas. The penance, the charitable gift and the death which men have at Dhanuṣkoṭi can destroy great sins, give salvation and accomplish all desires, O eminent Brāhmaṇas. There is no doubt about this.

82. A creature is oppressed by sins major and minor only as long as Rāmadhanuṣkoṭi, the bestower of salvation, is not seen (by him).

83. Of the person who visits Dhanuṣkoṭi, the knot (of *Avidyā*) in the heart is cut, all the doubts are cleared and all the sinful activities cease.

84-85. That very same line, the line made by Rāmacandra on the Setu on the southern sea for the welfare of Vibhīṣaṇa, with the tip of his bow, is the pathway to Kailāsa, is the road to Vaikuṇṭha and the world of Brahmā and the path to the heavenly world also. No doubt need be entertained in this matter.

86. A plunge in Dhanuṣkoṭi is on a par with Yajñas in regard to the merits and benefits. It is superior in merit to all the Mantras. It bestows the benefit of all charitable gifts.

87. In regard to the person who visits Dhanuṣkoṭi of what avail are the austerities that cause physical stress and strain to men? Of what benefit are the sacrifices, the Vedas and the scrip-

tures (to such a man).

88. If men have the opportunity to bathe in Dhanuṣkoṭi of Rāmacandra, of what use are the waters of Gaṅgā and Yamunā?

89. If a visit to Dhanuṣkoṭi of Rāmacandra can be made, why should the salvation after death at Kāśī be vainly sought by men?

90. There is no doubt about this that one will become poor by not taking a plunge in Dhanuṣkoṭi, by not observing fast for three days and by not giving away gold and cow (at Dhanuṣkoṭi).

91-92. Even by performing Agniṣṭoma and other Yajñas with plenty of monetary gifts, no man obtains that merit which one obtains by taking a bath in Dhanuṣkoṭi. It is true. I speak the truth. They know the Tīrtha named Dhanuṣkoṭi to be superior to all other Tīrthas.

93. There are ten thousand crores of Tīrthas on the earth, O excellent Brāhmaṇas; all of them are present in Dhanuṣkoṭi.

94-101a. All the following are always present in Dhanuṣkoṭi: eight Vasus, Ādityas, Rudras, Maruts, Sādhyas, Gandharvas, Siddhas, Vidyādharas and many other Devas.

In this Tīrtha Dhanuṣkoṭi, Brahmā is always present. Śiva, Viṣṇu, Umā, Lakṣmī and Sarasvatī also are always present here. By performing penance in Dhanuṣkoṭi, Devas and sages attained great Siddhis as a benefit thereof, O eminent sages.

A man who takes his holy bath there and offers libation to Pitṛs and Devas becomes liberated from all sins. He is honoured in the world of Brahmā.

A man who devoutly feeds one Brāhmaṇa here, attains infinite happiness in this world as well as in the other.

A man who does not subsist on greens, fruits and roots shall take his holy bath in Dhanuṣkoṭi for the purpose of achieving the benefit thereof. He who has no capacity to perform horse-sacrifice should take his holy bath in Dhanuṣkoṭi. Thereby he attains the benefit thereof.

101b-104. A Brāhmaṇa, a Kṣatriya, a Vaiśya or a Śūdra, O great sages, can avoid being born of despicable wombs, if he takes the holy bath in Dhanuṣkoṭi.

If a man takes the holy bath in Dhanuṣkoṭi in the month of Māgha when the Sun is in the Zodiac Capricorn, O Brāhmaṇas, I am not competent to describe his merit.

A man who takes the holy plunge in Dhanuṣkoṭi in the month of Māgha, O great sages, has really taken his holy bath in all the

Tīrthas including Gaṅgā. He shall attain eternal worlds as well as salvation.

105-106[1]. All the sins of a woman or a man incurred ever since her or his birth shall perish by taking the holy bath in the month of Māgha.

Just as Rāma, the scion of the family of Raghu, is the most excellent of all the Suras, so also Dhanuṣkoṭi is spoken of as the most excellent of all the Tīrthas.

107-114a. The holy bath there in the month of Māgha bestows all desired benefits. With great restraint the man should conquer his passions and take the holy bath in Dhanuṣkoṭi for all the thirty days in the month of Māgha for the prevention of rebirth.

One who takes only a single meal everyday, who has conquered anger and who takes the holy bath here in the month of Māgha, O eminent Brāhmaṇas, is liberated from the sin of Brāhmaṇa-slaughter.

The man should regularly take his holy bath in Dhanuṣkoṭi in the month of Māgha. At the end on the night of Śiva he should abstain from food and conquer his passions. He should perform the *Jāgaraṇa* rite at night. In every *Yāma* (i.e. three hours) he should perform a special worship of Rāmanātha, the great lord, in accordance with the injunctions. On the next day, at sunrise, he should take the holy plunge in Dhanuṣkoṭi. With great mental restraint he should take the holy baths in the other Tīrthas as well. He should then perform the daily round of holy rites. He should worship Rāmanātha according to his capacity, O excellent Brāhmaṇas. He should then feed Brāhmaṇas with cooked food and give them land, cows, gingelly seeds, foodgrains and monetary gifts according to his capacity. On being formally permitted by the Brāhmaṇas, he should take his food silently.

114b-117. To a person who performs thus, the great Lord Rāmanātha grants worldly pleasures and salvation after liberating him from all sins. Hence, by all means, O eminent sages, men desirous of salvation should take the holy bath in Dhanuṣkoṭi in the month of Māgha.

1. VV 105-114 describe the importance of taking bath at Dhanuṣkoṭi in the month of Māgha. The observance of Śivarātra (14th day in the dark half of Māgha) is described in vv 110-114.

O Brāhmaṇas, if a man takes the holy bath in Dhanuṣkoṭi in Setu at the time of the specific Yoga (astral conjunction) called *Ardhodaya*[1], his sins perish instantaneously. Holy bath during the specific Yoga called *Mahodaya*[2] here in also conducive to worldly pleasures and salvation.

118. If a man takes the holy bath during *Ardhodaya* and *Mahodaya* in Dhanuṣkoṭi, the three Devas Brahmā, Viṣṇu and Maheśvara come under his control.

119. The holy bath in Dhanuṣkoṭi during *Ardhodaya* and *Mahodaya*, O Brāhmaṇas, becomes the cause of the attainment of *Sāyujya*, even without the perfect knowledge of non-duality.

120. The holy bath there during *Ardhodaya* and *Mahodaya*, O Brāhmaṇas,(removes) the sins of sinners without expiatory rites. It has been spoken by Manu and other law-givers. It is true.

121-128a. If a man takes his holy bath here on the Setu in Dhanuṣkoṭi during *Ardhodaya* and *Mahodaya*, O Brāhmaṇas, he obtains the complete benefit of Yajñas without performing a Yajña. There is no doubt about it.

Even (the thousand-mouthed) Śeṣa is incompetent to recount the merits of that man who takes the holy bath here during solar and lunar eclipses.

Taking the holy plunge in Dhanuṣkoṭi during eclipses of the Sun and the Moon is mentioned as an expiatory rite for all the sins including that of Brāhmaṇa-slaughter.

The holy bath in Śrīrāmadhanuṣkoṭi during solar and lunar eclipses is said to be the bestower of *Sāyujya*. It yields the merit of (taking bath in) all the Tīrthas.

Men desirous of the benefit of worldly pleasures and salvation should take their holy bath here. Hence, O eminent sages, leave off everything and go to Dhanuṣkoṭi of great merit that gives the benefit of worldly pleasures and salvation. Go there and do offer rice-balls to Pitṛs.

128b-133. By offering rice-balls here Pitṛs will be contented for a period of a Kalpa.

---

1. When in the month of Pauṣa or Māgha, there is Amāvāsyā (New-Moon day) with Śravaṇa Nakṣatra and Vyatīpāta Yoga on Sunday, it is called *Ardhodaya Yoga.* (For details vide HD V, 1, pp. 261-62.)

2. If one requirement from Ardhodaya (viz. Pauṣa or Māgha Amāvāsyā, Śravaṇa Nakṣatra, Vyatīpāta, Sunday) is absent, it is called *Mahodaya Parva.*

"There is no doubt about this that one must strike when the army of the enemy is tired, frightened or engaged in taking food. It must be attacked at the time of marching out or entering the camp. All the armies must be assailed by the enemies when they are overcome with sleep at midnight, when they have set aside their weapons or when there is a split among the soldiers."[1]

After having taken this decision about the murder of sleeping warriors, that daring one, the son of Droṇa, wakened Bhoja and Kṛpa who were asleep on that night. After pondering for a short while, the son of Droṇa spoke to them thus:

Aśvatthāmā said:

58-60. King Suyodhana of great valour is dead. He, of good behaviour, has been killed by Pāṇḍavas of mean activities. The head of the king was kicked with his foot by the wicked Bhīma.

So, this night we will go over to the tent of the sons of Kuntī. With different kinds of weapons we shall kill them, when they are sound asleep.[2]

On hearing these words, O excellent Brāhmaṇas, Kṛpa said to him:

Kṛpa said:[3]

61-63. The massacre of sleeping persons is not a righteous act in the world. It is not approved. So also in the case of persons who have abandoned their weapons, chariots and horses. O dear one, listen to my words. Let this foolhardy activity be given up by you. We shall ask Dhṛtarāṣṭra and Gāndhārī, the chaste lady, as well as Vidura. We shall do what they ask us to do.

On being told thus, the son of Droṇa spoke to Kṛpa once again:

Aśvatthāmā said:

64-69. O my uncle, my father has been killed earlier in the battle fraudulently by Pāṇḍavas. This fact pricks and pierces all my vital parts.

How can I (quietly) hear the (boastful) words of Dhṛṣṭadyumna in the presence of all the people: "I am the slayer of Droṇa?" The

1. Cf Mbh, *Sauptika* 1.45-56.
2. Vide Mbh, *Sauptika*, Ch. 3.
3. VV 61-69 summarize Mbh, *Sauptika*, Chs. 4 and 5 up to v 37.

bounds of morality were broken by Pāṇḍavas first. In front of you all and all the kings my father who had cast off his weapons, was struck down by Dhṛṣṭadyumna. Similarly, Bhīṣma, the son of Śantanu, who had cast off his bow and had no other weapon was killed by Arjuna by keeping Śikhaṇḍin in front of him. Thus other kings too were killed by them fraudulently. In the same manner, I will carry out the murder of sleeping Pāṇḍavas at night.

70. After saying this, the son of Droṇa got into the chariot to which horses were yoked. Blazing with fury he went forward in the direction of his enemies.

71-76. As he went ahead, Kṛpa and Kṛtavarmā, both of them followed him. All of them went to their tent wherein all the people had gone to sleep.

After reaching the entrance of the tent the son of Droṇa stopped. At night he propitiated Mahādeva, the storehouse of mercy. From Mahādeva, the bestower of boons, he acquired a (bright) sword without impurities.[1] Then the son of Droṇa, the great warrior, asked Kṛpa and Kṛtavarmā to stand at the entrance and then he went within the tent. After the son of Droṇa had entered the tent, Kṛpa and Kṛtavarmā, the great archers, both of them stood alert at the entrance.

Then the extremely infuriated son of Droṇa seemed to blaze with his refulgence. Keeping the sword Vimala ('free from impurities') drawn, he wandered about in the tent at night. Then he slowly went to the tent of Dhṛṣṭadyumna.[2]

77. There Dhṛṣṭadyumna and others who had become weary and worn out were sound asleep with full confidence. They were surrounded by their respective soldiers.

78. After entering the tent of Dhṛṣṭadyumna, the son of Droṇa, conversant with missiles, looked closely at that exceedingly powerful (warrior) who was asleep on a splendid bed (with white bedsheet).

79-83. As he was sleeping the son of Droṇa kicked him furiously with his foot. On being kicked with his foot he woke up and got up from his bed. Thereupon, the hero saw the son of Droṇa standing in front of him. When he tried to get-up, the powerful son of Droṇācārya pulled him and dragged him by his hair. Then

1. Cf Mbh, *Sauptika* 7.66.
2. VV 76-88 summarize Mbh, *Sauptika* 8.17-132.

he hit him with both the hands and struck him down on the ground. On being thrashed and smashed by him, Dhṛṣṭadyumna became frightened. As he was blind with sleep and agonized by the kick, he could not move at all. The son of Droṇa trampled on his chest and fastened his neck by means of the bowstring. As he shouted and writhed with pain, he (Aśvatthāmā) killed him as though he was a beast. Similarly he killed all his soldiers.

84-88. He killed Yudhāmanyu, the exceedingly powerful Uttamaujas, the sons of Draupadī, the remaining warriors of Somakas, etc. With his sword he killed many others, the chief of whom was Śikhaṇḍin. Kṛtavarmā and Kṛpa killed all those soldiers who attempted to escape through the doorway because they were afraid of him (Aśvatthāmā). As the army was thus annihilated by those exceedingly powerful warriors, the tent became empty in an instant as the three worlds become a void at the time of the great deluge.

After killing everyone thus, the three (warriors) including the son of Droṇa came out of that tent. They were afraid of the sons of Kuntī. Because of their great dread, all of them swiftly fled to different places.

89-91. Then the son of Droṇa went to the charming banks of Revā, O Brāhmaṇas. Many thousands of sages, the expounders of the Vedas discussed many meritorious topics and performed excellent penance. The son of Droṇa went to the hermitages of those sages. The sages, the expounders of Brahman, knew the evil deeds of the son of Droṇa by the power of their Yoga. As soon as he entered (the hermitages) they spoke to him:

92-95. "O son of Droṇa, you are the basest of Brāhmaṇas. You are the sinner who killed sleeping warriors. Even by looking at you, we will become certainly fallen ones. Merely by talking to you we will incur ten thousand sins of Brāhmaṇa-slaughter. Hence, O vilest of men, get away from our hermitages."

The sages who were there said thus to the son of Droṇa, O Brāhmaṇas. On being told thus by the sages, the expounders of Brahman, the son of Droṇa became ashamed. He went away from that hermitage inhabited by the sages. In the same manner he went to the Tīrthas of great merit such as Kāśī, etc.

96. Everywhere he was censured by all the Brāhmaṇas of noble souls. With a desire to perform expiatory rites he sought refuge in Vyāsa.

97. He approached the great sage Dvaipāyana who was staying in Badarikā forest[1] and bowed down to him with great devotion.

98-99. Then Sage Vyāsa spoke thus to the son of Droṇācārya: "O son of Droṇa, get away at once from this hermitage. You have incurred great sin because of your evil deed of slaughtering sleeping warriors. Hence, if I were to converse with you I will incur great sin."

On being told thus, the son of Droṇa spoke these words to the sage:

Aśvatthāmā said:

100-102. O holy lord, I have been censured by all. Hence I seek asylum in you. If you also say thus who else shall be my refuge? O Brāhmaṇa, be merciful to me. Good people are compassionate to the wretched ones. O holy lord, lay down some means of expiation for me, to quell down the sin of slaughtering sleeping (warriors) since you are omniscient.

On being addressed thus by the son of Droṇa, Vyāsa meditated for a long time and spoke to him:

Vyāsa said:

103-107. No expiatory rite for the suppression of this sin has been laid down in the Smṛtis. Still I shall tell you the means of subduing this sin of yours. In the southern sea, on the meritorious Setu of Rāma, that bestows salvation, there is a great Tīrtha well-known as Dhanuṣkoṭi. It is highly meritorious, O son of Droṇa. It is destructive of great sins. It bestows heavenly pleasures and salvation to men. It purifies the sins of Brahmahatyā, etc. It is the most auspicious of all auspicious things. It bestows everything desired. It is the holiest of all holy things. It is the most excellent of all the Tīrthas. It dispels (the bad effects of) evil dreams. It is meritorious. It destroys the distress of Naraka.

108-112. It suppresses premature death. It increases the success of men. It removes poverty. It is the cause of increase in the life span of men. It bestows mental purity on men. It is the cause of

1. Vyāsa Āśrama is at Manal, a village near Badrinath in Garhwal in the Himalayas. (De 42).

the subjugation of the mind, sense-organs, etc.

Go to Dhanuṣkoṭi on the Setu of Rāma that bestows salvation, O son of Droṇa. Take your holy baths there continuously for a month. You will become purified immediately from the sin of slaughtering the sleeping (warriors). O son of Droṇa, carry out my suggestion quickly.

On being told thus by the great Sage Vyāsa, the son of Droṇa went to Rāmasetu and Dhanuṣkoṭi, the sanctifier. With the requisite rite of *Saṁkalpa* he took his bath continuously for a month.

113-114. He served (worshipped) Rāmanātha everyday during the three junctions (morning, noon and dusk). On the thirtieth day after taking the bath in the waters the son of Droṇa performed the Japa of the five-syllabled Mantra (*śivāya namaḥ*) at Dhanuṣkoṭi. On that day the son of Droṇa observed fast too.

115-116. In the night he remained awake in the presence of Rāmanātha. On the next day, he took his holy bath in Dhanuṣkoṭi along with the requisite *Saṁkalpa* rite. He served Rāmanātha after eulogizing him with great devotion. He danced in front of Śaṁbhu with tears of joy flooding (his eyes).

117. Then the delighted Lord appeared in front of him. On seeing Mahādeva Parameśvara he eulogized him:

The son of Droṇa said:

118-122. Obeisance to you, O lord of the chiefs of Devas. O merciful one! O Śaṅkara! O lord, your lotus-like feet are the raft for those who are sinking in the ocean of adversity.

O Mahādeva, O personification of compassion, O Dhūrjaṭi, O Nīlalohita, O Lord of Umā, O uneven (three)-eyed one, O moon-crested Lord, bow unto you.

O conqueror of Death, O three-eyed one, kindly protect me with your benign glance. Obeisance to you, to the Lord of Pārvatī. Hail to Śaṁbhu, the destroyer of the three Puras. Obeisance, obeisance to you, to the three-eyed one armed with the Pināka bow. O lord adorned with necklaces and other ornaments consisting of Ananta and other great serpents, O trident-bearing lord, obeisance to you. O Gaṅgādhara, O Mṛḍa, O immutable one, O lord, protect me compassionately from the cage of sins.

On being eulogized thus, the delighted Mahādeva said to the son of Droṇa:

Mahādeva said:

123-125. O Aśvatthāmā, the sin of slaughtering sleeping warriors committed by you has perished, because you have taken the holy plunge in Dhanuṣkoṭi. Choose your boon, O good performer of holy rites. When I am delighted, what is not accessible to men in all the worlds? Hence, choose what you desire from me now, O son of Droṇa.

On being told thus by Śaṁbhu the son of Droṇa spoke to Parameśvara:

126-128. "O Maheśvara, on seeing you I have become blessed and contented. To those devoid of merit your vision is unobtainable even in the course of a crore of births. Hence let my devotion to the lotus-like feet of yours be steady. O Śaṁbhu, grant me only this boon. Obeisance to you."

After saying "So be it" to the son of Droṇa, Maheśvara, the lord of Devas, vanished there itself even as the son of Droṇa was watching.

129-132. Aśvatthāmā too, O leading Brāhmaṇas, became rid of all his sins merely by taking his holy bath in Rāmacandra Dhanuṣkoṭi instantaneously. He was devoid of impurities. Ever since then all the great sages accepted the son of Droṇa, because he was pure, devoid of impurities and rid of all sins.

Thus, O Brāhmaṇas, how the son of Droṇa got rid of his sins, has been recounted to you. It was solely due to the glory of the holy bath in Rāmacandra Dhanuṣkoṭi.

He who reads this chapter or listens to it with mental purity and concentration, gets rid of all his sins here. He is honoured in the world of Śiva.

CHAPTER THIRTYTWO

The Glory of Dhanuṣkoṭi: Dharmagupta Gets Rid of his Madness

Śrī Sūta said:

1. I shall further recount the glory of Dhanuṣkoṭi, O residents of Naimiṣa forest, due to my respect for you.

2. There was a great king named Nanda, a descendant of the

lunar race. He righteously protected this earth extending up to the ocean.

3-8a. He had a son well-known by the name Dharmagupta.[1] Nanda entrusted his son with the burden of protecting the kingdom. He conquered his sense-organs and controlled his diet. He entered the penance grove.

When his father had gone to the penance grove, the king named Dharmagupta ruled the kingdom. He was fully conversant with holy rites and followed good policies and sound ethics. He worshipped Devas with Indra as their leader by means of Yajñas of many kinds. He gave wealth and many pieces of land to Brāhmaṇas. While he was administering the kingdom, all the people were engaged in their own duties. There were no harassments arising from thieves and others.

Once Dharmagupta mounted his excellent horse and entered the forest enthusiastically engaged in hunting, O prominent Brāhmaṇas.

8b-11. In that forest, all the directions were covered with tall trees of Tamāla (Indian cinnamon), Tāla (Palmyra), Hintāla (Phoenix trees), Kurava (Red Amaranth), etc. It was dreadful on account of lions and tigers. The humming sound of the inebriated swarms of bees spread everywhere in all directions. There were many lakes and tanks full of red, white and blue lotuses as well as lilies. It was (as if) adorned by ascetic-folk. While Dharmagupta, the king, was wandering through the forest, O Brāhmaṇas, night set in. The darkness thereof enveloped all the quarters.

12. After saying his Sandhyā prayers with strict observance of restraints in that forest, the king repeated the Gāyatrī Mantra, the mother of the Vedas.

13. As he was afraid of lions, tigers, etc. the king occupied a tree. Then a bear who was afraid of a lion came there.

14. The lion roaming about in the forest pursued that bear. The bear that was chased by the lion climbed on that (same) tree.

15. After climbing on the tree the bear saw that king of noble soul and great strength and valour seated on the tree.

16-18. On seeing the king the bear that had roamed about the forest spoke thus: "O great king, do not be afraid. I shall stay here

1. This Dharmagupta, the son of Nanda, is different from Dharmagupta, the son of King Satyaratha of Vidarbha, mentioned in *infra* iii.7.80,159.

for the night. A lion has come near the foot of this tree. He has great inherent strength. His body is very huge. He (i.e. his jaw) is full of great curved teeth. He is very terrible. You can sleep for half of the night protected by me first. Thereafter, O highly intelligent one, protect me when I sleep for (the remaining) half of the night."

19. On hearing these words of his, Nanda's son went to sleep. Then the lion spoke to the bear: "The king is asleep. Let him be pushed down."

20-23. The bear conversant with virtue spoke thus to the lion, O excellent Brāhmaṇas: "O king of beasts, wanderer over the forest, you do not know what is holiness and piety. Great pains and miseries befall those who betray confidence. Indeed the sin of those who are inimical to their friends is not destroyed even with ten thousand Yajñas. Somehow the means of expiation for Brāhmaṇa-slaughter and other sins can be had. But the sin of those who kill persons who trust, cannot perish even in the course of crores of births. O lion, I do not consider that Meru is the heaviest on the earth. I think that the person guilty of breach of faith is the most burdensome one in the world."

24. When this was spoken by the bear, the lion kept quiet. When Dharmagupta woke up, the bear went to sleep on that tree.

25-27. Then the lion said to the king: "Leave this bear to me." When this was spoken by the lion, the king unhesitatingly cast off that bear down to the ground, although he was asleep with his head placed on his own lap. Though dropped down by the king, the bear who stuck to the tree with his claws did not fall from the tree on the ground due to his merit. The bear approached the king and angrily spoke these words.

28-29. "I am born of the family of Bhṛgu. I can assume any form I wish. I have now assumed the form of a bear. Since you have dropped me down though I am sinless and was sleeping, O king, wander about as a mad person immediately after this (utterance of the curse to be a mad man quickly)."

30-37. After cursing the king, the sage then spoke to the lion: "Previously you were the great Yakṣa named Nṛsiṁha, a minister of Kubera. Once, accompanied by your wife you joyously indulged in sports near the hermitage of Gautama on the mountain Himavān. You were not aware that it was in the vicinity of the hermitage of Gautama. By chance, Gautama came out of his hermitage in order to bring sacrificial twigs. On seeing you naked he cursed you thus: 'Since you stayed naked in my hermitage, you will undoubtedly assume the form of a lion today.'

It was on account of this curse of Gautama that you became a lion previously. Formerly you were a Yakṣa and the minister of Kubera, named Bhadra. Indeed Kubera is righteous by nature. His servants too are like that. So why do you try to kill me, a sage living in the forest? O king of beasts, all this I know through meditation."

When this was said by Dhyānakāṣṭha (the sage in disguise), he left off his form of a lion immediately and re-assumed the divine form of a Yakṣa, the minister of Kubera. With palms joined in reverence he bowed down to Sage Dhyānakāṣṭha, and spoke thus:

38-41. "Today, O great sage, all those earlier incidents have been known by me. At the time of cursing, Gautama had indicated the termination too thereof: 'When you speak to Dhyānakāṣṭha in the form of a bear you will get rid of your leonine form.' Thus, O Brāhmaṇa, the great sage Gautama told me. Since my form of a lion has disappeared today, O great sage, I know you as the pure sage named Dhyānakāṣṭha who can assume any form as he pleases."

After saying thus, the eminent Yakṣa bowed down to Dhyānakāṣṭha. He then got into his excellent aerial chariot and went to the city of Alakā.

42-45. When the eminent Yakṣa had gone, the great Sage Dhyānakāṣṭha went about on the earth as he pleased, because his travel as he pleased was never impeded.

After Dhyānakāṣṭha, the sage who could assume any form he desired, had gone, Dharmagupta became mad as a result of the curse of the sage and went back to the city.

On seeing the king in the form of a mad man, the ministers brought him to his father on the beautiful and charming banks of Revā. To him they intimated the mental derangement of his son.

46. After coming to know of the actual state of his son, Nanda, his father, immediately went to Jaimini, taking his son with him. To him he recounted the details about his son from the beginning:

47-54a. "O holy Lord Jaimini, my son has turned mad. Tell me the means, O great sage, of dispelling his madness."

On being asked thus, Jaimini, the great sage, meditated for a long time. After meditating for a long time, he spoke to King Nanda: "Your son has become mad due to the curse of (Sage)

Dhyānakāṣṭha. I shall now tell you the means for liberating (him) from the curse. There is a very great Tīrtha well-known as Dhanuṣkoṭi in the southern sea on the meritorious Setu that is destructive of sins. It is the holiest of all holy things, the most auspicious of all that is auspicious. It is known through the Vedas. It is highly meritorious and purificatory of Brāhmaṇa-slaughter and other sins. O king, take your son there and bathe him. His madness will disappear instantaneously. There is no doubt about it."

On being told thus, Nanda bowed down to the great Sage Jaimini. He took his son with him and went to Dhanuṣkoṭi.

54b-60a. There he bathed his son along with the requisite observances of the rules and injunctions. Due to the holy plunge the son was immediately relieved of his madness. (Old King) Nanda too took his holy bath in Dhanuṣkoṭi with great devotion. The father stayed with his son there for a day. He adored Rāmanātha, the storehouse of mercy, the Lord with Goddess Aṁbā. Then Nanda took leave of his son and went to the forest for performing penance.

When the father had gone, O Brāhmaṇas, King Dharmagupta, the son, devoutly gave plenty of monetary gifts to Rāmanātha. He gave the Brāhmaṇas wealth, foodgrains and land. Thereafter, he went to his own city along with the ministers. He righteously administered his kingdom after getting rid of all oppressions. The extremely virtuous Dharmagupta ruled his hereditary kingdom, O Brāhmaṇas.

60b-65. Those men who are seized by wicked spirits and troubled by evil Planets or by ailments such as madness, epileptic fits, etc., O eminent Brāhmaṇas, become rid of them (their ailments) by taking the holy plunge in Dhanuṣkoṭi. It is true. I speak the truth. One who leaves off Dhanuṣkoṭi and goes to some other Tīrtha, abandons the cow's milk that he had already got and begs for the juice of *Euphorbia antiquorum* (Snuhīkṣīram), O Brāhmaṇas.

Men who repeat the word Dhanuṣkoṭi three times, O Brāhmaṇas, and take their bath in any water reservoir go to the region of Brahmā. Thus, O Brāhmaṇas, the splendid story of Dharmagupta has been recounted to you. Merely by listening to this, the sin of Brāhmaṇa-slaughter perishes. Other masses of sins such as the sin of stealing gold, etc. also perish.

CHAPTER THIRTYTHREE

The Glory of Dhanuṣkoṭi: Parāvasu Liberated from the Sin of Brāhmaṇa-Slaughter

Śrī Sūta said:

1-2. I shall further recount the glory of Dhanuṣkoṭi. It is very wonderful. It is a great secret. It is the sole thing that sanctifies all the worlds.

Formerly, a Brāhmaṇa named Parāvasu,[1] the most excellent one among those conversant with the Vedas, unknowingly killed his father and incurred the sin of Brāhmaṇa-slaughter. He took his holy bath in Dhanuṣkoṭi and instantly got rid of that sin.

The sages said:

3-4. How did Parāvasu kill his father previously, O Sūta? How did he get redemption, O sage, in Dhanuṣkoṭi? It behoves you to recount this to us who faithfully (listen to it).

Śrī Sūta said:

5. There was a king, a very powerful Emperor named Bṛhaddyumna. He righteously ruled the earth extending as far as the ocean.

6. He performed a sacrifice of long duration and worshipped Devas with Indra as their leader. The priest in his Yajña was Raibhya, an excessively righteous scholar.

7. He had two sons named Arvāvasu[2] and Parāvasu. They were masters of the Vedas with their six ancillary subjects. They were great experts in (the holy rites laid down in) Śrutis and Smṛtis.

8. They were proficient in the Vaiśeṣika system of philosophy, in Pūrva Mīmāṁsā, Sāṅkhya, Vedānta (Brahma Sūtras), Nyāya system, in the Yogic treatises and in the system of Grammar pro-

---

1. A son of Sage Raibhya, elder brother of Arvāvasu. The story given here is based on Mbh. *Vana* 138. The credit of his redemption from patricide by a bath in Dhanuṣkoṭi is the contribution of this Purāṇa to glorify the Tīrtha Dhanuṣkoṭi.

2. Arvāvasu: A famous sage, knower of Brahman (Mbh. *Anuśāsana* 150.30-32). Relieved his brother Parāvasu from the sin of patricide by his spiritual power (Mbh. *Vana*), not by bath in Dhanuṣkoṭi according to Mbh. He got spiritual power by propitiating Sun-god.

pounded by Pāṇini.

9-12. They were perfectly acquainted with the Smṛtis of Manu and others. They were masters of all scriptures. They were requested by Bṛhaddyumna[1] to assist in the Sattra (Yāga). On being permitted by their father Raibhya, the brothers who appeared like Aśvins in physical form, went to the Sattra of Bṛhaddyumna.

Raibhya remained in the hermitage along with the elder daughter-in-law. The two brothers went to the excellent Sattra of the king.

They performed the Yajña (Sattra) on behalf of King Bṛhaddyumna. Not a single slip did the brothers commit in the Sattra and in the holy rites with their subsidiary activities.

13-18. While the Sattra was being elaborately performed on behalf of King Bṛhaddyumna, all the sages invited by the king came there to witness it.

They were: Vasiṣṭha, Gautama, Atri, Jābāli, Kāśyapa, Kratu, Dakṣa, Pulastya, Pulaha, Sage Nārada, Mārkaṇḍeya, Śatānanda, Viśvāmitra, Parāśara, Bhṛgu, Kutsa, Vālmīki, Vyāsa, Dhaumya and many others.[2]

They came there surrounded by innumerable disciples and disciples' disciples.

On seeing them come, Bṛhaddyumna, the king, respectfully adored them with *Arghya* etc. Many kings accompanied by armies consisting of four divisions came there from different lands in order to witness the Sattra. They had brought with them gifts. Similarly many Vaiśyas and Śūdras too had come. People of all the four castes had arrived (then).

19. Religious students, householders, forest-dwellers and recluses came there to witness the Sattra of Bṛhaddyumna.

20-21. The excellent king honoured all of them befittingly. He gave cooked rice, ghee, sauce, etc. to all of them. He gave them garments, gold coins, many necklaces and jewels. Thus the king welcomed and entertained all those who had come for the Sattra.

22. At that time, O Brāhmaṇas, Arvāvasu and Parāvasu, the two sons of Raibhya, performed all the rites in connection with the sacrifice without any mistake.

---

1. A powerful king who employed the sons of Raibhya for his sacrifice (Mbh, *Vana* 138.1-2).

2. A traditional list of famous sages of old. They were not necessarily contemporaries.

23. On observing the skill of the sons of Raibhya, the sages, chief among whom was Vasiṣṭha, praised them nodding their heads in approbation.

24-27. After getting some rites performed at the end of the third Savana, O Brāhmaṇas, Parāvasu went to his hermitage to look after the duties at home. He went there without Arvāvasu in the evening. At that time, he saw his father Raibhya covered with deerskin, moving about in the forest. He was overcome with sleep. When there was blinding darkness at night, he suspected that a beast was about to rush at him in order to kill him. So Parāvasu killed his father in the great forest (mistaking him for a beast of prey).

28. It was with a desire to protect his body that his father was killed by the great sinner, but not with any other intention.

29. He came close to the person struck down and saw that it was his own father who was killed at night. With all sense-organs afflicted, he bewailed him.

30. Parāvasu performed all the obsequies for his dead father and returned to the Sattra of the king.

31. He reported everything done by him to his younger brother. On hearing that his father was dead, he too became grief-stricken.

32-35. The elder one then said to the younger one, O excellent Brāhmaṇas: "The great Sattra of King Bṛhaddyumna has begun. You are only a boy. You cannot by yourself bear the entire responsibility of the holy rite. Our father has been killed by me at night suspecting him to be a beast (of prey). Expiatory rite has to be performed for the purification of the sin of Brāhmaṇa-slaughter. O dear one, O my younger brother, perform those holy expiatory rites for my sake. I am capable of bearing the burden of the Sattra single-handed." On being told thus by his elder brother, Arvāvasu replied to him:

36. "O elder brother, let it be so. I shall perform the excellent holy rites for the purification of the sin of Brāhmaṇa-slaughter. You do bear the burden of the Sattra."

37-38. After saying thus to his elder brother, the younger brother went out of the chamber of the Sattra. After he had gone, the elder one performed all the rites of the Kratu. The younger one performed the expiatory rites for the sin of Brāhmaṇa-slaughter, O Brāhmaṇas, for a period of twelve years. Then he joyously returned to the place of the Sattra.

39-44. On seeing his brother, the elder one said to Bṛhaddyumna: "See here, the Brāhmaṇa-slayer Arvāvasu has come to your Sattra. O excellent king; expel him quickly from this Sattra. Otherwise you will lose the merit of the Sattra." On being told thus, he got him removed from the place of Sattra through his own servants.

While being expelled, Arvāvasu spoke to the king: "O sinless Bṛhaddyumna, this Brāhmaṇa-slaughter has not been committed by me. But, O lord, that murder of a Brāhmaṇa has been committed by my elder brother. It was for his sake that the expiatory rite for Brāhmaṇa-slaughter was performed by me."

Though he was told thus, the king expelled Arvāvasu from his Sattra at the instance of Parāvasu. He was condemned and reproached by the Brāhmaṇas and so he (Arvāvasu) quietly went to the forest.

45. Entering the penance grove filled with groups of ascetics, Arvāvasu performed a penance which is very difficult even for Devas to perform.

46-48. Performing the penance he worshipped Sun-god with mental concentration.[1] On account of his great penance, Sun-god became delighted in his mind. Bhāskara (Sun-god), the witness of all actions, the eye of the universe, the leader of all deities, appeared before him in a physical form, illuminating the surface of the earth by his own brilliance. Devas too appeared there with Indra at their head. O Brāhmaṇas, Indra and other Devas spoke thus to Arvāvasu:

49-56a. "O Arvāvasu, you are a *Pravara* (excellent man), on account of your penance and vow of celibacy, regular good conduct, learning and training in the Vedas and scriptural treatises. You were reproached and slighted much by Parāvasu. Still you suffered it patiently. You did not become angry with him. Since it was your elder brother who killed your father and you did not injure him at all, O highly intelligent one, since the expiatory rite for Brāhmaṇa-slaughter was performed by you on his behalf, we accept you and banish Parāvasu." After saying this, all those heaven-dwellers, the chief of whom was Indra, made Arvāvasu a *Pravara* and banished Parāvasu.

Again, keeping Sun-god in front of them the Devas including Indra said to Arvāvasu, "Choose your boon."

---

1. Vide ftn. 2, p. 209. Arvāvasu's propitiation of Sun-god has basis in Mbh, *Vana*.

He requested the Devas for the restoration of his father back to life and also making him and his father forget the slaughter. The Devas said "So be it" and added: "We shall grant you one more boon, O highly intelligent one, choose it."

56b-57a. On being told thus by the Suras, Arvāvasu spoke: "O heaven-dwellers, let my brother be free from the sin."

57b-61a. On hearing the words of Arvāvasu, the Devas spoke to him again:

"Since he has killed his father, a Brāhmaṇa, Parāvasu's is a great sin. If a man commits one of the five great sins, it cannot be dispelled by the expiatory rite performed by another. There is no redemption at all for one who kills his father or a Brāhmaṇa. Even by means of the expiatory rite performed by himself he has no redemption. Hence there is no redemption for your brother Parāvasu. Thus it is not possible for us to grant him freedom from the sins."

61b-71. Thereupon Arvāvasu spoke once again to the Devas, the leader among whom was Indra:

"Still, in view of your greatness and your favour, O excellent Devas endowed with mercifulness, do tell me how redemption can be had by my brother who has killed a Brāhmaṇa, i.e. my father."

On hearing these words of Arvāvasu the heaven-dwellers meditated for a long time. After coming to a decision they spoke thus:[1]

"We shall tell you the means that will dispel his sin. In the southern sea, on the meritorious Rāmasetu that bestows salvation, there is a Tīrtha well-known as Dhanuṣkoṭi. It yields salvation. It is destructive of the sins of Brāhmaṇa-slaughter, drinking liquor and stealing gold. It dispels the sins of defiling preceptor's bed as well as those of having dealings with great sinners. If a man takes the holy bath therein, even without any desire, it yields salvation. It dispels (the effects of) evil dreams. It is conducive to wealth. It destroys the distress of Narakas.

It helps in attaining Kailāsa and other regions. It grants the greatest of riches. It yields everything desired by men. It destroys indebtedness and poverty. By uttering the name*Dhanuṣkoṭi* three times it yields heavenly pleasures and salvation to men. It bestows great merits.

---

1. This glorification of Koṭitīrtha and its sanctifying efficacy are the additions of this Purāṇa.

If your elder brother Parāvasu goes there and takes his holy bath therein, he shall be liberated from the sin of Brāhmaṇa-slaughter at that very instant. This is a great secret means of expiation recommended by us."

After saying this to Arvāvasu, the Devas went to their own city.

72. Then Arvāvasu took his elder brother Parāvasu and went to Dhanuṣkoṭi, the bestower of salvation.

73. For the sake of purifying the sin, Parāvasu performed the *Saṁkalpa* rite on the Setu in accordance with the rules and took his bath in Dhanuṣkoṭi along with his brother.

74-75. When he took his bath and got up, an unembodied voice declared to him: "O Parāvasu, your sin of Brāhmaṇa-slaughter arising from the murder of your father, a Brāhmaṇa, has perished. The extremely dreadful sin of Brāhmaṇa-slaughter causing distress in Narakas has perished."

After saying this, the unembodied voice ceased.

76-77. Then, accompanied by his younger brother, O Brāhmaṇas, Parāvasu devoutly bowed down to Rāmacandra Dhanuṣkoṭi. Then they made obeisance to Rāmanātha Mahādeva with great devotion. Freed from his sins, O Brāhmaṇas, he went to the hermitage of his father.

78. At that time Raibhya got up from his state of a dead man. On seeing his sons come he became delighted in his heart. Therefrom he continued to live in his hermitage.

79. As Parāvasu's sin was now destroyed by his holy bath in Rāmacandra Dhanuṣkoṭi all the sages accepted him (received him cordially).

80. Thus the liberation of Parāvasu from the sin of Brāhmaṇa-slaughter has been recounted. His liberation from the sin merely on account of his holy bath in Dhanuṣkoṭi has been recounted to you, O eminent sages.

81. The sins of drinking liquor, etc. do perish by taking the holy plunge here. It is true. It is true. (I repeat) It is true. It is being declared by raising up the arms.

82-83. By taking the holy plunge here all the masses of great sins shall perish. If anyone reads this chapter on the liberation from the sin of Brāhmaṇa-slaughter, that sin of Brāhmaṇa-slaughter shall perish at the very instant. There is no doubt about this. Sins of drinking liquor, etc. shall also subside immediately.

CHAPTER THIRTYFOUR

The Glory of Dhanuṣkoṭi: Sumati's Liberation from Great Sins*

Śrī Sūta said:

1-4. I shall recount once again an ancient anecdote in praise of Dhanuṣkoṭi. It is (in the form of) a dialogue between a jackal and a monkey, O excellent ones.

Formerly, there was a jackal and also a monkey. Both of them could remember their previous births. In their previous human births they were friends. They were (re-)born in different species, namely, that of a jackal and that of a monkey. This jackal and the monkey again became close friends, O Brāhmaṇas.

Once, the monkey saw the jackal standing on a cremation ground. On seeing him at the cremation ground, he remembered his previous birth and so he spoke to the jackal thus:

The monkey said:

5. O jackal, what dreadful sin did you commit before (in your previous birth)? What is that sin whereby you eat dead bodies of foul-smelling and despicable nature on the cremation ground?

On being enquired thus by the monkey, the jackal spoke to him:

The jackal said:

6-12. In the previous birth, I was a Brāhmaṇa who had mastered the Vedas. My name was Vedaśarmā. I was a learned man conversant with all holy rites.

In that birth some money was promised by me to a Brāhmaṇa, but was not given to him. Hence, O monkey, I was born as a jackal. Therefore, I am now eating exceedingly despicable food like this.

Those wicked men who promise something but do not give the thing promised, O monkey, attain the exceedingly despicable species

---

* The object of this chapter and the next is to describe the efficacy of the Tīrtha in dispelling the following sins: (1) Backing out of a promise (of help, etc.), (2) Stealing, (3) The sin of Brāhmaṇa-slaughter, (4) Association with low-caste women, etc.

of a jackal.

If a man promises something but does not give it, whether small or big, all his hopes and ambitions shall perish like those of a eunuch, desiring to produce a child. After promising something to a Brāhmaṇa, O monkey, if anyone does not give the same, his merit acquired in the course of ten (previous) births perishes at that very instant. The sin that one incurs by not giving the thing promised, cannot be purified even by means of a hundred horse-sacrifices.

13-16. I do not know when this sin will perish. Hence the monetary gift promised should always be given by a learned man. By not giving after having promised once, one certainly becomes a jackal. Hence what is promised should be given by an intelligent and learned man.

After saying this the jackal asked the monkey again: "What sin has been committed by you whereby you are born a monkey? O monkey, you harass innocent birds of the forest. So tell me what that sin was, which has given you the state of a monkey."

On being told thus by the jackal, the monkey spoke to the jackal:

The monkey said:

17-21. In the previous birth I was a Brāhmaṇa known by the name Vedanātha. Viśvanātha was my father and Kamalālayā, my mother. O jackal, there was friendship between you and me even in the previous birth. You do not know everything. By the power of my merit, I know everything.

Formerly I had propitiated Lord Śiva by means of penance. With his favour I have acquired the perfect knowledge of the past and future even in the subsequent births.

O jackal, in that previous birth vegetable belonging to a Brāhmaṇa was taken away by me. I am born a monkey because of that sin. After experiencing the tortures of Naraka I am now born a monkey. The wealth of a Brāhmaṇa should never be taken away. If it is taken away, one will be cast into hell.

22. Thereafter, one will be born a monkey. There is no doubt about it. Hence the possession of a Brāhmaṇa should never be stolen by a learned man.

23-28. There is no greater sin than theft of a Brāhmaṇa's property.

A poison kills only him who drinks it. But the property of a Brāhmaṇa may burn one along with one's family.

The sinner who steals a Brāhmaṇa's property is cooked in the Kuṁbhīpāka hell. After experiencing the tortures of the hell, he is born in the species of monkey.

The wealth of a Brāhmaṇa should not be taken away. One must have forbearance in regard to them. Boys, poor people, wretched ones, those devoid of Vedic or scriptural knowledge—these Brāhmaṇas should not be despised. If they are infuriated, they are like fire.

O jackal, I have complete knowledge of the past and the future. But I don't have the knowledge of one thing—the means of purifying this sin.

Though you are capable of remembering previous births, you are not aware of the future tasks. Even in the matter of the past, your knowledge is restricted on account of obstacles. Hence you do not know the past or future entirely.

29. How long are we to experience this misery further, O jackal? Who will be our liberator from this sin?

30-32. While the monkey and the jackal were conversing thus, O Brāhmaṇas, due to the previous merits, the highly refulgent sage named Sindhudvīpa[1] came there by chance. He had applied Bhasma all over the body. There were Tripuṇḍra marks on his forehead. Rosaries of Rudrākṣa beads were his ornaments. He was engaged in repeating the names of Śiva.

On seeing the sage named Sindhudvīpa, the jackal and the monkey became delighted. They bowed down to him and asked him thus:

The jackal and the monkey said:

33-36. O holy lord conversant with all pious rites, O great sage Sindhudvīpa, do save us. Repeatedly look at us mercifully, joyously. Tell us that means whereby the state of being a monkey and a jackal may be dispelled. Indeed you are the most excellent one among meritorious persons. Good people always accord protection to the helpless, to the wretched, to the ignorant, to children and to people distressed on account of ailments. They are merciful. They do not expect any return (for their services).

* * *

1. A royal sage who attained Brāhmaṇahood by his penance at Pṛthūdaka (Mbh, *Śalya* 39.37). This famous name is connected with this story.

On being addressed thus by those two, the great sage Sindhudvīpa meditated mentally for a long time and spoke to the monkey and the jackal:

Sindhudvīpa said:

37-42. O jackal, O monkey, I know both of you very well. O jackal, in your previous birth you were a Brāhmaṇa named Vedaśarmā. After promising a Brāhmaṇa an *Āḍhaka* of food-grains, it was not given by you. On account of that sin, you are born a jackal.

You too, O monkey, were a Brāhmaṇa previously. Your name was Vedanātha. Vegetable was stolen from the house of a Brāhmaṇa by you. Hence you are born a monkey instilling fear in all birds.

I shall recount the means of subduing your sins. Both of you do go quickly to Rāmadhanuṣkoṭi in the southern sea. Take your holy bath here. Thereby, you will become liberated from your sins.

Formerly due to his association with a Kirāta (hunter) woman, the Brāhmaṇa Sumati[1] became addicted to liquor. He took his holy bath in Dhanuṣkoṭi and was liberated from his sin.

The jackal and the monkey enquired:

43-44. Whose son was Sumati? How did he become a drink-addict? How was he attached to a Kirāta woman, O highly intelligent Sindhudvīpa, kindly describe this in detail to us.

Sindhudvīpa said:

45-47. In the land called Mahārāṣṭra, there was a certain Brāhmaṇa who was a devout believer in Veda and God. He was well-known as Yajñadeva. He was a master of the Vedas and their ancillaries (Vedāṅgas). He was compassionate. He was hospitable to guests. He was a worshipper of Śiva and Nārāyaṇa.

That Yajñadeva had a son named Sumati. He abandoned his parents and his chaste wife and went away to Utkala land (Orissa), being devoted to a band of lecherous vulgar fellows.

48. A certain Kirāta woman who lived in that land enchanted all the youths. She used to tempt young men and seize all their

1. This Sumati-legend is a contribution of this Purāṇa. This Sumati is not known to other Purāṇas (PE 763).

riches. This went on for a long time.

49-52. Sumati, the base Brāhmaṇa, went to her house. That Kirāta woman did not welcome Sumati, a penniless Brāhmaṇa.

Although expelled by her, Sumati was excessively enamoured of her. He was eager to have a physical union with her. He stole much wealth from various places and handed it over to her regularly. Thus he began to have sexual dalliance with her for a long time. He used to take his food in her house. He used to drink liquor along with her from the same goblet. Thus, addicted to sensual pleasures, he sported with her for a long time. He never cared to remember his parents and wife.

53. Once he went in the company of Kirātas to commit robbery. The Kirātas went over to the land of Lāṭas (Southern Gujarat) for plundering their wealth.

54. He too adopted the guise of Kirātas. With a sword in his hand, he daringly entered the house of a certain Brāhmaṇa in order to take away the wealth by stealth or force.

55. That rash daring man killed the Brāhmaṇa, the master of that house, with his sword, took away a lot of wealth and went to the abode of the Kirāta woman.

56-57. As he went along, the dreadful Brahmahatyā (the ogress created by the sin of Brāhmaṇa-murder) closely followed him. She had red hair. She was exceedingly terrible. She was clad in blue robes. She roared and laughed boisterously making heaven and earth tremble. Pursued by her (the Brāhmaṇa Sumati) wandered all over the earth.

58. Wandering over the entire earth thus, O jackal, O monkey, once Sumati entered his own village in great fear.

59. Followed by Brahmahatyā, he became frightened and went towards his house. Chasing him, Brahmahatyā too entered the house along with him.

60. Sumati sought shelter in his father shouting "Save me, save me". Saying "Do not be afraid", the father attempted to save him. At that time Brahmahatyā spoke thus to his father.

Brahmahatyā said:

61-65. Do not give shelter to him, O Yajñadeva, O excellent Brāhmaṇa. He is a liquor-addict, a thief, a Brāhmaṇa-slayer, antagonistic to his own father and mother, a deserter of his wife and a great sinner. He is defiled on account of his contact with a Kirāta woman. I will not let him go, O Brāhmaṇa.

If you welcome and accept this son of yours, a very great sinner, O Brāhmaṇa, I will devour your wife, the wife of this son, you and your son as well as your entire family. Hence abandon this son. If you leave off this son of yours, I will spare you all now.

"O highly intelligent one, it does not behove you to destroy the entire family on account of one." On being told thus by Brahmahatyā, Yajñadeva said to her:

Yajñadeva said:

66. Filial affection compels me. How can I abandon him?

On hearing the utterance of the Brāhmaṇa, Brahmahatyā spoke to him:

Brahmahatyā said:

67-69. This son of yours has fallen down. He has been excluded from the four castes and stages of life. Do not be affectionate towards this son. His very sight is despicable.

After saying this, even as Yajñadeva was looking on, Brahmahatyā struck his son named Sumati with her palm.

Exclaiming "O father! O father!" he repeatedly wept to his father.

70-71. The father, the mother and the wife of Sumati cried then. In the meantime, as good luck would have it, Durvāsas, the Yogin born of Śaṅkara's part, came there, O jackal, O monkey.

On seeing that sage, the incarnation of Rudra, he bowed down to him with devotion. Yajñadeva sought refuge in him and requested for the same on behalf of his son.

The father said:

72-77. O Durvāsas, you are a great Yogin. You are directly born of a part of Śaṅkara. Persons without merit cannot have your vision.

This son of mine has become a Brāhmaṇa-slayer, a drink-addict and a thief. Brahmahatyā is present here. She has come to strike him. Tell me that means whereby my son shall become liberated from the great sins and also how this dreadful Brahmahatyā shall be quickly destroyed. Have pity on my son.

78. On being told thus, Durvāsas, born of a part of Śaṅkara, meditated for a long time and spoke to the excellent Brāhmaṇa Yajñadeva:

Durvāsas said:

79. O Yajñadeva, excessively grave sins have been committed by your son. Even by ten thousand expiatory rites his sin cannot be subdued.

80-83. Still, O Brāhmaṇa, I shall suggest an expiatory rite for suppressing the sin of your son. Listen to it without your mind straying elsewhere. If this son of yours takes his holy bath in Śrīrāmadhanuṣkoṭi in the southern sea, he shall be liberated from his sin instantly.

A Brāhmaṇa named Durvinīta took his holy bath there, O excellent Brāhmaṇa, and was at the same instant liberated from the sins of carnally approaching the wife of his preceptor.

This Dhanuṣkoṭi of Rāghava, Hari, himself shall destroy the mass of sins of your son merely by taking the holy bath.

CHAPTER THIRTYFIVE

The Glory of Dhanuṣkoṭi: The Jackal and the Monkey Liberated

Yajñadeva said:

1-2. O Sage Durvāsas, O highly intelligent one, O sage very clever in matters remote and proximate, who was this person named Durvinīta[1] who carnally approached the wife of his preceptor? Whose son was he? How did that Brāhmaṇa instantly get rid of

1. This story is a contribution of this Purāṇa to show how this Tīrtha absolves a person of the worst immoral acts. This Durvinīta is untraced in Mbh, VR, PI and PE.

the sin arising from sexual union with the wife of his preceptor by taking the holy bath in Dhanuṣkoṭi? It behoves you to recount this in detail to me, as I listen to it attentively.

Durvāsas said:

3-8a. Formerly, there was a Brāhmaṇa of vast learning named Idhmavāha in the land of the Pāṇḍyas. His wife was Ruci. He had a son named Durvinīta. Even while the son was only a child, the father died. So, Durvinīta performed the obsequial rites of his father and stayed for some time in the house with his widowed mother.

For twelve years there was no rain, and thus a great famine spread in the land. So he went to another land along with his mother. He came to Gokarṇa where there was plenty of food grains. There he stayed with his widowed mother for a long time.

8b-13. After the lapse of a long time, Alas! Durvinīta became more and more deluded in his intellect as a result of his sinful deeds of previous births. On account of lustful attachment, his mind went astray. He was assailed by the arrows of Kāma. Even as his mother went on protesting "Do not, do not" this sinner violently pulled her down. Lustful and deluded he had a sexual union with her, O excellent Brāhmaṇa.

After the discharge of the seminal fluid, Durvinīta became sad. He pondered over his sin and cried bitterly. He was extremely grief-stricken. He thought thus, 'Alas! I am the worst one among great sinners. I have committed a great sin, because under the influence of passion (Kāma) I have had sexual union with my own mother.' After thinking thus, he went to sages. Condemning himself, he spoke thus to the sages:

14-19. "O Brāhmaṇas, tell me the means of expiation for the sin of carnally approaching the wife of the preceptor. Do have pity on me. O Brāhmaṇas, conversant with the principles of scriptural texts, if I can have redemption by dying, I shall undoubtedly die. Whatever atonement is suggested by you, O Brāhmaṇas, whether death or anything else, I shall carry it out. It is true."

On hearing these words of his, some eminent sages, kept quiet. They came to the decision, 'Conversation with this fellow will bring about sins (to them).' So some sages kept quiet. Some sages shouted: "You are vicious. You have carnally approached your own mother. You are the worst among great sinners. Go away. Go away."

Those excellent Brāhmaṇas said these and many other similar words. The merciful, omniscient Kṛṣṇadvaipāyana who was a storehouse of mercy prevented them and spoke to Durvinīta:

20-26. "Go immediately to Dhanuṣkoṭi on Rāmasetu, along with your mother. When the Sun is in the Zodiac Capricorn in the month of Māgha, take your holy bath there along with your mother. There should be no break in the middle of the month. You should conquer the sense-organs and anger. You must avoid doing wrong to others. You must observe fast for the whole of the month. You will be purified of the sin of carnally approaching the wife of the preceptor. There is no sin which does not perish by the holy bath in the Setu. Dhanuṣkoṭi is praised in Śrutis, Smṛtis and Purāṇas as destructive of the five (great) sins.

Hence go quickly to Dhanuṣkoṭi along with your mother. O Brāhmaṇa, treat my words as authoritative like the words of the Vedas.

Even crores of great sins are not worthy of serious consideration of the person who has taken his holy bath in Śrīrāmadhanuṣkoṭi. O son of a Brāhmaṇa. Other means of atonement have been mentioned in Manusmṛti, etc. Therefore, go to Dhanuṣkoṭi that is destructive of great sins."

27-31. On being told thus by Vyāsa, O excellent Brāhmaṇa, Durvinīta bowed down to Vyāsa and left for Dhanuṣkoṭi along with his mother.

When the Sun was in the Zodiac of Capricorn in the month of Māgha, he observed fast continuously for a month along with his mother. He conquered his sense-organs and anger. He took his holy bath in Śrīrāmadhanuṣkoṭi with due performance of the rite of Saṁkalpa. He bowed down to Rāmanātha with devotion three times (everyday).

At the end of the month he performed the Pāraṇā rite (i.e. breaking the fast) and became purified in intellect. Accompanied by his mother he came back to Vyāsa in order to intimate to him the details. After bowing down to Vyāsa, Durvinīta spoke these words:

Durvinīta said:

32-34. O holy Sir, O ocean of mercy, O Dvaipāyana the Great

One, thanks to your mercifulness. I took my holy bath along with my mother in Rāmadhanuṣkoṭi in the month of Māgha. I carefully observed fast for the whole month. I bowed down to Maheśvara regularly.

Henceforth, O holy lord Vyāsa, fond of your devotees, what should be done by me? O sage, instruct me in this regard accurately.

On hearing these words of Durvinīta, sage Vyāsa who was a part of Nārāyaṇa, spoke to Durvinīta:

Vyāsa said:

35-40. O Durvinīta, your sin resulting from your union with your mother has gone today. The sin of your mother too arising from her union with you has perished. In this matter no doubt should be entertained. It is the truth that has been mentioned by me.

Your kinsmen, the folks connected with you and the other Brāhmaṇas—all these will accept you, O Durvinīta, along with your mother, due to my favour. You are pure now due to your holy plunge in Dhanuṣkoṭi.

Take a wife unto you and perform the holy rites of a householder. Avoid injuries to living beings. Resort to the eternal virtue. Serve the good and noble people always with a mind endowed with devotion. Do not eschew the daily rites, the chief of them being the Sandhyā prayers. Control the sense-organs. Worship Hara and Hari.

41. Do not speak ill of others. Do not be jealous at any cost. Do not be sad and aggrieved on seeing the prosperity of another man. It is futile.

42-48. Look at the wives of others always as though they were your mother. Never forget the Vedas that you have learned. Do not insult guests. Perform the Śrāddha rite on the day of the Pitṛs. Do not slander others even in your dreams. Read Itihāsas, Purāṇas, ethical treatises, Vedānta and Vedāṅgas. Repeat the names of Hari and Śaṅkara without hesitation and shyness. Apply Tripuṇḍra marks and smear the whole body with Bhasma repeating the Mantras of the Jābāla Upaniṣad. Always wear Rudrākṣa beads. Be devoted to the injunctions regarding cleanliness and good conduct. With Tulasī and Bilva leaves, worship Nārāyaṇa and Hara once, twice or thrice everyday.

Always eat the *Naivedya* food mixed with Tulasī leaves and sprinkled with the water with which the Lord's feet have been washed. Eat the *Naivedya* in front of the deities, Śaṁbhu and Nārāyaṇa. Perform the *Vaiśvadeva* rites and oblations for the purity of the cooked food.

49-54. Propitiate eminent ascetics devoted to Brahman with cooked foods when they visit your house. Similarly serve other old people, helpless persons, sick ones, religious students, etc.

Render service to your mother. Be devoted to religious meditation. Meditate upon the deities of the Mantras and perform the rite of Japa of the five-syllabled great Mantra (*namaḥ śivāya*) along with (preceded by) *Praṇava* (Oṁ) and also the eight-syllabled Mantra (*oṁ nārāyaṇāya namaḥ*) as well as other Mantras, O Brāhmaṇa, with purity (of mind and body).

Similarly always perform other holy rites prescribed in the Smṛtis. If you carry out all these things, you will attain salvation on death.

On being told thus by Sage Vyāsa, Durvinīta bowed down to him. After performing everything told by him, he attained salvation on death.

His mother too died in due course. Due to her holy plunge in Dhanuṣkoṭi, she attained the greatest salvation without any return to the earth or rebirth.

Durvāsas said:

55-56. Thus, O Yajñadeva, the salvation of Durvinīta and his mother, due to the holy bath in Dhanuṣkoṭi, has been recounted by me. You too, O Brāhmaṇa, take this son of yours for the sake of the purification of his sin of Brāhmaṇa-murder, and go to Dhanuṣkoṭi, the bestower of salvation.

Sindhudvīpa said:

57. On being advised thus by Durvāsas, Yajñadeva took his son and went to Rāmadhanuṣkoṭi, the bestower of salvation.

58. After going there, O jackal, O monkey, that Brāhmaṇa stayed there for six months with his son observing all restraints and curbs.

59. He took his holy bath in Dhanuṣkoṭi for six months along with his son. At the end of the six months, an unembodied voice spoke to Yajñadeva:

part of his Brāhmaṇahood is lost undoubtedly.

If the same continues for three days third (one-fourth) part is destroyed. There is no doubt about it. On the fourth day of this association, the final fourth part certainly perishes.

Beyond this (period) if one shares with them the same bed or seat or takes food with them, one too incurs great sins and shall become a sinner on a par with them. Thus, O Brāhmaṇas, Durācāra became bereft of Brāhmaṇahood. He was seized by a powerful and dreadful vampire.

14-20. Excessively harassed by that vampire, O Brāhmaṇas, he became helpless. He wandered from land to land and from one forest to another. Due to the previous merit, that Brāhmaṇa went to Rāmacandra Dhanuṣkoṭi that is destructive of great sins. He was still seized and pursued by that evil spirit. The Vetāla made him take his plunge in the waters of Dhanuṣkoṭi. Forced to enter the water of Dhanuṣkoṭi by that Vetāla, he came out immediately and became free from the Vetāla.

Having got up from the waters of Dhanuṣkoṭi, he regained normalcy and thought thus: 'What is this land on the seashore? I resided on the banks of Gautamī. How did I happen to come here?'

Agitated by these thoughts, he approached the noble-souled Dattātreya, an excellent Yogin, a resident of Dhanuṣkoṭi, and bowed down to him. Durācāra then spoke to him:

21-27. "I do not know, O holy lord, what this land is. Do tell me now. I am called Durācāra, a resident of (a place on) the banks of Gautamī. Kindly tell me, O Brāhmaṇa, how I happened to come here."

On being asked thus by Durācāra, that sage of good holy rites meditated for a short while. That sage, the storehouse of mercy, said to Durācāra: "Formerly you associated with great sinners. So your Brāhmaṇahood was lost. Hence a Vetāla seized you. Possessed by him, you became helpless and confounded in intellect and came here. The Vetāla made you take the holy plunge in the waters of Dhanuṣkoṭi. Solely because of your bath therein you were liberated from the sin. If men take their holy bath in the meritorious Dhanuṣkoṭi, all masses of five types of their sins perish. By the holy plunge in Rāmacandra Dhanuṣkoṭi your sin of association with great sinners has been absolved.

28-32. Since it (your sin) perished, the Vetāla too left you and got perished. The Vetāla that caught hold of you was a Brāhmaṇa formerly. He did not joyously perform the Mahālaya rite of the Pitṛs in accordance with the Pārvaṇa injunctions in the dark half of the month of Bhādrapada. Therefore, he was cursed by his Pitṛs and he became a Vetāla. Merely by visiting Dhanuṣkoṭi, he cast off his Vetālahood and attained the world of Viṣṇu.Thus those who, out of extreme greed, do not perform the Mahālaya rite of their Pitṛs in the dark half of the month of Bhādrapada, shall certainly become Vetālas possessed of great covetousness. There is no doubt about this.

33-34a. Hence, those who feed Brāhmaṇas, the knowers of the Vedas, according to their capacity with *Mahānna* ('great cooked rice') at the time of Mahālaya in the dark half of the month of Bhādrapada, never meet with adversity and mishap.[1]

34b-36. A man who, in accordance with his capacity, feeds one, two or three Brāhmaṇas in the Mahālaya rite during the dark half of the month of Bhādrapada, will never have misfortune.

This Brāhmaṇa did not duly adore the Pitṛs in the month of Bhādrapada. Hence he became a Vetāla who seized you when you were a sinner.

37-38. The period beginning with the month of Bhādrapada and ending with the Zodiac Scorpio (*Vṛścika*) has been said to be the period of Mahālaya by the sages who see the truth.[2]

The period of the month of Bhādrapada is particularly held sacred. There, O Durācāra, the dark fortnight is specially sacred (for rites of Pitṛs).

39-43a. If a man devoutly performs Mahālaya Śrāddha on the first *tithi* (day)[3] in that splendid dark fortnight, Lord Pāvaka (Fire-god), the sanctifier of all, becomes pleased with him. He attains the world of Fire-god and rejoices with Fire-god himself. To him Fire-god grants all prosperity. If any man does not perform Mahālaya

---

1. In vv 33ff the author discusses an important topic called *Mahālaya Śrāddha*. This Śrāddha is performed in the dark half of the month of Bhādrapada on the *tithi* (day) on which one's father passed away. The topic is discussed here and later in SkP VI.216 and VII.1. PdP (*Pātala* Ch. 101), *Bhaviṣya* I.183 and Nibandha writers like Aparārka deal with this.

2. There is a difference of opinion about the exact period about this Śrāddha (*vide* HD IV, 531-32 and Notes 1189, 1190).

3. VV 39-136 describe the importance and efficacy of performing Mahālaya Śrāddha on each *tithi* in the dark half of Bhādrapada.

Śrāddha rite on the first day, Fire may destroy his house, fortune, fields, etc. If a Brāhmaṇa, conversant with the Vedas, takes food on the first day, the Pitṛs become contented for ten thousand Kalpas.

43b-48a. If any man devoutly performs Mahālaya Śrāddha on the second day, Lord Īśvara, the lord of Goddess Bhavānī, becomes pleased with him. He attains Kailāsa and rejoices with Śiva. The delighted Maheśvara grants him vast wealth. If any man does not perform Mahālaya (Śrāddha rite) on the second day, the infuriated Śaṁbhu destroys his Brāhmaṇical splendour. He will give him the Narakas of Raurava and Kālasūtra.

If a Brāhmaṇa, well-versed in the Vedas, takes food in the Mahālaya rite on the second day, the Pitṛs become satisfied for twenty thousand Kalpas. With the favour of the Pitṛs his progeny flourishes.

48b-52. If any man devoutly performs Mahālaya Śrāddha rite on the third day, Lord Kubera, the lord of wealth, the guardian of the quarters, becomes pleased with him. Mahāpadma and other treasures come under his control. The three Devas, Brahmā, Viṣṇu and Śiva, become his followers.

If any man does not perform Mahālaya rite on the third day, the lord of wealth, Kubera, takes away his wealth instantly. He gives him poverty involving many miseries.

If any man performs Mahālaya rite on the third day, his Pitṛs become delighted for thirty thousand Kalpas.

53-57a. If a man devoutly performs Mahālaya Śrāddha on the fourth day, Lord Heraṁba, the son of Pārvatī, becomes pleased with him. With the favour of the Elephant-faced Lord, all his obstacles perish. If any man does not perform the Mahālaya Śrāddha rite on the fourth day, Lord Vighneśa always puts obstacles before him. He falls into the Naraka named Caṇḍakolāhala.

If a person performs Mahālaya Śrāddha rite on the fourth day, the Pitṛs become delighted for forty thousand Kalpas. To the performer of Śrāddha, they grant many sons.

57b-60. If any one does not devoutly perform the Mahālaya Śrāddha rite on the fifth day, Goddess Lakṣmī abandons his abode. A-Lakṣmī, the creator of quarrels, appears in his house.

If any man performs the Mahālaya Śrāddha rite on the fifth day, the Pitṛs become contented for fifty thousand Kalpas. On being propitiated, they grant him an unbroken line of progeny. Pārvatī becomes pleased with him and grants great riches.

61-62. If a man performs Mahālaya Śrāddha rite on the sixth day, the Six-faced Lord, the son of Pārvatī, becomes pleased with him. With the favour of the Six-faced Lord, his sons and grandsons are never harassed by evil Planets and evil spirits that torment children.

63-66. If a man does not devoutly perform Mahālaya Śrāddha rite on the sixth day, Lord Skanda Mahāsena shall undoubtedly become adverse to him. His progeny will perish soon after coming out of the womb. It is always troubled by the evil spirits such as Pūtanā, etc. He falls down into the Naraka called Vahnijvālāpraveśa.

If a person sincerely and faithfully performs Mahālaya Śrāddha rite on the sixth day, the Pitṛs become contented for sixty thousand Kalpas. They grant him sons and vast wealth.

67-72a. If a man performs Mahālaya Śrāddha rite on the seventh day, Sun-god with golden hands (rays) becomes pleased with him. With the favour of Sun-god he shall be free from ailments and be strong in every limb. The Golden-rayed Lord becomes delighted in his mind and grants to the performer of Mahālaya Śrāddha gold with his hand himself.

If any person does not devoutly perform Mahālaya rite on the seventh day, he is oppressed day and night by tuberculosis and other ailments. He falls into the Naraka named Tīkṣṇadhārāstraśayyā.

If a man devoutly performs Mahālaya Śrāddha rite on the seventh day, his Pitṛs become pleased for seventy thousand Kalpas. The groups of Pitṛs shall always grant him unbroken line of progeny.

72b-78. If a man performs Mahālaya Śrāddha rite on the eighth day, Śaṅkara, the conquerer of the god of Death, who is clad with elephant's hide, becomes pleased with him. With the favour of Śaṅkara salvation is within his reach. If the Three-eyed Lord himself is pleased with the Mahālaya Śrāddha, what object in all the fourteen worlds can be difficult of access to him?

If a person of deluded consciousness does not perform Mahālaya rite on the eighth day, he becomes always miserable and is plunged in the dreadful ocean of worldly existence perpetually. Never can he realize any of his desires on the earth. He remains in the Naraka called Vaitaraṇī as long as the moon and the stars shine.

If a man faithfully performs Mahālaya Śrāddha rite on the eighth day, his Pitṛs become contented for eighty thousand Kalpas.

The groups of Pitṛs make him flourish with their blessings. His obstacles are dispelled. They will grant him unbroken line of progeny.

79-80. If a person performs Mahālaya Śrāddha rite on the ninth day, Goddess Durgā, the consort of Śaṁbhu, becomes pleased with him. Durgā, the suppressor of demon Mahiṣa, becomes pleased with him and destroys the worthless goblins such as Pretas and Piśācas, (and ailments such as) *Kṣaya* (consumption), *Apasmāra* (epileptic fits), *Kuṣṭha* (leprosy), etc.

81-83. If a man does not perform Mahālaya rite on the ninth day, he shall be tormented with epileptic fits and Brahmarākṣasa (evil spirit of a former Brāhmaṇa). He will be perpetually harassed by Kṛtyās for black magic.

If a man performs the Mahālaya Śrāddha rite on the ninth day, his Pitṛs become contented for ninety thousand Kalpas. The groups of Pitṛs will perpetually grant him an unbroken line of succession.

84-88a. If a man performs Mahālaya Śrāddha rite on the tenth day, Moon-god of sixteen nectarine digits becomes pleased with him. When the Lord of (Medicinal) Herbs is propitiated by means of this Śrāddha, the plants and herbs shall always yield rice and other foodgrains.

If a person does not perform the excellent Mahālaya Śrāddha rite on the tenth day, the medicinal herbs and his agricultural activities shall be futile.

If a man performs Mahālaya Śrāddha rite on the tenth day, his Pitṛs become contented for a hundred thousand Kalpas. The groups of Pitṛs shall perpetually grant him an unbroken line of progeny.

88b-93. If a man devoutly performs Mahālaya Śrāddha rite on the eleventh day, Rudra, the annihilator of all the worlds, becomes pleased with him. With the favour of Rudra, the lord of the universe, the annihilator of everything, the performer of the Śrāddha shall always defeat his enemies. Ten thousand sins of Brāhmaṇa-murder committed by him, shall instantly perish. He attains the full benefit of the Yajñas including Agniṣṭoma.

If a man does not devoutly perform Mahālaya rite on the eleventh day, Rudra becomes averse to him. He does not become pleased at all. Enemies will increase all round him and harass him. Even if he were to perform Agniṣṭoma and other Yajñas with plenty of monetary gifts, they will become futile like the *Havya* (sacrificial oblations) deposited on ash.

94-95. On account of the sin of not performing the Śrāddha,

he will be on a par with slayer of a Brāhmaṇa. If a person performs Mahālaya Śrāddha rite on the eleventh day, his Pitṛs become contented for two hundred thousand Kalpas. The groups of Pitṛs shall perpetually grant him unbroken line of progeny.

96-101a. If a man performs Mahālaya Śrāddha rite on the twelfth day, Janārdana himself, the Lord of Lakṣmī, becomes pleased with him.

When Janārdana, the Lord of Devas, the lord of the chiefs is delighted, the entire world, mobile and immobile, becomes pleased undoubtedly.

The earth, the beloved of Hari, increases his foodgrains and vegetable produce. In his abode Lakṣmī, the beloved of Hari, flourishes.

The Iron Club named Kaumodakī held in Nārāyaṇa's hand always destroys the evil spirits of *Apasmāra,* etc. Similarly the Discus with sharp edges burns his enemies. The Conch too shall expel demons, ghosts, etc.

Thus Keśava prevents infliction of pain on him from all sides in every respect.

101b-105a. If a vulgar man does not perform Mahālaya rite on the twelfth day, his fields and riches will undoubtedly perish. *Apasmāra* and other evil spirits, enemies of great strength and demons harass him, because he is averse to Viṣṇu. He is cast into the Naraka named Asthibhedana. If a person devoutly performs Mahālaya Śrāddha rite on the twelfth day, his Pitṛs become contented for six hundred thousand Kalpas. The Pitṛs grant him unbroken line of progeny.

105b-110. If a person devoutly performs Mahālaya Śrāddha rite on the thirteenth day, Lord Kandarpa, the lover of Rati, becomes pleased with him. He always gets the objects of pleasure such as garlands, sandalpaste, charming ladies, etc. with the favour of Kāmadeva. Throughout his life from birth to death, he gets only happiness.

If a person does not perform Mahālaya Śrāddha rite on the thirteenth day, Kāmadeva shall be averse to him and shall destroy women and (other) means of enjoyment. He casts him into the Naraka named Aṅgāra-Śayyā-Bhramaṇa.

If with the Pitṛs in view, a person performs Mahālaya rite on the thirteenth day, his Pitṛs become pleased for a million Kalpas. The groups of Pitṛs grant him unbroken line of progeny.

accordance with the Pārvaṇa injunctions. In the Mahālaya Śrāddha the man should feed (and propitiate) the Pitṛs belonging to his mother's family in the same manner as the Pitṛs belonging to his father's family. He should do so joyously and it shall be conducive to welfare. He should give monetary presents in accordance with his capacity and befitting his affluence.

142-145. In the Mahālaya Śrāddha one should not be miserly in regard to the expenses. The Dakṣiṇā (monetary gift) of the Yajñas is called *Purogavā* (a leader, a predecessor). Just as the cart without the bullocks in front is of no use on the way, so also this Pitṛ Yajña without Dakṣiṇā is of no avail. It may even destroy everything. Hence at least a small amount of Dakṣiṇā should be given by one who knows (the religious rite). The Mahālaya Śrāddha rite should be performed by widowed women without sons with their husbands in view by feeding done on a large scale. Otherwise there will be loss of Dharma; they will fall into great Narakas.

146. If any person does not perform Mahālaya Śrāddha rite when the month of Bhādrapada arrives, his family perishes. He incurs the sin of Brāhmaṇa-slaughter.

147. If, with sincerity and faith, men perform Mahālaya rite on behalf of Pitṛs, their line of progeny never breaks. Their riches will be unimpaired (everlasting).

148. The word *Ālaya* indicates *Āspada* (abode). Welfare is called by the word *Mahā*. Since (this rite) is the cause of all auspicious things it is called *Mahālaya*.[1]

149. Hence a man should perform the Mahālaya rite for the attainment of welfare and auspiciousness. If he does not perform the Mahālaya rite it will be inauspicious for him.

150. Even if one does not perform the annual Śrāddha rites on the days of the anniversary of their death, one should be wise enough to perform Mahālaya Śrāddha rite without worrying about (other things).

151. If one is incapable of performing the Mahālaya Śrāddha rite, one should perform the Mahālaya rite to the Pitṛs even by begging.

---

1. Cf. another definition: Mahālaya is the *Ālaya* 'abode' of *Mahā* (Festival of Pitṛs).

152. One should beg for money and foodgrains only from excellent Brāhmaṇas. He should never take wealth or foodgrain from fallen persons.

153. If foodgrains, money, etc. are not available from Brāhmaṇas, the man should beg from excellent Kṣatriyas, if he has the desire to perform Mahālaya rites.

154-155. If no donor king is available, one should beg from Vaiśyas. If no Vaiśya donor too is available to him in the whole world, he should offer *Gogrāsa* (i.e. a morsel of grass or food to a cow) in the month of Bhādrapada for propitiating the Pitṛs. Or he shall go out into the forest and lament.

156. He should beat his belly with both the hands and shed profuse tears. The man should then announce thus loudly in those forest regions:

157-162. "May all the Pitṛs of my family listen to my words. I am a poor and wretched fellow. I am shameless. I am a doer of cruel deeds. The month of Bhādrapada has arrived. It increases the pleasure of the Pitṛs. But I am incapable of performing Mahālaya Śrāddha. Even after wandering over the entire earth nothing is obtained by me. So I do not perform the Mahālaya Śrāddha for you. Kindly forgive this (omission) on my part. Indeed ye all are excessively merciful."

The indigent fellow should lament thus in the forest regions. On hearing his lamentation the Pitṛs belonging to his family do become delighted and satisfied like Devas by drinking nectar.

By the offerings of *Gogrāsa* and by the (above) lamentation in the forest, the Pitṛs will have the same satisfaction as they will have when a number of Brāhmaṇas take food at the time of Mahālaya rite.

163. In the month of Bhādrapada, if there is any obstacle due to pollution caused by childbirth, etc., the devotee can perform it after the days of pollution are over till the end of the month of Vṛścika.

164-169. For the purpose of the rite of Mahālaya, a wise man should invite nine Brāhmaṇas. One of them is to be chosen for the sake of one's father and one for one's grandfather. The Brāhmaṇa should invite one Brāhmaṇa with the great-grandfather in view. For the sake of the maternal grandfather, he should invite one Brāhmaṇa. For the sake of mother's grandfather, he should invite one Brāhmaṇa. He should invite one Brāhmaṇa for the sake of mother's great-grandfather. For the sake of Viśvedevas he should invite two excellent Brāhmaṇas. For the sake of Viṣṇu he should invite one Brāhmaṇa very well-versed in the Vedas. Thus one should invite nine Brāhmaṇas in the Mahālaya Śrāddha.

Or for the sake of all the three Pitṛs of the father's side the devotee should choose (invite) one Brāhmaṇa. With (the three) beginning with maternal grandfather in view, he should invite one Brāhmaṇa. He should invite one for the sake of Viśvedevas and one for the sake of Viṣṇu.

170-176. Thus he should choose four Brāhmaṇas in the Mahālaya rite. A wise person should choose only those Brāhmaṇas who possess good character and who are well-versed in the Vedas. He who invites persons of vicious habit is indeed destroyer of the Śrāddha.

After the advent of the month of Bhādrapada, particularly in the dark half of it, if a man performs the Mahālaya Śrāddha sincerely and faithfully, O highly intelligent Durācāra, he is (on a par with) one who has taken his holy bath in all the Tīrthas, one who has performed a hundred Yajñas including Agniṣṭoma, one by whom charitable gifts, the most important among them being *Tulāpuruṣa Dāna,* have been made, and one by whom Cāndrāyaṇa and other Kṛcchra (expiatory) rites have been performed. He will obtain the benefit of the study of the four Vedas with their Aṅgas. He will get the merit of the Japa of the great Mantras such as Gāyatrī, etc. He shall get the benefit of the complete readings of the Itihāsas and Purāṇas.

There is no other meritorious thing on a par with Mahālaya on the earth. Through the Mahālaya rite, one can attain the worlds of Brahmā, Viṣṇu and Maheśāna.

177. Though Mahālaya and other Śrāddhas come under Kāmya rites (i.e those rites that are performed with some benefit in view), they are to be considered *Nitya* rites (compulsory daily rites). Thus if that rite is not performed it will lead to great obstacles.

178-180. By performing it (Mahālaya Śrāddha) one shall undoubtedly achieve what(ever) one desires. By performing the Mahālaya rite, evil spirits, vampires, etc., epileptic fits, evil Planets, groups of the witches, Śākinī, Ḍākinī, etc., demons, Piśācas (ghosts, etc.), dreadful Vetālas—all these and other evil beings perish instantly. By performing the Mahālaya rite one obtains vast fortune and glory.

181-182. On the advice of Vasiṣṭha,[1] King Daśaratha formerly performed Mahālaya Śrāddha rite at the advent of the month of Bhādrapada. (As a result thereof) he obtained the four sons like Rāma, who were highly honoured by the whole world. He got excellent renown and fortune and prosperity that surpassed those of everyone in the entire universe.

183-184a. It was by performing the Mahālaya rite that the excellent King Yayāti obtained all his great sons, the chief among them being Yadu, who perpetuated his line. Through the merit of the Śrāddha he obtained heavenly pleasures rarely attained by others.

184b. By performing the Mahālaya rite, Duṣyanta got Bharata.

185. By the performance of the Mahālaya rite, Nala, the husband of Damayantī, surmounted very great difficulties and regained the (lost) kingdom.

186. He could curb the dreadful Kali and the enemy Puṣkara. He obtained an exceedingly virtuous son named Indrasena.

187. By performing Mahālaya rites the great King Hariścandra, the most excellent one among the truthful ones, became free from the harassment caused by Viśvāmitra.

188-194. He obtained Candrāvatī as his wife and Lohitāśva as his son.

By performing the Mahālaya rite, the powerful son of Kṛtavīrya (Kārtavīrya Arjuna) obtained the overlordship of the eighteen islands.

By performing the Mahālaya rite in the Daṇḍaka forest Rāma killed Rāvaṇa in the battle and regained Sītā.

By performing the rite of Mahālaya, Yudhiṣṭhira, the son of Dharma, crossed the ocean of misery and killed the sons of Dhṛtarāṣṭra.

By performing the rite of Mahālaya the excellent sage Vasiṣṭha, and the other sages such as Atri, Bhṛgu, Kutsa, Gautama, Aṅgiras, Kaśyapa, Bharadvāja, Viśvāmitra, Agastya, Parāśara, Mṛkaṇḍu, etc. became superior to everyone in the universe. By performing the excellent Mahālaya Śrāddha in accordance with the injunctions they became the abodes of the eight supernatural powers, Aṇimā (Minuteness), etc., religious vows and austerities.

195. All of those excellent sages became living-liberated souls. Hence the Mahālaya Śrāddha rite should be performed by one who wishes for prosperity.

---

1. VV 181-95. As usual with Purāṇas, the fortunes or prosperity of legendary and Purāṇic figures is attributed to the performance of Mahālaya Śrāddha.

196. Thus, O Durācāra, if anyone has not performed Mahālaya rite till now, he will have great danger from evil spirits, vampires, etc.

197-203. By not performing Mahālaya rite, one shall attain the state of a vampire. This evil spirit that possessed you was a Brāhmaṇa in a previous birth. His name was Vedanidhi. He was the meritorious son of Bharadvāja. The noble-minded Brāhmaṇa stayed in the village named Kuśasthalī. He did not perform this Mahālaya Śrāddha in accordance with the injunctions. Hence due to the curse of the Pitṛs he attained the state of a vampire.

So, in the month of Bhādrapada, O Durācāra, on behalf of the Pitṛs, feed Brāhmaṇas devoutly with cooked food having all the six tastes. Thereby you can perpetually avoid poverty. You will be happy. Henceforth, do not associate with great sinners, since you have already experienced the misery resulting from possession by the Vetāla. Go to your own land; I have permitted you. Do not delay."

On being told thus by Sage Dattātreya, the Yogin, he bowed down to him and went back to his land with a satisfied and delighted mind.

204-206. After going home, O excellent Brāhmaṇas, the Brāhmaṇa Durācāra who had got rid of his sins and who was set free from the fear of the Vetāla followed the path indicated by Dattātreya. He became happy in his mind. He completely avoided association with sinners. He was devoted to the code of conduct befitting his stage in life. Due to the great efficacy of the holy plunge in Rāmacandradhanuṣkoṭi Tīrtha, Durācāra attained the greatest salvation on death.

Śrī Sūta said:

207-211. Thus the meritorious story of the liberation of Durācāra has been recounted to you. This meritorious Dhanuṣkoṭi is destructive of great sins. It is merely by taking his holy bath here that Durācāra was liberated.

How can one state the limit of the power (to purify) of Dhanuṣkoṭi. It destroys even those sins for which there is no atonement. All those sins devoid of expiatory rites, perish by one's taking the holy plunge in Dhanuṣkoṭi.

If a Brāhmaṇa bows down to a Liṅga or to Viṣṇu worshipped by a Śūdra, no atonement has been indicated for him by the great sages or the Smṛtis. But by taking the holy bath in Dhanuṣkoṭi even that sin of his shall perish.

212-216a. There is no means of atonement in the case of persons who censure Brāhmaṇas. There is no expiation for ungrateful persons and those who are guilty of breach of trust. There is no atonement for those who are enamoured of the wives of brothers, those who are fond of a Śūdra's cooked food, those who are engaged in decrying the Vedas, those who sell their daughters, O Brāhmaṇas, and those who sell horses, those who sell deities, those who sell the Vedas, the men who sell Dharma and those who sell their holy rites. There is no atonement for people who sell Tīrthas. But by taking the holy plunge in Dhanuṣkoṭi their sins perish.

216b-219. There is no means of expiation for those who take delight in harassing mothers, fathers and ascetics, those who are habituated to censuring preceptors and elders, those who are interested in censuring Śiva, Viṣṇu and ascetics, and those who denounce good stories. They shall be purified by taking the holy bath here in Dhanuṣkoṭi.

Thus, O Brāhmaṇas, the glory of Dhanuṣkoṭi has been recounted to you. On hearing about this the man is liberated from all the sins.

CHAPTER THIRTYSEVEN

Kṣīrakuṇḍa

Śrī Sūta said:

1-2. O ye all ascetics, residents of Naimiṣa forest, twenty-four Tīrthas beginning with Cakratīrtha and ending with Rāmadhanuṣkoṭi have been described by me now. In addition to these what do you wish to know?

The sages said:

3-5. We wish to hear about the glory of Kṣīrakuṇḍa,[1] O sage.

1. After describing the sacred Tīrthas on Rāmasetu ending with Dhanuṣkoṭi, the author describes a few miscellaneous Tīrthas. This Tīrtha is near Cakratīrtha (Tiruppullaṇi, called here 'Phullagrāma'). The *Pilgrims' Guide* does not mention it.

Earlier it was said by you that Cakratīrtha is near it. Where is that Kṣīrakuṇḍa? Of what sort is its glory? How did it become famous by the name Kṣīrakuṇḍa? It behoves you to narrate this in detail to us who faithfully listen to it.

Śrī Sūta said:

I shall describe it. Listen ye all with great concentration.

6. To the west of the exceedingly meritorious Devīpura and not far from it, there is a very great holy spot well-known as Phullagrāma.

7. The town named Phullagrāma from where Rāma began building his Setu on the great sea, is an exceedingly meritorious holy spot.

8-9. Kṣīrakuṇḍa too is there itself. It is destructive of great sins. On being seen, touched, meditated upon and glorified, it bestows salvation. I shall earnestly recount to you all including how that meritorious Tīrtha became famous by the name *Kṣīrakuṇḍa*. Listen to it faithfully.

10-14. Formerly there was a sage named Mudgala.[1] He followed the path of the Vedas. In the exceedingly sacred Phullagrāma, he performed an excellent Yajña, causing pleasure to Nārāyaṇa.

Completely gratified by his Yāga, Viṣṇu became delighted in heart, O excellent Brāhmaṇas. He appeared before him in that sacrificial chamber. Viṣṇu whose body was rendered splendid by Lakṣmī, who had the lustre of a dark cloud, who shone in his yellow garments, who was seated on Garuḍa, whose chest was beautified by the Kaustubha jewel and whose four arms shone with the conch-shell, discus, iron club and lotus, appeared before him.

On seeing him, overwhelmed with devotion, Mudgala whose body was thrilled (with joy) with hair standing all over his body then eulogized the Lord with words pleasing to the ears.

Mudgala said:

15-20. Obeisance to you, to Nārāyaṇa, to the Creator of the universe first, then to the Protector, and to the Annihilator there-

1. The story of Mudgala, how God Viṣṇu made the heavenly cow Surabhi fill the Kuṇḍa for Mudgala, is given to explain the name Kṣīrakuṇḍa. The Brāhmaṇa is one Mudgala, not the one mentioned in Mbh or in Purāṇas included in PI and PE.

after. Bow to the Lord in the form of fish, to (him in the form of) tortoise, to one of the nature of knowledge and consciousness. Obeisance to the Lord with the physical form of a boar. Hail to the Lord in the form of a lion. Obeisance to you, to Vāmana. Obeisance to you, to the son of Jamadagni. Bow to you, to Rāghava. Obeisance to you, to Balabhadra.[1] Obeisance to you, to Kṛṣṇa, to Kalki. Bow to the Lord in the form of perfect knowledge. Protect me, O ocean of mercy, O Nārāyaṇa, O Lord of the universe. I am a shameless wretch. I am slanderous, cruel, wicked, hypocrite and insignificant fellow. I am enamoured of other men's wives, wealth and fields. My mind is contaminated by feelings of jealousy. Kindly save me, O Hari.

21. On being eulogized thus directly by Mudgala, O excellent Brāhmaṇas, Hari said to Sage Mudgala, in a voice as majestic as thunder:

Śrī Hari said:

22-23. O Mudgala, I am pleased with this hymn of yours as well as by the sacrifice (*Kratu*). I have come to your sacrifice to partake of the *Havis* directly.

On being told thus by Hari there, Mudgala became delighted in his mind. The Brāhmaṇa, endued with great devotion, spoke to Viṣṇu:

Mudgala said:

24-29. O Hṛṣīkeśa, I am one who has attained his object. My wife too is blessed. Today my birth has become fruitful. My penance has become fruitful. My family has become fruitful. My sons have become fruitful. My hermitage has become fruitful. Everything belonging to me has become fruitful today since you have come to my sacrificial chamber to partake of the *Havis* directly. I directly perceive that Lord whom Yogins engaged in Yoga-practice, seek in their hearts. My *Kratu* has achieved its purpose.

* * *

1. In the list of ten incarnations of Viṣṇu, Buddha is omitted and Balabhadra, the elder brother of Kṛṣṇa, is included. It shows that Buddha was not then recognised as an incarnation of Viṣṇu—a significant factor in determining the date of this part of the Purāṇa.

are liberated from all bondages. They attain salvation. They are of meritorious deeds. Of what avail are Yāgas, the Vedas, pilgrimages to Tīrthas, Japa, observances of holy rites, to those who visit Kṣīrakuṇḍa?

57b-61. A man whose body is touched by the wind coming from Kṣīrakuṇḍa, O Brāhmaṇas, reaches the world of Brahmā and is liberated there itself. Those who have taken their plunge in this Kṣīrakuṇḍa disregard Yama. They may stand over his head blazing like fire.

To those who have had their holy bath in this Kṣīrakuṇḍa, the river Vaitaraṇī becomes cool. Surely all the Narakas become ineffective. Even when this Kṣīrakuṇḍa which is on a par with Kāmadhenu is present, if any man wanders elsewhere for taking holy bath, O excellent Brāhmaṇas, he goes (in search of) the juice of the *Arka* plant even when cow's milk is available.

62-63. There is nothing which is inaccessible to those who take their holy bath in this Kṣīrakuṇḍa. Salvation is secure in their hands. Why then talk much about other things? I proclaim with my hands raised; I tell you the truth; (I repeat) I tell you the truth.

He who reads this chapter or listens to this with attention, obtains the excellent benefit of holy bath in Kṣīrakuṇḍa.

CHAPTER THIRTYEIGHT

The Glory of Kṣīrakuṇḍa: Kadrū's Expiation for her Deceitful Action

The sages said:

1-2. O Sūta, how was Kadrū liberated by taking her holy bath in Kṣīrakuṇḍa?[1] How did she act fraudulently towards her co-wife? Whose daughter was that Kadrū of sinful resolve? Whose co-wife was she? Why did Kadrū defeat her co-wife with deceitful

---

1. The story how Kadrū deceitfully enslaved her co-wife Vinatā is found in Mbh, *Ādi* 20.2-23 and other Purāṇas (PI, I, 304). But the expiation of that deceitfulness by a bath in the Kṣīrakuṇḍa is a contribution of this Purāṇa to enhance the glory of this Tīrtha.

ing with their heads down from that branch. He became afraid lest they should fall. Garuḍa then caught hold of that branch.

As Garuḍa, son of Vinatā, moved through the sky holding that branch as well as the elephant and the tortoise, his father said to him, "O son of Vinatā, let go this branch on a deserted mountain."

On being told thus, the bird placed the branch on a deserted mountain and began to eat the elephant and the tortoise. At that time a portent occurred in the sky foreboding a calamity.

70. On seeing the portent, Indra repeatedly asked his preceptor, "O Jīva (i.e. Jupiter), what is the cause of this portent?" Then, O excellent Brāhmaṇas, Bṛhaspati told Indra:

Bṛhaspati said:

71-76. Formerly, O Indra, Sage Kaśyapa performed a *Kratu*. He despatched all the sages, Suras, Siddhas, Yakṣas, Gandharvas, and Kinnaras for gathering the requisites for Yajñas.

On seeing Vālakhilyas of a short thumb-like size, who had collected together the requisites and who were about to sink in the water in the pits made by hooves of cows, you laughed (at them). On being insulted by you, O Indra, Vālakhilyas became angry then. With their faces blazing with anger, they performed *Homas* in the sacrificial fire (praying), "May a son who instils fear in Devendra, be born to Kaśyapa." His son Garuḍa is now eager to take away nectar. He is on his way to this place. These ill omens forebode that."

On being told thus, Indra spoke to the Devas, Agni and others:

77. "A bird is coming to take away nectar. Let it be guarded."

Urged and directed by Indra thus, the Devas equipped with weapons protected the nectar.

78. The king of birds came face to face with the Devas armed with weapons. On seeing the exceedingly powerful Garuḍa, those Suras trembled.

79. A great fight ensued between the Suras and Garuḍa. Bhauvana, the keeper of Nectar, was pierced with the snout of the bird.

80-84. Then the Devas struck Garuḍa with many weapons. Garuḍa was excessively pained and harassed by the Devas armed with weapons. With (flapping of) his wings, he cast off the Devas, the leader among whom was Agni. The Devas who were hit by his wings became extremely furious. They hurled *Nārācas* (iron arrows), *Bhindipālas* (javelins) and many other weapons. Then with great force, with his wings, Garuḍa, the son of Vinatā, raised a lot of dust that blinded the eyes of the Devas. The excellent Devas got the dust storm stopped by wind. With his wings and snout, O Brāhmaṇas, Garuḍa harassed Rudras, Vasus, Ādityas, Maruts and other Suras.

85-90. When the Devas fled, Garuḍa saw Fire-god blazing in front of him. Then he attempted to extinguish the fire that blazed all round.

He adopted a thousand snouts (mouths), drank up hundreds of rivers and with those waters he put out that fire quickly. Thereafter, he saw a discus that whirled round and round. It had sharp edges and it closely guarded the nectar. On seeing it he assumed a tiny form and entered it through the space between two spokes. Thereupon he saw two serpents of exceedingly terrible size with their mouths open. Even merely glanced at by them one would be reduced to ash. But Garuḍa struck and cut them with his wings and snout. Then he seized the nectar and flew up breaking the mechanical device. Mādhava spoke to Garuḍa as he flew up, "O lord of birds, I am pleased with you. Choose a boon, O bird of firm vows."

Then the bird replied to Hari, the Lord of Kamalā:

91-94. "Let there be no old age or death unto me. Let me be able to stay above you (as your flag)." Hari said, "It will be so." (Then the bird said:) "Let a boon be received from me." On being told thus Hari said: "You, be my vehicle, O son of Vinatā. Also be my emblem above my chariot."

The bird too said, "So it will be" to Acyuta, the Lord of Kamalā.

On hearing that the bird had taken away the nectar Indra quickly rushed after him and struck the wing of the bird with his thunderbolt. Thereupon Garuḍa laughingly spoke to Indra:

95-101. "I am not at all pained by being struck with the thunderbolt, O Indra. But, O leader of Suras, let your blow with the thunderbolt be fruitful." Saying this he dropped down a feather from his wing. Garuḍa became well-known as Suparṇa because his *Parṇa* (wing) was splendid.

Everyone was surprised on seeing Garuḍa completely golden in colour. Then, O excellent Brāhmaṇas, Grauḍa spoke to Indra: "I have the unfailing power, O Devendra, to bear the (burden of) entire universe consisting of mobile and immobile beings along with you, forever. A thousand Indras cannot be a match unto me in battle."

As Garuḍa spoke thus, Indra asked him thus: "What have you to do with nectar? Let the nectar be given (back) to me. Those people to whom you give this nectar, O son of Vinatā, will become free from old age and death by drinking the nectar. They may become superior to us in strength. They may then harass Devas."

102-107. As Indra spoke thus, O Brāhmaṇas, Garuḍa said to him: "You may come to the place where I keep this and snatch it away quickly." On being told thus, Indra said to Garuḍa: "I am pleased with you, O highly intelligent one. I shall grant you a boon. Choose it." Garuḍa said to Indra when he was addressed thus, "In making my mother a slave (to their mother) the reptiles had employed deceitful means. O Indra, the slayer of Vṛtra and Pāka, let these serpents be my food forever." On being told thus by Garuḍa, Indra said to him, "It will be so."

Then Garuḍa who held (the pot of) nectar went on his way, O Brāhmaṇas. As he proceeded ahead, Indra who was eager to retrieve the nectar swiftly followed him, O excellent Brāhmaṇas. After approaching his mother, the lord of the birds spoke to the serpents:

108-113. "O serpents, the nectar is now being kept here on the Darbha grass. Take your holy bath and partake of it calmly when you have become pure. O serpents, let my mother be released from slavery." The serpents then said to Garuḍa, the son of Vinatā, "It will be so".

At that moment itself, O excellent Brāhmaṇas, Vinatā was liberated from slavery. Those serpents then went for their holy bath to prepare for the consumption of nectar. At that very time, Indra took away (the pot of) nectar. The serpents returned after their bath. They could not see (the pot of) nectar there. Since the pot of nectar had been placed on the Darbha grass, they began to lick the Darbha grass. Since then their tongues were torn asunder by the tips of Darbha. Therefore, O excellent Brāhmaṇas, they are called *Dvijihvas* ('Double-tongued') ever since then. Due to the contact with nectar Darbha grass attained sanctity.

114. After liberating his mother from slavery Garuḍa who was furious, cursed Kadrū who had defeated his mother by fraudulent means:

115-125. "O Kadrū, you have defeated my mother by fraudulent means. Hence you do not deserve to render service to your husband."

After cursing Kadrū thus, Garuḍa went away as he pleased. Kadrū and Vinatā both approached their husband. Kaśyapa turned away his face from Kadrū and spoke to her angrily: "O Kadrū, since you had defeated Vinatā in a deceitful way, you are unworthy of rendering any service unto me, O wicked woman. If a man or a woman defeats another man or woman by using fraudulent means, he or she shall be a great sinner. By holding conversation with a person who gains victory by means of deceit, one will become (similar to) a Brāhmaṇa-slayer.

It has been declared by sages that a person in association with a thief, drink-addict, defiler of teacher's bed is contaminated by that association and should be known to be on a par with them. By holding conversation with you, I shall incur a sin that will land me in hell. Hence, O dreadful Kadrū, go away from my presence.

One will immediately fall into the ocean of Naraka by talking to that person on the earth, who takes food in the same row along with someone who gains success by deceitful means.

If one looks at a person who gains victory by deceitful means (one incurs a great sin). To subdue that sin, one should look at the sun, water or fire.

No other person should stay in the hermitage or abode where a cheat or a person who gets success deceitfully lives. If he stays there, he falls into Naraka.

Hence get away, get away from the very path of my sight and from my hermitage. You had defeated this simple-minded Vinatā (by deceit)."

126-130. After reproaching Kadrū, Kaśyapa of great intellect quickly accepted (honoured) Vinatā of excellent conduct. On being told thus harshly by Kaśyapa, Kadrū became exceedingly distressed. Crying (much) she fell down at his feet. Even after seeing her falling at his feet, Kaśyapa, the great sage, did not accept Kadrū, remembering the sin committed by her.

Then Vinatā bowed down to Kaśyapa and spoke these words: "O holy lord, O storehouse of mercy, accept (honour) this sister of mine. Out of ignorance this erring and childish Kadrū has committed a sin now. It behoves you to forgive everything. Indeed good people are kind-natured."

131-133. On being requested thus by the mother of Garuḍa,

Sage Kaśyapa said: "O Vinatā, without the expiatory rite I will not accept this woman of wicked behaviour. I solemnly proclaim it thrice on my honour."

On hearing the words of Kaśyapa, Vinatā said again: "O Brāhmaṇa, do tell me what atonement has to be performed by my sister for her sin so that she will become one worthy of rendering service unto you."

134. On being spoken thus by her, O Brāhmaṇas, Kaśyapa, the son of Marīci, meditated for a short while. Afterwards he spoke thus:

135-137a. "On the shore of the Southern sea, in Phullagrāma that bestows salvation, there in a Tīrtha named Kṣīrasaras. It is destructive of sins.[1] Merely by the holy bath in that Tīrtha, her sin will perish. This sin of hers will not perish even by ten thousand expiatory rites without the holy plunge in that Tīrtha. So let her go to that lake."

137b-139. When this was said by her husband, Kadrū bowed down to that excellent Brāhmaṇa. Instantly she went to Kṣīrasaras with the help of her sons. After a few days Kadrū reached that meritorious lake Kṣīrasaras. With great purity and the sense-organs controlled she performed the *Saṁkalpa* rite and took the holy bath in Kṣīrakuṇḍa in accordance with the rules.

140. She observed fast for three days and then bathed in the waters of that Kṣīrasaras. When she was performing the rite of ablution with eagerness on the fourth day, O excellent Brāhmaṇas, there was heard an unembodied voice from the sky:

141-146. The unembodied voice said: "O Kadrū, you are now liberated from the sin of gaining victory by deceitful means, due to your holy plunge here. You are worthy of rendering service to your husband. There is no doubt about it. By taking the holy bath here, the curse imprecated by Garuḍa has gone. Go to your husband. He will accept you." After saying this the ethereal unembodied voice stopped. Kadrū became delighted in her mind. She bowed down to that voice. She circumambulated the Tīrtha and bowed down to it along with her sons. Along with them, she went to her husband with a desire to serve him.

On seeing her arrived after having taken the holy bath in the waters of Kṣīrasaras and realizing that she was rid of all her sins

1. Thus this story from Mbh is used by SkP for the glorification of Kṣīrakuṇḍa.

by means of meditation, Kaśyapa accepted her as his wife and considered her worthy of serving himself.

147-150. Thus, O Brāhmaṇas, it has been recounted to you how Kadrū was rid of her sins by taking the holy plunge into the meritorious waters of Kṣīrasaras which bestows salvation to men.

One who listens to this chapter or reads this obtains the excellent merit of the holy bath in Kṣīrakuṇḍa. He enjoys the entire benefit of the Yajñas including horse-sacrifice. He is (on a par with) one who has taken holy bath in all the Tīrthas including Gaṅgā. He who reads this chapter in praise of Kṣīrakuṇḍa obtains the complete merit of those who make a gift of a thousand cows.

CHAPTER THIRTYNINE

The Glory of Kapitīrtha: Raṁbhā and Ghṛtācī Liberated from their Curse

Śrī Sūta said:

1-8. Henceforth, I shall recount the glory of Kapitīrtha.[1] That Tīrtha was formerly created by all the monkeys on Gandhamādana for helping everyone, O Brāhmaṇas. After Rāvaṇa and other demons were killed, the monkeys made the Tīrtha and joyously took their baths there. The monkeys, who could assume any form they desired, granted this boon unto the Tīrtha:

"All those who take their holy bath in this Tīrtha with their minds devotionally inclined, shall attain salvation. They will be liberated from great sins. Those who take their holy plunge here in this Tīrtha need not be afraid of Narakas. All the men who take their holy bath here, will never meet with poverty. Those who take their holy plunge here in the Tīrtha will not be harassed by Yama. He who always utters "I shall go to Kapitīrtha", and goes a hundred paces, O Brāhmaṇas, shall attain the highest region. A Tīrtha on a par with this Tīrtha has never existed before nor will there ever be."

9-10a. After granting this boon to this Tīrtha, all the eminent

---

1. This Tīrtha is a tank at Pamban.

monkeys bowed down to Rāma, the son of Daśaratha and requested him: "O lord, let some wonderful boon be granted to this Tīrtha by you."

On being requested by the monkeys, O Brāhmaṇas, Rāmacandra became delighted very much. In order to please the monkeys, he granted this boon:

10b-13. "Those who take their holy plunge here in this Tīrtha will attain the merit of holy bath in Gaṅgā. They will get the merit arising from holy bath in Prayāga as well as the benefit of all the Tīrthas. They will get the excellent merit of Agniṣṭoma and other Yāgas. They shall get the merit of reciting Gāyatrī and other great Mantras. The people will attain the unimpaired merit of those who make the gifts of a thousand cows. They will get the merit of reciting the four Vedas. They will get the merit of the worship of Brahmā, Viṣṇu, Maheśa and other Devas."

14-18. Thus Rāma granted the boon to Kapitīrtha, O Brāhmaṇas. When the boon was granted by Rāma thus, the following persons began to praise the Tīrtha to which Rāma had granted the boon: the three-eyed Lord Śiva, Brahmā, Indra, Yama, Varuṇa, Agni, Vāyu, Kubera, the Moon-god, the Sun-god, Nirṛti, Sādhyas, Vasus, all other Devas, Viśvedevas and others, Atri, Bhṛgu, Kutsa, Gautama, Parāśara, Kaṇva, Agastya, Sutīkṣṇa, Viśvāmitra and many other sages, Sanaka and other Yogins as well as Nārada and other celestial sages. All these praised the Tīrtha in various ways.

19-22. They took their holy bath in that Tīrtha that bestows all desired objects. All those Devas and sages said this also: "Since this excellent Tīrtha has been created by the monkeys, it will become famous in the world as Kapitīrtha."

Hence all those who are desirous of salvation should certainly go to Kapitīrtha. Raṁbhā who was turned into a stone by the curse of Kauśika[1] formerly, O Brāhmaṇas, took her bath there and regained her own form and went to heaven. I cannot adequately recount the greatness of this Tīrtha.

The sages said:

23. Why did Kauśika curse Raṁbhā, O Sūtanandana? How did the celestial damsel who had become a stone go to Kapitīrtha? Describe all this in detail, O excellent sage.

---

1. For the story cf VR. I. 64.1-15; Mbh. *Anuśāsana* 3.11.

Śrī Sūta said:

24-29. Formerly there was a king named Viśvāmitra in the family of Kuśika. Once that powerful great king who was eager to see different kingdoms, wandered over the earth, surrounded by his army.

After wandering over many lands, he went to the hermitage of Vasiṣṭha. He was invited by the noble-souled Vasiṣṭha to enjoy his hospitality. The king agreed and prostrated before him like a rod.

Due to the power of Kāmadhenu, O Brāhmaṇas, Vasiṣṭha, son of Brahmā, extended his hospitality to Viśvāmitra, the king. On knowing the power of Kāmadhenu, the scion of the family of Kuśika requested Vasiṣṭha for Kāmadhenu, the bestower of whatever is desired. When it was refused by Vasiṣṭha, Viśvāmitra dragged the cow by force.

30-33. He was defeated by the Mlecchas and others sent forth by Kāmadhenu.[1] Then the king propitiated Mahādeva and secured many missiles from him. He went to the hermitage of Vasiṣṭha (again) and discharged all the missiles and miraculous weapons as well as the Brahmā missile. By the power of his penance, Vasiṣṭha, son of Brahmā, struck down all those miraculous weapons with a single Brahmadaṇḍa (divine rod of Brahmā). Viśvāmitra who was defeated became extremely ashamed. In order to achieve Brāhmaṇahood for himself, he went to forest for performing penance.

34-38. He performed penance in the three quarters beginning with the East and ending with the West. In all those three quarters (viz. East, South and West) Kauśika (i.e. Viśvāmitra) had to face great obstacles.

Thereupon he went to the northern quarter on the Himālaya mountain devoid of impurities. He performed a very great penance on the meritorious banks of the river Kauśikī that absolves one of sins. For a period of a thousand divine years, he abstained from food. He conquered his sense-organs. He did not see anything. He curbed his breath. He controlled his anger. He was steady (in penance).

During summer, he stood in the middle of five fires. During

1. This quarrel with Vasiṣṭha and Viśvāmitra's defeat by Kāmadhenu is described in VR, I, cantos 52-54, 19-23 and also Mbh, *Ādi* 174.1-45.

winter, he stood in waters. During rainy season, he stood under the open sky. With his arms raised up, he stood thus without any prop. Thus he performed a very great and severe penance for achieving Brāhmaṇahood. Thereby the heaven-dwellers, Devas accompanied by Indra spoke to Raṁbhā these words:

Devas said:

39-43. O Raṁbhā, do tempt by means of your seductive movements, Sage Viśvāmitra who is engaged in penance on the banks of Kauśikī (modern Kosi) on the Himālaya mountain. Do anything to cause obstacles to his penance.

On being told thus by Devas of whom the leader was Indra, Raṁbhā replied to all the Suras, after bowing down to them with the palms joined in reverence.

Raṁbhā said:

Viśvāmitra, the great sage, is extremely cruel and wrathful. He will curse me in a fit of anger. I am, therefore, afraid of him, O Suras. Save me mercifully. I am your maid-servant.

On being told thus by Raṁbhā, Indra spoke to her:

Indra said:

44-48. O Raṁbhā, you need not be afraid of Viśvāmitra, the ascetic. I too shall come to assist you along with Kāmadeva. Vasanta (Spring) too, sweet on account of the chirping sound of cuckoo, will come. Exceedingly beautiful in form as you are, you do tempt the great sage.

On being told thus by Indra, Raṁbhā went to the hermitage of Viśvāmitra. She assumed a graceful form. Standing within the range of his vision, she tempted the sage by means of her graceful movements. At that time the cuckoo cooed delighting the minds (of all). On hearing the note of the cuckoo and on seeing Raṁbhā, the eminent Sage Viśvāmitra, the ascetic, became suspicious in his mind. On realizing that it was the work of Indra, the sage, rich in penance, cursed Raṁbhā in his anger.

Viśvāmitra said:

49-55. I am desirous of controlling anger. Yet you make me furious. So, O Raṁbhā, become a stone here and remain here for ten thousand years. Should you be saved in the meantime by any Brāhmaṇa, you will attain salvation.

On account of the curse of Viśvāmitra, she became a stone just after. She remained in his hermitage, O Brāhmaṇas for a long time in the form of a stone.

Viśvāmitra of righteous soul again performed a great penance. On the recommendation of Vasiṣṭha, he attained Brāhmaṇahood inaccessible to kings.

Raṁbhā remained in his hermitage for a long time in the form of a rock. In that very meritorious hermitage one honoured disciple of Agastya, the sage named Śveta, performed a great penance as he was desirous of salvation. While that great sage was performing the penance for a long time, a certain demoness, notorious by the name Aṅgārakā, came to his hermitage. She was extremely cruel. Her loud voice resembled thunder.

56. That terrible demoness defiled the hermitage with urine, blood, faeces and other filthy things. She harassed that sage in various other modes of nuisance.

57. The infuriated Sage Śveta fitted the stone, the result of the curse of Viśvāmitra, with a missile having Wind-god for its presiding deity and discharged it against the demoness.

58. When the Vāyavya (having Wind as the presiding deity) missile was aimed at her, the demoness fled. She was pursued by the stone fitted to the Vāyavya missile.

59-60. The frightened demoness fled to the shore of the southern sea. The rock fitted to the miraculous missile chased the fleeing demoness. As she jumped into Kapitīrtha and sank into it, the stone fell on her head and she died by the impact of the stone.

61-66. Thus Raṁbhā, who had been cursed by Viśvāmitra, discarded the form of a stone as it plunged into Kapitīrtha. She regained her form as Raṁbhā.

The charming lady was incessantly showered with flowers by the Devas. She got into a divine aerial chariot. She shone in her divine robes. She was bedecked in necklaces, armlets, bangles and nose-ornament. She was surrounded by her companions, the celestial damsels including Urvaśī. She repeatedly praised the glory of Kapitīrtha.

After serving Rāmanātha, the moon-crested Lord Śaṅkara, she went back to Amarāvatī, the beautiful city of Indra.

The demoness (who harassed Śveta) was Ghṛtācī, the celestial courtesan who had been turned into a demoness by the curse of the extremely powerful Pot-born Sage.[1] By taking the holy bath in the waters of Kapitīrtha, she too regained her original form.

67-69. Thus, by taking the holy plunge in Kapitīrtha, O excellent Brāhmaṇas, with favour of Śveta, the disciple of Agastya, Raṁbhā and Ghṛtācī cast off their forms of a rock and a demoness and regained their original form. Hence by all means, one should take the holy bath in Kapitīrtha.

One who listens to this chapter or reads it, attains the excellent merit arising from the holy bath in Kapitīrtha.

CHAPTER FORTY

The Glory of Gāyatrī and Sarasvatī Tīrthas[2]

Śrī Sūta said:

1-4. Henceforth, O sages, I shall recount the glory of Gāyatrī and Sarasvatī (Tīrthas) that sanctify the worlds. It bestows salvation on men, and destroys the great sins of those who listen to it or read it. It yields great merits to men and destroys the tortures of Narakas. If men joyously take their holy bath in Gāyatrī and Sarasvatī (Tīrthas), they will no longer stay in a womb. They will certainly be liberated.

These two rivers (Tīrthas) are called so because of the proximity of the two wives of god Brahmā, Gāyatrī and Sarasvatī, on the Gandhamādana mountain.

The sages said:

5. How did it happen that Gāyatrī and Sarasvatī came to be present on the Gandhamādana mountain? O Sūta, describe it to us.

---

1. New information in this Purāṇa.
2. These Tīrthas are in the garden behind the Hanumān Temple.

Sūta narrated:

6-8. Prajāpati (i.e. Brahmā) was formerly deluded, O Brāhmaṇas. He desired like a lover his own daughter named Vāc (Speech) joyously.

This daughter of Prajāpati bacame ashamed on noticing his lecherous love for her. Hence she assumed the form of a Rohita deer. Inclined to have sexual dalliance with her, Brahmā too took the form of a deer. As she went ahead in the guise of a female deer, he too followed her.

9-10a. On seeing him intent on having sexual intercourse with his daughter, all the deities condemned him: "This Brahmā is committing a deed that should not be done, i.e. (attempt to have) sexual union with one's own daughter." Thus they censured the creator and the Lord of the worlds.

10b-12. On seeing Parameṣṭhin (Brahmā) engaged in the forbidden act, Lord Hara took up the Pināka bow and assumed the form of a hunter. He fitted one arrow to his bow. He drew the bow string as far as his ear and hit Brahmā with his sharp arrow. Struck down by the arrow of the Annihilator of the three Puras, Brahmā fell down on the ground.

13. A great luminous refulgence rose up from his body. It became the constellation named Mṛgaśīrṣa of great lustre in the sky.

14. Assuming the form of the constellation Ārdrā, Hara pursued him inflicting pain on the constellation named Mṛgaśīrṣa, the form of Brahmā.

15. Even now, O Brāhmaṇas, the Annihilator of the three Puras is clearly seen in the sky in the form of a hunter of deer, near Mṛgaśīrṣa.[1]

16-19. When Parameṣṭhin was thus slain by Śaṁbhu, Gāyatrī and Sarasvatī who were bereft of their husband became extremely sad. With a desire to resuscitate their husband, O excellent sages, they consulted each other: "What shall we do to revive our lord?"

In order to regain their lost husband, Gāyatrī and Sarasvatī went to Gandhamādana, the most excellent holy spot of Śiva, the bestower of all desires of men. They were inclined to perform penance.

1. This is generally attributed to the destruction of Dakṣa's sacrifice when Firegod flew in the heaven and Śiva followed him as a hunter.

They observed all the restraints in order to perform the penance with Śiva in view.

20. For their holy bath, O Brāhmaṇas, Gāyatrī and Sarasvatī made two Tīrthas after their own names, destructive of all sins.

21-26. They joyously took their holy baths thrice everyday there. They performed their penance abstaining from food for a long time. They were free from (the bad feelings of) lust, anger, etc. They practised very severe observances and restraints. They were absorbed in meditation on Śiva. They were auspicious. They strictly adhered to the recitation of the great five-syllabled Mantra. Thus, for the sake of resuscitating their lord, Gāyatrī and Sarasvatī performed the penance with Mahādeva in view.

Delighted with their penance, Mahādeva, the great lord, presented himself there in his great form with a desire to grant them the benefit of their penance.

On seeing Śaṁbhu, Lord Śiva, the lover of Pārvatī, present there, attended on either side by Gaṇeśa and Kārttikeya, Gāyatrī and Sarasvatī became extremely pleased. With many hymns and prayers they eulogized Mahādeva, the storehouse of mercy, worthy of being eulogized.

Gāyatrī and Sarasvatī eulogized:

27-33. Obeisance to the sole cause of the destruction of the darkness of unavoidable worldly existence. Bow to the lord who consumed the Kālakūṭa poison dreadful on account of the blazing flames.

O lord who fascinate the universe, obeisance to you, the sole cause of the destruction of the body of Kāmadeva equipped with five missiles. Obeisance to you, O annihilator of the ruthless Yama who destroys the worlds. Bow to the lord who wears a cluster of matted hair washed by the waves of Gaṅgā. Obeisance to you, O lord with uneven (three) eyes. Hail to the lord wearing the crescent moon. Obeisance to the lord who frightened the dwellers of the three Puras by means of the dreadful twanging sound of the Pināka bow; bow to you, the lord who cut off the head of the creator of the universe full of things of diverse kinds and shapes. O lord who protected Mṛkaṇḍu's son with compassionate vision, peaceful and devoid of impurities. Obeisance to you, O lord of the Daughter of the Mountain. We have sought refuge in you, protect us both. O Mahādeva, O lord of the universe, O Śaṅkara,

O destroyer of the Tripuras, O Vāmadeva, O Mahādeva, we have sought refuge in you. Protect us both.

On being eulogized by them both, Śambhu, the great lord, the lord of Devas, became pleased. He spoke to Gāyatrī and Sarasvatī.

Mahādeva said:

34-35. O Sarasvatī, O Gāyatrī, I am pleased with you both. Choose a boon from me, whatever may be in your minds.

On being addressed thus by Hara, Gāyatrī and Sarasvatī spoke to Mahādeva, the lord of Pārvatī, the storehouse of mercy:

Gāyatrī and Sarasvatī said:

36-42. O lord, O merciful lord of all, kindly resuscitate our husband, the Four-faced Lord. O lord, you are our father. We are your two daughters. Hence, O Destroyer of the Three Puras, save us by giving back to us our husband.

On being thus requested by both of them, O eminent Brāhmaṇas, Śambhu said to Gāyatrī and Sarasvatī, "It will be so". He was eager to unite the same body of Brahmā with his head.

O sages of virtuous conduct, Śambhu got the body of Brahmā along with his heads there itself through the Bhūtas, the chiefs of whom were Nandī and Bhṛṅgī. In a moment in the presence of Vāṇī (Sarasvatī) and Gāyatrī, Śaṅkara united those many heads with his body. Thus joined by Hara, the Four-faced Lord of the universe got up immediately, O Brāhmaṇas, as though he was getting up from his sleep. On seeing the moon-crested Lord Śaṅkara, Prajāpati (i.e. Brahmā) eulogized him with excellent words along with his wives.

Brahmā said:

43-47. Obeisance to you, O lord of the chiefs of Devas, O merciful Śaṅkara. Protect me, O ocean of mercy. Save me from committing forbidden actions. By your mercifulness, let there be no inclination in me towards the commission of forbidden acts henceforth. Further, protect me always.

The Lord of the Daughter of the Mountain said to Brahmā: "Let it be so. O Brahmā, henceforth do not commit any similar blunder. I am the perpetual chastiser of all persons who go astray."

After saying this to the Four-faced Lord, O excellent Brāhmaṇas, Mahādeva said to Gāyatrī and Sarasvatī:

Mahādeva said:

48-51a. Due to my favour, O Gāyatrī, O Sarasvatī, the Four-faced One, your husband, has come back alive. Go to the world of Brahmā along with him. Let there be no delay. Since you two will be perpetually present in these two sacred Kuṇḍas, men will attain salvation in the form of *Sāyujya* by taking the holy bath here. This Tīrtha will become famous permanently all over the world by your names, Gāyatrī and Sarasvatī.

51b-53. Of all the Tīrthas, this pair of Tīrthas will be more efficacious as the bestowers of purity, destructive of great sins, cause of great peace, and givers of all desired objects unto men. They will cause pleasure to me and to Viṣṇu also. There never was nor will ever be a Tīrtha on a par with these two Tīrthas.

54-57. Indeed by taking the holy bath everyone will realize every desire. These two sacred Kuṇḍas created by you two are very great. They will become famous by your names. They will bestow salvation. Those who do not regularly perform the *Upāsti* (meditation and worship) of Gāyatrī, those who are devoid of Vedic studies and recitation, those who are without *Aupāsana* (sacrificial rites), those who do not perform the five daily Yajñas—all these shall attain the respective merits by taking the holy bath in your Kuṇḍas. Others who commit great sins and do not perform the daily devotional rites shall, by taking the holy bath in these two Kuṇḍas, become pure and excellent, O Brāhmaṇas.

58. After speaking thus to Sarasvatī and Gāyatrī Maheśvara instantly vanished there itself, even as all were watching.

59-61. After getting back their husband, Gāyatrī and Sarasvatī became joyous. Along with him, they went to the world of Brahmā, O excellent Brāhmaṇas.

Śrī Sūta said:

Thus it has been recounted to you, O Brāhmaṇas, how and why

Gāyatrī and Sarasvatī happened to be present at Gandhamādana Parvata.

He who listens to this chapter or he who reads this with devotion, shall undoubtedly attain the merit of taking the holy bath in these two Kuṇḍas.

CHAPTER FORTYONE

The Glory of Gāyatrī and Sarasvatī Kuṇḍas: Destruction of Kāśyapa's Sin

Śrī Sūta said:

1-2. Henceforth I shall relate a story of great sanctity concerning Gāyatrī and Sarasvatī (Tīrthas).

A Brāhmaṇa named Kāśyapa took his holy bath formerly in these two Tīrthas, and became absolved of a great sin that would have sent him to Naraka.

The sages said:

3-4. O sage, what sin did this (Brāhmaṇa) named Kāśyapa commit, from which he was instantly liberated by taking the holy bath in these two Tīrthas? Narrate this mercifully, O Sūta, to us who are faithful. Persons who are satisfied with the nectar of your words, do not feel even thirst.

Śrī Sūta said:

5. I shall describe the legendary story[1] that illustrates the glory of Gāyatrī and Sarasvatī and that is destructive of the sins of those who listen (to it).

---

1. The story how King Parīkṣit was cursed to be bitten by Takṣaka for his insult of Sage Śamīka and how the Brāhmaṇa Kāśyapa who was going to save him from Takṣaka-bite was bribed by Takṣaka, is told in details in Mbh, *Ādi* Chs. 40 to 43. This Purāṇa borrows this story from Mbh and uses it to glorify the above Tīrthas by stating how that Brāhmaṇa Kāśyapa was absolved of his sin (complicity in Parīkṣit's murder) by bathing in these Kuṇḍas and was respectably rehabilitated in social Brāhmaṇical status.

6. The son of Abhimanyu, the king named Parīkṣit, stayed in (occupied) the city of Hastināpura protecting the earth righteously.

7-8. Once when the king was sixty years old, he went to the forest for hunting. Wandering (here and there) he became afflicted with hunger and thirst. He was in search of a deer (which escaped after being hit). While searching for it enthusiastically, he saw a sage in bark garments engaged in meditation and spoke to him:

9-12. "A certain deer was hit by me in this forest now, O sage. It ran away in extreme fright, O learned man. Was it seen by you?"

As the sage was engaged in meditation and hence adopted silence, he did not say anything in reply. Thereupon the king became angry. With the tip of his bow (he lifted) a dead serpent and placed it on the shoulders of the great sage. The king went away to the city.

The sage had a son named Śṛṅgī. He had a friend named Kṛśa, O excellent Brāhmaṇas. That friend named Kṛśa said to his companion Śṛṅgin:

13-15. "Your father holds a dead serpent on his shoulders. O friend, do not be proud. Do not be haughty in vain."

The infuriated Śṛṅgin desirous of cursing the king said thus: "Let that man of deluded mind, who placed the dead serpent on my father's body, die within seven days, on being bitten by the serpent Takṣaka."

Thus the son of the sage cursed Parīkṣit, the son of Subhadrā's son.

16-21. His father named Śamīka heard that the king had been cursed by his son. The great sage said to his son Śṛṅgī:

"Why did you curse the king, the protector of all the worlds? How will we be able to stay properly in a world without the king? A sin has been committed by you in anger. You will not be happy. He who dispels the rising anger by means of forbearance attains great happiness here and hereafter. Only persons endowed with forbearance derive excellent welfare."

Then Śamīka said to his disciple named Gauramukha:

"O Gauramukha, go to king Parīkṣit and tell him about this curse uttered by my son, that he would be bitten by serpent Takṣaka. Then, O highly intelligent one, come back to me quickly."

22-25. On being told thus by Śamīka, Gauramukha went to

the king. Approaching King Parīkṣit, the grandson of Subhadrā, he said to him thus:

"On seeing the dead serpent placed by you on the shoulders of his father, Śṛṅgī, the son of Śamīka, cursed you in anger: 'On the seventh day from today, the son of Abhimanyu shall be bitten by the great serpent Takṣaka. He shall be burned by the fire of poison.' O king, Śṛṅgī, the son of that sage, has cursed you thus. His father has sent me to you in order to tell you this."

26-30. After saying this to the king, Gauramukha returned immediately.

After Gauramukha had gone, the grief-stricken king got a pavilion made in the middle of Gaṅgā. It had only one pillar. It was very lofty. It scraped the sky. It was capacious.

With great concentration and care he made every effort to get the poison of Takṣaka quelled by physicians who knew medicines and Mahāgāruḍa Mantra. He was accompanied by many excellent celestial sages, Brāhmaṇical sages and saintly kings. The king who had great devotion to Viṣṇu sat in that lofty pavilion.

At that time a Brāhmaṇa named Kāśyapa who was an excellent *Māntrika* (one well-versed in Mantras) set out in order to save the king from the great poison of Takṣaka on the seventh day.

31-34. The eminent Brāhmaṇa was poor. So he was (naturally) desirous of some wealth. In the meantime, Takṣaka too had set out assuming the form of a Brāhmaṇa. On the way, he met Kāśyapa and spoke to him: "O Brāhmaṇa, O great sage, where are you going? Tell me."

On being asked thus, O Brāhmaṇas, Kāśyapa spoke to Takṣaka: "Takṣaka will bite Parīkṣit, the great king today, and burn him by means of the fire of his poison. I am going to him in order to quell it (the poison)."

As the Brāhmaṇa said thus, Takṣaka said to him once again.

35-40. "I am Takṣaka, O excellent Brāhmaṇa. It is not possible to cure a person bitten by me by means of ten thousand great Mantras in the course of a hundred years. If you have the power to cure one bitten by me I shall bite this banyan tree which is many Yojanas tall. Revive it. Then (I shall admit) that you are really competent."

After saying thus, Takṣaka bit that tree. That tree which was extremely tall was reduced to ash. Earlier a man had climbed on it. He was burned by the poisonous flames of Takṣaka, but neither

Takṣaka nor Kāśyapa was aware of it. Even as Takṣaka listened, Kāśyapa proclaimed thus: "O ye all Brāhmaṇas, witness the power of our Mantra now."

41-46. After saying this, Kāśyapa, the most excellent one among Māntrikas, resuscitated by the power of his Mantra, that tree which had been reduced to ash by the poisonous flame. Along with the tree, that man too was revived. Then Takṣaka said to Kāśyapa who was an expert in the employment of Mantras: "O Brāhmaṇa, do everything in such a manner as not to falsify the utterance of the sage. I shall give you twice the amount that the king may possibly give you. O excellent Brāhmaṇa, return quickly."

After saying this, Takṣaka gave him very valuable jewels and gems. Thus he made that Brāhmaṇa Kāśyapa who was an expert in Mantras, return.

With the power of the vision of knowledge Kāśyapa realized that the king was not destined to live long. So he quietly went to his hermitage after receiving the gems and jewels from Takṣaka.

At the same time Takṣaka called all the serpents together and said:

47-51a. "All of you adopt the guise of sages and go to that king. Give Parīkṣit fruits in the form of present."

All those serpents said, "So it shall be". They gave the king fruits as presents. Takṣaka assumed the form of worm and entered a jujube fruit in order to bite the king.

King Parīkṣit gave away all the fruits handed over by the serpents in the guise of Brāhmaṇas to those elderly persons efficient in the employment of Mantras. The king eagerly took up a big fruit in his hand. At that time, the sun set behind the Western mountain.

51b-55. All the men there, the Brāhmaṇas and the kings said to one another, "Will not the utterance of the sage be false?" Even as all of them were saying thus, a red worm was seen by all of them and by King Parīkṣit. The king then said: "Perhaps this worm may bite me now; will it?" After saying this, O excellent Brāhmaṇas, he placed that fruit on his ear along with the worm. Takṣaka who had concealed himself earlier within that fruit in the form of a worm, immediately came out of that fruit, and twined round the body of the king. When the king was encircled by Takṣaka all those who were at his side fled out of fright.

56-61. Thereafter, O Brāhmaṇas, the king was burned to ash by the poisonous flame of Takṣaka. He was reduced to ash along with his palace by the powerful poison of Takṣaka.

The ministers and the priests performed the obsequies of the king. They crowned his son named Janamejaya as the king in the realm, with a desire to protect the entire universe.

The Brāhmaṇa named Kāśyapa, O excellent sages, who had come to protect the king from Takṣaka, was condemned by all the people (because he did not do so). He wandered over the different lands. He was censured by all the honourable people. He did not get any (permanent) place (of rest) either in a village or in a hermitage. To whatever land he went, he was expelled by the leading public men of those lands.

Ultimately he sought refuge in Śākalya.[1] Kāśyapa who was censured by the people bowed down to Sage Śākalya. He said these words to the noble-souled Śākalya:

Kāśyapa said:

62-66. O holy lord Śākalya, conversant with all holy rites, O favourite of Hari, sages, other Brāhmaṇas and friendly people censure me. I do not know the reason thereof. Why do these men condemn me? I have not committed Brāhmaṇa-murder, liquor-drinking, sexual intercourse with my preceptor's wife or theft (of any sort). Nor am I defiled by association with these sinners at any place. Nor other sin has been committed by me, O sage. Still the people, the kinsmen and others, condemn me in vain. If you know, O Śākalya, tell me the fault committed by me.

On being told thus by Kāśyapa, the great sage Śākalya meditated for a short while, O excellent Brāhmaṇas, and spoke to Kāśyapa:

Śākalya said:

67-73. You proceeded (to Hastināpura) in order to save Parīkṣit, the great king, from Takṣaka. But on the way you had been prevented by Takṣaka. If a person, competent to cure one who is afflicted with poison, ailment, etc., does not save him due to covetousness, people call that person a Brāhmaṇa-slayer. O great Brāhmaṇa, he who does not save a man afflicted with poison or ailment because

1. Mbh does not know this Śākalya. But PE (667) records this episode and Śākalya advises Kāśyapa to bathe in the Godāvarī river (instead of Gāyatrī Kuṇḍa).

of anger, lust, fear, covetousness, jealousy or delusion, is (on a par with) a Brāhmaṇa-slayer, a drink-addict, a thief, a defiler of the preceptor's bed and one who is contaminated by association with these. There is no means of atonement for him.

Indeed there is some means of expiation mentioned in the scriptures in regard to one who sells a girl, one who deals in selling horses and even an ungrateful person. But if a person competent to save does not save one who is afflicted with poison and ailments, no means of atonement has been laid down for him. He cannot make amends even by means of ten thousand expiatory rites. A meritorious person shall not take food along with him in the same row.

74-80. No one should talk to him. No one should look at him in any place. Merely by talking to him one will incur great sin.

That great King Parīkṣit was a righteous person of renown. He was a great Yogin and a devotee of Viṣṇu. He was a defender of the discipline of the four castes. He heard the story of Hari from the son of Vyāsa (i.e. Śuka) with great devotion.

At the instance of Takṣaka you returned without (even attempting) to save him. Therefore, you are abused and condemned by leading Brāhmaṇas and kinsmen. Although the great King Parīkṣit was one destined to be short-lived, it is essential on the part of learned men, to continue the medical treatment till death.

Persons who have mastered the ocean-like science of medicine as physicians have uttered this verse in days of yore: "In the case of a man on the verge of death, treatment should be continued as long as the vital airs are at his throat. The movement of god of Death is crooked (and unpredictable)."

Though you are capable of treating, you abstained from administering any antidote. You retraced your steps after coming half the way and thereby you killed him.

On being told thus by Śākalya, Kāśyapa replied:

Kāśyapa said:

81-86. O sage of good holy rites, tell the means of subsiding this evil of mine, so that my kinsmen and friendly people will accept me (respectfully), O Śākalya. O favourite of Hari, take pity on me.

On being told thus by Kāśyapa, the great sage Śākalya meditated for a short while, and then said sympathetically to Kāśyapa:

CHAPTER FORTYTWO

Ṛṇamocana and Other Tīrthas

Śrī Sūta said:

1-6. Henceforth, O eminent sages, I shall recount the glory of all the Tīrthas situated in the middle of the Setu, but not described so far.

There is a Tīrtha of great merit named Ṛṇamocana.[1] If men take their holy plunge here, all their three debts become cleared. As soon as a Brāhmaṇa is born, he incurs three debts, viz. (the debt) to the Sages, to the Devas and to the Pitṛs, O excellent Brāhmaṇas.

If he does not practise the vow of celibacy (and study the Vedas), he gets into debt to the Sages. If he does not perform Yajña, etc. he becomes a debtor to the Devas. If he does not beget sons, he is in debt to the Pitṛs.

Without (observing) the vow of celibacy, without performing Yajña and without begetting any son, men shall attain liberation from indebtedness to the Sages, the Devas and the Pitṛs by merely taking the holy bath in the Tīrtha named Ṛṇamokṣa ('Release from debts').

7-13. The Sages, the Devas and the Pitṛs are not so much pleased with the vow of celibacy, Yajña and the birth of a son, as they attain matchless pleasure by the holy bath in the (Tīrtha named) Ṛṇamokṣa.

Further, by taking the holy bath here, poor persons and persons who are in debt become free of all debts and rich (also). There is no doubt about it.

Since the men who take their holy plunge here are liberated from indebtedness, this Tīrtha is known by the name Ṛṇamocana. Hence all persons in debt should take their holy bath here for extricating themselves from the same. There has never been a Tīrtha on a par with this, nor will there ever be one.

There is another great Tīrtha here created by Pāṇḍavas.[2] Here

---

1. This Tīrtha is near Thangachimadana near Ekānta Rāma Temple.

2. Pāṇḍava Tīrtha is not one Tīrtha called Dharma Tīrtha, but a group of five Tīrthas named after the five Pāṇḍava brothers Dharma, Bhīma, Arjuna, Nakula and Sahadeva. They are near Gandhamādana Parvata. Mbh does not support this act of Pāṇḍavas. Gandhamādana mentioned here is on the southern ocean, while Gandhamādana mentioned in Mbh, *Vana* Chs. 144, 155, 158 is a part of the Himalayas.

the five Pāṇḍavas including the eldest Dharmaputra performed a Yajña formerly with this Tīrtha in view, (as) it yields both worldly pleasures and salvation. Ten thousand crores of excellent Tīrthas are always present in this Tīrtha of the five Pāṇḍavas.

14. Ādityas, Vasus, Rudras, Sādhyas and groups of Maruts are always present in the great Tīrtha of the Pāṇḍavas.

15. He who takes the holy bath here and offers libations to the Pitṛs and the Devas, shall be rid of all sins. He is honoured in the world of Brahmā.

16. If anyone feeds at least one Brāhmaṇa on the banks of this Tīrtha devoid of impurities, he rejoices here and hereafter on account of this holy act.

17. A Brāhmaṇa, a Kṣatriya, a Vaiśya or a Śūdra or anyone else who takes his holy bath in this excellent Tīrtha, does not take a debased birth.

18. The man who takes his holy bath in the great Tīrtha of Pāṇḍavas during auspicious conjunctions (of stars, etc.) becomes the most excellent of all men. He never sees Naraka.

19. If a person remembers the great Tīrtha of Pāṇḍavas in the morning and in the evening, it is as good as if he had taken his holy bath in Gaṅgā and all other Tīrthas. There is no doubt about it.

20. There is another Tīrtha on Gandhamādana named Devatīrtha, where Indra and other Devas performed Yajñas for the purpose of subduing Daityas.

21. By taking the holy bath in Devatīrtha a man is liberated from all sins. He shall attain eternal worlds and all his desires.

22. The sin committed by a man or a woman ever since his birth, perishes immediately after taking the holy bath in this Devakuṇḍa.

23. Just as the Slayer of Madhu is the first and foremost among all the Suras, so also the excellent Devakuṇḍa is the first and foremost among all Tīrthas.

24-28. If a man performed Agnihotra for full hundred years and if another man takes the holy bath in this Devakuṇḍa casually once, their merits are on a par with each other. There is no reason why anyone should doubt this.

Charitable gifts and residence in this Devakuṇḍa are rarely obtained. Going to Devatīrtha and taking holy bath therein, are very rare achievements. One who goes to Devatīrtha and propitiates the Devas, the Sages and the Pitṛs, obtains the merit of a horse-sacrifice. He goes to the world of Viṣṇu. If a person stays on the banks of Devakuṇḍa, destructive of Naraka, for two, three, five or six days, he no longer stays in the womb of any mother. He attains the excellent Siddhi.

29-33. By taking the holy bath here for three days, one gets the merit of the Vājapeya sacrifice. By remembering Devatīrtha a man is immediately liberated from sins.

By worshipping the Devas and the Pitṛs on the banks of this Tīrtha, a man shall fully attain all his desires and (also) the benefit of all the Yajñas.

There has never been a meritorious Tīrtha on a par with this Tīrtha nor will there ever be one. Hence those desirous of salvation should of necessity take their holy bath in Devatīrtha.

Similarly those men who are desirous of achieving the benefit of this and the next world, should take their bath in Devatīrtha. The glory of Devatīrtha has been succinctly recounted, O Brāhmaṇas. It is impossible for me to describe it in detail.

I shall (now) describe Sugrīvatīrtha[1] on Rāmasetu that bestows salvation.

34-40. By devoutly taking the holy bath here a man obtains the world of the Sun. By taking the holy bath in Sugrīvatīrtha, one shall get the merit of a horse-sacrifice. Expiation for Brāhmaṇa-slaughter and other sins is caused hereby. By proceeding towards Sugrīvatīrtha, one shall get the merit (of the gift) of a thousand cows.

By remembering it one shall get the merit of reciting the Vedas. By merely observing a fast for a day on the banks of this Tīrtha, O Brāhmaṇas, great sins will be destroyed even without a (formal) expiatory rite. One who takes the holy bath there, should offer libations to the Pitṛs and the Devas. He will get eight times the merit of the Yajña (named) Āptoryāma. By taking the holy bath in Sugrīvatīrtha one shall obtain the merit of human sacrifice.

By taking the holy bath in Sugrīvatīrtha, a man will be able to remember (events of the past) births. O Brāhmaṇas, go to Sugrīvatīrtha for the attainment of what is desired. Thus, O Brāhmaṇas, the glory of Sugrīvatīrtha has been recounted to you.

Now I shall recount the glory of Nalatīrtha[2] to you.

---

1. This Tīrtha is on the way to the Gandhamādana Parvata.
2. This is (now) a well in the compound of Mādhava Shrine (3rd Prākāra—West) in the Rameśvara Temple premises.

41-46a. By taking the holy bath in Nalatīrtha a man obtains the heavenly world. By taking the holy bath once in Nalatīrtha, one shall be liberated from all sins and shall obtain the excellent merit of the sacrifices Agniṣṭoma, Atirātra, etc.

One who stays there for three days and offers libations to the Pitṛs and the Devas, O Brāhmaṇas, shines like the Sun and obtains the merit of a horse-sacrifice.

I shall now recount Nīlatīrtha[1] which is destructive of great sins. It has been made by Nīla, the son of Agni, on the Setu. It yields salvation. By taking the holy bath in Nīlatīrtha, a man shall be released from all sins and he obtains hundred times the merit of the Yāga named Bahuvarṇya.

By taking the holy bath in Nīlatīrtha that bestows all desires, a man attains the world of Agni. He shall amply realize all his desires.

46b-50. There is a Tīrtha on the Gandhamādana mountain, made by Gavākṣa.[2] By taking the holy bath in it, one can avoid falling into a hell.

There is a Tīrtha on the Setu made by Aṅgada.[3] It bestows salvation. By taking his holy bath here a man attains the status of Devendra.

There are other Tīrthas made by Gaja, Gavaya,[4] Śarabha of great prowess, Kumuda, Hara and Panasa, the strong one. There are Tīrthas made by other monkeys also on the exceedingly meritorious Rāmasetu on the Gandhamādana mountain. He who takes his holy bath in those Tīrthas attains immortality.

51-55a. There is a Tīrtha made by Bibhīṣaṇa (Vibhīṣaṇa). It liberates one from sins. It subdues great miseries. It dispels great ailments. It is excellent. It is like fire unto the heaps of great sins. It is the destroyer of the torture of Kuṁbhīpāka and other Narakas. It destroys evil dreams. It is conducive to wealth. It removes great poverty. One who takes his holy bath there never incurs any sin. He attains Vaikuṇṭha from where no one returns (to the earth).

There are four Tīrthas made by Vibhīṣaṇa's ministers. By tak-

---

1. This Tīrtha is near Nalatīrtha in the same premises.
2. This Tīrtha is in the same premises as the Nala- and Nīla-tīrthas.
3. This is on the way to Gandhamādana Parvata, outside the Rāmeśvara Temple.
4. This Tīrtha is near Nala-, Nīla-tīrthas in the same premise (compound of Mādhava Shrine).

ing his holy bath there a man is liberated from all sins.

55b-60a. The river Sarayū, O Brāhmaṇas, (comes to and) remains on the Gandhamādana mountain always to serve Rāmanātha, the great lord. By taking their holy bath there, all men become relieved of all sins. They shall attain the merit of resorting to all Tīrthas and performing all penances.

Ten thousand crores of Tīrthas reside on this extremely meritorious Gandhamādana mountain, O excellent Brāhmaṇas. Similarly the rivers including Gaṅgā, the seven oceans, the meritorious hermitages of the sages, the meritorious forests and excellent holy spots of Hari and Śaṅkara are always present on the Gandhamādana mountain.

60b-61. The Four-faced Lord has spoken of another Tīrtha called Upavītāntara (?).

At the bidding of Lord Rāmacandra the thirty-three crores of Devas reside on the Setu along with groups of Pitṛs, all the sages, Yakṣas, Siddhas and the Kinnaras.

Śrī Sūta said:

62-63. Thus, O excellent Brāhmaṇas, the glory of the Tīrthas has been recounted by me. He who reads or listens to this, is liberated from a host of miseries. He attains salvation from which there is no return (to worldly existence).

CHAPTER FORTYTHREE

*The Glory of Rāmanātha**

Śrī Sūta said:

1-7. Henceforth, I shall recount the glory of Rāmanātha, on hearing which a man on the earth is liberated from all the sins.

If a man sees once the Liṅga installed by Rāma, he attains salvation in the form of Sāyujya with Śiva.

In Tretāyuga, men obtain in one year that much of merit which

* Rāmanātha and Rameśvara are the two names of the same Liṅga installed by Rāma. The Southerners (the author of this Māhātmya is presumably so) prefer to call it Rāmanātha while we from the North called it Rameśvara.

The great Liṅga Rāmeśvara dispels the agony of men in adversity. The lord should be listened to, glorified and remembered by learned men.

He who offers villages to Lord Rāmeśvara becomes Śiva himself at the destruction (death) of the body, as destined.

Rāmanātha, the great lord, is the most excellent one among the deserving for religious charity (Dāna). By offering (gifts) to him, O Brāhmaṇas, one attains infinite pleasure. It is true.

Sin (exists) only till one visits the great Liṅga of Rāmanātha. By giving him anything the man (donor) shall certainly become an emperor.

126b-132a. Those men who offer fans, flags, umbrella, sandalpaste, aromatic gum resin as well as copper, brass, silver, gold or bejewelled pots for the ablution of Rāmanātha are born as overlords of the whole world in their next birth.

Those who produce flowers for worshipping Rāmanātha certainly obtain the merit of a horse-sacrifice and other sacrifices.

There is nothing difficult of access if the great Liṅga Rāmeśvara is worshipped, bowed down to, remembered, heard and seen, O eminent Brāhmaṇas.

Masses of sins of a person become frightened immediately on seeing him proceeding on to serve and resort to the great Liṅga Rāmanātha.

If Rāmanātha, the great lord, is seen by men, of what avail are the Vedas, scriptural texts and resorting to Tīrthas?

132b-133. He who offers sandalpaste, saffron, Koṣṭha (?), musk, aromatic gum resin and resin of the pine to Rāmeśvara becomes very rich in the world and also one who has mastered the Vedas.

134. One who offers pearls, ornaments, costly garments, etc. to Rāmanātha, never becomes distressed or miserable.

135. One who bathes the great Liṅga Rāmanātha with the waters of Gaṅgā (specially) brought for that purpose, is worthy of being worshipped even by Śiva. There is no doubt about it.

136-137. Before one dies, before one is assailed by old age, before one is faced with the defects and deficiencies of the sense-organs, O excellent Brāhmaṇas, Mahādeva Rāmanātha, Śiva, should be saluted, worshipped, mentally pondered over and eulogized regularly.

138. There is no other holy rite on a par with the worship of

the great Liṅga Rāmeśvara in all the Purāṇas and in all scriptural texts.

139. Those who devoutly worship Lord Rāmanātheśvara, the exceedingly merciful lord, become ever happy in this terrestrial world.

140. They enjoy worldly pleasures yielding great happiness along with their wives and sons. When this body perishes, they will attain perpetual salvation.

Śrī Sūta said:

141-142. Thus, O Brāhmaṇas, the glory of Rāmanātha has been recounted to you all. He who listens to this always and recites this with devotion, obtains the excellent merit of doing service to Rāmanātha. He attains the merit of taking the holy bath in the great Tīrtha of Dhanuṣkoṭi.

CHAPTER FORTYFOUR

The Installation of the Liṅga of Rāmanātha

The sages said:

1-4. O Sūta, O knower of the true meaning of the Vedas, you have crossed the ocean of (i.e. have attained mastery over the vast learning of) the Purāṇas. You have dispelled all inauspicious things by prostrating at the lotus-like feet of Vyāsa. You help all living beings by teaching them the contents of the Purāṇas. We have been blessed by you by your narration of the Purāṇas.

Now, O sage, by your narration of the greatness of Setu, we have become exceedingly blessed and contented, O highly intelligent disciple of Vyāsa. We wish to hear how Rāma, the son of Daśaratha, installed the Liṅga. Narrate it to us now.

Śrī Sūta said:

5. O eminent Brāhmaṇas, I shall now recount why the Liṅga was installed by Rāmacandra on the Gandhamādana mountain.

6-10. After his wife had been abducted by the powerful Rāvaṇa from the forest, Rāma, who was courageous and had great strength, reached Mahendra mountain along with Lakṣmaṇa and the army of the monkeys.[1] He surveyed the ocean. The scion of the family of Raghu built the Setu on that boundless ocean. Thereby he went to the city of Laṅkā defended by Rāvaṇa.

Early in the full-moon night, after the sun had set, O Brāhmaṇas, Rāma climbed on the Suvela mountain along with his army.

Then, at night, the powerful son of the Sun-god saw the ruler of Laṅkā standing in the mansion and caused his crown to fall down. The demon whose crown was smashed, went within the abode.

11-16. After the lord of Laṅkā had gone within his abode, Rāma got down from the mountain top in the company of his younger brother (Lakṣmaṇa), Sugrīva as well as his army. The heroic Rāma deployed the army around Laṅkā.

As the (army of) monkeys were being arranged and established, the followers of Rāvaṇa, viz. Parvaṇa, Pūtana, Jṛmbha, Khara, Krodhavaśa, Hari, Prāruja, Aruja, Prahasta and others rushed at them.

They were fully armed. They had huge bodies. They were accompanied by their soldiers. They attacked (the monkeys) while keeping themselves invisible. Then Bibhīṣaṇa dispelled the invisibility of those vicious ones (i.e. made them visible).

Being perceptible now to the powerful monkeys who could leap long distance, they were all killed by them. They fell down dead. Unable to brook this, Rāvaṇa set out with his army.

17-20. Removing those monkeys (from their positions) he destroyed them with his arrows. Rāghava then set out with his army well-arrayed and fought with the ten-headed demon, with great vehemence.

Then duels took place there. Indrajit, the son of Rāvaṇa, fought with Lakṣmaṇa. Virūpākṣa fought with Sugrīva. Kharvaṭa fought with Aṅgada, son of Tārā. Pauṇḍra fought with Nala. Puṭeśa fought with Panasa. The other monkeys too, of great heroism, fought duels with the Rākṣasas. The whole battle was tumultuous increasing fright within the cowards.

21. Shattered thus by the monkeys of dreadful valour, the

---

1. VV 6-57 are a brief resumé of the war between Rāma and Rāvaṇa (cf VR, VI, cantos 20-108).

Rākṣasas fled from the battlefield immediately to Laṅkā defended by Rāvaṇa.

22-23. When all the soldiers were thus shattered, Rāvaṇa sent his son Indrajit, O Brāhmaṇas. Rāma and Lakṣmaṇa, the two sons of Daśaratha, were struck in the battle by Indrajit with exceedingly dreadful serpent-missiles. They were then liberated by the noble-souled son of Vinatā (Garuḍa).[1]

24. Prahasta came there speedily. Hardy in battle that he was, he roared loudly and struck Bibhīṣaṇa with an iron club.

25. Though hit with that iron club of dreadful velocity that mighty and intelligent Bibhīṣaṇa did not tremble. He remained firm like the Himālaya mountain.

26. Bibhīṣaṇa took up a huge Śakti fitted with eight bells, consecrated it with Mantras, and hurled it at his head.

27. The head of that demon was taken away by that Śakti as it fell on him, just as the crown of a tree is smashed by the thunderbolt. The demon thus resembled a tree uprooted by (stormy) wind.

28. On seeing the demon Prahasta killed in battle, Dhūmrākṣa speedily rushed against the monkeys.

29. When he saw that the army of the monkeys had fled, the son of Wind-god (i.e. Hanumān) immediately struck down Dhūmrākṣa with an arrow in the battle ground.

30. On seeing that Dhūmrākṣa was killed, the demons who survived reported to King Rāvaṇa everything as it happened.

31. Then the lord of Laṅkā awakened Kumbhakarṇa who was lying down asleep. When he got up, Rāvaṇa, sent him to the battle front.

32. As Kumbhakarṇa came to the battlefield, the infuriated Lakṣmaṇa[2] hit him with the Brahmā Missile. He fell down lifeless.

33. Vajravega and Pramāthī, the younger brothers of Dūṣaṇa, who were on a par with Rāvaṇa in the battlefield, were killed by Hanumān and Nīla.

34. Nīla, the son of Viśvakarman, killed Vajradaṁṣṭra. Kumuda, a great monkey, killed Akampana.

35. On the sixth day, the king (Rāvaṇa) was defeated and he entered the city. Atikāya and Triśiras were killed by Lakṣmaṇa.

---

1. Cf. VR, VI.50.38-65.
2. According to VR VI.67 it was Rāma and not Lakṣmaṇa who killed Kumbhakarṇa.

36. Devāntaka and Narāntaka were killed in battle by Sugrīva. The two sons of Kuṁbhakarṇa were killed in the battle by Hanumān.

37. Makarākṣa, the son of Khara, was killed by Bibhīṣaṇa. Thereupon Rāvaṇa directed his son Indrajit.

38-40. Indrajit made the brothers Rāma and Lakṣmaṇa unconscious in the battlefield. His vehicle was destroyed by Aṅgada with dreadful arrows. Staying in the firmament he struck down all the monkeys along with Kumuda, Aṅgada, Sugrīva, Nala, Jāṁbavān and others. Having struck down Rāma and Lakṣmaṇa thus in the battlefield, the exceedingly powerful Meghanāda vanished in the sky.

41. With palms joined in reverence, Bibhīṣaṇa bowed down to Rāma, the ornament unto the family of Ikṣvāku, again and again and spoke these words:

42-48. "At the bidding of Rājarāja (Kubera) a Guhyaka has brought some sacred water, O Rāma, the suppressor of enemies. He has brought it to you. O great king, Kubera has given this water to you. O scorcher of foes, he has sent it to you to enable you to see invisible beings. When you apply this water to your eyes, you will be able to see the living beings that have vanished and become invisible. To whomsoever you may give this, he too will be able to see the living beings that have vanished in the sky."

Saying "yes", Rāma accepted that water with great deference and purified his eyes with it. So also Lakṣmaṇa of great strength, Sugrīva, Jāṁbavān, Hanumān, Aṅgada, Mainda, Dvivida, Nīla and all other monkeys (washed their eyes) with the water offered by Rāma; all of them became pure-eyed. They saw the heroic son of Rāvaṇa who had vanished in the sky. As he came into view, Lakṣmaṇa rushed at him.

49-54. Lakṣmaṇa got his eyes sanctified by means of the water sent by Kubera and became dignified. He became infuriated and struck Indrajit. Thereupon, a great fight took place between Lakṣmaṇa and Indrajit. It was exceedingly wonderful and mysterious like the fight between Indra and Prahlāda. Then on the third day, O Brāhmaṇas, Indrajit was killed in the battle by the powerful Lakṣmaṇa with great effort. Then the entire original (main) army was killed by the wise Rāma.

When his favourite son was killed, the Ten-headed One was furious. Seated in his chariot and accompanied by many soldiers, he came out of the city. When Rāvaṇa attempted to kill Sītā, he was prevented by Vindhya.

Then Mātali, the charioteer of Indra, approached Rāma in the battlefield with a chariot that had the refulgence of the Sun and that was fitted with reddish-brown horses.[1]

55. Seated in the chariot of Indra Rāma, the most excellent one among the upholders of righteousness, struck down the heads of the great Rākṣasa by means of Brahmā missile.

56-57. The delighted Devas, Sages, Siddhas and Vidyādharas eulogized Rāma, the son of Daśaratha, who killed the ten-headed demon. They blessed (and greeted) him with (shouts of) victory. They showered the lotus-eyed Rāma with flowers.

58-62. After crowning Bibhīṣaṇa as the king of Laṅkā, Rāma got into the aerial chariot Puṣpaka accompanied by all the groups of Suras, surrounded by the armies and accompanied by Sītā and Lakṣmaṇa. Rāma who was accompanied by the army of the monkeys, went to the Gandhamādana mountain. On the mountain Gandhamādana, he tested the chastity of Sītā.

Rāma, the lotus-eyed one, was surrounded by the monkeys. The hero who had killed the lord of Laṅkā was accompanied by his wife, his younger brother and Bibhīṣaṇa. He was served by groups of Devas and leading sages. The sages residing in the Daṇḍaka forest came to see Rāma at this juncture. With Agastya as their leader, they eulogized the lord of Sītā.

The sages said:

63-68. Obeisance to you, to Rāmacandra who blessed all the worlds. You (the Lord) are incarnated on the earth to make the universe free from Rāvaṇa. Obeisance to the lord who annihilated Tāṭakā's body; to the lord who guarded the sacrifice of Viśvāmitra. Bow to you who conquered Mārīca, to the lord who slew Subāhu. Obeisance to the lord, the dust particles from whose lotus-like feet granted salvation to Ahalyā. Hail to you who sportingly broke the bow of Hara. Obeisance to you who became enthusiastic to grasp (in marriage) the hand of the daughter of the king of Mithilā. Bow to you, to the lord who defeated Reṇukā's son (i.e. Paraśurāma). Bow to the lord who came to the forest in order to make his father's promise true, (the promise concerning) the two boons granted to Kaikeyī, to the lord who came to the forest accompa-

1. Cf. VR, VI.102.

nied by Lakṣmaṇa and Sītā. Obeisance to you who gave away the pair of his sandals to Bharata at his request. Bow to you, the sole cause of the acquisition of heaven by Śarabhaṅga.

69-74. Obeisance to the annihilator of Virādha. Bow to you, to the friend of the king of vultures (Jaṭāyu). Obeisance to the lord who split the limbs of the cruel Mārīca who had assumed the form of the false deer.

Obeisance to the lord who burned (cremated) Jaṭāyus who lost his body in fight with the lord of Laṅkā who abducted Sītā; obeisance to the lord who granted salvation to him. Obeisance to the slayer of Kabandha. Obeisance to the lord whose feet were worshipped by the Śabara woman. Bow to you who entered into companionship with Sugrīva, to you who killed Vāli. Hail to the lord who made a Setu on the ocean, the abode of Varuṇa. Obeisance to the annihilator of all the Rākṣasas. Bow to the slayer of Rāvaṇa. Obeisance to you whose lotus-like feet become the raft for crossing the ocean of worldly existence. Obeisance to the destroyer of the agony of devotees. Hail to the lord, the embodiment of existence, knowledge and bliss. Obeisance to you, to Rāmabhadra. Obeisance to the cause of the prosperity of all the worlds. Bow to the lord who dispels the sins of those who repeat the meritorious names beginning with Rāma.

75-77. Obeisance to you, the cause of creation, sustenance and annihilation of all the worlds. Bow to you, the embodied form of mercy. Obeisance to you ready for protecting the devotees. Obeisance to you accompanied by Sītā, O lord, the bestower of happiness on Bibhīṣaṇa. Indeed, O Rāma, the universe is protected by you by slaying the lord of Laṅkā. Protect, protect, O Lord of the universe. Protect us, O Lord of Sītā.

After eulogizing thus all the sages became silent, O excellent Brāhmaṇas.

Śrī Sūta said:

78. He who devoutly recites during the three junctions (of the day) this hymn uttered by the sages, obtains worldly pleasures and salvation.

79-81. If anyone recites this at the time of starting on a journey, he will have nothing to be afraid of. By reading this hymn evil spirits, vampires, etc. perish. Ailments perish. Heaps of sins perish. One who is desirous of having a son, gets a son. A virgin gets a good husband. He who is desirous of salvation attains salvation. He who is desirous of wealth, gets wealth. One who devoutly recites this hymn, obtains all his desires.

82-86. Then Rāma bowed down to the sages and said to them with palms joined in reverence:

"I have to be attained by all men for the sake of sanctity. A living being within the range of my vision is entitled to perpetual salvation. Still, O sages, I bow down to holy, honourable and noble men who with their minds full of devotion are perpetually contented, who are pleased with the realization of their own souls, who are great friends of all living beings, who are devoid of arrogance and egotism, who strictly observe the vow of celibacy and are quiescent.

Since I am a Deva favourably inclined towards Brāhmaṇas, I always honour and adore Brāhmaṇas. I ask you all something. Answer it after due deliberation.

I have incurred sins, O Brāhmaṇas, by slaying Rāvaṇa. Tell me the means of expiation for the same, i.e. the sin arising from killing the descendant of Pulastya. By carrying it (the expiation) out, O great sages, I shall be absolved of that sin."

The sages said:

87-94. O lord of the worlds, O truthful one, O bearer of the burden of protection of the worlds, O Rāma, perform the worship of Śiva for the sake of rendering help to all the worlds. Perform the installation of the Liṅga of Śiva on the peak of Gandhamādana which is highly meritorious and yields salvation. Perform the installation of the Liṅga of Śiva with a desire for the welfare of the worlds. Perform this, O Rāma, for dispelling the sin arising from killing the Ten-headed Demon.

Even the Four-faced Lord is not competent to recount adequately the merit accruing from the installation of the Liṅga. Then, O lord, how can a man be competent to do so?

Visiting the Liṅga that is to be installed by you on the Gandhamādana mountain, shall be far more beneficial than visiting the Liṅga at Kāśī. There is no doubt about this that it will be a crore of times more meritorious. Let this Liṅga be known after your name.

It is destructive of both merits and sins. It is on a par with fire for the fuel named merits and sins. This Liṅga will become famous in the world as Rāmeśvara. Hence do not delay in regard to the holy rite of the installation of the Liṅga, O Rāmacandra of great fortune, who are full of mercy.

Śrī Sūta said:

95-96. After hearing these words of the sages, O great ascetics, Rāma, the lord of the universe, consulted about an auspicious hour which lasted two Muhūrtas. He then sent Hanumān to Kailāsa, the abode of Śiva. The scion of the family of Raghu wanted him to fetch a Liṅga of Śiva for installation.[1]

Rāma said:

97-103a. O Hanumān, the son of Wind-god and Añjanā, O highly powerful one, go to Kailāsa quickly and bring a Liṅga. Do not delay.

On being commanded thus by Rāma, the powerful lord of monkeys stroked his arms. Understanding (fully) that the auspicious hour extended only to two Muhūrtas, he leaped up with great velocity making Gandhamādana shake (from top to bottom) even as all the Devas and the noble-souled sages were watching.

Crossing the aerial path, he went to the Kailāsa mountain. The monkey did not see Mahādeva in the form of the Liṅga. For the sake of acquiring the Liṅga, the son of Añjanā, with full attention and concentration performed a penance on that auspicious Kailāsa mountain protected by Śaṅkara. He was seated on the Kuśa grass with their tips towards the East, O great ascetics. He had nothing to support him. He lifted up his arms. He held up his breath and conquered his sense-organs. Hanumān propitiated Mahādeva and acquired the Liṅga.

---

1. Kaṁba, the great Tamil poet, has given this story in his Rāmāyaṇa.
This work (SkP) is probably Kaṁban's source as the author of this Māhātmya and Kaṁban are Southerners. There is a close similarity in these accounts of the installation of Rāmanātha (Sand-Liṅga prepared by Sītā), Hanumān's late arrival, his attempt to uproot the Rāmeśvara Liṅga and the priority of paying respects to the Liṅga brought by Hanumān (in this and the following chapters).

103b-110. In the meantime, O **Brāhmaṇas**, the sages, the seers of the truth realized that there was only very little time left of the auspicious hour and that Hanumān had not come back. So they said thus to the highly intelligent Rāma:

"O Rāma, O Rāma, O mighty one, the time is passing off now. O lord, Jānakī has sportingly made a Liṅga of sand. It is a great and excellent Liṅga. Install it now."

On hearing these words, Rāma tied the auspicious thread (*Kautuka maṅgala*) (round his wrist) in the company of Sītā and the sages. He installed the Liṅga when there were ten very auspicious Yogas (astral and planetary conjunctions). It was the tenth day in the bright half of the month of Jyeṣṭha. The day was Wednesday. The constellation was Hasta and there was Vyatīpāta when the Karaṇa was Garānanda. The Moon was in the Zodiac of Virgo. The Sun was in the Taurus Zodiac. He installed Mahādeva Hara in the form of Liṅga on the highly meritorious Gandhamādana in the middle of the Setu. Rāma installed the excellent Śivaliṅga of Īśāna, wearing the elephant hide and holding Gaṅgā and the crescent Moon. Rāghava worshipped Īśvara along with Aṁbā stationed in the Liṅga.

111-114. Śaṅkara, the great lord, stationed in the Liṅga accompanied by Pārvatī appeared in person and granted an excellent boon to the noble-souled Rāghava, the refuge of all the worlds:

"O scion of the family of Raghu, whoever sees the Liṅga installed by you here, will get rid of his sins even if he be defiled by great sins. All the sins, even great sins, perish, O great King Rāmacandra, by taking the holy plunge in Dhanuṣkoṭi and by viewing the Rāmaliṅga. There is no doubt about it."

115. The lord, lord of Aṁbikā, granted this boon to Rāma. At the front, Rāghava installed Nandikeśa.

116-118. For the sake of the ablution of the lord, O Brāhmaṇas, Rāghava pierced the ground with the tip of his bow and made a well. He took water from it and bathed Śaṅkara. That meritorious excellent Tīrtha is called Koṭitīrtha. The glory thereof has already been recounted by us, O leading sages. The Devas, Sages, Serpents, Gandharvas, groups of celestial damsels and all the monkeys—everyone made a Liṅga eagerly.

Śrī Sūta said:

119-121. Thus, O Brāhmaṇas, how the Śivaliṅga that yields

worldly pleasures and salvation was installed by the intelligent Rāma has been recounted to you.

He who listens to or reads this installation of the Liṅga, shall obtain the merit of serving Rāmeśvara Liṅga. Due to the power of Rāmanātha, he shall attain *Sāyujya* too.

CHAPTER FORTYFIVE

Rāma's Discourse on Philosophy

Śrī Sūta said:

1-4. When the Liṅga was installed thus by Rāma, the doer of pleasant things, Hanumān came there all of a sudden, taking an excellent Liṅga with him. After bowing down to the heroic Rāma, the son of Daśaratha, Hanumān bowed down to Sītā, Lakṣmaṇa and then Sugrīva.

On seeing the scion of the family of Raghu engaged in worshipping that sand-Liṅga of Sītā along with the sages, the son of the Wind-god became angry.

With his effort gone in vain, he became excessively dejected (through exhaustion). Hanumān, the son of Añjanā, said to Rāma, the knower of Dharma:

Hanumān said:

5-11. I am unfortunate and wretched, O Rāma. I am born in the world only to experience distress. I have been subjected to great stress and strain by the Rākṣasas of cruel activities in various ways.

Would that no other lady should give birth to a son like me. For boundless misery has been experienced by me in this ocean of worldly existence.

Formerly, I was distressed due to service, still move due to the war, but far more than that my misery is endless now, because you slight me.

O scion of the family of Raghu, you have been served by Sugrīva for the sake of his wife, and by the Rākṣasa, the younger brother of Rāvaṇa, for the sake of the kingdom. O Rāma, you have been served by me without any particular motive (or personal interest), O highly intelligent one.

I alone from among many monkeys have been commanded today by you to bring a Śivaliṅga from Kailāsa, the most excellent mountain. I promptly went to Kailāsa but did not see the Pināka-bearing Lord.

I propitiated the Bull-emblemed Lord accompanied by Aṁbā, by means of penance and obtained the Liṅga and have hurriedly come back, O Scion of the family of Raghu.

12-15. You have now installed another Liṅga made of sand, O lord, and you are worshipping the same along with the Devas, Sages and Gandharvas.

This Liṅga which has been brought by me from the Kailāsa mountain has been futile. Alas! I am unfortunate. My physical body is only a burden unto the earth, O great king, O Lord, O lover of Sītā. I am unable to bear this grief, O Scion of the family of Raghu. What shall I do? Where shall I go? I have no (other) goal. Hence I shall abandon this body as I have been slighted by you.

Śrī Sūta said:

16-17. Thus, O Brāhmaṇas, he lamented in various ways. The son of Wind-god prostrated on the ground like a log. He bacame agitated due to anger and grief.

On seeing him, the leader of the family of Raghu said this laughingly. Even as all the Devas, Sages, monkeys and Rākṣasas stood watching, he mollified the feelings of Hanumān and dispelled his misery.

Śrī Rāma said:

18-23. I know every activity of myself as well as of others; of everyone born, dead or yet to be born, O monkey. A creature is born and dies alone due to its own acts. It goes to hell. The Great Ātman (Paramātmā) is devoid of Guṇas. Knowing this truth do not grieve, O monkey. Always see that the Ātman is free from the three Liṅgas (? genders). It is unsullied, single, luminous like a flame. It is self-dependent (requiring no other support). It is free from modifications. Why do you feel grief that is an obstacle unto the knowledge of truth. Be firmly established in the knowledge of truth, O excellent monkey. Always meditate upon the Ātman that is self-luminous, O monkey. Get rid of the sense of my-ness for the physical body, etc. It is a hindrance to the knowledge of truth.

24-30a. Resort always to Dharma. Avoid injury to living beings. Serve good and honourable men. Curb all the sense-organs. Always avoid magnifying the faults of others. O monkey, always perform the worship of Śiva, Viṣṇu and other Devas. Speak the truth always. Avoid grief, O monkey. The ignorance of the identity with the Immanent Soul arises from objects of delusion. Splendid and inglorious illusion has been imposed on this as though it were real. This illusion by its power makes the objects appear splendid. When men are ignorant and deluded, O excellent monkey, they become attached (to worldly objects). Those who are bound by the force of attachment and hatred become subject to the control of Dharma and Adharma. Such people, Devas, animals, human beings, etc. fall into hell. Sandalpaste, Agallochum, Camphor, etc. are exceedingly splendid objects. (But) They become dirty by contact with the physical body. Then how can that body be conducive to happiness?

30b-35. All foodstuffs and edible objects are very excellent. But they are turned into faeces by contact with the physical body. How can that body be conducive to happiness? Water is fragrant and cool. But it is turned into urine due to contact with the physical body. Hence how can that lump (body) be splendid? O monkey, tell me now.

Clothes are extremely pure and white. But they become dirty due to contact with the physical body and sweat. How can it (the body) be splendid?

Let the highest truth be heard from me, O Hanumān, O son of Wind-god. In this deep abyss of worldly existence, there is no happiness at all. First a creature attains its birth. Then it goes through the stages of infancy and childhood. Afterwards it attains youth. Thereafter it meets with old age. Afterwards it dies and then undergoes rebirth.

36-40. It is the power of ignorance that makes man subject to misery. If that ignorance disappears, he obtains excellent happiness. The termination of ignorance is possible only through knowledge and not through action. Knowledge is indeed the knowledge of Supreme Brahman, which arises from the Vedāntic statements.

That knowledge comes only to the one who is unattached and not to anyone else. It is the truth that the one (the disciple) acquires through the favour of the Ācārya (Preceptor) who is the most important authority. When all the desires that are lurking in his heart become eliminated, the man becomes immortal. He attains Brahman here itself. Whether this man is awake or asleep, taking food or standing by, the cruel god of Death always (at any time) drags him.

41. All hoardings end with destruction; all risings end in fall. Unions end in separation and life ends in death.

42-43. Just as ripe fruits have nothing to be afraid of except falling down, so also all men have nothing to be afraid of except dying. Just as a house, though it may have strong pillars, crumbles in due course into ruins, so also men being subject to old age and death, perish.

44. As days and nights pass, so the life span of men terminates. Bewail yourself; why do you bewail others?

45-51. Life passes away whether one stands steady or runs about, O eminent monkey. Death walks along (with us). Death sits along (with us).

After wandering in far-off lands, one returns along with death. Wrinkles occur on the body. The hair turns white. On account of old age, asthma, cough and other ailments, the body becomes worn out and shattered.

Just as one log of wood comes into contact with another in the great ocean, O monkey, and after coming into contact, they may get separated after a lapse of some time, so also is the case with wives, sons, kinsmen, fields and riches. To some places they go together, again they go elsewhere (i.e. are separated).

Just as someone standing on the road says to another traveller as he goes along, "I shall also come along with you" and they may then go together for some time, but afterwards, they may go elsewhere, in the same manner, O monkey, the association of wives, sons and others is transient. Along with the birth of the body, death too is certainly born.

52-58. In the case of death which is certain to take place, there is no means of avoidance. When this body perishes, the soul, in accordance with its Karma, O dear one, attains another body and so leaves the previous one. O monkey, all living beings do not remain in one place forever. In accordance with their respective Karmas, living beings get separated from one another. The physical bodies of living beings are born and perish too, O excellent monkey, but the Ātman is neither born nor does it die.

Hence, O son of Añjanā, think about the pure Brahman which is devoid of grief, is non-dual, which is perfect knowledge. It is of the nature of existence. Think about (it) day and night.

The action performed by you is the same as that performed by me. That performed by me is the same as that performed by you. Hence, O monkey, my installation of the Liṅga is your own installation of the Liṅga. Since the auspicious hour was soon passing off, the Liṅga was made of sand by Sītā and it was installed by me here. Hence do not be angry or sad. On this very auspicious day install the Liṅga that has come from Kailāsa.

59-60. Let this Liṅga become famous in all the three worlds by your name. The Liṅga installed by Rāma (Rāghaveśvara) should be seen only after seeing the Liṅga installed by Hanumān (Hanumadīśvara). Multitudes of Brahmarākṣasas have been killed by you, O monkey. Hence, by installing the Liṅga in your own name, you will become liberated.

61. Visiting the Śiva (Liṅga) given by Hara himself, the Liṅga named after Hanumān, and then visiting Rāmanātha, a man having his own objective achieved becomes blessed.

62. If one remembers the Liṅga of Hanumān and Rāmanātheśvara even from a distance of a thousand Yojanas, one shall attain Sāyujya.

63. If the Mahādevas, i.e. Hanumadīśvara and Rāghaveśvara, are seen by anyone, all the Yajñas have been performed by him. All penances have been performed by him (He gets the merit of these).

64-67. Śiva himself shines in eleven forms. He is always present in the following eleven Liṅgas: the Liṅga installed by Hanumān, the Liṅga installed by me, the Liṅga pertaining to Sītā, the Lakṣmaṇeśvara Liṅga, the Liṅga established by Nala the builder of the Setu, the Liṅgas installed by Aṅgada, Nīla and Jāmbavān, the bejewelled Liṅga installed by Bibhīṣaṇa and the Liṅga that has been made by Indra and others and installed by Śeṣa and others.

68-72a. Hence in order to purify your sins, install Maheśvara. If, O highly fortunate one, you uproot this Liṅga made by Sītā and installed by me, I shall install the Liṅga brought by you.

The Liṅga that has been installed by me stands piercing through Talātala, Rasātala and Vitala and reaches Sutala and Pātāla. Who can be strong enough to break the Liṅga installed by me. Get up, O monkey, uproot this Liṅga installed by me. Install the Liṅga brought by you quickly. Do not be grieved.

72b-74a. On being told thus, the monkey who was ignorant of his own strength bowed to him and thought thus:

'I shall quickly take out the excellent Sand Liṅga and install the Liṅga brought from Kailāsa eagerly. What trouble can there be to me in uprooting this Sand Liṅga?'

74b-79. After thinking thus mentally, Hanumān, the son of Wind-god, the powerful monkey, caught hold of that Sand Liṅga with his hand, even as all the Devas, Sages, monkeys, Rākṣasas, Rāmacandra, Lakṣmaṇa and Sītā were watching. He caught it with all his strength. Hanumān shook it with great effort, but he could not move the Sand Liṅga with his strength. Then the great monkey produced a chattering sound, lifted up his tail and pulled at (the Liṅga) with both the hands using all his strength.

Thus although the monkey, the son of Wind-god, tried to move the Liṅga in various ways, he was not able to move it.

80. The monkey, the son of Wind-god, encircled the Liṅga with his tail. He touched the ground with both the hands. Then he suddenly leaped into the sky.

81-83. But Hanumān, O Brāhmaṇas, fell on the ground at a distance of a Krośa (three kilometres) from the Liṅga and swooned. (As he fell) the entire earth consisting of the seven continents and mountains quaked. He vomited blood. His entire body trembled. As the son of Wind-god fell, O excellent Brāhmaṇas, a stream of blood flowed from his mouth, pair of eyes, nostrils, ear-cavities and anus. It became a pit of blood.

84-86. There was a great hue and cry among all the Devas, Asuras and human beings. Rāma and Lakṣmaṇa rushed to the place along with the monkeys and Sītā. They became very sad and grief-stricken, O Brāhmaṇas. Surrounded by the monkeys and accompanied by Sītā, those two powerful heroes shone on that Gandhamādana mountain like the Moon and the Sun accompanied by the stars at night.

87-90. They saw Hanumān with his entire body shattered to pieces. He had fallen unconscious on the ground and was vomiting blood through his mouth.

On seeing him all the monkeys cried "Alas! Alas!" and fell

down on the ground.

Saying "O dear one, O dear one", Sītā kindly stroked with her hands Hanumān, the son of Wind-god, who had fallen on the ground.

On Seeing Hanumān, the great monkey, fallen down Rāma placed him on his lap. He stroked his body with both the hands, O Brāhmaṇas. Shedding tears from his eyes, he spoke to the son of Wind-god.

CHAPTER FORTYSIX

The Reason for the Installation of Rāmanātha

Śrī Rāma said:

1-6. We were in a miserable condition in the Paṁpā forest, O great monkey. You brought about our friendship with the son of Sun-god (i.e. Sugrīva) and consoled us. Seeing you, we do not remember our father, mother Kausalyā and kinsmen and all others. Much help had been rendered by you. For my sake, the ocean extending to many Yojanas was crossed (by you). Maināka, an excellent mountain, was struck (down) with the palm. Surasā, the mother of serpents, was subdued for my sake. You killed the cruel demoness Chāyāgrahā. In the evening, you reached Suvela, struck Laṅkā with your hand and entered the abode of Rāvaṇa for my sake, O great monkey. You searched for Sītā fearlessly throughout Laṅka at night. Not seeing her anywhere else, you went to the Aśoka grove thereafter.[1]

7-13. You bowed down to Sītā and presented her the token ring. For my sake you took from her the crest jewel.

You broke down and shattered the trees in the Aśoka grove, O great monkey. Thereafter, for my sake, you killed the eighty thousand Rākṣasas named Kiṅkaras who were on a par with Rāvaṇa in battle. They were exceedingly powerful and had a great many foot-soldiers, horses, elephants and chariots.

Then you killed Jambumālī, the son of Prahasta, who had come (to fight with you). Then you killed the seven sons of ministers

1. For the incidents mentioned here see VR, V, cantos 1, 2, 3, 4, 5, 7, 14.

who had the refulgence of fire.

Subsequently, you despatched five generals to the abode of Yama. Thereafter, you killed Prince Akṣa in the course of a fight.

Afterwards you were taken to the splendid audience chamber of the king of Rākṣasas by Indrajit. There you slighted and insulted verbally the king of Laṅkā. Then, O son of Wind-god, for my sake you destroyed the city of Laṅkā. Thereafter, you returned to Ṛṣyamūka, a great mountain.[1]

14-16. These and other great miseries have been undergone by you for my sake. You now lie down on the ground causing great grief unto me. If you die, O son of Wind-god, I will discard my life.

What have I to do with Sītā? With Lakṣmaṇa, my younger brother? What have I to do with Bharata? What with Śatrughna or with fortune and prosperity? I have nothing to do with the kingdom, if you are dead, O monkey.

17-19. O Hanumān, O dear one, why do you lie down on the ground? Make my bed, O mighty monkey, for me to sleep. Bring bulbous roots, fruits and roots for my food. I will now go to bathe. Fetch me the pot quickly. Offer me deerskin, garments and Darbha grasses. When I was bound by Brahmā missile, O monkey, it was by you that I was set free.

20-24. I was liberated (brought back to consciousness) along with my brother Lakṣmaṇa by fetching the medicinal herbs. You are the life-giver unto Lakṣmaṇa.[2] You are the destroyer of the arrogance of the descendant of Pulastya.

With you as my assistant in the battle, I was able to kill the exceedingly powerful Rākṣasas, Rāvaṇa and others and got back the daughter of the king of Mithilā. O Hanumān, O son of Añjanā, O destroyer of the grief of Sītā, why have you left me, Lakṣmaṇa and Sītā? Why have you gone away yourself without taking us back to Ayodhyā? Where have you gone, O great warrior, O thorn unto the great Rākṣasas?

After saying these words, the scion of the family of Raghu, stopped speaking. He stared silently at his face. Crying, he drenched the son of Wind-god with profuse tears.

---

1. For these incidents in these verses see VR, V, cantos 36, 38, 41-48, 54, 55.
2. Cf, VR, VI, cantos 101.30-42.

25-30. The son of Wind-god then slowly recovered from his swoon, O Brāhmaṇas. He saw Rāma who was the unborn Lord Nārāyaṇa who had come (to the earth) for protecting the world that had been terrorized by the descendant of Pulastya (Rāvaṇa). The Lord had taken human form and incarnated thus. He saw Rāma who was accompanied by Sītā and Lakṣmaṇa. He was surrounded by monkeys. He resembled a black cloud (in complexion). He was completely covered with the dust from the battlefield but was looking glorious due to the matted hair. His eyes were as large as (the petals of) a white lotus. He was highly vexed and strained due to the battle.

On seeing Rāma, the son of Daśaratha, who slew his enemies and was eulogized by Devas, Sages, Pitṛs and Kinnaras and whose mind was full of mercy, that monkey (became happy). The whole of his body became all right when Rāma touched it with his hands.

The eminent monkey fell down on the ground like a log of wood, O Brāhmaṇas. With palms joined in reverence he eulogized the Lord of Sītā with hymns pleasing to the ears.

Hanumān said:[1]

31-36. Obeisance to Rāma, to Hari, to Viṣṇu, the powerful one, to the lord, to the primordial lord, to the ancient one, to the wielder of the iron-club. Bow to the noble soul stationed perpetually in the Puṣpaka (Aerial Chariot). Obeisance to you whose lotus-like feet are served by the delighted army of monkeys. Hail to the lord who crushed the great Rākṣasa; to the lord who performed what was pleasing to the universe. Bow to the thousand-headed one and to the thousand-footed one. Obeisance to the thousand-eyed pure Rāghava, to Viṣṇu. Obeisance to you, the dispeller of distress of devotees. Hail to the lord of Sītā. Obeisance to Hari, to the Man-lion who tore up the king of Daityas, Obeisance to you, to the (divine) Boar, O lord, who lifted up the earth by means of your curved teeth. Bow to Trivikrama; to you who destroyed the Yajña of Bali. Obeisance to the lord in the form of Vāmana. Obeisance to the supporter of Mandara (in the form of a Tortoise).

1. The eulogy of Rāma and Sītā shows the belief in Rāma being Viṣṇu's incarnation and Sītā, that of Lakṣmī.

37-43. Obeisance to you of the form of Fish, the protector of the Vedas. Bow to Paraśurāma, to you who annihilated Kṣatriyas. Obeisance to you, the destroyer of Rākṣasas. Obeisance to you in the form of Rāghava. Bow to you who broke the exceedingly dreadful, great bow of the great Lord (Śiva). Obeisance to the lord who inspired fear in the cruel Bhārgava (i.e. Paraśurāma) who annihilated Kṣatriyas.

Obeisance to the dispeller of the distress of Ahalyā. Bow to the destroyer of sins. Obeisance to the destroyer of the physical body of Tāṭakā possessed of the strength of ten thousand elephants. Obeisance to the lord who split and pierced the broad chest of Vāli as hard as a rock. Hail to the lord who crushed the deer created by Māyā. Obeisance to the lord, to the dispeller of ignorance. Obeisance to the lord who dried up the ocean of distress of Daśaratha like Agastya who dried up the briny sea.

Bow to the destroyer of the arrogance of the vast Ocean surging with many waves. Obeisance of the lord who delights the mind of Sītā like the Sun that delights the lotus. Obeisance to the witness unto the world. Obeisance to you, to the eminent king, O Hari. Obeisance to you, to the lord of Sītā. Obeisance to you, to Brahman that redeems. Obeisance to you, O lotus-eyed one.

44-50a. Obeisance to Rāma, to Rāmacandra. Obeisance to the excellent one, of the nature of happiness. Bow to the lord, a favourite of Viśvāmitra. Obeisance to the slayer of Khara.

Be pleased, O lord of the chiefs of Devas, O bestower of immunity from fear to the devotees. Save me, O ocean of mercy; O Rāmacandra, obeisance to you. Save me, O Rāghava who are beyond the pale of the words of even the Vedas. Protect me mercifully. I seek refuge in you. O heroic scion of the family of Raghu, dispel my great delusion now.

While bathing, while drinking, while taking food, during the stages of wakefulness, dream and deep slumber, protect me in all the conditions and stages everywhere.

Protect me, O descendant of Raghu. Who alone are competent in all the three worlds to eulogize your own glory adequately? You alone know your greatness, O descendant of Raghu.

After eulogizing Rāmacandra, the storehouse of mercy, the son of Wind-god eulogized Sītā too with a mind fully steeped in devotion:

50b-52. "O Jānakī, I bow to you, the destroyer of all sins. I bow down to the destroyer of poverty and indebtedness; to the goddess who bestows what is desired by the devotees; to the daughter of the king of Videhas, to (the lady) causing delight unto Rāghava.

I bow down to the daughter of the Earth, to Vidyā, to Prakṛti, to Śivā. I bow down to the destroyer of the riches and prosperity of the descendant of Pulastya; to the beloved one of the devotees; to Sarasvatī.

53-57. I bow down to you, the daughter of Janaka; to the foremost one among chaste ladies; to the goddess disposed to bless; to the spotless Ṛddhi (prosperity); to the beloved one of Hari.

I bow down to the spiritual knowledge in the form of the three Vedas; to the one in the form of Umā. I bow down to Lakṣmī, the splendid daughter of the Ocean of Milk, who is inclined to (grant) favour.

I bow down to the sister of the Moon-god; to Sītā who is beautiful in every limb. I bow down to the goddess with Dharma for her abode, (the embodiment of) compassion, the mother of the Vedas.

I bow down to Sītā with the lotus for your abode; with a lotus in your hand; to the goddess with the broad chest of Viṣṇu for your abode; I bow down to Sītā with the moon for your abode; to the goddess with face resembling the moon.

I bow down to Siddhi, the embodiment of bliss; to Śivā; to the cause of welfare; to Satī (i.e. Pārvatī). I bow down to the mother of the universe; to the beloved wife of Rāmacandra. I worship always with my heart Sītā whose limbs are blameless."

Śrī Sūta said:

58-63. After eulogizing devoutly Sītā and Rāmacandra, O excellent Brāhmaṇas, Hanumān remained quiet, shedding tears of joy. He was drenched in tears.

One who daily reads this hymn to Rāmacandra and Sītā, the hymn that was composed by the son of Wind-god, the hymn that destroys sins, attains great prosperity. He obtains whatever he desires.

He always gets many fields and foodgrains, milch cows, long span of life, learned sons and a charming wife.

Even a person who recites this hymn once, obtains all these

things, O Brāhmaṇas. There is no doubt about it. By reading this hymn one never falls into a hell.

Even very great sins such as that of Brāhmaṇa-slaughter, etc. perish. Being liberated from all sins on death one attains salvation.

64. On being eulogized by the son of Wind-god thus, Rāghava, the Lord of the universe, O Brāhmaṇas, who was accompanied by Sītā, spoke to Hanumān thus:

Śrī Rāma said:

65-71a. This foolhardy action was committed, O excellent monkey, by you due to ignorance. This Liṅga that has been installed by me, cannot be uprooted by Brahmā, or Viṣṇu or Indra and other Devas. It was because you offended Mahādeva that you fell down unconscious.

Henceforth let not any offence against the Trident-bearing Lord accompanied by Aṁbā be committed by you. From today onwards this Kuṇḍa (Pit) shall become famous after your name in all the three worlds. The place where you fell down, O excellent monkey, shall be a holy spot.[1] By taking the holy plunge here masses of great sins shall perish.

Gautamī that originated from the matted hair of Mahādeva is the most excellent one among rivers. On the men who bathe therein, it bestows the merit of a thousand horse-sacrifices.

The merit of bathing in Gaṅgā, Yamunā and Sarasvatī is hundred times greater. The holy bath in that place where these three rivers flow together, O monkey, is known as giving thousand times that merit.

71b-75. By taking the holy bath in this Kuṇḍa of yours one undoubtedly obtains that merit, O monkey, which men get by taking the holy bath in all these rivers.

After attaining human birth that is rarely achieved if a person does not perform Śrāddha on the banks of Hanumatkuṇḍa with a mind fully endowed with devotion, O monkey, his Pitṛs become angry and go away disappointed.

Sages too become angry with him. Devas including Indra and Cāraṇas are also angry with him. If no charitable gift is made, or

1. This is Hanumānkuṇḍa Tīrtham (Hanumatkuṇḍa) to the north of Rāmeśvaram Temple.

if *Homa* is not performed, the life of that person is futile. He will be miserable both here and hereafter. If water libation is offered along with gingelly seeds in the vicinity of Hanumatkuṇḍa, the Pitṛs rejoice. They drink from canals of ghee.

Śrī Sūta said:

76-77. On hearing these words uttered by Rāma, O Brāhmaṇas, the son of Wind-god joyously installed the Liṅga brought by him to the north of Rāmanātha (Liṅga) at the bidding of Rāmacandra.

78-80. Hara bears the three folds of skin as a result of being encircled by the tail of the monkey.[1] This is clearly perceptible to everyone. In the northern direction thereof he joyously installed Gaurī too.

Śrī Sūta said:

Thus, O Brāhmaṇas, it has been recounted unto you all, why the Liṅga was installed on the Setu by Rāghava. It yields worldly pleasures and salvation.

He who reads this chapter or listens to it with concentration shall rid himself of all sins. He is honoured in the world of Śiva.

CHAPTER FORTYSEVEN

Rāma's Sin of Brahma-hatyā

The sages said:

1-4. O Sūta, O great Sage, how did the noble-souled Rāghava incur the sin of Brāhmaṇa-slaughter by slaying Rākṣasa Rāvaṇa.

O Sūta, the sin of Brāhmaṇa-slaughter is incurred only when a Brāhmaṇa is killed. The ten-headed demon was not a Brāhmaṇa. How then did this happen? O sage, tell us. How could Rāmacandra, the intelligent one, commit the cruel sin of Brāhmaṇa-slaughter?[2]

---

1. The story explains why there are three curls round the Rāmeśvara Liṅga.
2. This story explains why Rāvaṇa and his brothers are regarded as Brāhmaṇas. VR, I, 20.18 tells us that Rāvaṇa's father Viśravas was a Brāhmaṇa. Hence his Brāhmaṇahood, though his mother Kekasī was of Rākṣasa clan.

We listen attentively; kindly tell us about it now.

On being asked thus by those residents of Naimiṣa forest, Sūta began to give an excellent answer to their question.

Śrī Sūta said:

5-6. There was a son of Brahmā, of great brilliance, called Pulastya, O Brāhmaṇas. His son Viśravas was very well-known. That son of Pulastya, Viśravas, O eminent sages, performed a penance for a long time. It was one which was very difficult to be performed even by Devas.

7. While he was engaged in the penance, a Rākṣasa named Sumālī came to the terrestrial world from the nether worlds. He wandered over the entire earth.

8. He wore armlets made of gold coins. His complexion was of the colour of a black cloud. He had taken with him his virgin daughter who was like goddess Lakṣmī but without the lotus.

9-11. As he was wandering over the earth thus, once he saw Kubera, the son of Viśravas and the lord of wealth, seated in his aerial chariot named Puṣpaka. Then, O eminent Brāhmaṇas, that Rākṣasa Sumālī thought thus: 'If we had a son like Kubera, we would all flourish. All the Rākṣasas would be free from fear from everywhere.'

After thinking thus the lord of Rākṣasas spoke to his daughter:

12-17. "O my splendid daughter Kaikasī! Now that you have attained youth, the time of giving you away in marriage has arrived. You are to be given away to a bridegroom.

If daughters are not given away (in marriage), fathers will be distressed. Further, O my splendid daughter, you have all the good qualities like Lakṣmī. You are very excellent. O splendid girl, it is due to the fear of being refused that you are not being wooed by men. Indeed the state of being the father of a girl brings misery to all men desirous of honour.

I do not know who that bridegroom will be, O dear girl, who intends to woo you. (I suggest that) you yourself approach the Brāhmaṇa Sage Viśravas, the son of Pulastya. He is born of the family of Brahmā. You court him of your own accord. There is no doubt about this that sons on a par with Kubera will be born to you."

On hearing his words, the girl Kaikasī of pure smiles accepted his suggestion out of deference to her father.

18. She went to the hermitage of Sage Viśravas, O excellent ascetics, and stood near him blushing with the face downwards.

19. At that time, O Brāhmaṇas, the intelligent son of Pulastya resembling a blazing fire was engaged in performing *Agnihotra* (the worship of Fire-god).

20-21. Without considering the fact that it was the exceedingly cruel hour of the dusk, the lady of beautiful eyebrows approached that sage out of deference for the directives of her father. She stood there with downcast eyes marking lines on the ground with the tip of her big toe. On seeing Kaikasī who was slender-waisted and whose face resembled the full moon, O Brāhmaṇas, Viśravas spoke to her smilingly.

Viśravas said:

22-24. O splendid lady, whose daughter are you? From where have you come here? O lady of pure smiles, what is that purpose for which you are here? Speak everything truthfully to me now, O praiseworthy one.

On being told thus, O Brāhmaṇas, that virgin Kaikasī joined her palms in reverence. She spoke to the sage humbly and politely:

25. "O sage, the illuminator of the family of Pulastya, due to the power of your penance, you can know perfectly well my purpose (of coming) today.

26-27. I am the daughter of Sumālī, O sage, and my name is Kaikasī. I have approached you, O Brāhmaṇa, at the bidding of my father. The rest you can know with your vision of knowledge. There is no doubt about it."

Sage Viśravas meditated for a short while and said to Kaikasī:

28-32. "O lady of excellent eyebrows, the desire within your heart has been known by me. O splendid lady, you have come to me now with a desire for sons. Since you approached me now during the cruel hour of dusk with a desire[1] for sons, I have to tell you this, O lady, listen attentively. O uncensured (i.e. praiseworthy) Kaikasī you will give birth to Rākṣasas of ruthless activi-

---

1. The cruel demoniac nature of Rāvaṇa and his brothers is attributed to the 'cruel nature of the time' of their conception.

ties. They will be dreadful with terrible features. They will be fond of terrible people."

On hearing his words, Kaikasī bowed down to the son of Pulastya, O Brāhmaṇas, and said to him with palms joind in reverence:

"O holy lord, it is not proper that I should get sons like these from you."

33-39. On being told thus, that sage said to Kaikasī, the lady of excellent waistline: "Your youngest son will be one with good qualities, befitting my family. He will be righteous. He will be conversant with the scriptures. He will not indulge in demoniac activities."

Kaikasī was told thus, O Brāhmaṇas. After the lapse of some time, she gave birth to a son in the form of a dreadful Rākṣasa, who had ten heads and twenty hands. He was evil-minded and frightful. His lips were copper-coloured. His face was dark. His moustache and hair were red in colour. He had huge curved teeth. His body too was very huge. He caused perpetual terror to all the people. He was called by the names of Daśagrīva and Rāvaṇa.

After Rāvaṇa, the son named Kuṁbhakarṇa was born. Thereafter, the cruel demoness named Śūrpaṇakhā was born. Thereafter the last son of Kaikasī, well-known as Bibhīṣaṇa was born. He was intelligent and virtuous. He was conversant with the Vedas and scriptures. O Brāhmaṇas, thus these sons of Viśravas, Daśagrīva and others, were Brāhmaṇas.

40-43. So due to the killing of Kuṁbhakarṇa and Daśagrīva, Rāma, of unwearied activities, incurred the sin of Brāhmaṇa-slaughter. In order to dispel the same Rāma installed the Liṅga named Rāmeśvara in accordance with the injunction in the Vedas.

So by killing Rāvaṇa, the intelligent Rāmacandra, the favourite of all the people, had incurred the sin of Brāhmaṇa-slaughter.

Thus how the sin of Brāhmaṇa-slaughter was incurred, has been recounted to you all. It was to expiate this sin that Rāma himself installed a Liṅga.

44. After installing the Liṅga, the exceedingly virtuous Rāmacandra considered himself blessed and contented, O Brāhmaṇas, along with Sītā and his younger brother.

45. A Tīrtha named Brahmahatyā-Vimocana[1] arose in the place

1. Now this is a well in the second north Prākāram of the Rāmeśvaram Temple.

where the sin of Brāhmaṇa-slaughter of King Rāmacandra was dispelled.

46. The holy bath there is highly meritorious. It is destructive of the sin of Brāhmaṇa-slaughter. Even now, Rāvaṇa is seen there in the form of a shadow.

47-52. Further ahead of it, there is a hole (leading to) the world of serpents. It is very huge. The lord of Sītā took the powerful sin of Brāhmaṇa-slaughter arising from the killing of Rāvaṇa to that hole. Above that hole he made an excellent pavilion. For the sake of guarding it Rāghava established Bhairava there.

Frightened of the command of Bhairava, the dreadful sin of Brāhmaṇa-slaughter could not come out of that hole, O excellent Brāhmaṇas. That Brahmahatyā who was unable to do anything, remained in that hole itself.

To the south of Rāmanātha, the great Liṅga, there stays joyously the Daughter of the Mountain who forms half the body of the Supreme Bliss, Śiva.

On either side of the Trident-bearing Lord are the Sun and the Moon. Fire-god is in front of Lord Rāmanātha.

53. Indra is in the east. Fire-god is in the south-east. The attendant of Rāmanātha in the south is Yama.

54. Nirṛti is on the south-west of Śaṅkara, O Brāhmaṇas. In the west Varuṇa devoutly serves Rāghaveśvara (Rāmanātha).

55. To the north-west of Śiva is Wind-god and Dhanada (Kubera) is in the north of Rāmanātha.

56-59. To the south-east of the lord, O Brāhmaṇas, is Maheśa. Vināyaka and Kumāra, the two sons of Mahādeva, stay in their respective places in the temple of Rāmanātha now. All the leaders of the Gaṇas of Maheśvara, Vīrabhadra, etc., always stay in their respective places in the temple of Rāmanātha. Sages, serpents, Siddhas, groups of Gandharvas and Apsaras live as they please in the vicinity of Śiva with contented hearts. They stay there for the sake of rendering service to Rāmanātha with great devotion.

60. For the sake of worshipping Rāmanātha, Raghupati established many Brāhmaṇas well-versed in the Vedas, as the priests.

61-66. One should adore the Brāhmaṇas established by Rāma by means of *Havya* and *Kavya*. If they are pleased, all the deities along with the Pitṛs shall be pleased.

The Lord of Sītā gave them many villages yielding much wealth. For the Naivedya of the great Lord Rāmanātha, the elder brother of Lakṣmaṇa gave many villages and much wealth. The son of Daśaratha gave necklaces, armlets, bracelets and other ornaments, gold coins, many silk garments and different kinds of fine fabrics to Lord Rāmanātha.

Gaṅgā, the meritorious Yamunā, Sarayū and Sarasvatī worship Lord Rāmeśvara on the Setu for suppressing their own sins.

By reading this chapter and by listening to this, a man shall be liberated from all sins. He attains *Sāyujya* with Hari.

CHAPTER FORTYEIGHT

Cessation of Great Sins Incurred by King Śaṅkara

Śrī Sūta said:

1-5. With reference to (Lord) Rāmanātha, O excellent sages, I shall recount a story that destroys sins. Listen to it with great concentration.

Formerly, there was a king of the Pāṇḍya land, named Śaṅkara. He was favourably disposed towards Brāhmaṇas. He was righteous and truthful in speech and a regular performer of sacrifices. He was conversant with the truths of the Vedas and the Vedāṅgas. He annihilated the armies of the enemies. He righteously protected the people of the four castes and stages of life. He was devoted to the conduct of life in accordance with the Vedas. He had mastered Purāṇas and Smṛtis. He always worshipped Śiva and Viṣṇu, and worshipped other deities as well. He used to make great gifts to noble-souled Brāhmaṇas.

Once that intelligent king went to a penance grove for the purpose of hunting.

6-7a. It was very dreadful on account of such cruel animals as lions, tigers, elephants and buffaloes. It had a terrible noise of crickets and was infested with reptiles. It was full of dreadful beasts of prey. It was terrible on account of forest-fires.

7b-11. Śaṅkara, the crest-jewel among kings, was accompanied by many soldiers. He had with him a big number of hunters. His feet were protected by sandals. He wore a red turban and green garments. He had put on the protectors of leather for his fingers as well as palms. He was armed with a bow and arrows. A great sword was kept fastened at his side. He was seated on an excellent white horse. He was dressed in an excellent manner. He was well accoutred. He was surrounded by foot-soldiers. Entering the great forest, the young king of lion-like strength, roamed about here and there along with his armies in the forest, beautiful mountains and caves and crossing big streams, he hunted the animals.

12-17. "See here, a swift deer is running ahead in the forest. Let it be bound or killed." When the soldiers shouted thus Śaṅkara, the great king, jumped down himself, entered the forest region and killed the deer. While slaying the lions, boars, buffaloes, elephants, Śarabhas (eight-footed fabulous animals) and other wild animals, King Śaṅkara mistook a quiescent sage of controlled mind for a tiger, because he (the sage) wore a tiger's skin and stayed in a certain cave in the forest region. The king quickly killed him with a flat-jointed arrow. The arrow was very swift, O eminent Brāhmaṇas, and it killed his wife too who was seated near him and who loved her husband like her own vital airs. On seeing his parents killed in the forest, their frightened son who was exceedingly distressed, cried and lamented bitterly.

18-25. "O father! O mother! where have you both gone now, leaving me here? Where should I go? Who will be my refuge? O father, who will teach me the Vedas and the scriptural texts? O mother, who will give me food along with moral instructions? O father, as you are dead now, who will give me training in the rituals and in the general conduct of life? O mother, when I become excited with anger, who will fondle me? Both of you are sinless. Still, who is that sinner by whom you two have been killed with arrows, you who were steadfastly engaged in austerities, and had been my very vital breath and, my elders (father and mother) in this forest?"

Thus their sons, O Brāhmaṇas, cried very bitterly. Śaṅkara who was wandering in the forest heard this lamentation. So he immediately proceeded towards the mouth of the cave in the direction from which the sound had come. The sages of the places nearby too came to that hermitage quickly.

On seeing the sage killed with an arrow and the wife too killed, the king (standing there) holding the bow and also the son lamenting, all those sages became agitated very much. Saying "Do not cry", they pacified the frightened son.

The sages said:

26-27. O dear one, the king of the dead behaves equally towards all living ones, whether rich or poor, whether learned or foolish, whether stout or lean. Whether in the forest or in the city, whether in the village, on the mountain or in any other place, all creatures have to succumb to (god of) death.

28-33a. O child, those who are in the womb, those who are born, the youths, the old people—everyone has to go to the city of Yama. O son of a Brāhmaṇa, when the time comes, the body has to be abandoned by religious students, householders, forest-dwellers and recluses, O highly intelligent son of a Brāhmaṇa. All people have to go to the abode of the dead ones, whether they be Brāhmaṇas, Kṣatriyas, Vaiśyas, Śūdras or people of mixed castes. Devas, Sages, Yakṣas, Gandharvas, Serpents, Rākṣasas, Brahmā, Viṣṇu, Hara and others as well as all other creatures shall die. It does not behove you to bewail. The non-dual Brahman of the nature of existence, knowledge and bliss, mentioned in the Upaniṣads has no birth or growth or dissolution, O excellent one.

33b-38. If anyone considers the physical body to be splendid, he is deluded and vicious. This physical body is a vessel of dirt and filth. It has nine pores and exits. It is the abode of putrid lymph and blood. It is in the form of a bubble. It is full of (millions of) worms and germs. It causes lust, anger, fear, malice, delusion and jealousy. It is enamoured of other men's wives, and craves for fields and riches belonging to others. It is full of violence, envy and foul matter. It is a mere receptable of faeces and urine.

This body is like a pot with a number of holes. It is always filthy. Can the air named Prāṇa (vital breath) stay there for long? Hence do not feel grieved over your mother and father. Due to their own Karmas they have gone somewhere leaving their abode. Due to your Karmas, you still stay on the earth.

39-42. When your Karmas are exhausted, you will also die. A ghost that is about to die bewails a ghost that is dead. You were not born at the time when your parents were born. Therefore the fates of yours (as well as theirs) are different. If, O highly intelligent one, your fate and theirs were similar, you too would have gone to that place where those two dead ones have gone. If the kinsmen of the dead people shed tears on the earth, the dead ones and those whose funeral rites are not performed, will have to drink those tears certainly in the other world.

43-46. Hence give up your grief. Take courage. With great concentration perform the obsequies in accordance with the Vedic injunctions. Since your mother and father died after being struck down by an arrow, you have to dispel the evil arising from it. Collect together their burnt bones and deposit them in Rāmasetu that yields salvation. It is in the holy spot of Śiva (named) Rāmanātha. So also perform Śrāddha, Sapiṇḍīkaraṇa and other rites there itself. Perform it, O son of a Brāhmaṇa, for the sake of purifying them. Thereby the evil of ill-fated death shall perish, not otherwise.

Śrī Sūta said:

47-52. On being told thus by the sages, O Brāhmaṇas, that son of Śākalya named Jāṅgala deposited the bones of his parents in the holy spot of Rāmeśvara in the manner mentioned by the sages. He performed Śrāddha and other rites as well.

He performed the various rites there, till the first anniversary of their death. The only son of the sage, named Jāṅgala, remained there for a year. On the last day of that year, at night, the Brāhmaṇa saw in his dream his mother and father holding a conch, discus and an iron club. They were seated on Garuḍa. They were adorned with lotus-garlands. They shone in the garlands of Tulasī leaves with refulgent fish-shaped ear-rings.

53-59. Kaustubha jewel adorned their chests. They shone brilliantly in their yellow robes. On seeing them thus, Jāṅgala, the son of the sage, was highly delighted in his mind.

He returned to his hermitage, O Brāhmaṇas, and lived there happily. The boy Jāṅgala recounted to those Brāhmaṇas the details of his parents as seen in the dream. He was extremely delighted.

On hearing this the sages too were pleased in their minds.

On seeing the king, all those sages became very furious, O Brāhmaṇas. Cursing King Śaṅkara, they spoke thus:

"O king of Pāṇḍya state, O highly foolish one, O ruthless Brāhmaṇa-slayer, since the murder of a Brāhmaṇa and the murder of a woman has been committed by you, you have to cast off your body into fire. Otherwise there is no redemption for you even by means of hundreds of expiations. Merely by speaking with you, one will incur ten thousand sins of Brāhmaṇa-slaughter. Oh! you have sullied the fair race of Pāṇḍyas."

60-66. On being told thus by the sages, O eminent Brāhmaṇas, Śaṅkara, the Pāṇḍya king said: "Let it be so. I shall cast off my body into the fire in the presence of you all for purifying the sin of Brāhmaṇa-murder. O excellent sages, may you (be pleased to) bless me. May my sin perish by casting my body off." After saying this to all those sages, Śaṅkara, the king of Pāṇḍyas, called his ministers together and spoke these words:

"O my ministers, the murder of a Brāhmaṇa (couple) has been committed by me unwittingly. The murder of a woman is very heinous. It bestows a dreaded Naraka. In order to wipe off this sin, I shall cast off my body into a well-kindled fire of huge flames. Bring wood and fuel quickly. Let the fire be kindled with them. Crown my son Suruci in the kingdom ere long. O ministers, do not feel sad. Fate cannot be transgressed."

67-69. On being told thus by the king, the ministers began to cry: "O great king, O lord of Pāṇḍyas, friendly even to the enemies, indeed we have always been protected by you as though we were your own sons. Without you we will not enter the city that is comparable to the city of Devas. We too shall enter the fire kindled with huge pieces of wood."

On hearing their words of lamentation, Śaṅkara, the Pāṇḍya king, spoke thus to all the ministers pacifying them:

Śaṅkara said:

70-77a. What will you do with me, O ministers? I am a great sinner. It is not proper on my part to sit on the throne and rule the earth extending to the four oceans. So install my son Suruci immediately on my throne. Bring fuel quickly so that I can enter fire. O my excellent ministers, don't delay now.

On being told thus those ministers brought the fuel in a moment. On seeing the fire well kindled, King Śaṅkara took his holy bath and performed the *Ācamana* rite. In the vicinity of the sages, thus purified in soul he circumambulated the fire and those sages quickly. He bowed down to the fire and the sages and meditated on Lord Umāpati (Śiva) in the presence of those sages. Then the king calmly began to leap into the fire.

At that time, O Brāhmaṇas, even as the sages continued to

listen, there was heard an unembodied voice roaring fearfully:

77b-83. "O King Śaṅkara, do not enter the fire now. O highly intelligent one, may you not be afraid of the sin of Brāhmaṇa-slaughter. I will give you this secret instruction embedded in the Vedas. Listen attentively, O king. What is spoken by me may be carried out by you.

On the shore of the Southern Sea on the Gandhamādana mountain, on the highly meritorious Rāmasetu highly destructive of great sins, there is the Liṅga Rāmanātha of Maheśvara installed by Rāma. Serve him three times a day with great devotion and continue the same for a year. Perform the rites of circumambulation and obeisance. May the great ablution rite of Rāmanātha be performed by you. Let the *Naivedya* of different kinds be made everyday. Worship Rāmaliṅga with sandalpaste, agallochum and camphor. Perform the ablution rite with ghee produced from cow's milk. The ghee should weigh two *Bhāras*.

84-89. Everyday perform the bathing rite for the Liṅga of the Lord with cow's milk weighing two *Bhāras* as well as with a *Droṇa* of honey. Perform the *Naivedya* everyday with milk pudding and cooked rice. Perform the propitiation of the lord by means of lights everyday with gingelly oil. If you perform all these rites to the Trident-bearing Rāmanātha, O great king, your sins of woman-murder and Brāhmaṇa-murder shall perish instantly.

O lord, by visiting Rāmanātha hundreds of sins of Brāhmaṇa-slaughter, ten thousand sins of drinking liquor, ten thousand sins of stealing gold, ten thousand sins of sexual intercourse with the preceptor's wife as well as the evil due to association with these sinners perish instantly. All those sins that are as heinous as the great sins (like Brāhmaṇa-slaughter) shall also perish by serving Rāmanātha.

90. If an opportunity to render great service unto Rāmanātha is got by men, of what avail is Gaṅgā, Gayā, Prayāga or any sacrifice?

91. Therefore go to Rāmasetu, regularly worship Rāmanātha. O lord, do not delay. Hasten to go there."

92-96. After saying this the unembodied voice ceased. On hearing it, all the sages made the king to hurry up. "Go quickly, O great king, to Rāmasetu that bestows salvation. It was due to our ignorance of the glory of Rāmanātha that we advised you to cast off your body in a well-kindled fire now."

On being permitted thus by the excellent sages, that King Śaṅkara hurriedly despatched the army consisting of the four divisions to his city. He then bowed down to all the sages with the extremely delighted inner soul and taking with him ample cash, surrounded by only a few soldiers, he went to Gandhamādana for the purpose of serving Rāmanātha.

97-101. He stayed for a year in Rāmasetu that bestows sanctity. He took food only once a day. He subdued his anger, controlled his sense-organs. During the three junctions, he devoutly served Rāmanātha. He joyously gave Rāmanātha ten Bhāras (of gold) and cash.

Everyday he performed the great worship of Rāmanātha. Everyday he devoutly took his holy bath in Dhanuṣkoṭi. He joyously gave food to Brāhmaṇas. He carried out everything suggested by the unembodied voice. He performed all the rites of worship too.

Even as he performed everything thus, O Brāhmaṇas, a year passed by. At the end of the year, Śaṅkara who was delighted in his mind, had attained purity. He then eulogized Rāmanātha, the supreme lord, the storehouse of mercy.

Śaṅkara said:

102-107. I bow down to Rudra, the lord, Rāmanātha, the lord of Umā. Kindly protect me, O lord. Burn down my sin of the Brāhmaṇa-slaughter. O Mahādeva, the destroyer of the three Puras, O swallower of the poison Kālakūṭa, protect me, O ocean of mercy; release me from (the sin of) woman-murder, O Gaṅgādhara (one who holds Gaṅgā on his head), of uneven eyes, O Rāmanātha with three eyes.

Protect me with your merciful glance. O Lord, dispel my sins. O enemy of Kāma, O bestower of all desired things on the devotees, O Rāghaveśvara!

Cast the benign glance at me, O Dhūrtaṭi; purify me, O Mṛtyuñjaya, O protector of Mārkaṇḍeya from fear, O immutable Śiva.

Obeisance to you half of whose body is occupied by the Daughter of the Mountain. Make me free from sins permanently. O Śaṅkara, the moon-crested lord with the rosary of Rudrākṣa beads as ornament!

108-113. Make me fully fit to practise the ideal conduct as laid down in the Vedas. Obeisance to you. Obeisance to you who broke the teeth of Sun-god and who cut off the nose of Bhāratī. Obeisance to Lord Rameśvara; be the bestower of purity on me. I bow down again and again to the bull-emblemed Lord Rāmanātha. Bliss personified, O embodiment of existence, knowledge and bliss! May my sin perish.

Even as he eulogized Rāmanātha, the great lord, thus with great devotion, the extremely terrible sin of Brāhmaṇa-slaughter issued forth from the mouth of that king. It was excessively dreadful with deep-red hair. It was clad in blue garments.

At the bidding of Rudra, Bhairava struck with his trident the hideous Brahmahatyā that came out of the mouth of the king.

When the Brahmahatyā was killed at the bidding of Śiva by Bhairava, Rāmanātha who was delighted in his mind, spoke to the king:

Śrī Rāmanātha said:

114-121. O Pāṇḍya king, O sinless great ruler; I am delighted with this hymn of yours. I shall grant you a boon. Choose the boon you desire.

The evil that you had incurred through the murder of a woman and a Brāhmaṇa has vanished. You are pure. You are rid of all your sins. Rule the kingdom as before.

I destroy even ten thousand Brahmahatyā-sins of those men who serve me here with a mind endowed with devotion. There is no doubt about it that I destroy other sins too, such as ten thousand sins of drinking liquor, ten thousand sins of indulging in sexual intercourse with the preceptor's wife, ten thousand sins of stealing gold and ten thousand sins of associating with these sinners. Those men who serve me, O king, do not undergo (the sufferings of) worldly existence. They undoubtedly attain salvation in the form of *Sāyujya.*

I shall destroy the mass of great sins of those who devoutly eulogize me with this prayer, O lord of men, I am delighted with your devotion and this prayer of yours. Request for any boon from me as you please. O king, I am the bestower of boons.

On being told thus by Śiva, Śaṅkara, the great king, spoke to Śaṅkara, the storehouse of mercy, Lord Rāmanātha:

The king said:

122-125. O Maheśvara, I am contented and blessed with your vision. More than this I have nothing to request for. Your pair of feet that dispelled the distress of the son of Mṛkaṇḍu has been seen by me, O Lord Mahādeva. There is nothing else to be requested for. Let my devotion to the lotus-like pair of your feet be steady. Let me not be reborn in the filthy belly of mothers. O lord, let those men who recite this prayer composed by me be liberated from all their sins. Let them attain the merit of service unto you.

Śrī Sūta said:

126-128. Saying "So be it", O excellent Brāhmaṇas, Rāmanātha blessed him. The Blue-throated Hideous (three)-eyed Lord vanished in the Liṅga form. The king who was blessed by Rāmanātha bowed down to Rāmanātha with fully contented inner soul. Surrounded by the army, he went to his city with delight.

129-133. He reported this incident to the sages who lived in the forest. Delighted in their minds, those sages crowned the king in the kingdom. Accompanied by his sons and wives after attaining the kingdom free from thorns (i.e. obstacles or enemies), O Brāhmaṇas, he protected the earth for a long time along with his ministers.

When the last days of his life arrived, he meditated on Śiva Rāmeśvara. On death he derived the splendid *Sāyujya* (type of liberation) with Rāmanātha.

Thus, O Brāhmaṇas, the glory of Rāmanātha has been recounted to you and also the meritorious narrative of the king named Śaṅkara.

Listening to this or reading this chapter with great reverence, a devotee shall be rid of all sins. He attains Rāmanātha.

CHAPTER FORTYNINE

Eulogy of Rāmanātha

Śrī Sūta said:

1. Henceforth, I shall recount the chapter of prayers of the Trident-bearing Lord Rāmanātha.[1] It is highly meritorious, O Brāhmaṇas, listen.

2-4. When the Liṅga was installed, Rāma eulogized Parameśvara. So also did Lakṣmaṇa and Sītā, the daughter of Janaka, Sugrīva and other prominent monkeys, Brahmā and other Devas, and the great sages including the Pot-born Sage Agastya. All of them eulogized Rāghaveśvara severally with great devotion.

I shall recount the same in the proper order. Listen with great respect. O Brāhmaṇas, merely by listening to this, a man shall become liberated.

Śrī Rāma said:

5. Obeisance to you, to the noble-souled one, to the Trident-bearing Lord of great Māyā; to the dispeller of the distress of the devotee; unto the lotus-like pair of his feet; to the lord with serpents for his necklace.

6. Bow to the overlord of Devas, to the Lord Rāmanātha, the witness. Obeisance to the lord comprehensible only through the Vedānta texts; to the giver of truth to the Yogins.

7. Bow to Lord Śaṁbhu, to the lord of the universe, eternally filled with bliss. Obeisance to the lord, the dust particles of whose lotus-like feet cause destruction of the fear of devotees.

8. Obeisance to you, the lord of all. Obeisance to the Supreme Ātman himself. Hail to you of wonderful power; to the destroyer of great sins.

9. Bow to you, the destroyer of Kāla, Kāla (himself), one who transcends Time. Obeisance to the destroyer of Avidyā (Nescience), the dispeller of sins.

10. Hail to you, the sole cause of dispelling the distress of those who are tormented by Saṁsāra. Bow to you, the destroyer

---

1. Although the author takes every opportunity to eulogize Rāmeśvara, this is a special chapter in which prominent ancient personalities are shown to have praised that god. Most of the epithets here are taken from *Rudrādhyāya*.

of my sin of Brāhmaṇa-slaughter, the swallower of (Kālakūṭa) poison.

11. Obeisance to you, O Lord of Pārvatī, O immutable lord with Kailāsa as the abode. O Gaṅgādhara, O hideous-eyed one; protect me from all miseries.

12. Bow to you, the wielder of Pināka bow, the destroyer of Madana. Repeated salutations to you always in all conditions.

Lakṣmaṇa praised:

13. Obeisance to you, to Rāmanātha, to Śaṁbhu, to the destroyer of the three Puras. Obeisance to the Lord of Pārvatī, to the lord with Gaṇeśa and Skanda as sons.

14. Obeisance to the lord with matted hair, with the Sun-god, the Moon-god, and the Fire-god, for the three eyes. Obeisance to Śiva accompanied by Umā, Obeisance to the destroyer of the fear of Mārkaṇḍeya.

15. Obeisance to the cause of creation, sustenance and annihilation of the entire universe. Bow to Ugra (the fierce one), to Bhīma (the terrible one), to Mahādeva, the witness.

16. Obeisance to the omniscient one, to the most excellent one, to the bestower of boons, to the most excellent one. Obeisance to you, to Śrīkaṇṭha, to the destroyer of the five sins.

17. Obeisance to you, to the embodiment of the supreme bliss, truth and perfect knowledge. Obeisance to you, O destroyer of the ailment called worldly existence. Obeisance to the lord of sinews(?).

18. Obeisance to you, to the lord of Taskaras (thieves). Obeisance to the lord of the forests. Obeisance to you, to the lord of Gaṇas, to the cosmic-formed one, to the witness.

19. O Śaṁbhu, let me be devoted to your pair of feet wherever I may be born on being induced by my Karma.

20. Let me not be attached to or interested in improper path; with your compassion, let me be drawn to the conduct of life in accordance with the Vedas. Obeisance to you.

Sītā said:

21a. O Śaṅkara, O supreme cause, O Dhūrjaṭi, who are rendered splendid by the saffron colour from the breasts of the Daughter of the Mountain.

21b. May my mind be always (absorbed in or devoted to) my husband and never to another man.

22. O Gaṅgādhara of hideous eyes, O blue-red-complexioned Śaṅkara, O Rāmanātha, obeisance to you; protect me, O compassionate one.

23. Obeisance to you, O lord of the chiefs of Devas. Bow to you, O abode of mercy. Obeisance to you, O lord, the destroyer of the fear of worldly existence of those who are afraid of Saṁsāra.

24. O lord, O Śaṁbhu, by meditating upon your lotus-like feet, the son of Mṛkaṇḍu got rid of the fear of the god of Death and he attained eternity (eternal life). O great lord, what cannot be achieved by resorting to you (i.e. everything can be)?

25. O great lord, O supreme bliss, O protector of those who seek refuge in you, Grant me perpetual chastity. Repeated obeisance to you.

Hanumān said:

26-27. O lord of Devas, O lord of the universe, O Rāmanātha, O storehouse of compassion, let my devotion to the lotus-like feet of yours be steady.

Salute to Rāmanātha, to Śaṁbhu without whom there will not be existence of the world, nay not even its appearance. Obeisance to him whose form is the manifestation of Reality.

Aṅgada said:

28. Obeisance to that Rāmanātha, to Śaṁbhu, due to whose refulgence the universe becomes perceptible. The universe does not manifest itself without his brilliance.

Jāmbavān said:

29. Obeisance to this Rameśvara who is the embodiment of the supreme bliss, whose bliss is the bliss of all and shines forth in reality.

Nīla said:

30. Obeisance to that Rameśvara whose form is non-different, which is always non-dual, which is not differentiated by the difference of land, space, time, etc.

Nala said:

31. Obeisance to you, to Rāmeśvara who are free from Avidyā, but out of whose Avidyā are evolved Brahmā, Viṣṇu and Maheśāna.

Kumuda said:

32. Obeisance to Rāmanātha, to Śaṁbhu, to the cause (unto all). It is due to the ignorance of his real form that the world is supposed to be evolved with Pradhāna (i.e. Prakṛti) as the cause.

Panasa said:

33. The states of wakefulness, dream and deep slumber are the results of the ignorance of his real nature. Obeisance to him devoid of wakefulness, etc., to the lord in the form of knowledge.

Gaja said:

34. It is due to the ignorance of his form that atoms are wrongly regarded as the cause of effects by wretched Tārkikas (Logicians).
35. I perpetually worship that supreme bliss Rāmanātha, the great lord in the form of Ātman. He is the witness unto all.

Gavākṣa said:

36. I always seek refuge in Śiva Rāmeśvara, the quiescent one, the lord who liberates the Paśus (i.e. individual souls) from Pāśa (bondage) or *Malas* of ignorance.

Gavaya said:

37. I salute Rāmanātha Śiva, who is the support of the frightened universe, who is the lord of Umā, has the moon for his crest and who is the antidote for the ailment of worldly existence.

Śarabha said:

38. I bow down to Rāmanātha, the Ātman. People deluded and ignorant of this Ātman say that the *Antaḥkaraṇa* (internal sense, the mind) is the Ātman.

Gandhamādana said:

39. For the sake of the purification of all sins, I worship

Rāmanātha, the lord of Umā, the lord of the Gaṇas, the three-eyed lord, the lord of the universe.

Sugrīva said:

40-42. I have fallen into the ocean of worldly existence which causes fear, which has birth and death for its waters. It (Saṁsāra) has the surging waves in the form of sons, wives, wealth and fields. It is the ocean (or Saṁsāra) in which the entire Cosmic Egg is immersed. I have not reached the other shore. I am helpless. I am lamenting. I am wretched. I am frightened of the tiger of sensuous objects. I am afflicted by the crocodiles of diseases. I am agonized by the fishes in the form of the three *Tāpas* (afflictions of three types). Protect me, O Lord of the Daughter of the Mountain. Obeisance to you, O Rāmanātha.

Vibhīṣaṇa said:

43-45. I am in distress in the middle of the forest of worldly existence where I have lost my path which (i.e. this wrong path) has thieves in the form of ailments; where anger is like a lion; birth is like a tiger; death is like serpents; childhood, youth and old age are dreadful deep wells; anger, covetousness and malice are like fires; where the sensual objects are the cruel mountains. It is full of thorns causing terror. Take me now to the splendid path, O Śaṁbhu, O Rāmeśvara.

All the monkeys said:

46-48. We were born in many wombs (species) censurable or otherwise, in all places. We had fallen in Kuṁbhīpāka and other Narakas. We are born again in many indecent wombs due to the remnants of Karmas. We are now in the ocean of worldly existence. We are helpless and wretched. We cry, O Śaṅkara, O storehouse of mercy, O Rāmanātha; save us. Obeisance to you, O Rāmanātha, O ocean of mercy, O great lord.

Brahmā said:

49. Obeisance to you, to the lord of the worlds, to Rāmanātha, to Śaṁbhu. Be pleased with me, O lord of all. Destroy my ignorance.

Indra said:

50. I salute Śaṅkara, lord of Umā, Rāmanātha whose Śakti is Goddess Umā, identical with the three Vedas, the mother of the universe.

Yama said:

51. For the sake of dispelling all ignorance I serve Rāmeśvara whose sons are Gaṇeśa and Skanda and whose vehicle is the bull.

Varuṇa said:

52. I worship with my heart Rāmanātha, the conqueror of the god of Death. Due to the power of the worship of this lord the son of Mṛkaṇḍu conquered death.

Kubera said:

53. Obeisance to Rāmeśvara, to the lord whose ears shine with (the ornaments of) ear-rings, and whose body is pink-coloured like lac.

Āditya said:

54. Obeisance to you, O great lord, O three-eyed Rāmanātha. Salute to you, the destroyer of Dakṣa's sacrifice. O Śiva, do protect me.

Soma said:

55. Obeisance to you, to the trident-bearing lord who is smeared with ash, to the lord having serpents for garlands, O Rāmanātha, O ocean of mercy. Obeisance to the lord with the cremation-ground as your abode.

Agni said:

56. O lord whose lotus-like feet are served by all the Guardians of the Quarters including Indra; perpetual obeisance to the pure one, to Rāmanātha having the quarters for garments (i.e. naked).

Vāyu said:

57. Obeisance to you, O Rāmanātha, to Hara identical with

Hari in form, to the lord having tiger-skin for garments. Be the bestower of my desired objects.

Bṛhaspati said:

58. O Rāmanātha, obeisance to you, the perpetual witness unto the Ego; to the non-dual inner being; destroy my ignorance quickly.

Śukra said:

59. Obeisance to one who is difficult of access to those who deceive; to the lord whose form constitutes the meaning of the great Mantras. Obeisance to one free from duals, to Rāmanātha, to Śaṁbhu.

Aśvins said:

60. Obeisance to you, O Rāghaveśvara who shine in the hearts of Yogins perpetually in the form of Ātman; to the lord who cannot be comprehended through any other means of manifestation.

Agastya said:

61. O primordial lord, O great god, O lord of the universe, O immutable Śiva, O Rāmanātha, lord of Aṁbikā, O bull-emblemed lord, be pleased (with me).

62. Forgive a thousand faults of mine, O Moon-crested lord. Relieve me of my sense of possession in sons and others as "This is mine", etc.

Sutīkṣṇa said:

63. Neither fields, nor jewels, neither riches nor wives, neither friends, nor garments nor cows, horses and sons can be of any help indeed, O Rāmanātha. Hence grant me detachment.

Viśvāmitra said:

64. If a man has no devotion to you, O Lord Śrī Rāmanātha, O Śiva, certainly his learning of scriptures is futile, even the Vedas learned by him are fruitless.

Gālava said:

65. It is definite that if men do not bow down to you, O Rāmeśvara, their charitable gifts, their performance of Yajñas, their observances of restraints, their austerities and their plunges in Gaṅgā and other Tīrthas are useless.

Vasiṣṭha said:

66. People may commit all the sins but, O Rāmeśvara, if they devoutly approach you and bow down to you, they (sins) will be certainly dissolved like the darkness which is clearly dispelled by the brilliance of the Sun.

Atri said:

67. After visiting you, O Rāmeśvara, once, after touching and bowing down to you the lord, a man does not attain any womb (birth) further, but becomes non-different from you.

Aṅgiras said:

68. If any man approaches you, O Rāmanātha, and bowing to you remembers his kinsmen, he redeems even them from all the sins. There is no wonder in his being contented.

Gautama said:

69. O Lord Śrīrāmanātha, this is a great secret. It dispels grief. Those who serve the men who worship the soles of your feet are also blessed.

Śatānanda said:

70. This should be understood by persons desirous of salvation, who are conversant with the secret of the perfect Vedāntic knowledge. Discarding all the scriptural texts, O Raghuvīra-Nātha, (they should) serve you.

Bhṛgu said:

71. O Rāmanātha, a person who has got rid of all his sins by meditating upon the pair of your lotus-like feet, fearlessly attains the refulgent non-dual reality and happiness that is solid consciousness which is never futile.

Kutsa said:

72. O Rāmanātha, service unto your feet bestows always the boon of worldly pleasures and salvation on men. It is destructive of Raurava and other Narakas. Which man, desirous of grasping (getting) pleasure, would not worship it?

Kāśyapa said:

73. In regard to the persons who serve your feet, O Rāmanātha, of what avail are observance of holy rites, austerities and sacrifices? Of what avail is the thought of Japas and discussion of Vedas and scriptures? Of what avail is the water of the Celestial River?

74. At the time when my soul departs from my body, O Śrīrāmanātha, you do come quickly along with Bhavānī and enable me to attain your lotus-like feet devoid of grief and delusion, having the form of *Cit* (consciousness) and happiness.

Gandharvas said:

75. O Rāmanātha, you alone are the goal unto us who worship you. In the ocean of worldly existence which is boundless and which has waves in the form of miseries, we do not have any other goal except you.

Kinnaras said:

76. O Rāmanātha, in the wild forest of worldly existence, dreadful on account of the tigers in the forms of ailments, there is no one to guide us excepting you.

Yakṣas said:

77. O Rāmanātha, the oppression of our enemies (in the form of) the sense-organs is always unbearable to us. O Dhūrjaṭi, assist us in subduing them.

Serpents said:

78. O Rāmanātha, you are one of unimaginable glory and we are of inferior intellect. O lord of Aṁbikā, how shall we be competent to eulogize you adequately?

Kiṁpuruṣas said:

79. Obeisance to you, O Rāmanātha. Do destroy our frequent deaths and births in different wombs (species). Destroy our ignorance as well.

Vidyādharas said:

80. Obeisance to you, to the lord of Aṁbikā, to the noble-souled, to you, to Rāmanātha. O bull-emblemed one, be pleased.

Vasus said:

81. Obeisance to you, to the lord of the Gaṇas, to Rāmanātha, to the lord whose feet are worshipped by the multitudes of Gaṇas; obeisance to Gaṅgādhara, to the *Guhya* (the mysterious one); obeisance to you. Always protect us.

Viśvedevas said:

82. Obeisance to Rāmanātha accompanied by Aṁbā; to you, the noble-souled, the unattached one. Bow to you, the bestower of salvation on excellent Yogins strictly adhering to *Jñapti* (knowledge) alone. O Śaṅkara, protect us.

Maruts said:

83. Obeisance to you, to Rāmanātha, the supreme principle, to the genuine essence of all the principles. Obeisance to Śaṁbhu, the self-luminious one.

Sādhyas said:

84. Obeisance to Lord Rāmeśvara, to the lord who has none apart from himself (i.e. the all-pervading lord), to the lord, the assigner of existence to the universe; salute to the destroyer of Avidyā.

All the Devas said:

85-91. All of us always think in our minds of Rāmanātha for the purification of our sins—Rāmanātha who is full of existence, knowledge and bliss; who is devoid of a dual; who is of the nature of Brahman; who is self-manifest; and has neither beginning nor middle nor end. He has no aberration or deterioration, no attachment, is pure and eternal, is the witness unto Ether and other evolutes, is the greatest immortal one.

He is beyond knowledge. He is the giver of enlightenment even to the means of right knowledge. He is always bereft of appearance, disappearance, shrinkage, etc. He is the witness unto this world superimposed on himself. He is unaffected. He is supreme bliss. He has given up all activities. He is great bliss, the supreme soul; he is of the form of consciousness and is bereft of sensual enjoyment. We are desirous of knowing our own Ātman and bliss. O Rāmanātha, protect us; O ocean of mercy, obeisance to you.

Obeisance to Rāmanātha, to Rudra. Obeisance to the dispeller of worldly existence, to the lord who has differentiated himself in the forms of Brahmā, Viṣṇu, etc. through his own Māyā.

The Ministers of Vibhīṣaṇa said:

92. Obeisance to you, to Rāmanātha, to the bestower of boons, to the excellent one, to the three-eyed lord, to the trident-bearing one. Obeisance to the eternal lord worthy of being meditated upon by Yogins.

Sūta said:

93-96. On being eulogized by Rāma and others, O excellent Brāhmaṇas, Śiva, Rāmeśvara called Rāma and all the others and said to them: "O Rāma, O Rāma of great fortune, O lord, O lover of Jānakī, O Lakṣmaṇa, O splendid Jānakī, O Sugrīva and others, O Brahmā and others, listen with great concentration.

The man who listens to or reads or imparts to others this meritorious *Stotrādhyāya* ('Chapter on Prayers') composed by you, with great reverence, shall have the merit of worshipping me. There is no doubt about it.

97-100. They will have the merit of taking the holy bath in Rāmacandradhanuṣkoṭi. They will derive the merit of residing on Rāmasetu for a full year. They will have the merit of taking the holy baths in all the Tīrthas on Gandhamādana. There is nothing to doubt in this."

After saying this, Rāmanātha vanished in his Liṅga. The man who recites this meritorious chapter of prayer always shall be rid of death and old age. He shall be free from the miseries of (frequent) births. There is no doubt about this that he will attain the salvation of *Sāyujya* (type) with Rāmanātha.

CHAPTER FIFTY

The Story of Puṇyanidhi

Śrī Sūta said:

1-5. Henceforth, I shall recount the glory of Setumādhava.[1] Listen, O sages, with devotion. It is highly meritorious and destructive of sins.

Formerly there was a king born of the lunar race, named Puṇyanidhi. He ruled Madhurā graced by Hālāsyeśvara.

Once, that king installed his son in Madhurā and went to Rāmasetu accompanied by his army consisting of the four divisions. He was followed by the members of his Antaḥpura and all the attendants. He was eager to take his holy bath. After reaching that place, he took his holy bath in Dhanuṣkoṭi with the requisite *Saṁkalpa* rite.

The excellent king took his holy bath in the other Tīrthas too located there. With great devotion, he served Lord Rāmeśvara.

6-8. Thus, for a long time he stayed there happily. Staying in the meritorious Rāmasetu on the Gandhamādana mountain, once the king performed a Yajña that was highly pleasing to Viṣṇu. At the end of the Yajña, eager to have his *Avabhṛtha* (valedictory bath), the king joyously took his bath in Rāmadhanuṣkoṭi along with his wives and attendants. After serving Rāmanātha, O Brāhmaṇas, he went to his abode.

9-11. While King Puṇyanidhi continued his stay thus, once Lakṣmī had a playful quarrel with Hari. In order to test the devotion of the king, she stipulated certain conditions with Hari. Lakṣmī, the goddess with lotus for her abode, was sent by Viṣṇu from Vaikuṇṭha. In the guise of a girl of eight years, she went to the Gandhamādana mountain. Goddess Lakṣmī came to Dhanuṣkoṭi and stood there waiting.

12. At that time, O Brāhmaṇas, king (Puṇyanidhi), the storehouse of good qualities, went to Rāmadhanuṣkoṭi to take his holy bath along with his wives and soldiers.

13-14. After going there, the king took his holy bath with due observance. He made the full gifts such as *Tulāpuruṣa,* etc. Desirous of returning to the abode, he saw a certain girl of eight

1. This legend is introduced here to explain why Setumādhava (Viṣṇu on the Setu) came to be installed in this place specially holy for Śiva.

years, with pure smiles and of excessive beauty.

15. On seeing her who had beautiful eyes, smiled sweetly and had splendid teeth, her lips resembling the Biṁba fruit (*Momordica monadelpha*), and whose waistline was slender, the king asked that girl:

Puṇyanidhi said:

16. Who are you, O girl? Whose daughter are you? From where have you come here? O dear girl of beautiful smiles, what is your purpose in coming here?

17. Thus the king asked that girl with eyes like lotus. On being asked thus, O Brāhmaṇas, the girl spoke to that king:

18. "I have neither mother nor father. Nor have I any kinsfolk. I am without a protector, O great king. I shall become your daughter.

19-20. I shall stay in your house, O father, looking at you, always. If anyone holds me by the hand and violently pulls at me, O king, you shall chastise him. In that case, I shall stay in your place as your daughter for a long time, O father, O storehouse of good qualities."

21-24. On being told thus, the king, the storehouse of good qualities, said to the girl:

"I shall do everything mentioned by you, O splendid girl. I have no daughter. I have a son, the support of the family. I shall give you whatever appeals to you. Come to my house, O girl. Live in my Antaḥpura as the daughter of my wife. O uncensured (praiseworthy) girl, live here as you please."

On being told thus by the king, that girl of lotus-like eyes said to the king: "That's right". She went to his abode along with him.

25-26. The king handed over that splendid girl to his wife. The king told his wife Vindhyāvalī then: "O splendid queen Vindhyāvalī, this is your daughter. Protect her in every respect, O dear lady, from all other men."

27. On being told thus by the king, Vindhyāvalī, the wife, said "Of course", and grasped that girl, her daughter, by the hand.

28. That girl was brought up and nurtured by the king like his own son. Always fondled (by them), the girl lived in the king's palace happily.

29. Then in order to search for Lakṣmī, O Brāhmaṇas, Viṣṇu,

the Lord of the universe, eagerly rode on his Garuḍa and set out from Vaikuṇṭha.

30. Going out from Vaikuṇṭha, he traversed the ethereal path. He wandered over many lands. But he did not see Lakṣmī in those places.

31. Then he went to Rāmasetu on the Gandhamādana mountain. Searching for Indirā, he wandered all over Rāmasetu.

32. At that very time, that girl went to the trees in the garden of the palace, eager to gather flowers, accompanied by her companions.

33-36. She began to collect the flowers in the forest along with her companions. Viṣṇu came there, O Brāhmaṇas, assuming the form of a Brāhmaṇa. He held (a pot of) Gaṅgā water on his shoulder. He held an umbrella in his hand. He had adopted the dress and the guise of a Brāhmaṇa who regularly bathed in Gaṅgā. In his right hand, he had the Pavitra made of Kuśa grass. He had applied Bhasma all over his body. He shone with his Tripuṇḍra mark. He repeated the names of Śiva. He wore a garland of Rudrākṣa beads. He had the upper cloth. O Brāhmaṇas, thus Janārdana came there in a neat guise.

37. On seeing the Brāhmaṇa the girl stood stunned. He saw his beloved in the form of a girl of eight years gathering flowers.

38. On seeing that sweet-voiced girl, the Garuḍa-emblemed Lord in the form of a Brāhmaṇa hurriedly seized her by the hand.

39. Then along with her companions in the forest, the girl shouted loudly. On hearing that shout, the king too came there.

40. The king went to the park of the palace accompanied by a few soldiers. After going there, the king asked the girl and her companions too:

41-42. "O girl, what for did you shout and cry out loudly along with your companions now from this palace park? Let the reason thereof be told. O my daughter, by whom have you been teased? Did anyone seize you by force?"

On being asked thus, the girl said to the king, the storehouse of good qualities, with her eyes full of tears. She had been annoyed and was sad. She had been frightened much.

The girl said:

43-46. O king of Pāṇḍyas, it was this Brāhmaṇa who violently seized me. O dear father, quite undaunted he is standing there under that tree.

On hearing her words, the intelligent king, the storehouse of good qualities, caught hold of the Brāhmaṇa with force. He took him to the shrine of Rāmanātha. The king was not aware of the real power of the Brāhmaṇa. He bound him with fetters and noose and took him to the pavilion. The king then consoled his daughter and took her to the Antaḥpura.

47-53. The great king went to his beautiful mansion. During his sleep the king saw that Brāhmaṇa in his dream. He was adorned with a conch, discus, iron club, lotus and garland of sylvan flowers. His chest was embellished with the Kaustubha jewel. He was Hari clad in yellow garments. He was brilliant with the complexion resembling a black cloud. He was seated on Garuḍa. He had beautiful teeth and splendid smiles. His ear-rings resembling Makara, shone well. He was attended upon by Viṣvaksena and other servants. He lay on the couch (of the body) of Śeṣa. He was eulogized by Nārada and other sages; (further) he saw his own daughter standing in a full-blown lotus. In her hand there was a lotus flower. Her hair was black, curly and glossy. She had her abode in the broad chest of Viṣṇu. Her breasts were lifted up and protruding. Her limbs were showered upon by the elephants of the cardinal points. She was dark-complexioned and clad in yellow garments. Her tresses were embellished with garlands made of golden lotuses. She appeared rich with the splendour of divine ornaments. She was bedecked in beautiful necklaces.

54-58. She appeared very splendid in her nose ornaments made of costly jewels. Gold coins (wreathed together) constituted her ornament. She shone with her girdle and anklets. The king thus saw his daughter that night in the form of Mahālakṣmī. On seeing his daughter as well as that Brāhmaṇa in the dream thus, the king got up suddenly from his bed and went to the abode of his daughter. There he saw his daughter in the same form as he saw in his dream. When the sun rose, the king took his daughter and went to the temple of Rāmanātha where he had kept the Brāhmaṇa. There in the excellent Maṇḍapa he saw the Brāhmaṇa in the form of Hari exactly as he had seen in the dream, marked with the garland of sylvan flowers, etc. After knowing him to be Viṣṇu, the king eulogized Lord Hari.

Puṇyanidhi said:

59-65. Obeisance to you, O lover of Lakṣmī. Be pleased, O Garuḍa-emblemed one. Obeisance to you, O lord with the Śārṅga bow in your hand. Forgive my offence. Obeisance to you, O lotus-eyed one, O Lord of Śrī having the discus in your hand. Bow to the lord marked and adorned with Kaustubha jewel; obeisance to the lord with Śrīvatsa scar; obeisance to you with Brahmā as your son; to the lord who crushed multitudes of Daityas. Hail to the lord with a lotus in (i.e. growing from) the navel, the abode of all the worlds. Obeisance to the destroyer of Madhu and Kaiṭabha; obeisance to you, to the destroyer of Rāvaṇa. Bow to you, to the protector of Prahlāda. Obeisance to the lord of the earth, to the lord devoid of attributes, to Viṣṇu, to the incomprehensible one, to the witness of the intellect (of all). Obeisance to you; to Śrīnivāsa; to the creator of the universe; to the Supreme Ātman. Bow to Lord Nārāyaṇa, to Kṛṣṇa, the enemy of Madhu. Obeisance to the lotus-navelled one, to the lotus-eyed one. Obeisance to the husband of Goddess Lakṣmī with the lotus in her hand. Hail to the lord with lotus-like feet.

66-74a. Again and again obeisance to you, O lord of the universe. Obeisance to one with lotus-garlands. Obeisance to you, O mercy personified. Forgive my offence, O slayer of Madhu, I have offended you with these fetters and nooses. O lord, this has been committed by me without knowing your real form and nature. Hence my offence should be forgiven, O slayer of Madhu.

After eulogizing Mahāviṣṇu thus, O Brāhmaṇas, King Puṇyanidhi joyously eulogized Lakṣmī, the mother of all living beings:

"Obeisance to you, O mother of the universe, O goddess with Viṣṇu's broad chest for your abode. Obeisance to you, O Daughter of the Ocean, O Mahālakṣmī, O beloved of Hari. Perpetual obeisance to Siddhi, Puṣṭi, Svadhā and Svāhā. Repeated obeisance to Sandhyā, to Prabhā, to Dhātrī, to Bhūti. Obeisance, Obeisance to Śraddhā, to Medhā and to Sarasvatī. O Yajñavidyā ('science of sacrifice'), O Mahāvidyā, O Guhyavidyā ('science of the secret things'), O highly splendid one, O Ātmavidyā ('science of Ātman'). O goddess of Devas, O bestower of salvation on all the embodied beings, O mother of the universe, O goddess, the embodiment of three Vedas, O protectress of the universe! Save me by your benign glance, O goddess, the cause of creation, sustenance and annihilation. Again and again, obeisance to you, O mother of Brahmā, O great goddess."

74b-78. After eulogizing Mahālakṣmī thus, he prayed to Mādhava: "Out of ignorance, offence has been committed by me against you, O Viṣṇu, by tying your feet with fetters. Let that offence be forgiven by you.

All the people of the worlds are your children, O Hari. You are the father of all the worlds, O Madhusūdana; the offence of the sons should be forgiven by the fathers.

You have given even your own form to the offending Daityas, O Viṣṇu. Forgive this offence of mine. O lord, formerly Pūtanā had approached you with a desire to kill you. Still you took her to your region. Therefore, O storehouse of mercy, protect me. O Keśava, the lover of Lakṣmī, cast at me your merciful glance."

Śrī Sūta said:

79. On being entreated thus by that king, O excellent Brāhmaṇas, Viṣṇu spoke these words to King Puṇyanidhi in a majestic voice.

Viṣṇu said:

80-86. O king, you need not entertain any fear as a result of keeping me in bondage. I have revealed unto you the fact that I am completely subject to the control of the devotees. You have performed a Yajña causing great delight unto me. Hence you are my devotee. Being bound down with the noose of devotion, I have become subject to your control.

O suppressor of enemies, I always forgive the faults of my devotees. This goddess was despatched by me, because I was desirous of knowing your devotion. Lakṣmī, my beloved, was protected by you now, O king. Therefore, I am delighted with you. This goddess has always my form. She is identical with me. One who is a devotee of hers in this world is called a devotee of mine. One who is averse to her, O king, will always be remembered as one who hates me. Since with great devotion you have worshipped her, my worship also has been performed by you, for she is not different from me.

87-91. Hence, O ruler of men, no offence has been committed by you against me. But worship alone has been performed by you to me by worshipping her. With my wife you came to an agreement earlier. It was to honour that agreement that you bound me. Therefore, I am pleased with you, O king. Lakṣmī has been protected now. Lakṣmī is one with my form. She is the mother of the universe. She is identical with the Vedas. In the course of according protection to her, O king, you bound me. That bondage is delightful unto me, O eminent king. Let not fear be entertained by you. Really this Lakṣmī is your daughter. There is no doubt about it.

When this was spoken by Hari, Lakṣmī said to the king:

Lakṣmī said:

92-97. O king, I am also pleased with you, because I have been protected by you in your abode. It is to test your power of devotion that both of us, Viṣṇu and I have come here, O king, shamming a playful quarrel. Both of us are pleased with your yogic power and devotion, O scorcher of foes. With our favour, O king, may you have perpetual happiness. May you certainly have all the riches of the entire sphere of the world forever. May you have steady devotion unto our feet. On death, O king, may you have *Sāyujya* with me without further return (to Saṁsāra) forever, O king. May you not have evil-mindedness at all. Let there always be devotion to Viṣṇu. Let your mind be inclined towards Dharma forever.

After saying this to the king, Lakṣmī went to her abode on the broad chest of Viṣṇu.

Then, O eminent Brāhmaṇas, Viṣṇu spoke to the king these words:

98-106a. "O excellent king, I shall stay here by the name Setumādhava in the manner in which I have been fettered by you. This Setu has been built by me. I shall be here for its protection from the multitudes of Bhūtas and Rākṣasas and for subduing all sorts of fears. Brahmā too lives here day and night for protecting the Setu. Śaṅkara named Rāmanātha permanently stays here on the Setu. Indra and other guardians of the worlds too stay here with great joy. Hence, I will also stay here under the name Setumādhava for the purpose of protecting the Setu and to suppressing all troubles, for the purpose of fulfilling the desires of everyone and quelling all sins. Those men who serve me here where I have been fettered by you, will attain *Sāyujya* with me, O king, and realize all their desires.

Those who read this narrative of mine, of Lakṣmī and of yours, will never become poor. They will get all riches. Those who read or listen to or joyously write this prayer to Lakṣmī and to me composed by you, O king will never return from my world."

106b-108. After saying this to King Puṇyanidhi, Hari became permanently present there.

After bowing down to Viṣṇu in the form of Setumādhava and after devoutly performing the great worship of the lord, and after serving Rāmanātha, he went to his abode.

109. O Brāhmaṇas, King Puṇyanidhi stayed in that excellent holy spot Setu throughout his life. At Madhurā he installed his son as the ruler.

110. Staying there, the king on his death, attained salvation. Vindhyāvalī, his wife, died after him. The chaste lady loving her husband as much as her own vital breath, attained good goal.

Śrī Sūta said:

111-113a. Those who perpetually serve Setumādhava here with devotion, will never return from Kailāsa. Those men who do not serve Setumādhava here, cannot have success in their worship of Rāmanātha too.

113b-117. If a man takes sand from Setu and scatters it in Gaṅgā, that man shall stay in the city of Mādhava in Vaikuṇṭha.

One who is desirous of going to Gaṅgā, O Brāhmaṇas, shall perform the *Saṁkalpa* rite in the presence of Setumādhava. He should then go to Gaṅgā. His pilgrimage shall be fruitful. He should bring the water of Gaṅgā and bathe Rāmeśvara with that. He should deposit all his problems and burdens on the Setu. He shall certainly attain Brahman.

Thus, O Brāhmaṇas, the glory of Setumādhava has been narrated to you all. One who reads this or listens to this attains Vaikuṇṭha.

CHAPTER FIFTYONE

Pilgrimage to Setu

Śrī Sūta said:

1. Henceforth I shall recount the procedure for pilgrimage to Setu, O Brāhmaṇas. On hearing it, one is liberated from all sins instantly.

2-6. The intelligent devotee should remain pure in soul. He should take his holy bath and perform the *Ācamana* rite as well as all the routine duties of the day. For propitiating Lord Rāmanātha as well as giving delight to Rāghava, he should feed some Brāhmaṇas in accordance with his capacity. He should feed those Brāhmaṇas who have mastered the Vedas. He should smear the body with Bhasma (holy ash) and have the Tripuṇḍra mark on his forehead. Or he can smear his body with Gopīcandana and sandal-paste and have the Ūdhvapuṇḍraka on his forehead. He should wear a necklace of Rudrākṣa beads and have a *Pavitra* (ring made of kuśa) round his finger. Making himself pure thus, he shall devoutly perform the rite of *Saṁkalpa*, 'I shall perform the pilgrimage to the Setu'. Without speaking anything (to anyone), he should set off from his house. He should repeat the eight-syllabled Mantra (*oṁ nārāyaṇāya namaḥ*) (or) the five-syllabled Mantra (*namaḥ śivāya)* with perfectly controlled mind. He should take food only once a day. He should take the *Haviṣya* (food) only. He should subdue and control anger and the sense-organs.

7. He should not have (any) footwear or umbrella. He should avoid chewing betel leaves. He should not take oil bath. He shall never have physical contact, etc. with women.

8. He should strictly adhere to the norms of cleanliness and good conduct. He should regularly perform the Sandhyā prayers. He should repeat the Gāyatrī Mantra during the three junctions and meditate on Rāma.

9. On the way, he should respectfully read the glory of Setu everyday. Or he should read the Rāmāyaṇa or any of the Purāṇas.

10. He should avoid unnecessary talks and utterances. He should thus proceed to the Setu for the sake of purity. He should not accept any monetary gifts, nor should he give up any of the good customs and manners.

11. He should perform the worship of Śiva, Viṣṇu, etc. on the way in accordance with his capacity. He should perform the holy rites of *Vaiśvadeva,* etc. according to his capacity.

12. He should perform the sacred rites of *Brahmayajña,* etc. and worship the holy fire. He should offer food, beverage, etc. to guests as much as he can.

13. To the ascetics too he should give alms without being stingy. On the way, he should repeat the names of Śiva, Viṣṇu, etc. and recite the hymns and prayers.

14. He should always do what is righteous and avoid prohibited activities. Strictly adhering to these and other restrictions and observances, he should go to Setumūla.

15. At the outset, he should offer pieces of rocks (stones) with great concentration after going there. He should invoke the Ocean there, and bow down to it thereafter.

16. He shall offer *Arghya* to the sea. Thereafter he should offer prayers. Then he should have the *Anujñā* (formal granting of permission by the Sea). Then he should take his bath in the great sea.

17. He should mentally meditate on Hari and offer libations to the sages, Devas, monkeys and Pitṛs, O Brāhmaṇas.

THE NUMBER OF PĀṢĀṆAS (PIECES OF ROCKS)

18. The devotee should offer seven *Pāṣāṇas* or (at least) one, O eminent Brāhmaṇas. By offering the *Pāṣāṇas* the holy bath shall become fruitful and not otherwise.

THE MANTRA FOR OFFERING THE PĀṢĀṆAS

19. "O Kṛtyā (Evil Spirit), O terror of all the worlds originating from Pippalāda, the *Pāṣāṇas* have been given to you. May these be utilised for your meal."

THE MANTRA REQUESTING FOR THE PRESENCE

20. "You are Viśvācī, you are Ghṛtācī, O Viśvayānā ('Having the universe for the vehicle'). O lord, O king, for my sake, be present in the briny sea."

THE MANTRA FOR OFFERING NAMASKĀRA

21. "Obeisance to you, the lord remaining hidden in the uni-

verse. Obeisance to you, O Viṣṇu, O lord of the waters. Obeisance to the lord with golden horns (?). Obeisance to the lord of rivers. Obeisance to the munificent ocean."

After uttering thus the devotee should prostrate (himself).

THE MANTRA FOR ARGHYA

22. "O glorious one, O great sea, O mine of all gems! You are the chief one with all gems. Accept the *Arghya*."

THE MANTRA FOR ANUJÑĀPANA (OFFERING THE FORMAL PERMISSION)

23. "O lord, the support of the entire universe, O lord holding the conch, the discus and the iron club, grant me permission to resort to your Tīrtha."

THE MANTRA OF PRAYER

24-27. "One should remember Sugrīva in the East, Nala in the South, the one named Mainda in the West and Dvivida in the North. One should remember Rāma, Lakṣmaṇa, Sītā of great reputation, Aṅgada, Hanumān, the son of Wind-god, and Vibhīṣaṇa in the middle."

O great Sea, grant me the merit of holy bath in all the Tīrthas of the earth that have entered you. Save me from all the sins.

With the two (?verses) beginning with "*Hiraṇyaśṛṅga*" the devotee should remember Nārāyaṇa in the navel.

28. Meditating upon Lord Nārāyaṇa in the rites such as the holy bath, etc., one attains the world of Brahmā. He is not reborn here.

29. Thereby one would have done atonement for all the sins. The devotee should with single-minded devotion think about Prahlāda, Nārada, Vyāsa, Aṁbarīṣa, Śuka and other devotees of the Lord.

THE MANTRA FOR THE HOLY BATH

30-36. "You are the source of the Vedas (?), the origin of Veda and Vasiṣṭha, O Ocean, you are the lord of the rivers, the origin of all gems. (You are) fire, the refulgence, the earth, Viṣṇu, the navel of Amṛta (?), the lord discharging the *Retas* (semen). This water of yours is not like other waters, those waters that enter the ocean. Having approached (and immersed) my head, I shall cast off all my sins from the body like the serpent that casts off the decaying slough."

Again, O Brāhmaṇas, he should make obeisance to the munificent ocean. Then he should utter thus: "One should bow down to the pure Ocean, the lord of rivers, who is full of all Tīrthas. There are two oceans." After uttering this, he should take the second bath.

"O Sun, O harbinger of the day, all the Tīrthas within the Cosmic Egg are touched by your rays. Due to this truth, grant me the Tīrtha on the Setu." Then the devotee should remember in the order mentioned before, 'Sugrīva in the East', etc. Thereafter, O Brāhmaṇas, he should take the third holy dip.

If the man undertakes the pilgrimage starting from Devīpaṭṭaṇa, he should take the holy bath in the ocean in the middle of the nine rocks in Setu, the bestower of salvation. He should take the holy bath for quelling his sins.

37. If he goes to the Setu, the bestower of salvation, through the path of "Darbhaśayyā" he shall take his bath directly in the ocean for attaining salvation.

THE PROCEDURE FOR OFFERING LIBATIONS

38-43. The devotee should offer libations to the following,[1] three times for each[2], uttering the Mantra: Pippalāda, Kavi, Kaṇva, Kṛtānta, Jīviteśvara, Manyu, Kālarātri, Vidyā, Ahargaṇeśvara, Vasiṣṭha, Vāmadeva, Parāśara, Umāpati, Vālmīki, Nārada, the sages Vālakhilyas, (the monkeys such as) Nala, Nīla, Gavākṣa, Gavaya, Gandha, Ṛṣabha,

---

1. It appears that there were two ways of starting the pilgrimage VV 15ff show that one starts from Devīpaṭṭaṇa (called Devīpaṭnam), a coastal village about ten miles from Rāmanāthapuram. It is so-called as there is a famous shrine of Devī in the village. The village is called 'Navapāṣāṇam' as nine stones (one for each Planet) were installed here by Rāma to formally inaugurate the building of the Setu. Hence pilgrims are asked to deposit one stone here.

It is generally after the pilgrimage to Rāmeśvaram that pilgrims go to Darbhaśayanam or Tirupullaṇī, a coastal village about 7 miles from Rāmanāthapuram railway station. Here Rāma is said to have stayed on a bed of Darbha grass to propitiate Sea-god to give him the way to Laṅkā through him. From v 37, it appears that people started from Darbhaśayanam also at the time of the Purāṇa writer.

2. The list of libations includes ancient sages as well as prominent figures from Rāmāyaṇa.

Sugrīva, Hanumān and Vegadarśana. Then to Rāma, Lakṣmaṇa and Sītā, the highly fortunate and exceedingly renowned. The names should be uttered in the Dative Case, O Brāhmaṇas. The libations unto Devas, Sages and Pitṛs shall be duly offered with water and gingelly seeds. The names may be uttered in the Accusative Case also, O Brāhmaṇas, and the libations can be offered.

44. The devotee should stand in the water with a pleasant mind and offer the libations with a *Pavitra* round his finger. By the offerings of the libations, he shall attain the merit of holy bath in all the Tīrthas.

45-48. After the *Tarpaṇa* rites, he should come out of the water. Casting off the wet clothes he should wear dry clothes. He should perform the *Ācamana* rites and wear the *Pavitra*. He should then perform the Śrāddha duly. He should offer rice-balls to the Pitṛs in accordance with the injunctions along with gingelly seeds and raw rice-grains.

This is the Śrāddha of the weaker man (a poor one) in the society that I am describing, O excellent Brāhmaṇas. A rich man should perform the Śrāddha by means of cooked rice with (dishes of) six tastes. The prosperous and the rich man should make charitable gifts of cows, plots of land, gingelly seeds, gold, etc. In Rāmacandra Dhanuṣkoṭi also he shall do like this.

49. He should perform everything beginning with the offerings of *Pāṣāṇa* and ending with *Tarpaṇa,* O Brāhmaṇas, exactly in the same way as he performs in Setumūla in accordance with the injunctions.

50. Then he should go to Cakratīrtha[1] and take the holy bath there too. Then he should see Lord Hari, Nārāyaṇa, the lord of the Setu.

51. Going along the western path, the devotee should take the holy bath in Cakratīrtha there itself. Then he should devoutly see Lord Darbhaśaya.

52. Then he should go to Kapitīrtha and perform the rite of ablution there. Then he should proceed to Sītākuṇḍa and take the holy bath there too.

53-54. Then he should proceed to Ṛṇamocanatīrtha that grants great merit and take his holy bath. After bowing to Lord Rāma,

1. The locations of the Tīrthas mentioned here are indicated in the respective chapters of their glorification.

the lover of Jānakī, he should go to Lakṣmaṇatīrtha. Shaving off all the hair above the neck he should take the holy bath there too thinking about his evil deeds.

55-56. After taking the holy bath in Rāmatīrtha he should proceed to the temple. Then he should take his holy bath in Pāpavināśa, Gaṅgā, Yamunā, Sāvitrī, Sarasvatī, Gāyatrī and Hanumatkuṇḍa granting great merit, O excellent Brāhmaṇas. Thereafter he should go to Brahmakuṇḍa and perform the rite of ablution in accordance with the injunctions.

57-59. Then the man should proceed to Nāgakuṇḍa that is destructive of the tortures received in the Narakas. Gaṅgā and all other rivers and all the Tīrthas stay in Nāgakuṇḍa always for quelling their own sins. This salvation-granting excellent Tīrtha has been made by the eight great serpents Ananta, etc. It is a Tīrtha on Rāmasetu and it causes welfare.

Thereafter the devotee should go to the very excellent Agastya Kuṇḍa and take his holy bath.

60. Then he should go to Agnitīrtha which is destructive of all evil Karmas. The devotee should take his holy bath, offer libations to the Pitṛs, duly perform the Śrāddha rite and remember the Pitṛs.

61. By making the charitable gifts of cows, plots of lands, gold, food-grains, etc. to Brāhmaṇas in accordance with his capacity on the banks of Agnitīrtha the devotee is liberated from all sins.

62-63. Or the devotee can take his holy bath in due order in those Tīrthas, the chief one among them being Cakratīrtha, as spoken before, O Brāhmaṇas, or in accordance with his taste he should take his bath in any of them. After taking the holy bath in all the Tīrthas thus he shall perform Śrāddha and other rites.

64-67. Afterwards he should go to Rāmeśvara and resort to (i.e. worship) Parameśvara. He should then come to Setumādhava (and visit) Rāma, Lakṣmaṇa, Sītā, Hanumān and other excellent monkeys.

After taking the holy bath in all the Tīrthas there in accordance with the injunctions, he should bow down to Rāmanātha, Rāmacandra and others. After performing the obeisance the man should go to Dhanuṣkoṭi for taking the holy bath. There he shall observe the rites of offering stones, etc. as mentioned before. He should make charitable gifts in Dhanuṣkoṭi in accordance with his monetary capacity.

68. He should respectfully give pieces of land, cows, rice-grains, clothes and other things to Brāhmaṇas well-versed in the Vedas in accordance with his financial position.

69. Then he should go to Koṭitīrtha and take the holy bath in accordance with the injunction. Then he should bow down to Rāmeśvara, the Bull-emblemed Lord.

70-74. If one is affluent, one should give gold as monetary gift. In accordance with one's monetary capacity one shall make gifts of gingelly seeds, foodgrains, cows, pieces of land, rice-grains, clothes and other things. One should not be greedy or stingy.

He should offer incense, lamps, food, accessories to worship, etc. to Lord Rāmeśvara according to his wealth.

After eulogizing Lord Rāmeśvara and devoutly bowing down to the lord, he should take the formal permission and go to the presence of Setumādhava.

After offering him incense, etc. and taking the formal ritualistic permission of Mādhava strictly adhering to the holy observances mentioned before, he should come back to his own house. He should feed Brāhmaṇas fully with cooked food consisting of the six tastes.

75. Thereby Lord Rāmanātha will be delighted with him and give what he desires. He will never fall into Naraka (Hell). His poverty will perish.

76. The line of progeny of that man increases, O excellent Brāhmaṇas. He shall get rid of worldly existence quickly and attain *Sāyujya* form of salvation.

77-80. If anyone is unable to come here, O Brāhmaṇas, he should read or make others read, those collections of texts and passages in Śrutis, Smṛtis and Āgamas that are highly meritorious, that glorify Setu and destroy great sins. Or he should read with great devotion this glory of Setu (given here).

Thereby he obtains the merit arising from holy bath in the Setu. There is no doubt about it. This has been recommended by learned men to the blind, the lame, etc.

Śrī Sūta said:

Thus, O Brāhmaṇas, the procedure of the pilgrimage to Setu has been recounted to you. One who reads this or listens to this, shall be liberated from all miseries.

CHAPTER FIFTYTWO

The Glory of Setu

Śrī Sūta said:

1. Out of deference to you, O prominent sages, I shall recount the glory of Setu further. Listen.

2. Of all the holy places this is the greatest. It is said that Japa or Homa performed here is everlasting. Penance performed and charitable gift made here are of everlasting benefit.

3. By taking the holy bath in Dhanuṣkoṭi in this great holy spot, one shall attain the merit of staying in Vārāṇasī for ten years.

4. After taking the holy bath in Dhanuṣkoṭi in that sacred place and after visiting Lord Rāmeśvara Śiva, O Brāhmaṇas, one should reside there for three days with great devotion.

5. Thereby, O eminent Brāhmaṇas, one attains that merit which results from staying for ten years in the city of Puṇḍarīka.[1] It is destructive of great sins.

6. By reciting the original six-syllabled Mantra (*oṁ namaḥ śivāya*) one thousand eight times in this place with devotion, the man shall obtain *Sāyujya* with Śiva.

7-13. If a man joyously takes his holy bath in the month of Māgha in the glorious Dhanuṣkoṭi, there is no doubt about it that he will get the merit of staying for a year in the following holy spots of Śiva or Viṣṇu:[2] Madhyārjuna, Kuṁbhakoṇa, Māyūra,

---

1. As will be seen from the list, most of these places are in Tamil Nadu and Andhra. It shows that the author is a southerner.

Puṇḍarīkapura also mentioned in NP II.73 is noted for the Liṅga of Mahādeva installed by Jaimini. But De147 identifies it with Pandharpur in Solapur District of Maharashtra. But Pandhapur is famous for its Viṭṭhala (Viṣṇu) shrine and not for Jaimini's Mahādeva.

2. The following are the locations of the holy places mentioned here:

Madhyārjuna: Tiruvidaimaruḍūr, six miles east of Kumbhakonam and 20 miles from Tanjore, Tamil Nadu. It is famous for its temple. It was visited by Śaṅkarācārya (De 116).

Kuṁbhakoṇa or Kuṁbhaghoṇa: An ancient centre of learing in Tanjor District, Tamil Nadu. A celebrated temple of Śiva and a sacred tank called Kuṁbhakarṇa Kapāla are the special features of this sacred place (De 107).

Māyūra: Māyāpurī or Haradwar U.P. (De 129).

Śrīparvata: In Karnool District, Andhra Pradesh.

Vedāraṇya: A forest in Tanjor with the hermitage of Agastya. It is 5 miles north of point Calimere (De 28).

Śvetakānana, Hālāsya, Gajāraṇya, Vedāraṇya, Naimiṣa, Śrīparvata, Śrīraṅga, the glorious Vṛddhagiri, Cidambara, Valmīka, Śeṣādri, Aruṇācala which is the glorious southern Kailāsa, Veṅkaṭa mountain, the holy spot of Hari, Kāñcīpura, Brahmapura, Vaidyeśvarapura and other similar places sacred to Śiva or Viṣṇu, O excellent Brāhmaṇas.[1]

There is a Vedic verse beginning with "*dvau samudrau*". It refers to Setu. It is eternal and is the mother (as it were). O eminent sages, there is another Vedic verse, beginning with "*ado yaddāru*". It describes the activities of Viṣṇu and praises the Setu. There is another verse too beginning with "*tad viṣṇoḥ*".

14. Itihāsas, Purāṇas and Smṛtis, O ascetics, confirm the glory of Setu in similar statements.

15. One who takes the holy bath in the Setu during eclipse of the Sun or the Moon, shall attain the merit of taking the holy bath in Gaṅgā for ten years in Avimukta (i.e. Kāśī).

16. Sin acquired in the course of a crore of births (by him) perishes instantaneously. He gets the excellent merit of a thousand horse-sacrifices.

17-19. Merely by visiting the Setu on the Viṣuva days (equinoctical days), on the days of the transit of the Sun (from one Zodiac to another), on Mondays and on Parvan days, the sin acquired in the course of seven births perishes. O eminent Brāhmaṇas, he attains heaven.

By taking the holy bath in Dhanuṣkoṭi for three days when the Sun has just risen, in the month of Māgha, when the sun is in the Zodiac Capricorn the man becomes free from sins. He shall attain the merit of taking the holy bath in all the Tīrthas including Gaṅgā.

20. The man who takes the holy bath in Dhanuṣkoṭi for five days, O excellent Brāhmaṇas, shall obtain the merit of a horse-sacrifice, etc.

Śrīraṅga: Two miles north of Trichinopoly, Tamil Nadu. It is famous for the Viṣṇu (Śrī Raṅgam) Temple.

Cidambara: Tamil Nadu. It has the sky (*Vyoma*) aspect of the Śiva-Liṅga.

Aruṇācala: Tiruvannamalai in South Arcot Dist., Tamil Nadu. The Śiva Liṅga hereof is the *Teja* (Fire) form of Śiva.

1. Most of these places are identified previously. A few more are added here.

Kuraṅgaka: Koringa near the mouth of Godāvarī (De 109).

Madhurā: Madurai, Tamil Nadu.

21. He shall obtain the merit of performing *Cāndrāyaṇa* and other *Kṛcchra* rites of atonement. Similarly he will attain the merit of reading (reciting) the four Vedas.

22. By having the holy bath in Dhanuṣkoṭi for ten days in the month of Māgha, ten thousand sins of Brāhmaṇa-slaughter will perish. There is no doubt about it.

23. The man who performs the holy ablution in Dhanuṣkoṭi for fifteen days in the month of Māgha shall obtain Vaikuṇṭha.

24. One who takes the holy bath in Rāmasetu for twenty days in the month of Māgha, attains the *Sāmīpya* (proximity) (salvation) with Śiva. He rejoices along with Śiva.

25. One who takes the holy bath for twenty-five days shall attain *Sārūpya* type salvation. One who takes the holy bath for thirty days shall certainly obtain *Sāyujya*.

26. Therefore, O excellent Brāhmaṇas, the learned man should take the holy bath certainly in Rāmasetu in the month of Māgha when the Sun has risen a little.

27-28. The man who takes the holy bath in Rāmasetu during a lunar or solar eclipse, at the time of *Ardhodaya* or *Mahodaya*, does not suffer from various distresses which one undergoes in the womb. It is glorified as destructive of Brāhmaṇa-murder and other sins.

29. It is glorified as annulling (the stay in) all the Narakas. It is proclaimed as the cause of all the riches.

30-34. It yields *Sālokya* (i.e. stay in the same world) with Indra and other gods.

A holy plunge in Dhanuṣkoṭi during lunar as well as solar eclipse and during *Ardhodaya* and *Mahodaya* is definitely certain (to lead to salvation). This was formerly created by Rāma for the sake of destroying Rāvaṇa. It was resorted to by Siddhas, Cāraṇas, Gandharvas, Kinnaras and serpents. Bathing here was performed by Brāhmaṇa-sages, celestial sages, saintly kings and groups of Pitṛs. It has been devoutly performed by groups of Devas including Brahmā.

Even if a person remembers Rāmasetu, the meritorious holy spot, O Brāhmaṇas, and takes his bath in any lake or other water reservoir, he will never incur any sin.

35. By giving handfuls (of grains) in the Tīrthas stationed in the middle of Setu, all ailments disappear. So also the sins of foetus-murder, etc.

36. If a man sees the holy line drawn by Rāma by means of his bow, he will never return from Vaikuṇṭha.

37. It is destructive of sins. It is well-known in the world as Dhanuṣkoṭi. This was made by the intelligent Rāma at the request of Vibhīṣaṇa.

38-41. Dhanuṣkoṭi is highly meritorious. After devoutly taking the holy bath therein, the devotee should make charitable gifts of money, lands, cows, gingelly seeds, rice-grains, foodgrains, milk, clothes, ornaments, pulses, cooked rice, curds, ghee, water, vegetables, pure sugar, greens, honey, sweetmeats, sweet pies and other things. The charitable gift of these things in Rāmasetu, O Brāhmaṇas, is mentioned as yielding all desired things.

42-45. Hence one should make gifts in Rāmasetu without any covetousness for wealth. The gifts made, the *Homa* performed, the penances performed, the *Japas*, the observances of restrictions, etc. at Śrīrāmadhanuṣkoṭi shall yield infinite merit. Thereby the Vedas are pleased, the Pitṛs become contented and all the sages are satisfied. Brahmā, Viṣṇu and Śiva are pleased. Serpents, Kiṁpuruṣas and Yakṣas are certainly delighted. By visiting Dhanuṣkoṭi one shall become purified oneself. He shall sanctify all the men born in his own family. He will sanctify his grandfathers.

46-50. By visiting Dhanuṣkoṭi he shall liberate (from Saṁsāra) the entire family. By taking the holy plunge in the line drawn by the tip of Rāma's bow crores of the five great sins shall certainly perish at that very moment. He who sees the line drawn with the tip of Śrīrāma's bow never undergoes stay in the womb that is full of distress.

If anyone takes holy plunge in the Kuṇḍa where Sītā entered the fire, hundreds of the sins of destroying foetus perish, O Brāhmaṇas, within a moment. As Rāma, so is Setu; as Gaṅgā, so is Hari. If a man utters "O Gaṅgā, O Hari, O Rāmasetu" and takes the holy bath anywhere in the open, he attains the greatest goal.

51-53. The devotee should take his holy bath in the Setu on the Gandhamādana mountain at the time of *Ardhodaya* (*Parva*) and offer piṇḍas of the size of mustard seeds to the Pitṛs. Then the Pitṛs become contented as long as the Moon and the Sun (shine).

If the *Piṇḍa*, even if it be of the size of a Śamī leaf (*Mimosa suma*), is offered by a Brāhmaṇa with the Pitṛs in view, if it is offered with devotion, he shall be rid of all sins. The Pitṛs in the heaven attain salvation and those in Naraka shall go to heaven.

54. In the holy spots of Setu, Padmanābha, Gokarṇa and Puruṣottama the holy bath can be taken in the waters of the ocean at all times.

55. He who desires for progeny should not take his bath in the saline waters on Tuesdays, Fridays and Saturdays anywhere else except in the Setu.

56. One who has not concluded the obsequies or one whose wife is pregnant should not knowingly take bath in the ocean anywhere else except in the Setu.

57. In regard to the Setu, there is no question of waiting for any particular time. Taking the holy bath in it everyday is praiseworthy. The rules and restrictions in regard to the days of the week, the lunar days and the Constellations, O Brāhmaṇas, are applicable to the seas elsewhere except in the Setu.

58-65. One can take the holy bath on behalf of another living man and not of a dead man. He should make the replica of the person concerned with Kuśa grass and bathe him with the waters of the Tīrtha uttering the following Mantra with calm sense-organs and mind:

"You are Kuśa. You are holy. You were formerly held by Viṣṇu. If you take your holy bath, he too has taken the holy bath—he who is represented by these tied knots (of Kuśa grass).

Everywhere the ocean is holy at the time of Parvan days. In the Setu, in the place where a river joins the ocean, the place of confluence of Gaṅgā and sea, in Gokarṇa and in Puruṣottama (Jagannātha Purī) daily bath is laid down. In other places, one shall not touch the ocean except on Parvan days.

Even as the Pitṛs, all the Devas and the Sages were listening, Rāma, accompanied by Sītā and Lakṣmaṇa, took a vow:

"All those men who take their holy bath here in this Setu built by me will with my favour never have rebirth. By visiting my Setu all the sins do perish. Even in the course of hundreds and crores of years I cannot (adequately) describe the glory of Rāmanātha and the power of my Setu."

66. On hearing these words of Rāma, the Devas and the great sages became delighted. They praised his words saying, "Very well! Very well!".

67. At the bidding of Īśvara, the Four-faced Lord in the company of all Devas, occupies the middle of the Setu for the sake of protecting it always.

68-71. For the sake of guarding Rāmasetu, Mahāviṣṇu occupies it by the name of Setumādhava. He is bound by fetters as it were.

Great sages, Pitṛs, expounders of Dharmaśāstra, Devas, Gandharvas, Kinnaras, great Serpents, Vidyādharas, Cāraṇas, Yakṣas, Kiṁpuruṣas and all other living beings stay here day and night.

This Rāmasetu, O excellent Brāhmaṇas, protects (all) from all the sins, if it is seen, heard, remembered, touched or plunged into.

72. The holy bath in the Setu at the time of *Ardhodaya* causes the attainment of joy. It yields salvation. It is highly meritorious. It is destructive of great Narakas.

73-79. In the month of Pauṣa when the Sun is in the Constellation of Viṣṇu (i.e. Śravaṇa), on Sundays when the Sun has risen a little, if it is in conjunction with the new-moon day, if there is *Vyatīpāta,* and on the Constellation of Viṣṇu, there shall be the meritorious *Ardhodaya*. During *Ardhodaya* the bath in the Setu is conducive to the achievement of *Sāyujya*.

One new-moon day is remembered (i.e. held) to be on a par with a thousand Vyatīpātas. If that is a Sunday, the merit is that of ten thousand new-moon days. If the Constellation of Śravaṇa is in conjunction with Sunday, it should be considered highly meritorious due to the mutual contact. Each of these yields immortality through the holy bath, charitable gifts, Japas and worship. When all the five are in conjunction, nothing need be said in praise of its sanctity.

Śravaṇa star is the most excellent of all luminaries. The new-moon is the most excellent one among the lunar days. Vyatīpāta is the most excellent one among the Yogas. The day of the Sun is the most excellent among all the days of the week. If all these four came together when the Sun is in the Zodiac of Capricorn and if the man takes his holy bath in Rāmasetu at that time, he never stays in the womb of a mother thereafter. He shall attain salvation of the type of *Sāyujya*.

80. A holy time on a par with *Ardhodaya* has never been before nor will there ever be (hereafter). Similarly the time of *Mahodaya* is proclaimed to be a sacred period.

81-85. Charitable gift in the Setu during these holy periods is glorified.

A Brāhmaṇa having the following good qualities is said to be a person who deserves charitable gifts: good conduct, penance,

Vedic knowledge, listening to Vedāntic discourse, worship of Śiva, Viṣṇu and others and the ability to expound the topics of the Purāṇas.

In the Setu, the devotee should make charitable gifts to that deserving Brāhmaṇa.

If a suitable person endowed with good conduct is not available in the Setu, the devotee should mentally decide upon another deserving person and hand it over to him after returning to the village.

Hence no gift should be made to a base man by persons who deserve merits. The excellent (treatise on) the glory of Setu should be given to the expounder and not to anyone else.

In this connection I shall recount a traditional legend mentioned by Vasiṣṭha. He told this excellent legend to the great King Dilīpa who wanted to know the person deserving charitable gifts.

Dilīpa said:

86. To whom should gifts be made, O son of Brahmā, O my priest. Recount this factually, O great sage, to me, your disciple.

Vasiṣṭha said:

87. The most excellent one of all deserving persons is one who is devoted to good conduct and study of the Vedas. A person still more deserving is one who has not partaken of food of Śūdra.

88-89. A person who has mastered the Vedas, Purāṇas and Mantras, who worships Śiva, Viṣṇu and others, who regularly performs the duties and observes the rules pertaining to his caste and stage of life, who is poor but has a large family, is mentioned to be the most excellent and deserving person. What is given to that deserving person bestows virtue, wealth, love and salvation.

90. (*Defective Text*) Particularly in a holy spot, charitable gifts should be made to a very deserving person. Otherwise it is despicable. The guilty person will be a chameleon during ten births.

91. He shall be a donkey during three births, a frog during two births, a Cāṇḍāla during a single birth and then he is born as a Śūdra.

92. Thereafter, he is successively born as a Kṣatriya, a Vaiśya and a Brāhmaṇa. Then he shall be poor and afflicted with many diseases.

93. Thus there are many kinds of defects resulting from making gifts to undeserving recipients. Hence, by all means, one should make gifts to the most deserving ones.

94-95. If a deserving person is not readily available, the devotee should think of a very deserving person and pour water on the ground with that person in view. If that person is dead, the gift should be handed over to his son. If he too dies, the gift should be dedicated to Mahādeva. Hence no gift shall be made to a base recipient, and particularly so in a holy place.

Śrī Sūta said:

96-99. On being told thus by Vasiṣṭha, O excellent Brāhmaṇas, Dilīpa, from that time onwards, gave the excellent charitable gifts to the most deserving person.

Hence in a sacred place, here, in the Setu too, if a deserving person is available, one should make monetary and other gifts. If he is not available, the devotee should think of a very excellent deserving person. He shall with great devotion pour water on the ground with that person in view. Afterwards on returning to his own village, he should hand it over to that deserving person.

100. He should hand over the sum thought of before to that person. Otherwise he shall be guilty of omission of duty. (By making the gift) he will never again be miserable. He shall attain *Sāyujya*.

101-106. A period on a par with *Ardhodaya* has never been before nor will there ever be.

Shaving off the head and observing fast have been glorified in the following holy spots: Kumbhakoṇa, Setumūla, Gokarṇa, Naimiṣa, Ayodhyā, Daṇḍaka forest, Virūpākṣa, Veṅkaṭa, Śāligrāma, Prayāga, Kāñcī, Dvārāvatī, Madhurā, Padmanābha, Kāśī the abode of Viśveśvara, all the rivers and oceans and the mountain Bhāskara.

If a man does not do so out of greed or delusion, and goes back to his abode, all the sins accompany him to his house.

There are twenty-four Tīrthas on the Gandhamādana mountain. Shaving off the head there in the Lakṣmaṇa Tīrtha is said to be meritorious by the sages. The hair should be cast off on the banks of Lakṣmaṇatīrtha according to the command of Śiva.

107-110. After shaving off the head alone and after making monetary gift, the devotee should take his holy bath in Lakṣmaṇatīrtha and visit (Lord Śīva called) Lakṣmaṇa Śaṅkara. Thereby, the man becomes liberated from all sins and he attains Śaṅkara.

At the time of *Ardhodaya* the devotee should always take the holy bath in Setu thus.

There is no Tīrtha on a par with Setu. There is no penance on a par with Setu. There is no merit on a par with Setu. There is no goal on a par with Setu.

Ardhodaya is said to be an auspicious time on a par with a thousand eclipses. There is no other period on a par with *Ardhodaya*, a period that liberates one from the worldly existence.

111. According to all scriptures, there is no bath as auspicious as the holy bath that is taken on Rāmasetu at the time of *Ardhodaya*.

112-113. By taking a single holy bath, particularly at the time of *Ardhodaya* as well as *Mahodaya*, in Rāmasetu, one shall certainly achieve as much merit as one is able to achieve by plunging into Bhāgīrathī for sixty thousand years, O eminent sages. The merit is declared as much by the sages.

114-115. There is no doubt about this, O Brāhmaṇas, that a man by taking a single holy plunge in Rāmasetu at the time of *Ardhodaya*, obtains that merit which one obtains by means of a thousand holy baths during the holy months of Māgha when the Sun is in the Zodiac of Capricorn at Prayāga which is destructive of sins.

116. By taking the holy bath only once during *Ardhodaya* in Setu one gets the same merit as is obtained by the people who have taken their holy bath in all the Tīrthas existing in the three worlds.

117-123. It is certain that the following sinners can atone for their sins in the Setu by bathing at the time of *Ardhodaya*: those who are devoid of the knowledge of Brahman, wicked and ungrateful persons, great sinners, as well as other types of sinners.

In other holy spots, ungrateful and treacherous people do not get any redemption of any nature. By taking the holy bath in the Setu at the time of *Ardhodaya*, even they can have redemption.

Those who do not take the holy bath in the Setu at the time of *Ardhodaya*, due to delusion, get immersed in worldly existence. They meet with downfall like blind men.

By taking the holy bath in the Setu at the time of *Ardhodaya*, the devotees can break (their way) through the solar disc. They then go to the world of Brahmā. No doubt need be entertained in this regard.

When there is *Ardhodaya*, a man should take the holy bath in the Setu, the bestower of salvation. He should then properly meditate on Rāghava, the lord of the universe, along with Sītā. He should meditate on Mahādeva called Rāmeśvara and the monkeys, chief among whom were Sugrīva and others.

After meditating on these the devotee should offer water libations to the Devas, the sages, as well as the groups of Pitṛs. He should propitiate them all for getting release from his own impoverished state.

124. The devotee should worship the Lord of the universe who is devoid of impurities and who is called *Ardhodaya*. He should worship him at the time of *Ardhodaya*. Keśava is delighted thereby.

125-130a. He shall offer *Arghya* at the time of *Ardhodaya* with separate Mantras as follows:

"O Divākara (Sun-god), O mass of brilliance, O lord of the universe, obeisance to you."

"O Sudhākuṁbha (Pot of Nectar i.e. the Moon-god) born of the family of Atri, O Brother of goddess Lakṣmī, O holy lord, accept the *Arghya*. Obeisance to you."

"O Vyatīpāta, the great Yogin, O destroyer of great sins, O thousand-armed, one identical with all, accept the *Arghya*. Obeisance to you."

"O great lord, the deity of lunar days, constellations and days of the week, O lord in the form of months, accept the *Arghya*. O lord in the form of Kāla, obeisance to you."

After offering the Arghyas separately thus by separate Mantras, the man should offer presents to Brāhmaṇas in accordance with his wealth. He should propitiate fourteen, twelve, eight, seven, six or five Brāhmaṇas, offering them food and drink in accordance with his capacity. He should repeat the Mantras separately.

130b-132. The devotee should take a new brass vessel or a wooden vessel and fill it with milk. He should place it in front of the Brāhmaṇas along with fruits, jaggery, ghee, betel leaves and monetary gifts. He should make a gift of this to the Brāhmaṇas along with a sacred thread and a milch cow together with her calf. The Brāhmaṇas should be adorned in accordance with the capacity of the donor. He should repeat the following Mantras:

133. "O Keśava, O lord of the universe, let what has been offered by me to the suppliants bring everlasting merit. It has been offered on the day with the Śravaṇa Constellation, the Constellation of your birth.

134. O lord of the Constellations, O bestower of nectar to the Devas, O lover of Rohiṇī, save me, O (lord) of entire digits. Obeisance to you.

135. O lord of the universe, O lord of the poor and wretched, O lord of digits, O merciful one, let my devotion to the pair of your lotus-like feet be steady.

136. O Vyatīpāta resembling the moon, the sun and fire, obeisance to you. Whatever has been given, such as charitable gift, etc., let that bring inexhaustible merit.

137. O Hari, O Vāsudeva, O Janārdana, you are the (wish-yielding) Kalpa tree unto the suppliants. O lord of the units of Time, viz. month, season and (half-yearly) transit, quell my sin."

138-139. After having worshipped thus, O eminent Brāhmaṇas, the devotee should perform the Śrāddha with gold, uncooked (rice, etc.) or cooked food as offering.

Thereafter, he should perform the Pārvaṇa (pertaining to the holy *Parvan* days). He should not hesitate to spend money. Afterwards, he should worship (i.e. honour) the Ācārya (Preceptor) with clothes, ear-rings and other ornaments.

140. The replica should be handed over to him. A cow, an umbrella and a pair of footwear should also be given to him. Thus, O excellent Brāhmaṇas, the devotee should perform the holy rite on the Setu during *Ardhodaya*.

141. He may be contented with that alone. There is no further duty binding him. Even in other holy spots, the devotee should perform the holy rite during *Ardhodaya*.

142-143. The Setu was made by Rāma on the ocean on Gandhamādana. By glorifying its name, by repeating "Setu", O wise men, at the time of bathing, crores of human sins perish instantaneously. The devotees go over to the region of Acyuta.

144. The servants of Yama are incompetent to come within the range of vision of a man who stands on the Setu for even a moment or half a moment.

145-147. One shall be liberated from all miseries and one shall attain the greatest region by mentally remembering Rāmasetu, Dhanuṣkoṭi, Rāma, Sītā, Lakṣmaṇa, Rāmanātha, Hanumān, Sugrīva and other monkeys, Bibhīṣaṇa, Nārada, Viśvāmitra, the Pot-born Sage (i.e. Agastya), Vasiṣtha, Vāmadeva, Jābāli and Kāśyapa as also other devotees of Rāma.

148-153. Sins perish by having holy baths in the following

holy spots: Satyakṣetra, Harikṣetra, Kṛṣṇakṣetra, Naimiṣa, Śālagrāma, Badarī, Hastiśaila, Vṛṣācala, Śeṣādri, Citrakūṭa, Lakṣmīkṣetra, Kuraṅgaka, Kāñcika, Kumbhakoṇa, Mohinīpura, the meritorious Śvetācala pertaining to Indra, the great holy spot Padmanābha, the holy spot named Phulla, the mountain Ghaṭika, Sārakṣetra, Haristhala, the great holy spot Śrīnivāsa, the great holy region of Bhaktanātha, the great holy place named Alinda, Śukakṣetra, Varuṇa, Madhurā, Harikṣetra, Śrīgoṣṭhī, Puruṣottama (Jagannātha Purī), Śrīraṅga, Puṇḍarīkākṣa as well as other holy spots of Hari. O excellent Brāhmaṇas, all those sins (perishing at the above holy places) certainly perish due to the holy bath at the Setu.

154. If men do not take their holy bath in the Setu made by the scion of the family of Raghu and resorted to by great sages, they do not get rid of the ocean of worldly existence.

155-161a. O eminent sages, those men who never listen to, utter or remember the auspicious five-syllabled Mantra *namaḥ śivāya,* those who do not remember or recite the eight-syllabled Mantra, *namo nārāyaṇāya*, along with Praṇava (i.e. *oṁ namo nārāyaṇāya*), O excellent men, those who do not recite, listen to, or remember the six-syllabled Mantra of Śrīrāmacandra shall take their holy plunge in Rāmasetu. Their sins do perish thereby.

Those who do not observe fast on the auspicious day of Hari (Ekādaśī), those who do not apply Bhasma all over their bodies or in the form of three parallel lines on the forehead, or on their heads, etc. by reciting the seven Mantras of the *Jābāla Upaniṣad*, O eminent Brāhmaṇas, those who do not worship Śiva, Keśava or other Suras in the way prescribed in the Vedas, should take their holy plunge in Rāmasetu. Their sins get quelled thereby.

161b-164. O excellent Brāhmaṇas, those who do not devoutly offer incense, light, sandalpaste and flowers to Śiva, Viṣṇu and other deities, those men of sinful minds who do not perform the rite of ablution to Śiva, Viṣṇu and other Devas through the Mantras of *Śrīrudra, Camaka*, the holy *Puruṣasūkta*, *Pāvamānya* and other Sūktas (hymns), *Trimadhu*, *Trisuparṇa*, the five Śānti Sūktas as well as other Mantras should take their holy plunge in Dhanuṣkoṭi. Their sins perish thereby.

165-167a. Those men whose intellect has been sullied by sins and who do not make obeisance to or circumambulate Śiva, Viṣṇu and other Devas devoutly, those who do not perform the worship of Śiva, Viṣṇu and other Devas along with great *Naivedya* offerings early in the morning in the month of Dhanus, shall take their holy plunge in Rāmasetu. Their sins perish thereby.

167b-171a. Those who do not glorify the names of Viṣṇu or Hara, those men who, out of delusion, do not worship Śāligrāma stones, Śivanābha (particular form of Śivaliṅga) or Dvārakācakra, O Brāhmaṇas, those deluded men who do not apply on their chest and forehead the clay from Gaṅgā, the mud (from the roots) of Tulasī plant, one who does not wear Rudrākṣa bead or Tulasī twig cleanly round the arms and the neck for subduing all the multitudes of sins, should take their holy plunge in Dhanuṣkoṭi and their sins perish thereby.

171b-177a. O Brāhmaṇas, one should get up from sleep in the Brāhma Muhūrta. With a delighted mind one should meditate on the names of Hari and Śaṅkara and recite the hymns pertaining to them. One should always think of the special Mantra. One should then take the holy plunge in Dhanuṣkoṭi. Thereby one's sins perish.

O excellent sages, a man should go to a tank (river, etc.) early in the morning, take his holy bath and ceremoniously sip the water with purified intellect. He should be delighted in his mind. If any man does not perform his *Sandhyā* prayer and the worship of *Gāyatrī*, the mother of the Vedas, if men do not perform carefully the rites of *Aupāsana* both in the morning and in the evening, if those who are sullied by the sins, do not perform *Mādhyāhnika* (midday) rites, if they do not perform Brahmayajña, Vaiśvadeva and the rites of honouring guests at midday and if they do not worship guests in the evening too, they should take their holy plunge in Dhanuṣkoṭi and their sins perish thereby.

177b-183a. Those men who do not offer alms to ascetics at midday, O Brāhmaṇas, those evil-minded ones who forget the Vedic text learnt by them, those who do not study the Vedas or the ancillaries to the Vedas, those who do not perform the annual Śrāddha of their parents, those who, out of covetousness, fail to perform the Mahālaya Śrāddha, the Aṣṭaka Śrāddha as well as other types of occasional Śrāddhas, those persons whose intellect has been vitiated by greediness and who, for the gratification of Citragupta, do not offer Brāhmaṇas sweet drink, ripe plantains, milk puddings with sugar and jaggery, mango fruits along with jackfruits and other types of sweet fruits, betel leaves, sandals, umbrella, clothes, flowers, sandalpaste, etc. on the full-moon day in the month of Caitra, should take their holy plunge in Dhanuṣkoṭi. Thereby their sins get destroyed.

183b-186. Whether he be one of good conduct or one of evil conduct, one who resorts to Dhanuṣkoṭi is not born again. The worldly existence is cut off from him.

O eminent sages, if anyone wishes to cross the ocean of worldly existence, let him go to Rāmacandradhanuṣkoṭi without any delay.

I speak the truth; I speak what is beneficial; I speak the essence of what is conducive to (your) welfare: go ye to Rāmacandradhanuṣkoṭi for the sake of achieving salvation. One shall take the holy bath in Rāmacandradhanuṣkoṭi for the sake of liberation.

187-191. O Brāhmaṇas, there is no other means (of liberation). I say again and again. If men take their bath in Rāmacandradhanuṣkoṭi, they can, without any exertion, achieve the destruction of the fear of worldly existence.

There is no doubt about this that by taking the holy plunge in Dhanuṣkoṭi one shall attain the perfect eternal Brahman which is truth and (spiritual) knowledge and is infinite.

Śrī Sūta said:

Thus, O Brāhmaṇas, the excellent glory of Setu has been narrated to you.[1]

It subdues great misery. It dispels great sickness. It destroys bad dreams. It is meritorious and it prevents premature and accidental deaths. It causes great peace unto the men who read and listen to it. It bestows heavenly pleasures and salvation. It is meritorious. It bestows the merit of all Tīrthas.

192. He who glorifies this meritorious (text) or listens to it with great concentration and mental purity, obtains the complete merit of Agniṣṭoma and other Yajñas.

193. By glorifying the greatness of this (Setu), one obtains that merit which is obtained by reciting a hundred times the four Vedas along with their Aṅgas (ancillaries).

194. By reading or listening to a single chapter in this text, O eminent sages, one obtains the full merit of a horse-sacrifice.

195. By reading as well as listening to two chapters one obtains

1. The following verses give the detailed *Phalaśruti* of reading/reciting/hearing this Māhātmya.

the excellent merit of the Yajña named Gomedha (cow-sacrifice).

196. He who devoutly reads or listens to ten chapters attains the heavenly world and rejoices with Indra.

197. By reading or listening to twenty chapters, O eminent sages, one attains the world of Brahmā and rejoices along with God Brahmā.

198. By reading or listening to thirty chapters, O eminent sages, one attains the world of Viṣṇu and rejoices with Viṣṇu.

199. He who reads or listens to forty chapters, attains the world of Rudra and rejoices with Rudra.

200. He who reads or listens to fifty chapters attains Hara accompanied by Aṁbā, the crescent-moon-crested Śiva.

201. He who reads or listens to this entire excellent glory (i.e. 52 chapters) shall attain the same world as that of Sāṁba Śiva. There is no doubt about this.

202. He who reads or listens to this twice, O excellent sages, attains the vicinity of Śiva, riding on an excellent aerial chariot.

203. He who reads or listens to this three times with great concentration and mental purity, attains *Sārūpya* (identity of form) with Śiva, and Śiva is pleased with him.

204. He who reads or listens to this excellent glory four times, attains *Sāyujya* (union) with Śiva, the Lord of the Daughter of the Mountain.

205-208. If any man regularly reads everyday one verse, half of a verse, a quarter alone, a syllable or even a letter, his sin committed on that day perishes instantaneously.

If this entire Setu-māhātmya is read or listened to, as many sins of Brāhmaṇa-slaughter as there are letters in these verses perish instantaneously. Also, so many sins of imbibing liquor, so many sins of stealing gold, so many sins of carnally approaching the wife of the preceptor and so many sins of associating with these people perish instantaneously.

209-210. By reading or listening to this text, one obtains the merit of taking the holy bath in the twenty-four Tīrthas as many times as there are numbers of letters in this (text) of great merit, and also in the other Tīrthas situated in the middle of Setu.

211. He, by whom the excellent glory of the Setu has been written devoutly, shall attain *Sāyujya* with Śiva. All his ignorance shall be destroyed.

212. If this splendid (text) of the glory (of Setu) is kept in

manuscript form in any one's house, there is no fear from evil spirits, vampires, etc. in that house.

213-214. There is no affliction there due to sickness; there is no fear from thieves; there is no harassment by the Planets, the most important ones among them being Saturn and Mars.

O eminent sages, know that house to be Rāmasetu itself, in which this meritorious and excellent (text of the) glory (of Setu) is present.

215. All the twenty-four Tīrthas are present there itself. There itself is present the meritorious Gandhamādana mountain.

216. Brahmā, Viṣṇu and Maheśa are present there with great respect.

One should write out the glory of the Setu and offer it to a Brāhmaṇa. (It is as good as) the earth extending as far as the four oceans, has been gifted away by him.[1]

THE MANTRA FOR THE GIFT OF SETUMĀHĀTMYA:

217. All other charitable gifts do not deserve to be equal to even a sixteenth part of the gift of *Setumāhātmya*. Hence grant me peace. Of what avail is much talk? The three worlds are present in this.

218. If anyone reads out one chapter from (this text) at the time of Śrāddha, all the deficiencies of the Śrāddha are dispelled (compensated). The Pitṛs too get extremely delighted.

219. If at the times of holy Parvans, anyone reads out this text to the Brāhmaṇas, even an *Adhyāya* (chapter) or a verse of it, his cows and buffaloes become harmless. They will yield much milk. They will have many calves.

220. This meritorious (text) should be read in a holy temple, monastery, banks of rivers and lakes, or a holy forest region or in the house of Brāhmaṇas well-versed in the Vedas and never in any other place.

221. This should be particularly read on equinoctial days and on the days of the transit (of the Sun), on the holy Hari's day (i.e. Ekādaśī day), on the eighth and the fourteenth lunar day.

222. This should be read in the months of Śrāvaṇa, Bhādrapada, Dhanus as well as in the Uttarāyaṇa (northern transit of the Sun).

---

1. The fruit acquired by one who gets this Māhātmya written and gifts this (as a *dāna*) to a Brāhmaṇa is described in this chapter.

223. O Brāhmaṇas, this glory should be read while observing certain restrictions (i.e. restrictions should be observed while reading). The listeners shall also observe those restrictions and listen to this excellent (text).

224-227. In this (text of the) glory, many holy Tīrthas are praised. So also excellent saintly kings of meritorious conduct are commemorated. In this excellent text, sages of great fortune are glorified. Dharma and Adharma are described in this meritorious text, O eminent Brāhmaṇas. The three deities Brahmā, Viṣṇu and Rudra are praised in this. This is sacred. This is destructive of sins. This is supported by the meanings of the Śrutis. This is approved by the writers of Smṛti texts. This is liked by Sage Dvaipāyana. It should be listened to and read by one who desires his own welfare.

228. Something such as gold, etc. should be given to one who reads, in accordance with one's capacity. One should not be fraudulent in the matter of expenditure in this connection.

229. This Śrāvaka (the man who reads and expounds) should be honoured by giving clothes, gold, grain, plot of land or cow in accordance with their capacity by the people who listen to (him).

230. If the Śrāvaka is honoured, the Trimūrtis (Brahmā, Viṣṇu and Śiva) adored too are worshipped. If the Trimūrtis are worshipped, the three worlds are honoured.

231-234. Rāma, the son of Daśaratha who is Hari himself, incarnated on the earth accompanied by Sītā and Lakṣmaṇa, always bestows worldly pleasures here and salvation in the end, on the listeners and the expounder.

This extremely splendid *Setumāhātmya* has issued forth from the lotus-like mouth of Dvaipāyana. Accompanied by all his younger brothers, Bhīmasena and others, Dharmarāja Yudhiṣṭhira listened to this everyday along with his army even as the great sage Dhaumya, his priest, read it out. He strictly adheres(-ed) to the code of good conduct and holy observances.

Śrī Sūta said:

235-237. O ye all ascetics, residents of Naimiṣa forest, this sacred Māhātmya which is on a par with the Śruti has been heard by you all from me. You were observing all the restrictions. Read this respectfully always. Teach this always to your disciples who too strictly observe the restrictions.

After saying this to those sages, Sūta who experienced thrill and had hair standing all over his body, mentally remembered Vyāsa, his preceptor. He began to dance shedding tears (of joy).

238. In the meantime, the excessively learned great sage, the son of Parāśara, appeared there suddenly with a desire to bless his disciple.[1]

239-240. On seeing that the sage, the son of Satyavatī, had come, Sūta prostrated at the lotus-like feet of Vyāsa along with all those residents of Naimiṣa forest. The tears of joy flowed from his eyes.

241. The sage lifted up his prostrating disciple with his hands. He uttered words of blessings. He embraced him again and again.

242. Dvaipāyana, the ascetic of great splendour, sat on the excellent seat brought by the sages of Naimiṣa forest.

243. When the sages had reoccupied their seats, when Sūta too sat down at his bidding, the grandson of Śakti spoke to all those sages including Śaunaka:

244. "O residents of the Naimiṣa forest, all this was known by me that the excellent glory of Setu has been recounted to you all by Sūta, my disciple. It is destructive of sins.

245-246. This is the full and ultimate meaning of Śrutis, Smṛtis, Purāṇas, other Śāstras and Itihāsas. This glory (of Setu) is great. This is honoured by me in all the Purāṇas.

247-249a. At my bidding, Dharmarāja (Yudhiṣṭhira) listens (used to listen) to this always from Dhaumya. Hence you too should always read and listen to the excellent glory of the Setu. Teach this unto your disciples too."

On hearing these words of his, they said, "So it shall be, of course."

249b-250. Thereafter, accompanied by his disciple Sūta, Vyāsa took leave of all the sages and went to the Kailāsa mountain.

The sages with their abode in the Naimiṣa forest became contented. They listen to and read *Setumāhātmya* everyday.

:: End of Setumāhātmya ::

1. VV 238ff: an apt concluding glorification of this Māhātmya.

INDEX